THE MULTINATIONAL ENTERPRISE

*by John H. Dunning*

STUDIES IN INTERNATIONAL INVESTMENTS

# THE MULTINATIONAL
# ENTERPRISE

EDITED BY

## JOHN H. DUNNING

*Professor of Economics*
*University of Reading*

*London*

**GEORGE ALLEN & UNWIN LTD**

RUSKIN HOUSE   MUSEUM STREET

## ACKNOWLEDGEMENTS

We wish to record our sincere thanks to Shell International for generously providing the necessary financial support to sponsor a Conference on the Multinational Enterprise at Reading from May 28–30, 1970. Without their interest and encouragement this volume could not have been compiled.

First published in 1971
Second impression 1974

Printed in Great Britain
in 10 on 11 point Times Roman
by Lowe & Brydone (Printers) Ltd,
Thetford, Norfolk

# Contents

# Notes on Contributors

ROBERT Z. ALIBER
Graduate School of Business
University of Chicago

DAVID BARRAN
Shell International

JACK BEHRMAN
University of North Carolina

RICHARD E. CAVES
Harvard University

GERARD CURZON
Graduate Institute of International
Studies, Geneva

JOHN H. DUNNING
University of Reading

CHRISTOPHER FREEMAN
University of Sussex

JOHN GENNARD
London School of Economics and
Political Science

J. P. HAYES
Overseas Development Association
of the Foreign and Commonwealth
Office

JOHN HEATH
London Graduate School of
Business Studies

DAVID LEA
Trades Union Congress

ROBIN MURRAY
London Graduate School of
Business Studies

LIONEL NEEDLEMAN
University of Leicester

KEITH PAVITT
OECD

EDITH PENROSE
School of Oriental and African
Studies, London

DAVID ROBERTSON
University of Reading

MAX STEUER
London School of Economics and
Political Science

PAUL STREETEN
Queen Elizabeth House, University
of Oxford

J. F. SUDWORTH
ICI

H. W. WERTHEIMER
Economic and Legal Counsel

MICHAEL WHITEHEAD
Centre for European Industrial
Studies, University of Bath

# Introduction

This book is concerned with the impact of the multinational enterprise on the transfer of goods and factor inputs across national boundaries and the implication of this transfer on the welfare of nation states or sectors of nation states. Each of the contributions is written by a leading research specialist or practitioner in the field; each surveys the existing state of knowledge and suggests lines for future research. A number of the essays embody results of original research; others are more concerned with political considerations or are speculative in approach.

As both Paul Streeten and Jack Behrman emphasize in their chapters, the welfare of nation states affected by multinational enterprises is a synthesis of the welfare of its component parts, not all of which will be affected by their operations in the same way. As with other environmental issues, problems arise as much from balancing or reconciling *sectoral* costs and benefits within nation states as from securing the maximum net benefit of the whole. Mr Lea's chapter is a good illustration of this point. Nevertheless, the Reading Conference from which this book originated was more concerned with the general repercussions of the growth of multinational enterprises in the world economy. The intention was that participants should take stock of thinking on the subject and should suggest lines for future research.

As will be seen from the contents of this volume – and particularly from David Robertson's summary in Chapter 13 – the Conference was not primarily concerned with the internal operations of multinational enterprises. Instead it concentrated its attention on the impact of this particular phenomenon on the economic environment of which it is part.

Broadly speaking, the chapters divide themselves into four main sections. The first consists of three chapters. In a background review, Professor Dunning sets out some of the economic and conceptual issues surrounding the multinational enterprise. What is this particular phenomenon? Why is it worthy of study? What distinctive economic problems or challenges does it raise? How can these best be dealt with?

This essay is followed by two on the multinational enterprise as an agent of the transfer of factor inputs across national boundaries. Professor Aliber discusses the extent to which the pattern of growth of the multinational enterprise can be explained by the demarcation

11

of the world into various currency areas and the extent to which the operations of international companies – by their ability to move funds across national boundaries – affects the independence of monetary authorities in various currency areas. Mr Pavitt deals with the role played by foreign direct investment in transferring knowledge and technology, and draws upon the valuable data collected by the OECD in their 'Gaps in Technology' section. He also compares the role of the multinational enterprise in the transfer of technology to the less-developed areas with that to the developed countries.

The second series extends from Chapter 4 to 7 and is concerned with a selection of operational questions arising from international direct investment. Chapter 4 is a long contribution by Mr Steuer and Mr Gennard, and contains some of the results of an original piece of research undertaken by the authors and sponsored by the Board of Trade, into the effects of foreign direct investment in the UK. Mr Steuer has already published, or is about to publish, the rest of his findings – many of which are relevant to our theme. This contribution on industrial relations is especially welcome because it is one of the first pieces of work published on this aspect of the multinational enterprise. Later sections of the chapter also contain useful empirical material on the profitability and productivity of foreign enterprises in the UK.

This essay is followed by Mr Lea's chapter which, though perhaps somewhat less objective in its approach and orientation, fairly summarizes many of the concerns expressed by trade unions over the operation of multinational enterprises. Some commentators believe that many of the conflicts arising in the future will be in the area of labour/management relationships, particularly if, to meet the internationalization of business, the unions attempt to formulate global strategies. Such a bilateral monopoly could obviously have extremely wide implications which have not yet really been appreciated or worked out by the parties concerned – or received the attention they deserve from labour economists.

The following two chapters deal with the balance of payments and trade impact of foreign direct investment. Mr Robertson's is a comprehensive survey of the state of thinking on the subject, a field which is perhaps better documented than most and where economists have done the most empirical research. It is also one of the most hotly disputed subjects for, if nothing else, enquiries have revealed the difficulty of arriving at any sensible general conclusions, partly because of the wide differences between types of foreign investment and partly due to the difficulty of estimating what would have

happened had the investment not been made. Mr Sudworth's contribution, although perhaps not as forthcoming in statistical data as
one would have liked, is the more useful, because it does illustrate at
an individual enterprise level how one large multinational firm
considers its own investments have affected trade flows. Quite
unintentionally, it also illustrates one of the difficulties one has in
obtaining useful factual information from firms which, for very good
reasons of their own, are reluctant to provide data on their operations
in the way economists would like.

The third group of essays deals essentially with the relationship
between the multinational enterprise and host nations of which their
foreign operations are part. Professor Penrose and Mr Streeten are
concerned with the reactions of less developed countries to inward
foreign investment – Mrs Penrose concentrating on attitudinal and
organizational questions and Mr Streeten on the costs and benefits
of obtaining the ingredients of foreign investment by alternative
means. Both essays suggest that, even from an economic viewpoint,
it is very difficult to give any generalized answers to the problems
under review, though Mr Hayes, in his comments, questions
whether some of the alternatives Mr Streeten suggests are, in
practice, feasible.

In his contribution, Mr Murray surveys some of the implications
of the growth of international business for the system of national
states as they are at present organized in developed countries and,
in particular, the changes in political structures it may necessitate.

Professor Behrman's chapter is more concerned with the tensions
which may arise, both between nation states and the multinational
enterprise, and *within* nation states, as a result of the sharing out of
the operations of multinational enterprises and, in particular, from
the distribution of the costs and benefits they confer to host
countries. In examining these, he lists a variety of alternative government policies which might be pursued. Professor Behrman has
written extensively on this subject and is the author of a recently
completed study, *National Interests and the Multi-National
Enterprise*.[1]

The fourth section consists of a single paper. It stands on its own
as it is concerned with a rather different problem. Mr Whitehead is
a Research Fellow at the Centre of European Industrial Studies at
Bath University of Technology and is working with Christopher
Layton on the problem of multinational companies which are
owned and controlled by economic agents in two or more countries.

[1] Englewood-Cliffs, New Jersey, 1970.

His chapter attempts both to distinguish this brand of operation from others and also to give a first insight into the effects of one of the most recently set up of their enterprises, Afga-Gevaert.

Most of the contributions at the Conference were introduced by a participant other than the author, and we include in the volume the comments of several of these discussants who, like the authors, have worked or are working in this particular field. The volume concludes with a summary of the discussion recorded by David Robertson and some concluding impressions by Professor Heath.

Obviously, not all areas of the subject matter under review were covered in the two-and-a-half days of debate. Some of these (e.g. industrial structure) had been touched upon at other conferences,[1] while others – e.g. the theory of direct investment – have been dealt with fairly extensively in the literature.[2] Neither did we attempt to review the existing research being done on the multinational enterprise. For an idea of the work being done in the UK and North America the reader should consult an excellent summary recently produced by the British–North American Research Association.[3]

We hope that the growing number of people interested in the multinational enterprise will find the contents of this volume stimulating and informative – and a catalyst to further thinking and research.

[1] Notably the Conference on Mergers and Restrictive Practices organized by the Board of Trade and held at Cambridge in September 1969.

[2] See, for example, C. P. Kindleberger, *The International Corporation*, Cambridge, M.I.T. Press, 1969.

[3] *Research on the Multinational Enterprise*, by S. Webley and S. Lea.

PART ONE. THE MULTINATIONAL ENTERPRISE:
SOME GENERAL CONSIDERATIONS

*Chapter 1*

# THE MULTINATIONAL ENTERPRISE:
# THE BACKGROUND

JOHN H. DUNNING

## INTRODUCTION

Economic agents have long traded with each other across national boundaries; to this extent, the internationally-oriented enterprise is no new phenomenon. Similarly, the economic prosperity of nations has always been influenced by the terms on which they have exchanged goods and services among themselves. Since the early nineteenth century, an active international capital market has existed, while the international flow of knowledge has an even longer pedigree – dating back to the exodus of the Huguenots in the seventeenth century and the smuggling of drawings, designs and machinery out of Britain to the American colonies more than one hundred years later.

These observations underline the very familiar point that world trade in goods and factor inputs has always affected the economic welfare of participating nations, and that several countries owe the timing of their take-off in development directly to the inflow of foreign capital and expertise.[1] But until fairly recently, most international transactions had two things in common. First, each was generally undertaken independently of the other and by different economic agents. Admittedly, in the nineteenth century, trade often followed investment, and labour and capital sometimes migrated together, but these movements were usually separately initiated and diversely motivated.[2] Second, most transactions were between

[1] W. W. Rostow, *The Stages of Economic Growth*, London, Cambridge University Press, 1961.

[2] R. Nurkse, 'International Investment Today in the light of Nineteenth Century Experiences', *Economic Journal*, Vol. LXIV, March 1954.

unassociated buyers and sellers, and were concluded at market or 'arm's length' prices.

During the last half century, and particularly in the last twenty years, a new and separately identifiable vehicle of international economic activity has emerged as a result of the internationalization of the productive activities of many enterprises.[1] and its concomitant – the rapid expansion of foreign direct investment.

The distinctive features of foreign direct investment are twofold. First it embraces, usually under the control of a single institution, the international transfer of separate, but complementary, factor inputs, viz. equity capital, knowledge and entrepreneurship – and sometimes of goods as well. Nowadays direct investment accounts for 75% of the private capital outflows of the leading industrial nations,[2] compared with less than 10% in 1914. Payments for proprietary knowledge, e.g. royalties, technical service fees, etc. between related institutions, accounted for 54% of all such payments made across national boundaries by British enterprises in 1968,[3] and in the same year, about a quarter of their manufactured exports were sent directly to their foreign subsidiaries.[4]

The second unique quality of direct investment is that the resources which are transferred between countries are *not traded*, they are simply moved from one part of the investing enterprise to another; no market transactions are involved. Such prices as are charged may differ from arm's-length prices wherever, *inter alia*, it pays the investing enterprise to earn its taxable income in one country rather than another.

This, then, may be taken as a starting point to the concept of the international or multinational* producing enterprise (MPE), which we shall define simply as an enterprise which owns or controls producing facilities (i.e. factories, mines, oil refineries, distribution outlets, offices, etc.) in more than one country.† We distinguish

[1] J. Polk, 'The New World Economy', *Columbia Journal of World Business*, January/February 1968.

[2] International Monetary Fund, *Balance of Payments Yearbook*. Vol. 21, 1970.

[3] Board of Trade, 'Overseas Royalty Transactions in 1968', *Board of Trade Journal*, March 25, 1970.

[4] *Board of Trade Journal*, August 16, 1968.

* For the purpose of this paper we regard the terms international and multi-national as synonymous.

† A special case of multinational enterprise is the bi-national enterprise which is only involved (in some way or the other) with two countries. We might also classify nationally-oriented enterprises in similar ways (NPE, NTE, NOE, NCE).

such an enterprise from one solely engaged in international trade (MTE), which sells its domestically-produced output directly to other enterprises or individuals in other countries; and also from an internationally owned and/or (financially) controlled enterprise (MOE and MCE), the capital of which is owned or controlled by economic agents of more than one nationality. Most large enterprises are, to some extent, MOEs: only a very few, e.g. Unilever, Royal Dutch Shell, Agfa-Gevaert, are MCEs. These latter are also sometimes referred to as transnational enterprises.*[1]

It is, of course, possible for an enterprise to be multinational in more than one, or indeed in all, of the above senses, though in this paper we shall be mainly concerned with the economic issues surrounding the multinational producing enterprise (MPE), which is financially controlled by residents of one country.

From most standpoints, the distinction between foreign direct investment and the operations of the MPE is not an easy one to draw.[2] Nevertheless, there are some obvious differences. First, direct investment can be made by economic agents other than enterprises, though in practice the amounts involved are very small. Second, it incorporates foreign investment by all firms, irrespective of the *extent* to which they are involved in foreign activities – or indeed in domestic activities.[3] Third – and most important – while the value of direct investment only includes the capital of the foreign company actually *owned* by the investing enterprise, the economic role of the MPE is better expressed in terms of *all* resources under its *control*, including those of local origin.

Other writers have attempted more precise definitions of the MPE[4] but usually these either emphasize particular characteristics which may or may not be possessed by it, or treat the phenomenon from a specific viewpoint. The *producing enterprise*, for example, is likely to evaluate its degree of multinationalism in terms of the proportion its total employment, assets, sales or profits derived from

* To complete the picture there are a few multinational companies, e.g. Deltec and Adela, which are MOEs but where no substantial proportion of their capital is owned by any one shareholder in any one country.

[1] See also Chapter 12 in this volume.

[2] R. E. Caves, 'International Corporations: the Industrial Economics of Foreign Investment' in *Economica*, Vol. 38, February 1971.

[3] For example, many British-based companies in extractive industries do not operate production units in the UK at all.

[4] Some of these are summarized in the Committee on Invisible Exports, *The Role of International Companies and how their Management Affects Britain's Invisible Earnings*, London, 1970.

foreign operations.[1] Looked at from the angle of recipient *nation states*, or sectors within nation states, a more appropriate criteria might be the contribution of subsidiaries of foreign owned MPEs to domestic output or capital formation, or the impact of the foreign operations of domestically-owned MPEs on the balance of payments. A third and more functional approach is to look at the MPE according to the extent to which its constituent firms are subject to a common *management or operational strategy*.[2] Professor Perlmutter, for example, argues that only those enterprises which fully integrate their global activities and have a geocentric outlook can be considered as truly multinational.[3] On this definition, only a handful of the world's enterprises would currently qualify as MPEs; on the other hand, the numbers are growing and it is this particular form of the MPE which is attracting the most attention of nation states.[4]

In view of these diverse ideas about the nature of the MPE it may be questioned whether we can say anything useful about it. I think one can, for two reasons. First, as we have already observed, there are certain common features to all enterprises that produce in more than one country and, second, compared with nationally producing enterprises (NPEs), there are sufficient differences both in their behaviour and their economic impact to make this particular institution worth studying.

This chapter will seek to answer four groups of questions:

(a) What is the economic significance of the MPE? In what ways does its pattern of behaviour (or that of its constituent parts) differ from that of a NPE? To what extent is it a distinctive decision-taking unit? What determines the level and pattern of the activities of MPEs in the world today?

(b) What is the contribution of foreign and home-owned MPEs (or their subsidiaries) on the national economies of which they are part?

(c) What are the costs and benefits of these businesses (or their subsidiaries) from the viewpoint of investing and recipient countries? What is the nature and significance of the conflict of *objectives* between the MPE and nation states? – or sectors within

---

[1] N. K. Bruck and F. A. Lees, 'Foreign Investment Capital Controls and the Balance of Payments', New York University, Graduate School of Business Administration, *Institute of Finance Bulletin* No. 48/49, April 1968.

[2] R. Vernon, 'Multinational Enterprise and National Sovereignty', *Harvard Business Review*, March/April 1967.

[3] H. V. Perlmutter, 'The Tortuous Evolution of the Multinational Company', *Columbia Journal of World Business*, January/February 1969.

[4] See especially Chapter 11.

nation states? How, if at all, can conflicts of *interest* be resolved?
(d) What should government policy be towards the MPE (or its
subsidiaries)? Is there a case for establishing supra-national
institutions to deal with the international conflicts of interest
between the various interested parties?

## THE GROWTH OF THE MULTINATIONAL ENTERPRISE

The increase in the contribution of MPEs to world industrial output
is one of the most impressive economic features of the last two
decades. Though about three-quarters of this growth has originated
from US and UK owned and controlled enterprises, the greatest
percentage increases have been recorded by Continental, European
and Japanese firms,[1] which seem almost certain to increase their
share still further. A number of recent publications have analysed
these trends in some detail.[2] In this chapter we shall just highlight
one or two of the more outstanding facts.

First, the current position, in so far as one can estimate it. In 1968,
the book value of total assets owned by MPEs outside the country
in which they were first incorporated was about $94 billion, and their
total foreign sales (both exports and local output) were reckoned to
exceed in value the gross national product of any country except the
US and the USSR.[3] About 55% of these international assets were
owned by US enterprises, 20% by UK firms and the rest largely
by European and Japanese companies. About one-half of the
American companies with world-wide sales of more than $1 billion
in 1966 owned at least a quarter of their assets or derived at least
one-quarter of their sales outside the US.[4]

Second, the foreign output of MPEs is currently expanding at the
rate of 10% per annum, twice the rate of growth of world gross
national product and 40% faster than world exports. Moreover,
since the MPEs are concentrated in the technologically-advanced
and faster-growing industries, their share of the world output is
almost certain to rise in the future. This, coupled with the
economies of scale such enterprises enjoy over NPEs, has prompted

[1] J. H. Dunning and R. D. Pearce, 'The World's Largest Firms: A Statistical
Profile', *Business Ratios*, No. 3, 1969; S. Hymer and R. Rowthorn, 'Multinational
Corporations and International Oligopoly: the non-American Challenge' in
C. Kindleberger (ed.), *The International Coporation*, M.I.T. Press, 1970.
[2] S. Rolfe, *The International Corporation*, International Chamber of Com-
merce, 1969; J. Behrman, *Some Patterns in the Rise of the Multinational Enterprise*,
University of North Carolina research paper, 1969; Economist Intelligence Unit,
*The Growth and Spread of the Multinational Company*, London, 1971.
[3] J. Polk, *op. cit.*    [4] N. K. Bruck and F. A. Lees, *op. cit.*

some observers to make predictions that by the turn of the century the largest 200 or 300 MPEs will account for one-half of the world's output.[1] Whatever one's view of this prediction might be it would appear that, in recent years, the leading American MPEs have been growing appreciably faster than their more domestically-oriented counterparts. Of the largest 500 US industrial enterprises in 1967, those whose foreign sales and/or assets accounted for 25% or more of their total sales and/or assets grew by 64% during the preceding five years, while those whose overseas sales and/or assets were less than 25% recorded only a 53% rate of growth.[2]

The third point concerns the industrial concentration of MPEs. In 1967, 21% of the plant and equipment expenditure by US manufacturing enterprises was undertaken by their overseas subsidiaries.[3] But 85% of this was in four main sectors: vehicles, chemicals, mechanical engineering and electrical engineering. While certain industries throughout the world, e.g. rubber tyres, oil, tobacco, pharmaceuticals and motor vehicles are almost completely dominated by MPEs, in others, e.g. cotton, textiles, iron and steel, and aircraft they are largely absent. Why? This concentration has important implications for the theory of industrial organization, which we shall take up later.

Geographically, too, the impact of the MPE varies considerably. Of the developed countries most dependent on inward direct investment, Canada stands supreme. Some 55% of her industrial capital assets are owned by US or UK firms.[4] Of the 100 largest companies, 75 are foreign controlled. Australia is another example: 40% of her manufacturing and mining output is supplied by US firms, compared with less than 10% in Western Europe. MPEs are also active in many of the LDCs, particularly in the resource exploitation and intermediate technology fields.[5] Of the leading capital exporters, Switzerland, the Netherlands and the United Kingdom each derive more than 1% of their gross national product from income earned on foreign direct investment.[6]

Some countries are two-way investors. Britain is unrivalled here. While more than 30% of the profits of British owned enterprises are

---

[1] J. Polk, *op. cit.*    [2] J. H. Dunning and R. D. Pearce, *op. cit.*

[3] US Department of Commerce, *Survey of Current Business*, August 1968.

[4] M. Watkins, *Foreign Ownership and the Structure of Canadian Industry*, Report of the Task Force on the Structure of Canadian Industry, Ottawa, 1968.

[5] J. H. Dunning and R. D. Pearce, *Foreign Direct Investment in the Less-Developed Countries* (to be published as a PEP broadsheet 1971).

[6] J. H. Dunning, *Studies in International Investment*, London, Allen & Unwin, 1970.

derived from their overseas operations, foreign MPEs in the UK account for about 25% of manufacturing exports and, on present trends, are likely to supply the same proportion of manufacturing output by 1980.[1] The Netherlands, France, Sweden and, more recently, Germany and Japan also fall into this category.[2]

How can one explain these facts? Why do MPEs dominate certain industrial sectors? Why are they mainly of US and European origin? Why has the post-war growth of certain European economies been strongly influenced by American investment, while that of the Japanese economy has been largely independent of it?

We have already hinted at why, relative to other ways of conducting international business, foreign direct investment has become more attractive to enterprises, and particularly those in the technologically-advanced industries.[3] Basically this has to do, on the one hand, with the economics of the production of knowledge and its transmission across national boundaries and, on the other, with the conditions of international marketing. Increasingly, for one reason or another, enterprises have chosen to transmit abroad the knowledge of how to produce goods rather than the goods themselves, and to do this by setting up their own producing facilities rather than licensing foreign firms.

The above thesis essentially applies to MPEs in manufacturing industry but, equally important, are the activities of such enterprises in resource exploitation and tertiary industries. At this point it may be useful to distinguish between three types of MPE, the activities of which may be prompted by quite different considerations:

## 1 Backward Vertical (or Cost Oriented) Operations

These are of two varieties. The first represents the extension of the *purchasing* function of the investing firm and is undertaken to obtain cheaper or more reliable supplies of raw materials or processed goods for the investing company. The second type is undertaken, chiefly by firms in extractive industries, with the aim of supplying their output to world markets. Most operations of UK firms are now of this latter kind.[4]

[1] J. H. Dunning, *The Role of American Investment in the British Economy*, PEP Broadsheet No. 507, February 1969.

[2] International Monetary Fund, *op. cit.*

[3] W. Gruber, D. Mehta and R. Vernon, 'The Research and Development Factor in International Trade and Investment of US Industries', *Journal of Political Ecnomy*, Vol. LXXV, February 1967.

[4] W. B. Reddaway *et al.*, *Effects of UK Direct Overseas Investment*, London, Cambridge University Press, 1967 and 1968.

21

## 2 *Forward Vertical (or Market-Oriented) Operations*

These activities represent the extension of the *sales* function of the investing firm, the main purpose of which is to advance or protect its markets and facilitate *domestic* production. They do not usually account for large amounts of foreign capital, though quite a lot of the exports of the MPEs are channelled through them.

The factors influencing both these types of MPEs are fairly clear-cut as is their economic impact on host and investing countries.

## 3 *Horizontal Operations*

These largely comprise foreign manufacturing activities of MPEs which may or may not be harmonized with each other or with domestic activities. It is this type of operation which is currently attracting the greatest interest of both host and investing nations. These too may be variously classified, but perhaps the most useful division is between (*a*) high technology and (*b*) intermediate technology investments.

It now seems generally accepted that the explanation of the level and pattern of this kind of international activity is to be found in the theory of market behaviour and imperfect competition.[1] An enterprise develops foreign interests to exploit or protect a particular economic advantage it has over its competitors – or potential competitors.[2] In many cases this advantage can best be exploited by setting up a foreign operating subsidiary, rather than by any alternative route. In a static world of perfect competition and the free movement of capital there would be little or no incentive for direct investment. Imperfect competition, product differentiation and barriers to trade explain why the MPE exists at all.

Both Stephen Hymer and, more recently, Richard Caves have sought to explain foreign direct investment in these terms.[3] And, indeed, a quick look at the product and market structure of the leading MPEs in manufacturing industry shows that they tend to be concentrated in oligopolistic industries supplying branded or differentiated products. This is especially noticeable in the high technology industries, but it is also pronounced in some intermediate technology industries where, by today's standards, a fairly un-complicated and easily learned process of production is involved.

[1] C. P. Kindleberger, *American Business Abroad*, New Haven, Yale University Press, 1969.

[2] *Ibid.*

[3] S. Hymer, *The International Operation of National Firms: a Study of Direct Investment* (Ph.D. dissertation, M.I.T., 1960); R. E. Caves, *op. cit.*

Typical of these are cement, textiles, tobacco and soap. Here, the competitive imperfections mainly arise from import restrictions and/or high transport costs, and from the economies of experience and/or scale possessed by the investing company over its local competitors. Sometimes, because of its initial lead as an innovator and exporter, a foreign firm is able to retain its initial lead in local markets – particularly if the cost of indigenous competitors entering the market is a high one.

In the high technology industries it is the technology itself – or, perhaps, more correctly, the economic and institutional environment which generates this technology – which gives the foreign MPE an edge over its local competitors. The transatlantic technological gap is a very real phenomenon – however much one might believe its origins are, essentially, non-technological.

A particularly interesting feature about many MPEs in high technology industries is their attempt to closely integrate their world operating facilities. In the intermediate technology trades, each operating subsidiary in each country is more likely to produce similar products from start to finish, and there is comparatively little trade – either vertical or horizontal – between them.[1] By contrast, there appears to be much more international division of labour in the high technology industries. Sometimes this is vertical, with each subsidiary undertaking a particular process of production or supplying a range of components and parts of a particular product (or groups of products); sometimes it is horizontal, and subsidiaries trade finished products with each other; sometimes, in the case of some of the larger MPEs, e.g. IBM and Ford, it is a mixture of the two.

Such intra-enterprise product or process specialization, which appear to be increasing, has extremely important economic implications both for investing and host countries. This is partly because the operating strategy of each subsidiary is likely to be determined by the parent company (which is usually in the investing country) with the global interests of the enterprise in mind; partly because of the impact of such investment on trade flows; and partly because it is in this kind of MPE where the greatest opportunity for the manipulation of transfer prices occurs. For these reasons it is here where a conflict of interest between the MPE and the nation states in which it operates is most likely to arise. It is here too where national trades unions facing MPEs are most conscious of their weaknesses.[2]

[1] *Board of Trade Journal*, August 16, 1968; *Survey of Current Business*, May 1969.　　[2] See Chapter 5 of this volume.

THE MULTINATIONAL ENTERPRISE

We conclude. The level and growth of international direct investment reflects the costs and opportunities for investing firms to best organize their foreign operations in this particular way. The industrial pattern of such investment reflects the extent to which, for one reason or another, international competition is imperfect between firms in particular industries, and the attractiveness of foreign production as a means of overcoming these barriers to entry. The more significant the economies of scale and intra-enterprise integration; the more important enterprise-specific knowledge which cannot be transmitted on paper, the greater the need for product differentiation and the desire of the investing company to grow; then the more attractive international direct investment will be as a vehicle for international business.

Substantially the same approach may be used to explain the *geographical* origin and distribution of international direct investment, although here additional factors, e.g. risks associated with operating in a multi-currency world and political instability, are involved.[1] Just as the leading MPEs possess common features, so do the countries which invest the most outside their boundaries. These mainly fall into one (or more) of three types:

(a) Those countries which engage in foreign investment primarily to exploit market potentialities. Faced with a limited domestic market, enterprises within these countries seek to grow by diversifying their territorial interests. Switzerland and Holland are the classic examples here. Only four of Nestlés 189 plants – which account for 3% of its total sales – are in Switzerland, while Philips of Eindhoven derives more than 80% of its profits from its foreign operations.

(b) Those countries which invest mainly to secure materials for their manufacturing industries. This was the traditional *raison d'être* for UK firms venturing abroad in the nineteenth century, and it is still a very powerful inducement for many advanced industrial nations today. In 1968 the US obtained one-third of its imports of raw materials from its foreign subsidiaries, mostly in Canada and the developing countries.

(c) Those countries which invest primarily to exploit a comparative advantage which they have, or have acquired, in the ownership of certain kinds of resources – and hence in the production and/ or marketing of certain types of products. This kind of capital export is mainly *horizontal* within secondary industry, although

[1] See Chapter 2 of this volume.

the law of comparative costs holds no less for processes of production. Moreover, it is often two-way in character. While most post-war US investment in Europe, for example, reflects her comparative advantage in the innovation of research intensive products,[1] European investment in the US reflects her relative abundance of certain types of labour, and her more heterogeneous markets. The process by which this types of investment takes place has been traced by Raymond Vernon, Gary Hufbauer and others in their analysis of the *product cycle* and *technological gap* theories of trade.[2]

Little empirical research has been done in testing this more macro-approach to the theory of imperfect competition, though the general direction and composition of sales of MPEs of different nationalities would lend support to it.[3] Such macro-work so far published has tended to address itself to a rather different question, viz. what determines the flow of capital across national boundaries. The writings of Guy von Stevens, Alan Severn, R. d'Arge and others[4] have been mainly concerned with 'internationalizing' the theory of domestic investment, and specifying the relationship between foreign investment, profitability and other variables.[5]

This research, though providing us with a useful insight into the determinants of foreign direct investment, has generally much less to do with predicting the behaviour of MPEs. This is because the foreign capital owned by MPEs (which is usually taken as the dependent variable) is a poor proxy for the resources under its *control*. Since 1967, for example, the direct outflow of capital from US to finance the growth of American companies in Europe has been reduced, but the rate of expansion of assets *controlled* by US-affiliated companies has been maintained, as an increasing propor-

[1] W. Gruber, D. Mehta and R. Vernon, *op. cit.*

[2] For a summary of these and other modern trade theories, see G. Hufbauer, 'Theories of International Trade and Technological Progress', in R. Vernon (ed.), *Technological and International Trade*, National Bureau Committee for Economic Research, 1970.

[3] J. H. Dunning and R. D. Pearce, *Business Ratios, op. cit.*

[4] See particularly G. V. G. Stevens, 'Capital Mobility and the International Firm', and A. K. Severn, 'Investment and Financial Behaviour of American Direct Investors in Manufacturing': both papers presented at the Conference on International Mobility and Movement of Capital organized by the National Bureau of Economic Research, New York, January/February 1970.

[5] See also A. E. Scaperlanda and L. J. Mauer, 'The Determinants of US Direct Investments in the EEC', *American Economic Review*, September 1969, Vol. LIX, No. 4, Part 1.

tion of the resources used have been recruited locally or from the Euro-dollar market.[1] Probably not more than one-third of the growth of American subsidiaries since 1967 has been financed by new capital from the US and reinvested profits. Indeed, as has been frequently emphasized, the object of many MPEs appears to be to invest a minimum amount of equity in their foreign operations and to use this capital as a catalyst to obtain most of their resources locally. Obviously, this kind of 'geographical' gearing of capital has important implications for the balance of payments of the host and investing countries.

## THE ECONOMIC IMPACT OF THE MPE

We now turn to consider the contribution of MPEs or their subsidiaries on the economies of which they are a part, be they host or investing countries.

There are three sorts of data available for us to draw upon. First, at a macro-economic level, there is information, of varied quality and coverage, of the total foreign capital *stock* (both inward and outward), direct investment *flows* and/or earnings of most of the leading investing and recipient countries.[2] Even though it may still not be possible to derive anything like a complete matrix of international flows between countries,[3] one can estimate, with a reasonable degree of accuracy, the contribution of inward or outward investment to such magnitudes as gross national output, capital formation, and the balance of payments. Quite a lot of data has also been collected by private investigators on the role of foreign investment in particular sectors of host and investing economies[4] although, as one might expect, the further one moves from the macro to the micro level, the less comprehensive and reliable data becomes.

[1] See Chapter 3.
[2] Notably that published by US Department of Commerce, UK Board of Trade, Dominion Bureau of Statistics (Canada), Reserve Bank of India, Ministry of International Trade and Industry Materials (Japan), Commonwealth Bureau of Census and Statistics (Australia).
[3] S. Rolfe, *op. cit*; J. Behrman, *op. cit*; S. H. Robock and K. Simmonds, 'How Big is it: the Missing Dimensions', *Columbia Journal of World Business*, May/June 1970.
[4] For example, D. Brash, *American Investment in Australian Industry*, London, Cass, 1967; A. Safarian, *Foreign Ownership in Canadian Industry*, McGraw Hill, 1966; F. Stubenitsky, *American Direct Investment in the Netherlands Industry*, Rotterdam University Press, 1970; R. B. Dickie, *Foreign Investment in France: a Case Study*, Oceana Publications Inc., 1970.

From the viewpoint of the total activities of international firms, one is faced with a much less satisfactory situation, simply because the data of the kind required are not often separately collected. The most obvious starting point is the financial accounts of the firms. Unfortunately, even when these are available they are subject to a great deal of interpretative difficulty. Statistics of the output, employment, sales and exports of foreign or native owned MPEs are collected by even fewer countries, and these only infrequently. Only in 1970 was the Board of Trade able to produce for the first time an estimate (based on data collected in the 1963 Census of Production) on the contribution of foreign-owned enterprises to industrial output.[1] There are no comparable statistics for the US, although the US Department of Commerce regularly publishes fairly detailed analyses of the sales and trading patterns of its foreign subsidiaries. But the problem of reconciling data derived from widely different sources is a very real one, as anyone who has tried to relate the US Department of Commerce data to the production, sales and exports of indigenous firms will have found.

Thirdly, specially commissioned surveys, e.g. the Reddaway enquiry in the UK and the Hufbauer/Adler study in the US,[2] together with an increasing number of private research projects, are considerably adding to our knowledge of the role of international firms in particular industries or regions of various economies, and also of their size, age and market structure.[3] A good deal of preliminary work is also being done on the relationship between MPEs and employees' organizations in the countries in which they operate.[4]

From these sources of data, it is possible to classify countries (or sectors within countries) in one of four ways:

(a) Those which are substantial *net colonizers* of multinational operations, i.e. where the sales of the foreign subsidiaries of its domestic companies exceed, by a substantial margin, those of the foreign enterprises operating in it. Switzerland and the US are two countries which are in this category. Sometimes the *absolute* amount of net outward investment is large, while *relative* to domestic operations the foreign contribution is not of major importance, as in the US: sometimes the reverse is the case, as in

[1] Board of Trade, *Summary Tables*, 1963, Vol. 132. *Census of Production*, HMSO, 1970.
[2] G. Hufbauer and M. Adler, *Overseas Manufacturing Investments and the Balance of Payments*, US Treasury Dept., Washington, 1968.
[3] *Ibid.*, W. B. Reddaway *et al.*, *op. cit.*
[4] Trades Union Congress, *International Companies*, 1971.

Switzerland. In the UK the food, drink, tobacco and textile industries are among the leading net colonizers of multinational activity.

(b) Those which are both *colonizers* and are *colonized* by MPEs, i.e. which are important both as capital exporters and capital importers. The UK and Holland are the most long-standing examples of countries which are cross-hauliers of capital. Other European countries, e.g. Sweden and Germany, are more recent illustrations. The rubber-tyre industry of France, the pharmaceutical industry of Switzerland and the tobacco industry of the US are among sectors in which there is inward investment and which themselves operate overseas.

(c) Those which are *net colonized* by foreign-owned MPEs. Countries falling into this group are of two kinds. First, the high income but low-populated countries, e.g. Canada and Australia where, in spite of substantial indigenous resources and a highly-skilled workforce, small markets make it difficult for certain industrial sectors to operate on the scale necessary to exploit their full potential, or adequately finance research and development. Second, the less-developed countries, where the investment is in intermediate technology industries and in resource exploitation. As far as colonized sectors within an economy are concerned, the UK motor vehicles industry is a good example: in 1965, the (book) value of the foreign capital stake in the sector was £3,045 million, while British motor car companies owned about £150 million of assets abroad.

(d) Those countries and sectors may be added which, for one reason or another, neither attract inward investment nor invest themselves overseas. The countries include some LDCs, most communist countries and, until recently, Japan; the sectors (in most countries) include shipbuilding, woollen textiles and clothing, and aircraft.

Is it possible to explain why a country or sector should fall into one of these four categories? An analogy with the behaviour of firms may help. An enterprise is most likely to be colonized (i.e. taken over) by another firm whenever its assets are undervalued and/or whenever the buying enterprise believes it can use its resources and/or markets more profitably. The entry of national companies into overseas markets can be interpreted in similar terms, whether an existing foreign firm is purchased or a new enterprise set up. Since both the incentive and the ability of firms to be colonizers will vary between countries and industries, the level and pattern of activity by MPEs of different nationality will tend to differ. We have already explained the importance of knowledge as an agent of production, and the fact that it is expensive to produce. Yet, once produced, knowledge has a low marginal cost of exploitation. Rather than export the products of its knowledge or sell its knowledge to a foreign firm, the innovating firm may find it more profitable to exploit its advantage by colonization, particularly where the recipient country has a comparative cost advantage in the production or marketing of the goods in question. This sort of analysis certainly helps to explain why, for example, the motor vehicle and electronics industries in most countries of the world are *net colonized by* US firms. In other cases, particularly in the LDCs, the foreign penetration of an industry is better understood in terms of the marketing, financial or scale advantages of the colonizing firms.

There are, of course, a host of other factors – political, institutional and sociological – which might also influence the degree of colonization by MPEs, including the way the host economy is organized and the extent to which the benefits of particular MPEs can be obtained in other ways. The post-war experience of Japan is quite different from that of Germany. Its cultural background and strong nationalistic sentiments have largely determined its attitude towards foreign investment. There seems little doubt that had Japan followed the course of the UK and Germany in encouraging inward investment, several sectors of her economy would now be dominated by foreign (and particularly US) firms. The extent to which an importing country can absorb foreign capital is also influenced by its particular phase of growth (compare Australia now and before the war) and by the comparative efficiency of its firms *vis-à-vis* its international competitors.

Usually, of course, the comparative advantage of one nation over another does not apply across the board, nor is it necessarily maintained over time.[1] This helps to explain why two way currents in investment can and do occur. Canada is substantially a capital importer but in certain industries, viz. agricultural machinery, aluminium processing, etc. her own MPEs are among the largest in the world. Australia has substantial foreign investments in food processing and the Swiss in pharmaceuticals; Philips of Eindhoven is the fifth largest foreign company in the UK, while Japanese firms

[1] For the experience of British investment in the US, see T. C. Coram, *The Role of British Capital in the Development of the US 1600–1915*, M.Sc. (Soc. Science) thesis, University of Southampton, 1967.

are carving out an important share of the South American market in heavy iron and steel products. The UK insurance industry owns foreign assets considerably in excess of those possessed by other nationalities; at the same time, overseas banks in London account for 15% of all bank deposits in the UK.[1]

It is not, then, surprising that foreign investment tends to be concentrated in particular industrial sectors. Where the investment is also concentrated in the hands of a few firms, who use this capital as a catalyst to gain control over local resources, the impact of MPEs becomes that much greater and of more concern to host nations. And it is a fact that by far the larger part of international investment of all countries is undertaken by large firms competing under conditions of imperfect oligopoly.[2] Thus the impact of the MPE is considerably understated by the value of its foreign investment. The question now arises: to what extent is this impact different from that of a domestic firm of comparable size?

## THE ECONOMIC ISSUES INVOLVED

In this section we shall try and pinpoint some of the *economic* consequences of the presence of foreign-owned MPEs to nation states. These, of course, are not the only issues; indeed sometimes they may be secondary to political, social and cultural ones.

One thing which many studies of the multinational enterprise fail to establish is the extent to which any differences in its behaviour, compared with that of a national company, are due specifically to its 'multinationalism'. It is, for example, perfectly possible for an American subsidiary in the UK to perform more (or less) efficiently than a UK competitor for reasons, e.g. of size, product structure or technical expertise which have nothing to do with the fact that it is a subsidiary of a foreign enterprise. On the other hand, it could be *because* it is part of a MPE that its behaviour and impact in certain situations is quite different.

What, then, are the distinctive features of multinational businesses? We examine three aspects of the problem. First, the ways in which the MPE is analytically or conceptually different from a NPE. Second, whether or not its behaviour is likely to be different. And third, the extent to which its consequences on economic welfare are likely to be different.

[1] 'Foreign Banks in London', *The Banker*, November 1970.
[2] S. Hymer and R. Rowthorn, 'Multinational Corporations and International Oligopoly', in Kindleberger, *op. cit.*

## ANALYTICAL FEATURES

### (1) *The Theory of the Firm*

As a firm widens its territorial horizons, it changes its character to a certain extent. An enterprise which graduates from supplying a regional market to supplying a national market finds itself in competition with new firms and is faced with new market structures. Similarly, a firm with plants in more than one part of the country will have more flexibility in the organization of its activities than that possessed by a single plant firm. Depending on the importance of these differences, a plant operating in a particular location which is part of a multi-plant firm may be organized and perform differently than its single plant competitors, and its impact on the local region may also be different.[1]

As a firm goes 'international' in its operations these same considerations apply but they are intensified. (Compare, for example, the production and market conditions for rubber tyres in different parts of the UK with that in Pakistan.) The fact that the environment to which the new foreign investor is accustomed is different from that of its local competitors may give it certain advantages. If, for example, the host economy is becoming generally more capital-intensive in its production methods then, obviously, enterprises from countries more experienced in these methods will have the edge over local firms. Indeed, one of the most important competitive advantages of MPEs arises because they can draw upon their operating experience in different economic environments. This advantage is not only confined to production techniques. Knowledge gained in marketing, industrial relations, investment appraisal and so on may be equally valuable. As long as the MPE has the opportunity to make use of this experience – and chooses to do so – then it both increases its own efficiency and, because it is free to transfer its knowledge within its organization, that of the world economy as well.

In addition, there are differences between countries of a legal, political or cultural character which may also influence not only the amount of foreign investment undertaken, but the behaviour of investing firms. For, like the uncertainty surrounding the exchange rate, they may add a risk premium to foreign operations which, allowing for differentials in rates of taxation, may affect the way a MPE chooses (or would prefer) to allocate its profits between

[1] In a survey of some of the issues involved, see H. W. Richardson, *Regional Economics*, London, Weidenfeld & Nicolson, 1969.

31

countries. None of these problems really face the multi-plant domestic firm. Within a country there is usually unrestricted (though not costless) mobility of factor inputs and goods; there is a single currency and rarely will there be any substantial differences in the rate of profits tax between the regions.

The effects of these distortions on the activities of businesses are, of course, not confined to international firms. But the MPE is in a better position to overcome them. In order to minimize its world tax burden it is able to manipulate (or, at least, attempt to manipulate) its intra-group prices, both of goods and services, so as to record as high a profit as it can in low tax countries at the expense of profits in high tax countries. Neither this opportunity, nor those which arise from the ability of the MPE to organize the movement of goods and resources between countries to take advantage of the most favourable prices, are as readily available to NPEs.

Conceptually, there is no real difficulty in incorporating these new dimensions into the theory of the firm. On the other hand, it is possible that the utility function of managers of multinational businesses is different from that of managers of national enterprises. The motivation of local management may be influenced by local customs and constraints: indeed, in order to pacify host governments and avoid any charge of exploitation, the firm may adopt a 'satisfying' rather than 'maximizing' approach to projects. These differences in objectives are likely to be intensified where the subsidiary of the MPE is partly owned by local interests, the objectives of whom may not be the same as the foreign shareholders.[1]

## (2) *The Theory of International Trade*

Another area in which the activities of the multinational enterprise are different from that of the national enterprise is in the behaviour of trade flows. Almost all theories of international trade presuppose that trade is conducted between independent firms – the conditions and terms of which are determined by normal market forces – subject to macro-economic constraints.

The introduction of the MPE has affected trade flows in two ways. First, as we have seen, a substantial part of world trade, probably about one-eighth, is trade internal to MPEs. To be sure, some of this trade may well have taken place in any event – particularly the purchase of raw materials and sales of finished products; in other cases, the international spread of production facilities has been trade substituting. But a third type of trade which we might call cross-

[1] E. Kolde, *International Business Enterprise*, New York, Prentice-Hall, 1968.

32

horizontal trade is very much a product of the MPE and, in particular, of the way in which its world-wide operations are organized. To take one example, the world trade in electronic computers and related products is strongly influenced by the larger MPEs, which tend to be highly integrated in their operations and generate a considerable amount of *intra*-enterprise trade. The pattern of this trade would be quite different if each nation was self sufficient in its computer production and/or MPEs operated self-contained operating units in each country.

The second effect of the MPE on trade is much more difficult to assess. In spite of some quite sophisticated work by UK and US economists,[1] we still know very little about the extent to which the MPE affects *inter*-enterprise trade between countries. So much rests on the assumptions we make about the so-called 'alternative' position, i.e. what would have happened in the absence of the MPE. No generalization applicable to all situations seems possible,[2] although there is a strong presumption that MPEs have increased world trade since (*a*) international direct investment has almost certainly added to the level and quality of the world's real capital stock and hence world output, and (*b*) on average, the growth of world trade has kept pace with the growth of world output.

No one can doubt, however, that the geographical and industrial pattern of world trade has been very much affected by the operations of multinational enterprises. This can be seen *inter alia* by comparing the import and export performance of subsidiaries of MPEs with that of domestic companies.[3] It has been estimated, for example, that one-third of the increase in Europe's exports of technologically advanced products between 1955 and 1964 was accounted for by US-financed firms.[4] An even more dramatic impact is revealed by the composition of Canadian exports and some of those of the LDCs.[5] The full implications of these trends which partly reflect the

[1] W. B. Reddaway *et al.*, *op. cit.*; Hufbauer and Adler, *op. cit.*, and present research now being undertaken by the NBER.

[2] W. B. Reddaway, *op. cit.*

[3] For the UK experience, see *Board of Trade Journal*, August 16, 1968.

[4] J. H. Dunning, 'European and US Trade Patterns and US Foreign Investment', in C. P. Kindleberger and A. Shonfield (eds.), *North American and Western European Economic Policies*, Macmillan, 1971.

[5] A. E. Safarian, 'The Exports of American-Owned Exports in Canada', *Papers and Proceedings of the American Economic Association*, Vol. LIX, No. 3, May 1964 and L. Needlemam and others. Flow of provincial resources: balance of payments effects of private foreign investment. Case studies of Jamaica and Kenya UNCTAD document TD/B/C. 3/79. July 1970.

effect which MPEs have had on the comparative trading advantage of nations and partly the trading policies of MPEs (for example, since devaluation, the UK has become a more attractive base from which US firms can export to third markets) has not yet been worked out by international trade theorists, and there is a fruitful area for research here.[1]

There are various other branches of economic analysis which may need to be re-thought in the light of the growth of the international firm. The role of the MPE as a transmitter of factor inputs, particularly knowledge and entrepreneurship across national boundaries, and its impact on the economic development of host nations, is one of these; another is its implications for the theory of economic welfare of both investing and host nations; a third is the theory of wages and collective bargaining.

### (3) *Policy*

In the last resort, policy towards the MPE cannot be better than the policy-maker's understanding of the causes and effects of its behaviour. There are five main steps in the policy-formulating process:

(*a*) The recognition of a problem, or a phenomenon to be explained, e.g. that MPEs supply an important part of the output of a particular industry, or are instrumental in changing the pattern of a country's trade.

(*b*) The identification of the character of the problem, e.g. an evaluation of the net benefits (or costs) resulting from the presence of MPEs compared, for example, with those which would have occurred had the resources been obtained in a different way.

(*c*) An understanding of the factors influencing the behaviour of the main decision-taking units involved, e.g. in what way does the behaviour of the MPE differ from that of the NPE?

(*d*) A cost/benefit analysis of alternative policies which might be pursued either to affect the behaviour of the MPE, or of other economic agents, as a result of its effects.

(*e*) The choice of policy which is thought most likely to satisfy the policy-makers' objectives.

So far, thinking on these problems has advanced little beyond the first stage – yet all too often the policy makers choose to introduce measures and programmes based on hunches and prejudice rather than on substantive evidence.

[1] See also Chapter 6 in this volume.

Assume that there is something to be explained. How can one identify the characteristics of the problem? In what way are the economic objectives of governments advanced or hindered by the presence of foreign-owned firms. We have already suggested that only by comparing the actual behaviour and performance of MPEs with some alternative pattern of resource allocation can this question be properly answered. As a first shot let us make some very simple assumptions. The first is that governments of both host and investing countries pursue neutral policies towards the foreign operation of their MPEs; second, that corporate tax rates are identical for all countries and that there are zero risks associated with political instability or changes in the exchange rate. Third, that the utility functions of international firms (and their subsidiaries) are the same as those of NPEs.

Given these assumptions, in what ways might the impact of a subsidiary of a foreign-owned MPE on the local economy be distinctive? There are several possibilities, the more important of which are as follows.

(a) Its operating efficiency may be affected by the knowledge available to it from the rest of the enterprise of which it is part.

(b) As a result of (a), its methods of production, labour policies, marketing and purchasing techniques, financial strategies and so on may be different.

(c) Both the composition of the output it supplies, and the degree to which its operations are (internationally) vertically or horizontally integrated may be different.

(d) The level and pattern of its imports and exports may be different.

(e) The share of its value added, remitted (or credited) to non-resident shareholders will be greater.

(f) The external or spill-over effects, associated with its operations, e.g. the dissemination of knowledge, competitive stimulus, etc. may be more or less.

Each of these differences may affect, for good or bad, the economic welfare of the host country. In the short run, this will show itself in the level and structure of the domestic output and distribution of national income; over a longer period it may have far-reaching effects on the host country's international competitive position, the pattern of its economic growth and its relationships with the investing country.

If we now introduce an element of government intervention into

35

the situation, then this list of possible differences in the behaviour of the MPE is extended quite considerably.

First, if for whatever reason, the government of the investing company has the power, and uses the power, to influence the decision-taking of (or with respect to) the foreign subsidiaries of the MPE, then it is possible that the economic welfare of the host country may be affected. The favourite examples of extra-territorality usually quoted are the control of dividends policy and the constraints placed on US companies and their subsidiaries, on which countries they can trade with, and the extent to which they can associate with other firms. In each of these respects the policy of the US Government may not always be in accord with either the best interests of American subsidiaries or the policies of governments in host countries.[1]

Second, the fiscal, mainly taxation, policies pursued by governments of both investing and host countries will obviously influence the net profitability of the MPE and will cause it to arrange its intra-group trading in such a way as to earn profits where they are taxed the least. The *power* of companies to shift profits is the direct outcome of their multinational operations: the *incentive* to do so is due to the differential treatment by countries of income earned.

Third, because of these differences, multinational companies may well respond differently to the economic policies of host countries and, in some cases, may be able to avoid constraints on their conduct better than national firms. A credit squeeze in the UK may simply encourage US subsidiaries to obtain additional finance from their parent companies; the reactions of such firms to various incentives, e.g. investment allowances and the regional employment premium, may also differ from that of their native competitors.

### THE NATION STATE CONTROVERSY

It is these differences in the behaviour of international companies and their effects on national economic welfare which sometimes prompts a rather cautious attitude on the part of host governments towards them. Without detailed empirical research, one can say very little about the precise effects of such companies on particular recipient countries. But we do, perhaps, know enough to suggest under what conditions they are most likely to lead to an increase in

[1] Such as the measures taken by President Johnson in January 1968 to reduce the flow of new US foreign investment, which helped to exacerbate the balance of payments difficulties of a number of recipient countries.

economic welfare, and what might be done to maximize their net social benefits.

At the start, I think it important to accept there is almost certain to be a conflict between the *objectives* of a subsidiary of a foreign-owned firm and those of the host nation. To a certain extent, such a conflict exists between a domestically-owned MPE or NPEs and the nation state of which they are part: only very indirectly, for example, are such companies concerned with broader economic and social objectives. But because some of the resources of the subsidiary of a foreign company are owned outside the country in which it operates, an additional conflict arises. Profits (and interest) earned by a national firm contribute to the country's net income: profits (and interest) earned and remitted by a subsidiary of a foreign-owned firm contribute to the income of the *investing* country. This means that while the host country is concerned with minimizing the profit component of any given output generated by the MPE (i.e. maximizing the local value added – *lva*), the MPE may reasonably wish to maximize this component.

While accepting that, in practice, profit maximization may not always be the objective of MPEs, let us assume for the moment that their behaviour is geared to this end. Now, clearly, there are various ways by which the host government can try and keep the profits of international firms to the minimum consistent with maintaining their presence. Much of its policy towards monopolies and restrictive practices, to which foreign firms are as much subject as are domestic firms, has this aim. But because the foreign-owned subsidiary is sometimes able to increase the earnings remitted to the investing country by various devices not open to the domestic firm, some observers have suggested that more discriminatory measures are needed to ensure it conforms to national objectives.

There is some *non sequitur* in this argument. It does not necessarily follow, even if there is a conflict of objectives between the international enterprise and the nation state, that the final economic impact of the MPE, in the absence of government interference, might not be in the nation state's best interests. This entirely depends on whether, in its absence, the resources it uses could have been better deployed elsewhere; not whether the subsidiary is producing at maximum efficiency or its *lva* is as high as it might be.

Let us try and elaborate this argument. Suppose the host country has a single objective – to maximize its gross national product (GNP), or rate of growth of GNP, from the resources available. The contribution of foreign subsidiaries to this target is the increase in net output (i.e. above that which occurred in their absence), less the share of income accruing to the investing company, i.e. *lva*. This contribution will depend on (*a*) the efficiency of the subsidiary of the MPE, and the extent to which, by one means or another, it increases or decreases the productivity of other companies in the economy, and (*b*) on the share of the total value added remitted to the investing company. This includes not only the recorded profits and interests on capital invested, but also 'disguised' profits contained in royalties and fees paid for services rendered. These may be thought of as the 'price' which has to be paid by the host country to the investing country for the investment.

We have suggested that one reason why the *lva* of a foreign subsidiary might be lower than it could be is that its market position allows it to earn above competitive profits. Policy here, as with domestic firms in a similar situation, must obviously direct itself to stimulating competition or, at least, curbing the abuses of monopoly power. The peculiar feature of much American foreign investment in high technology industries, however, is that the size of most domestic markets outside the US does not permit more than one or two firms to derive the fullest advantages from the economies of scale, and because of the economies of large-scale research, larger firms often have the edge on their smaller competitors. This means that to maintain effective competition against the American challenge some host countries may need to encourage the merger of enterprises, not only within their boundaries but across boundaries.

A second and related problem arises from the diffusion of knowledge first introduced by MPEs. Only in certain circumstances will it be in the enterprises' best interest to encourage this. Certainly, the vertical dissemination of knowledge by US subsidiaries to their British component suppliers and their customers has been one of their most valuable spillover effects.[1] And the type of knowledge which is specific to the enterprise, but which cannot be patented or put down on paper, e.g. much of managerial, marketing and organization know-how, permeates into the economy in other ways. Again, however, it is difficult to see what the host economy can do except create the type of environment most conducive to the spread of this knowledge.

The contribution of foreign firms to economic growth will also depend on the type of activity in which they engage, as this affects the productivity of local resources used. We have dealt with one

[1] J. H. Dunning, *American Investment in British Manufacturing Industry*, London, Allen & Unwin, 1958.

aspect of this problem in another paper with Max Steuer.[1] Suffice here to make one general point. Anything which the MPE can do to improve the productivity of indigenous resources must be a good thing. If, for example, by dint of its superior knowledge, it is able to improve the skill of the labour it recruits, it will increase the *lva*. If, however, by undertaking research and development the foreign firm uses labour already trained from other sources then, although, if its productivity is higher, it may still increase the GNP, it is possible it may have made an even more valuable contribution by importing knowledge from the US, engaging only in simple production operations, and allowing indigenous firms to use the skilled labour. A lot more research needs to be done before one can say anything about the optimum structure of inward investment for a particular country.

Neither is it possible to generalize on the desirability of subsidiaries of MPEs purchasing their inputs from local suppliers rather than importing them. Much depends here on one's assumptions about the ability of the Government to maintain full employment, and whether or not the *lva* of the resources of UK firms in their present use is higher or lower than they would be if they produced parts and components for the foreign subsidiary. The case for local self-sufficiency is, however, strengthened wherever the presence of a foreign company produces a beneficial spillover effect on other firms and/or there are economies of vertical integration for the industry.

In the last resort, the policy of the host nation to maximize the *lva* of inward direct investment is constrained by the opportunities open to the investing firm to locate its production facilities elsewhere. In recent years, European governments have competed with each other to attract new US investment. This, in effect, has bid up the 'price' which incoming firms expect on their capital and, in consequence, has reduced their contribution to national output. Just as international machinery (in the form of GATT) exists to prevent unfair discrimination of one country to gain trade over another, it may well be in the long-term interests of government to formulate a code of good behaviour which will outlaw unfair discrimination (one way or the other) towards inward investment.[2]

Governments can affect the contribution of MPEs in two main ways. First, there is the issue of extra-territorality. By policies

[1] J. H. Dunning and M. Steuer, 'The Effects of US Direct Investment in Britain on British Technology', *Moorgate and Wall Street*, Autumn 1969.

[2] Joint Economic Committee of the US Congress, *The Multinational Corporation and International Investment*, Hearings, p. 27, 30th July 1970.

designed to protect its own economic welfare, the *lva* of the foreign subsidiaries of its MPE may be adversely affected. Such issues as these can only be satisfactorily resolved by discussions at an inter-government level. Secondly, use may be made of fiscal policies. On the one hand, a high rate of tax will increase the governments share of any given amount of profits or interest earned by a foreign subsidiary. On the other, it encourages the MPE to earn its profits in other countries where the tax rate is lower, by selling goods and services at below arm's length prices to its associated companies in these countries and buying from them at above arm's length prices.

Finally, the contribution of subsidiaries of MPEs to the GNP of host countries will be influenced by the proportion of equity capital locally owned. The Watkins Committee and others have emphasized the need for local economies to participate in the ownership of subsidiaries.[1] Most MPEs, however, particularly those of a geo-centric kind, appear to find joint ownership, due to a possible conflict of interest between the shareholders in the two (or more) countries, hampers their ability to operate as an efficient harmonized and co-ordinated unit.[2]

So far we have assumed the host country objectives can be expressed in terms of the level and growth of real national output. But clearly they are much more complicated than this. In some cases, for example, an argument similar to the infant industry argument for protecting a country against the import of goods may be put forward against foreign capital inflow. Here it is felt that the foreign firms, by their superior knowledge, inhibit local production from making a contribution to the nation's output which, in due course, might be greater than their own. In most cases this is a second best argument – but it is best discussed under the alternatives to the MPE.[3]

The other reasons why host countries might wish to restrict inward investment fall into two categories.[4] First, there are investments which are not welcomed because they are in industrial sectors over which it is desired to maintain complete independence and sovereignty. The obvious examples are communications and defence. It is really an extension of this argument to limit the extent of foreign investment in sectors vital to the economic well-being of the community, e.g. electronics, motor vehicles, oil. What the

[1] M. Watkins, *op. cit.*   [2] E. Kolde, *op. cit.*   [3] See pp. 42 ff.
[4] See H. G. Johnson, 'The Efficiency and Welfare Implications of the International Corporation' in C. P. Kindleberger (ed.), *The International Corporation*, M.I.T. Press, 1970.

trade-off is between the economic gain of such inward investment, and loss of national sovereignty or security this might imply, cannot be settled solely by economic analysis. It is probably true, though, that the higher proportion of any industry owned by foreign companies, the greater the potential economic gain of any new investment has to be to compensate for any loss of independence.

Secondly, host countries may be concerned about the effects of the operations of foreign companies on the distribution of the national output. Chief amongst these is the balance of payments impact. Since the war, the UK Government has particularly welcomed the contribution of inward investment where it seemed likely to benefit the balance of payments. Capital exporting countries have also been concerned about the payback on outward investment. The only comment we would make here is the obvious one that, as an economic phenomena, the balance of payments should not be regarded as an end in itself – though it may affect the extent to which wider economic objectives may be achieved. What is important to know is whether the level and/or rate of growth of GNP, after any adjustments to the balance of payments thought desirable as a result of foreign investment, is greater or less than that which would result from any alternative allocation of the same resources. This kind of sensitivity analysis might be used to evaluate the economic or social impact of foreign companies in other areas, e.g. the regional distribution of investment, industrial relations and trades union practices and so on.

In spite of what has been said, there is pressure from various sources in a number of countries to try and draw up guide-lines of good corporate behaviour for firms of foreign parentage. In general, I am as sceptical about the wisdom of doing this as for the laying down of such guidelines for national firms. Much depends, of course, on the objectives of such guidelines, and no one would deny that in specific instances they serve a useful purpose well. But if the aim of the host country is to ensure the maximum contribution to productivity from non-resident firms, then what is most required of governments is the creation of an economic and political environment by which such firms come nearest to achieving this by pursuing their own ends. It makes little sense to force the MPE to play a particular game differently from what it wants to, when what is really needed is for the rules of the game to be changed. Only when the net benefits of such a policy are shown to be less than those arising from the introduction of constraints would this latter policy be justifiable.

41

To summarize. One must accept that there will almost certainly be a conflict of objectives between the multinational enterprise and the nation states in which it operates. But this does not mean the community would be better off with less inward investment. To determine whether this is so or not, one needs first to specify one's social and economic goals; second, to formulate a model by which one can assess the contribution by the foreign-owned firms to these goals; and third, examine how this contribution could be improved upon by more effective micro- or macro-policies, or institutional reforms. Rather than criticize the foreign subsidiaries for any labour redundancies as a result of its intra-plant rationalization schemes, governments and trades unions in host countries might do better to study ways and means by which the hardship resulting from these redundancies might be minimized.

Where MPEs behave differently from national firms and it is desired to influence their behaviour, then specific rather than general policies may need to be implemented. In some cases multilateral discussions may be desirable to draw up international codes of conduct towards inward investment. As to the impact of MPEs on non-economic objectives, the most the economist can try and do is to estimate the cost of taking action which might conflict with economic goals, in terms of the extent to which these goals are less well achieved.

## ALTERNATIVES TO THE MPE

In the final analysis, the value of the contribution of the multinational enterprise must be judged in terms of their opportunity cost. Economists are principally interested in first best solutions. Even assuming everything had been done to ensure that a foreign-owned firm was contributing as much as it could to a particular host country, it might still be cheaper (in terms of resource usage) to obtain these benefits by other means. Whether or not this is the case cannot be settled on *a priori* grounds, but it is possible to make a few generalizations.

It is generally agreed that the main benefit of inward direct investment is that it offers a 'package deal' of complementary factor inputs, viz. knowledge, capital and entrepreneurship. The costs – or potential costs – are twofold: first, the price paid for these services and, second, the control of resources gained by the foreign-owned firm which, for reasons already given, may not be exercised to the maximum benefit of the host country.

The first of these costs must be set beside the costs of obtaining the individual components of the package deal in different ways, e.g. by domestic firms borrowing money on the international capital market and concluding management contracts or technological licensing agreements with foreign companies. In principle, one should be able to make a cost/benefit analysis of these various alternatives, which may include doing more indigenous research and development; presumably, some sort of calculation like this is carried out by domestic firms seeking to obtain (say) a new production process from abroad and foreign firms wishing to sell the process (including selling it via the medium of foreign investment). In practice, data limitations make it extremely difficult to make any precise evaluation of the alternatives.

It may be argued that the above issue is a non-problem. Why not allow the interested institutions to make the appropriate decisions? Providing these are correct, then the best alternative will be chosen. This is an interesting view and there might be something in it if market conditions approached the text-book state of 'perfect competition'. But, in this case, the market is clearly imperfect, with governments adding to these imperfections, e.g. by import controls, the subsidization of research and development and so on. Moreover, there is no reason to suppose that the external or spillover effects associated with these alternatives and impact will be the same.

Let me illustrate. Suppose the British consumer is interested in obtaining a particular drug at present manufactured in the US. Several choices are open. The finished product could be imported: British firms could produce it, but import (by one means or another) the necessary technology; a US firm might find it worthwhile to set up a subsidiary in the UK to manufacture the product; British firms could try and produce a similar product, using their own technology. Left to the market, it may be decided that a British firm should manufacture the product but buy the necessary technology through a licensing agreement. But this would not necessarily be in the best interests of the national economy. Compared with the setting up of a foreign subsidiary, the *direct* impact on GNP may be more favourable, but the technological spillover effects could be much less; and though a new product would be added to the range supplied by the UK pharmaceutical firms, the technological dependence on the US would be no less. For these reasons the host government may wish to intervene in the market process to tilt the choice of the nation towards inward investment.[1]

[1] Alternatively, the market might overrate the net benefits of inward investment, and rather more constraints on foreign firms might be called for.

Even so, there is a further question: what kind of inward investment? It should be clear from what has been written that the impact of the subsidiary of a foreign firm – even within a particular industry – on the GNP of the recipient economy may differ considerably – according to both the way in which it is financed and how its activities are integrated with those of the rest of the enterprise of which it is part. The technological spillover effects of a foreign subsidiary in the machine-tool industry may be no greater if it is 100% financed rather than 51% financed, but they may differ considerably according to the extent to which its operations are vertically integrated. The financing issue has two implications. From the host country's viewpoint, the question is what is the minimum amount of equity capital which must be invested by the foreign-owned MPE to generate a given increase in GNP? Other things being equal, the larger the proportion of local shareholding, the more will be the contribution of the foreign subsidiary to the domestic economy. In this case, assuming that there is shortage of domestic savings, then it is clearly better to import loan capital and encourage local participation in the equity capital either of the foreign subsidiaries or of their parent companies.

Nor is it possible to get very far with a macro cost/benefit analysis. By studying the ways in which different industries (or size of firms) obtain their technology and expertise, it may be possible to formulate general principles as to the conditions in which the subsidiaries of multinational enterprises are most likely to maximize the GNP of host countries compared with licensing agreements.[1] An obvious example is where the knowledge is of a kind which cannot be embodied in drawings, specifications, machines and so on, and is more concerned with management and organizational skills. Where, too, one wishes to inject more efficiency into an industry, the encouragement of inward investment may be preferable to propping up native firms by government aid. On the other hand, where an industry is already largely controlled by foreign-owned MPEs, a case may be made out for government help to assist domestic firms to compete more effectively. Sometimes, it may be in the best interests of a country to encourage a subsidiary to produce a complete line of products: in another to specialize and engage in the maximum amount of intra-enterprise trade in the world.

If the avoidance of foreign financial control is a key objective of

---

[1] Similarly, with the alternative forms of the *outflow* of resources, though this paper has concentrated very much on the effects of the inward transfer of resources.

governments, then clearly all the other alternatives to foreign direct investment have their merits, though it does not follow that these will allow the host country more economic *independence*. There is a lot of misunderstanding about the independence issue. It is true that the MPEs affect the geographical pattern of resource utilization. But no less does international trade. For example, American enterprises have always influenced the level and structure of resource utilization in the UK by their demands for British goods. Though US subsidiaries in Britain make a more direct demand for labour, land and capital, in each case, the UK is economically 'dependent' on the US: the principles are essentially the same.

The control issue is rather different, and concerns the long implications of inward direct investment. Equity capital accumulates and since it tends to be concentrated in the faster-growing sectors and backed by local capital – this gives foreign companies increasing control of the host countries resources. For example, only about one-quarter of the increase in the capital stake of American-based companies since 1950 has been financed from capital exports from the US: the balance has been made up of reinvested profits and local debt capital.

This fear of growing financial control has led many' countries to insist on a local equity shareholding in all foreign associated companies, or to limit foreign investment in some way or another. In some developing countries an impasse has occurred between investing enterprises, who are reluctant to relinquish the security of a 100% financial control, and recipient countries who welcome the benefits of inward investment but who wish to be in complete control of their economic destiny. In many developed countries, too, governments are tending to become more sensitive on this issue, the cordiality extended to foreign investment varying almost inversely with the amount of foreign participation already existing.

One thing seems certain. The multinational enterprise, though generally an instrument of growth and efficiency, does require an economic environment which is receptive to the consequences of change. Like a country dependent on foreign trade, an economy influenced by the MPEs, both foreign and locally owned, is potentially less stable, at least in the short term, than one which is self-sufficient. Though there is little evidence that foreign firms have engaged in widespread closures of plants in Europe due to international rationalization schemes, isolated cases have been reported which have a marked impact on particular industries or regions.[1]

[1] Though, again, such schemes have been minor compared with those involving only domestic firms.

Moreover, however closely the subsidiary of a foreign-owned firm may be identified with the host country, the parent company can never be as wholly identified as can a parent company of a local-based MPE. While, then, the host Government can, by one means or another, constrain the behaviour of a foreign subsidiary, in the last resort, it has the power either to withdraw from the economy, or cut back its plans for expansion. It may do this, of course, for reasons quite unconnected with the economic climate of the host country, e.g. due to conditions at home or in other countries where it has its subsidiaries. To this extent, its behaviour is likely to be more volatile than that of domestic businesses – although in a period of prosperity and expansion, this characteristic may be concealed.

This volatility of behaviour is an additional price which a host country may have to pay for the benefits of the MPE. It is a price which, at times, and to particular sectors of the economy, may appear a heavy one[1] (although this can be cushioned by appropriate government policy towards redeployment and retraining), but it is one which has to be paid by any economy which seeks to keep pace with changes in world technology and conditions of demand.

## CONCLUSIONS AND POLICY IMPLICATIONS

The growing contribution of multinational enterprises to world economic output is likely to continue in the foreseeable future. It is also likely to pose a variety of problems. This paper has sought to identify the character of these problems in so far as they are different from those arising from the operation of national companies, or in the normal course of trade. These problems are sometimes exacerbated by xenophobia – the special pleading of particular interests, but they essentially arise because of a certain conflict of objectives between the MPE and the nation states of which they are part, and the fact that the MPE, *because* it is *multinational*, may use devices to achieve these objectives – which may not always be in these same nation states. Accepting that the policy of governments of nation states is usually designed to maximize the net benefits of the inflow of resources, there are various forms of action it might take.

First, host governments should try and formulate general principles as to the kinds of foreign investment most likely to be beneficial to economic welfare. This implies that they should be aware of the causes and consequences of different types of inward investment,

[1] For an examination of the attitudes of trades unions, see Chapter 5 in this volume.

and that it should ensure that any decision to invest, rather than to license, is taken in the light of full information both to investing firm and potential UK licensees.

Second, governments should strive to create the economic environment so that locally-owned MPEs and subsidiaries of foreign MPEs can operate as efficiently as possible. Where appropriate, governments should take the initiative to help national firms to be an effective countervailing power to powerful foreign financed companies, while encouraging the diffusion of knowledge throughout the economy.

Third, and more specifically, governments should seek to identify possible areas of conflict which might arise from decisions taken by MPEs – in particular regions, sectors or areas of economic activity – and, again, introduce the appropriate measures either to minimize the conflicts or the adverse effects of their consequences. This may include a selective approach to inward investment and policies which may affect the behaviour of MPEs.

Fourth, governments should aim, by one means or another, to minimize 'unfair' transfer pricing; they should negotiate with investing governments on the question of extra-territorality, e.g. anti-trust policy, export embargoes. I am less enthusiastic for laying down general guide-lines for good *corporate* behaviour – partly because what is *good* corporate behaviour will differ according to circumstances – and partly because if it is followed literally, and by all countries, the international company may become such an emasculated institution that it can no longer produce the beneficial effects it does.

In this paper we have concentrated on some of the economic issues surrounding the MPE. We recognize, however, that there are other considerations relating to national sovereignty, and in the end these may be the more decisive ones. But the economist can still make a contribution to assessing the economic significance of an increasing foreign participation in a particular industry by providing the decision-takers information with the size and character of the 'trade-off'.

In general, we take the view that the case has not been proven for the setting up of a supra-national authority to control the operations of MPEs as they are at present organized. If supra-national action is needed, we consider it should be directed towards three objectives: first, the curtailment of international monopoly power of MPEs by the encouragement of countervailing power (cf. the work of the Industrial Reorganization Corporation in the UK);

this may only be possible by further economic integration. Second, to encourage individual governments to consult on ways and means of rationalizing their own policies towards the MPE, e.g. in respect of extra-territorality and tax systems. Third, to foster more research in the ways by which the individual countries in which subsidiaries of MPEs operate can be better identified with the prosperity of the whole organization of which they are part. One suggestion is that the equity shareholding in the capital of MPEs should be shared between the different countries in which they operate according to the proportion of the total sales or assets accounted for by them.

It is accepted by most economists that, in the long run, the unhindered movements of goods and factors of production best serves the world's economic interests and that of individual countries – though, in certain circumstances, and in the short run, certain constraints may be necessary to protect economies against some of the vagaries of the free market. There is much to be said for countries adopting the same basic attitude towards the operations of multinational enterprises, and for governments, sometimes in conjunction with another, to create the economic environment which enables them to contribute most to the GNP, and only intervene when there is some reason to suppose that market is unable to produce a 'first best' solution to resource allocation in which they are involved.

*Chapter 2*

# THE MULTINATIONAL ENTERPRISE IN A MULTIPLE CURRENCY WORLD

## ROBERT Z. ALIBER

### INTRODUCTION

The growth of the multinational firm has been a major development in the international economy. For several hundreds of years – since the founding of the East India Company and the Hudson's Bay Company – firms based in one country have engaged in production and sales in other countries. Usually those firms, like those in mining, petroleum and plantation enterprises, were vertically organized, frequently with the market in the country in which the firm was based. The uniqueness of direct foreign investment in the recent period has been that the activities of the firms in various parts of the world are sometimes much more closely co-ordinated because of increases in the speed and reductions in the costs of communication and transportation. Productive activities under one management in various countries may more fully involve horizontal integration. The scope of the market has increased because of these same developments in communication.

This chapter discusses the two aspects of the relationship between the multinational producing enterprise and a world of multiple currencies. The first involves the extent to which patterns in the growth of the enterprise can be explained by the demarcation of the world into various currency areas. The second involves the extent to which the international corporation affects the independence of the monetary authorities in various currency areas. These firms may be in a better position to alter the currency mix of their cash positions, and thus affect the distribution of foreign exchange reserves of central banks in a pegged exchange rate system, or the level of spot exchange rate in a floating rate system.

### THEORIES OF DIRECT FOREIGN INVESTMENT

Several years ago I suggested a theory of direct investment based on the division of the world into numerous currency areas.[1] The motivation for the development of this theory was the need to find some element of 'foreignness' in a direct foreign investment – some factor which was qualitatively different from those which explain the expansion of regional firms into national firms, a factor which could be attributable to the existence of national boundaries. The traditional theory of foreign investment – the Hymer–Kindleberger view – suggested that firms with a monopolistic advantage expanded into foreign markets to exploit their advantage abroad.[2] As foreign firms expanded into the domestic market of others, so there resulted a great web with firms based in each country invading the domestic markets of foreign firms. Caves hypothesized that firms in oligopolistic industries in each country encounter limits to increasing the sales of their traditional product in the domestic market; to continue their growth rate, they must choose between expanding across a product boundary in the domestic market or expanding across a national border with their traditional product.[3] In both the Hymer and Caves views, the foreignness tends to be identified with economic distance.

The industrial organization approach to direct investment did not explain why the firm chose to exploit the foreign market through investment rather than through exporting or licensing. Subsequent articles suggested the market for advantages might be imperfect.[4] The traditional theory has other shortcomings – it offers little explanatory power for the country pattern of foreign investment (why so many countries are host countries and so few are source countries), nor could it explain the industrial pattern of foreign investment (why there is so much foreign investment in aluminium and so little in steel). Finally, the traditional theory could not explain direct foreign investment through takeovers.

Theories of foreign investment should be directed at the observed pattern of penetration of foreign markets – most firms intially satisfy the foreign demand by exporting from domestic production; the

[1] Robert Z. Aliber, 'A Theory of Direct Foreign Investment', in C. P. Kindleberger (ed.), *The International Corporation*, M.I.T. Press, 1970.

[2] S. Hymer, *The International Operations of National Firms, A Study of Direct Foreign Investment*, Ph.D. dissertation, M.I.T., 1960; C. P. Kindleberger, *American Business Abroad*, New Haven, Yale University Press, 1969.

[3] R. E. Caves, International Corporations: *the Industrial Economics of Foreign Investment Economica*, Vol. 38, February 1971.

[4] S. Hymer, 'The Multinational Corporation: An Analysis of Some of the Motives for International Business Integration'; a French version was published in *La Revue Economique*, 1968.

economies of scale in domestic production more than offset the cost of transport and the tariffs in the importing country – as long as the market in this country is small. As the foreign market expands, some economies of scale may be realizable by producing abroad. This market may be exploited by a host-country firm or by a foreign firm.

Most approaches to the theory of direct foreign investment assume that the host-country firm has an inevitable advantage in his domestic market over foreign firms. This advantage reflects that the foreign firms incur additional costs of co-ordination and communication that the host-country firm avoids. They may be subject to tax disadvantages. The host-country firm might earn higher profits than the source-country firm on activities in the same market, since they both face the same demand functions and buy their factors in the same markets. If the costs of co-ordination and communication are high, the host-country firm may buy the advantage from the source-country firm: this is what licensing is all about. If the source country sells its advantage, the income must be higher than the income from exploiting the advantage by production. Given that the source-country firm always operates at a cost disadvantage in the host-country market, the question arises why the source-country firm invests abroad rather than selling its advantage to a host-country competitor. Some anecdotal evidence is cited about the imperfection in this market, but there is also substantial evidence that licenses are sold as firms intially expand abroad and that thereafter, as the foreign market grows, they seek to invest rather than license. Since the likelihood that the market for advantages becomes less perfect as the size of the foreign market grows is low, an explanation is needed for the desire to move from licensing to direct investment as a way to exploit the advantage.[1]

I suggested that direct foreign investment could be explained even if the market in advantages were perfect – that the source-country firm might pay a higher price for the same income stream than the host-country firm because the source-country firm had an advantage in the capital market. In the market for debt, the source-country firm may be able to borrow at a lower interest rate than the host-country firm. In the equity market, the shares of the source-country firm may be capitalized at a higher rate than the earnings of the host-country firm. Indeed the distinction between source-country firms

[1] See L. Franko, *Strategy Choice and Multinational Corporate Tolerance for Joint Ventures with Foreign Partners*, an unpublished thesis, Graduate School of Business Administration, Harvard University, August 1970.

and host-country firms may be largely in terms of the difference between the capitalization rate applied by their market to their shares.

The systematic basis for the difference in capitalization rates for source-country and host-country firms is explained in terms of investor pricing of exchange risk. Because of exchange risk, assets which are alike in all respects except currency denomination have somewhat different yields. The difference in yields reflects two factors. One is expected changes in the exchange rate; the other is uncertainty about expected changes in the exchange rate. Because of uncertainty the difference in yields on assets denominated in sterling over those denominated in US dollars has exceeded the depreciation of sterling in terms of the US dollar. This difference may be considered the payment demanded by investors for bearing uncertainty about exchange risk. The explanation for an international bond market – why firms based in one country issue debt denominated in a foreign currency (why Canadian firms issue debt denominated in the US dollar) is that these firms believe that lenders have overpriced exchange risk. These firms elect to carry the exchange risk in the belief that the reduction in their borrowing costs more than compensates for the additional risk. In a world without an exchange risk premium, borrowers would incur the additional costs of denominating debt in a foreign currency, for the difference in interest rates would reflect fully the expected changes in the exchange rate.

The first part of this hypothesis for direct foreign investment assumes that the world market of investors attaches a different exchange risk premium to equities denominated in different currencies. Just as differences in interest rates reflect expected changes in exchange rates, so will differences in equity yields; and just as differences in interest rates reflect uncertainty about exchange risk, so will differences in equity yields – and hence in the capitalization ratios of equities. The countries with the high capitalization rates are the source countries.

The second element in the hypothesis is that a higher capitalization rate is applied to a host-country stream when the income stream is earned by a source-country firm rather than by a host-country firm. But this element seems inconsistent with the search for an explanation which is consistent with the perfect market assumptions. These investors might acquire an income stream in the host country directly; presumably when acquiring the shares of a source-country firm, investors would adjust for the income streams in foreign currencies received by the firm. This difference in the capitalization rates might reflect several factors – one is that the source-country firm might be more efficient in hedging the exchange risk. Or the source-country firm may provide the investors with a diversified portfolio at a lower cost than the investors can acquire on his own. Finally, investors may be ignorant about the share of the source-country firm earnings that come from foreign sources; investors may tend to apply the source-country capitalization rate to the company's earnings, unless a substantial portion of its earnings are from foreign sources.

On a conceptual basis, this theory of foreign investment has greater explanatory power than the theories based on monopolistic competition. The advantage of the source-country firm is explained; this advantage reflects in the demaraction of the world into multiple currency areas. The basis for the distinction between the source countries and the host countries is explained, and this demarcation has an element of foreignness that the monopolistic competitor theories lack. Moreover the exchange risk approach can explain foreign investment through take-overs which the monopolistic competition approach cannot do. In the end, the test of theories of direct foreign investment is their predictive power. Few empirical studies have been made, and none has been directed to a comparison of the two approaches.[1]

A variety of data suggests that the source-country firms earn higher profits in the host country than many of their host-country competitors in the same industry. The reliability of this data is questionable, for the allocation of profits among branches and between branches and home office is very much what the firm wishes them to be. But even if the branch of the source-country firm earns higher profits than its competitors, the inference is unclear; it may be that the branch can extract rents from its factors more effectively than its competitors.[2]

Occasionally it is asserted that the effective *a priori* or intuitive test is the appeal of the explanations for cross-hauling – why British and German firms invest in the United States at a time when US firms are investing abroad. In fact there is relatively little cross-hauling, and much of it is explainable in historical terms – the British firms that are strong overseas are those that engaged in direct investment over a period when the exchange risk hypothesis

---

[1] One empirical approach is that of T. Horst. See *American Participation in Canadian Markets: A Multinational Firm Approach*, Harvard Institute of Economic Research, January 1970.

[2] On the issue of foreign profitability, see D. T. Brash, *American Investment in Australian Industry*, London, Cass, 1967, especially Chapter X.

favoured firms with shares denominated in sterling. This factor aside, most cross-hauling involves a few individual firms and is not a pervasive phenomena – there are perhaps three or four Dutch firms, one or two Swedish firms, one Belgian firm, etc. The monopolistic competition approach suggests that these European firms expand abroad because further expansion domestically in their traditional industry is too costly; it is sometimes asserted that they wish to 'spoil' the profits of their foreign competitors in their competitors' backyard. The exchange risk hypothesis says that these foreign firms expand in the US market for two reasons – the first is to reduce their borrowing costs by making it easier to borrow the preferred currency, the dollar. And the second, and perhaps more important, is that they hope that by acquiring a dollar income stream, investors will attach a higher capitalization rate to the firms' earnings.

### MONEY FLOWS AND THE MULTINATIONAL ENTERPRISE

The development of firms with production and sales facilities in numerous countries has had an important impact on the stability of the system of pegged exchange rates, and the relationships among various national central banks. Almost inevitably these firms will have financial assets and liabilities – as well as credit lines denominated in currencies of the countries in which they have a production or sales activity. Various functions of these firms will be dispersed around the world. A few activities, including the long-term planning and the treasurer's function tend to be centralized. The treasurer (occasionally the title may be controller – the function is important, not the name) will be concerned with the management of the firm's cash position – the currency mix of its short-term assets and liabilities. In the normal course of business, he will face different rates on assets and liabilities denominated in the various currencies; he may also be confronted by expectations of changes in the exchange rates. The constellation of interest rates in different countries constitutes the set of opportunities available to the firm. These interest rates may differ depending on currency of denomination, in reflection of estimates about the exchange risk attached to assets denominated in different currencies and of the political risk attached to holding assets of a given currency denomination issued in various centres. The firm compares the markets' estimates of the risks attached to different types of assets with its own estimates of these risks.

The firm concludes that the spreads in interest rates on assets denominated in various currencies differs from the spreads it believes consistent with its own estimates of risk. The payments between the home office and subsidiaries may be speeded or slowed, and the cash may be shifted among various centres and among various currencies. The term 'leads and lags' is applied to these shifts of funds in response to changes in the interest rate pattern when the stability of the pegged exchange rates is not in question; the firm borrows more in the centre with the lower interest rates and lends more in the centre with the higher interest rate. When the stability of a pegged exchange rate is in doubt, the terms 'hedging' and 'speculation' are applied to similar shifts in the firm's cash position.

Firms with production and sales solely in one country may engage in the leads and lags, in hedging and speculation. The advantage of the firm with sales investments in several or many countries is that the affiliates provide a continuous flow of information on the opportunities and risks available in holding funds denominated in several currencies; these transactions are simpler to execute. Another advantage of the multinational corporation is the multiplicity of banking connections that such firms have in various centres.

If movements in the short-term interest rate differentials followed a random walk – if there were no runs in the times series in the data – there would not be any advantage to the firm to change the currency mix of its short-term position. But there are runs in the data, for the central banks seek to maintain short-term interest rates at a particular level for an extended period to achieve domestic monetary objectives. And because firms have to worry only minimally about changes in the exchange rate peg, they can shift funds to take advantage of the interest rate differential. The much greater willingness of firms to shift funds complicates the achievement of independent monetary policies by the various central banks.

Under a system of floating exchange rates, new information would be continually discounted in the current exchange rate and the firm would have minimal reason to expect continuity in the exchange rate from one day to the next; they would be less likely to shift the currency mix of their cash position in response to changes in expectations about exchange rates in the future. Under the currency system of pegged exchange rates, firms can profit from anticipated changes in exchange parities that have not yet occurred, for the exchange rate pegs are changed after some delay. Many participants in the exchange market are confident that the parity will be changed before the government authorities make the change. Moreover, under the existing system, the costs of being wrong in cases where the expectations are not realized are low, while the possible gains from being right are substantial.[1]

In the 1965–70 period, the parities of three of the major European currencies – sterling, the mark, and the French franc – were changed, while the parities of three other important currencies – the guilder, the Belgian franc and the Italian lira – were under great pressures. Various estimates place the shift away from sterling at $3–5 billion. The French lost substantial reserves between the May 1968 student riots and the August 1969 devaluation, much of which must have reflected a change in the portfolio position of private firms. The shift by private parties into marks in anticipation of a possible revaluation at the time of the September 1969 election probably exceeded $5 billion. While the data are weak for the point of view of comparisons, one plausible inference is that the volume of funds which are shifted in response to an anticipated change in the exchange is increasing. And this suggests that firms respond faster to changes in expectations about future exchange rates. One possible consequence is a widening of interest rate differentials.

CONCLUSIONS

This chapter has discussed the causal relationship between two different systems – one is the monetary system with a large number of independent central banks, each with its own currency; the other the system of large firms with co-ordinated activities in many parts of the world. The multiple currency system means that firms with equities denominated in a currency favoured by world investors have an advantage relative to firms with equities denominated in other currencies; in a competitive world, this advantage may give the former a dominant position. The system of co-ordinated firms places the monetary system under strain, since the firms may alter the currency mix of their past position very rapidly.

[1] This paragraph should not be read as an argument for floating rates. Rather, it is a descriptive statement about one possible cost of a system of pegged exchange rates in a world where numerous central bankers have a Hamlet complex about changing the exchange rate pegs.

# COMMENT ON THE CHAPTER BY PROFESSOR ALIBER

## JOHN H. DUNNING

Professor Aliber's chapter is a succinct analysis of the importance of certain considerations influencing the investment decisions of a multinational enterprise which are both unique to international investment and absent from many of the traditional explanations. As far as it goes, I am fully persuaded that the factors he mentions – noticeably that the world market of investors may attach a different exchange risk premium to equities denominated in different currencies and hence evaluate investment opportunities differently – should be incorporated in any generalized theory of investment behaviour. Where I part company with him is his suggestion that this theory is a substitute for the Kindleberger/Hymer (=monopolistic competition) hypothesis or indeed that it 'has greater explanatory power' (p. 53) than this theory. Indeed, it seems to me that it is a variant of the monopolistic competitive hypothesis but, in this instance, the imperfections arise in the capital market due to differences in the value of currencies differently denominated, and of the evaluation of risks and capitalization rates in different markets (p. 52).

Any satisfactory explanation of foreign direct investment must contain both necessary and sufficient conditions. I am not persuaded that Aliber's approach satisfies either of these conditions, any more than those theories which concentrate solely on product or market advantages. It is perfectly possible to envisage a situation where the conditions he postulates as influencing foreign investment are absent, just as he points out that foreign investment may take place if the market in advantages were perfect (p. 51). It is not essential that in order to allow direct investment to take place the 'source-country firm should have an advantage in the capital market' (p. 51). In any case, viewed in a dynamic context, these same advantages may be the outcome of imperfect competitive forces. The fact that the source country may be able to borrow at a cheaper rate than the host-country firm either indicates that there is some imperfection in the capital market or that, in some way, lenders in source countries are prepared to lend at a lower rate of interest. This, in turn, could be because of certain advantages the firm possesses over its competitors.

Similarly with the differences in capitalization of shares denominated in different currencies. This is not *only* a question of exchange risk; it could equally reflect the comparative advantage of source *v.* host-country firms in the view of the investor. Nor must it be the case that a 'higher compensation rate is applied to a host-country stream when the income stream is earned by a source-country firm than by a host-country firm'. I would be the first to admit this *may* be the case – indeed, Max Steuer and I have used a similar argument to explain the takeover of UK firms by foreign companies[1] – but I question whether it must necessarily be so.

Professor Aliber also claims that his theory 'can explain foreign investment through a takeover which the monopolistic competition approach cannot do'. I confess I am not clear on the nature of the problem. Accepting Aliber's own formulation (para. 3 on p. 52) then the theory of foreign investment is primarily concerned with explaining why a firm invests £x million in one country rather than another, independently of the form the investment takes. It is perfectly true that the relative price of a takeover compared with the establishment of a new enterprise may influence this decision, but I do not see how the process of decision taking differs from that faced by a domestic firm: it is a straightforward case of investment appraisal. One does not need a special theory of *foreign* investment to explain *the means* by which the investment is made – only the fact of it. Why cannot the Kindleberger/Hymer approach be suitably modified to incorporate imperfections in the capital and exchange market? Or again, how does the Aliber theory help to explain why takeovers occur in some industries rather than others? I would have thought that the *exchange* risk element is independent of the type of industry.

Aliber criticizes the Kindleberger/Hymer view that it does not explain why a firm chooses to exploit the foreign market by foreign investment rather than by other means. I agree with this criticism, but it is not difficult to incorporate these elements into any theory. In any case, I would not accept that host-country firms have an 'inevitable advantage' over foreign firms (p. 51). This implies that *ceteris paribus* the two groups of firms are equally efficient and this need not be the case. Of course, the foreign firm is faced with certain additional costs not faced by the domestic firm, but what matters is whether or not these costs are outweighed by cost advantages in other directions, e.g. from integrated production. Taking these into

[1] J. H. Dunning and M. Steuer, 'The Effects of US Investment on UK Technology' in J. H. Dunning (ed.), *Studies in International Investment*, Allen & Unwin, 1970.

account, I would have thought that the Kindleberger/Hymer theory does offer quite a good explanation of both the geographical and the industrial pattern of foreign investment within countries. The case of aluminium and steel (p. 50) cited by Aliber is a case in point – although here historical and environmental factors are very interwoven. The Japanese are, in fact, exploiting the steel market through direct investment. But there is much more imperfection of competition in aluminium than in steel. I certainly cannot see how the Aliber thesis can explain patterns of investment in a *particular country*.

Moreover, if one accepts the theory of comparative advantage suitably adapted to take account of both technological change and imperfections in capital and currency markets, I would have thought this also adequately explained the geographical structure of investment. Professor Aliber claims that the monopolistic competition theory fails to explain cross-hauling (of which I believe there is a good deal more than he implies) but then goes on to make the point that foreign firms invest in the US today because they can borrow the preferred currency (the $) more easily and investors will attach a higher capitalization rate to the firm's earnings (p. 54).

Why, then, do UK firms invest in Europe and other areas at the same time? Why do US firms invest in the UK? Is it also because investors will attach a higher capitalization rate to their firm's earnings or because in this case the preferred currency is the pound, the mark or the franc? Or is it rather that the multinational firm has an advantage in operating in a multi-currency world independently of the denomination of its currency?

I can see no evidence that there is any relationship between flows of direct investment to particular countries and the strength of their currencies. Indeed, the trend towards increased investment by European countries in the US is taking place when, comparatively speaking, the $ is less strong than it used to be.

The growing diversity of international direct investment fits in with the product cycle theory of Raymond Vernon and why, until 1950 or so, the US and UK did tend to dominate in certain fields. This is no longer the case, and in the 1970s I suspect that the multinational enterprises which grow the most will be non-European in origin. The Vernon theory also helps to explain the structure of US investment in the UK – and to quite a large extent the structure of UK investment overseas.

In his book *American Business Abroad*, Kindleberger writes, 'For direct investment to thrive there must be some imperfection in markets for goods and factors . . . or some interference in competition by government or by firms which separates markets. If one incorporates the currency market as one of the factors, then I would have thought this definition would be acceptable as a *necessary* criteria for foreign investment – though not necessarily a *sufficient* criteria.' For this, one should add . . . 'and it is more profitable for exploiting a market than other means'.

I feel that Professor Aliber is on considerably stronger ground in the second half of his chapter. He has spelied out well the advantages of a multinational firm in operating in a multi-currency world (some of these advantages also operate with firms marketing in different countries but not producing there) and compares the implication of MPE's operating under fixed and variable exchange rates. I also think he is right when he suggests that the extent to which firms are shifting funds in anticipating changes in exchange rate is increasing. Partly, this has been aided and abetted by the emergence of new instructions e.g. the Euro-dollar and Euro-bond markets.

## Chapter 3

# THE MULTINATIONAL ENTERPRISE AND THE TRANSFER OF TECHNOLOGY*

### KEITH PAVITT

It is very difficult to dissociate any discussion of the multinational firm from technology, and vice versa. Both have upset the classical theory of world trade, suggesting that there are new factors of production that must be looked at, and that assumptions about their international mobility may be wrong. Both began to emerge as economic phenomena around the beginning of this century, and both have grown with tremendous rapidity in the 1950s and 1960s. Expenditure on scientific research and development now amounts to between 1·5% and 3·0% of GNP in the industrially advanced OECD countries,[1] while Dr S. Rolfe has estimated that world output of foreign subsidiaries of multinational firms in 1966 are about double the volume of exports of the major trading nations.[2]

Furthermore, technology and the multinational firm are mutually dependent. Most industrial research and development (R & D) is performed in large – and therefore probably multinational – firms. In eight industrially advanced OECD countries, eight firms account for between 30% and more than 50% of all industrial R & D; and in the Netherlands, the first five firms account for nearly 65% of the total. And while multinational firms employ a very high proportion of technological resources in the OECD area, their management and operation have been considerably facilitated by technological

* Unless otherwise indicated, the factual information used in this paper is drawn from a series of studies undertaken by the OECD under the general title *Gaps in Technology*. In addition to the general report, there were a series of industry reports, viz. electronic computers, electronic components, non-ferrous metals, pharmaceuticals, plastics and scientific instruments – and an analytical report.

[1] *The Overall Level and Structure of R & D Efforts in OECD Member Countries*, OECD, Paris, 1967.

[2] S. Rolfe, 'The International Corporation in Perspective' in *The Multinational Corporation in the World Economy*, London, Praeger, 1970.

advances in communications, transportation and – more recently – information.

It would be altogether wrong, however, to conclude that large multinational firms have an exclusive control over new technology. Certainly, they have been responsible for most important innovations in such areas as commercial EDP computers, pharmaceuticals, plastics and nuclear energy. But the past twenty years are full of examples of large firms – including the best managed amongst them – which have missed important and profitable innovations in sophisticated and fast-moving technologies, where new or small firms have made the running (e.g. xerography, instant photography, advanced electronic components, large and small computers).

This situation can be explained partly in terms of the organizational and behavioural difficulties of pushing radical change through large, established organizations, and partly in terms of the very considerable technological and market uncertainties associated with radical innovation: witness General Electric's experience in advanced components and computers. None the less, it is worth noting that many of the small firms which have exploited radical innovations have been started, or greatly assisted, by scientists and engineers with previous work experience in the laboratories of large firms, and that large firms are very often customers for the products of these small firms when they start. This means that these small firms tend to stay geographically in the technologically sophisticated environment on which they feed – initially at least. It also means that the large – and often multinational – firm must be seen not only as a source of technological innovation, but also as a source of technical entrepreneurship, the benefits of which it does not necessarily reap itself.

Neither technology nor the multinational firm are exclusively American phenomena. As much as anything else, the almost exclusive concentration of attention on US multinational firms reflects the poor statistics available for countries other than the USA: estimates made for the Development Assistance Committee suggest that the USA accounts for about 60% of OECD countries' direct foreign investment.[1] And with regard to technology, the data on R & D collected by the OECD have often been misinterpreted. The USA certainly undertakes considerably more R & D than Europe, when measured in monetary terms, and when including government financed defence and space research. But when such research is excluded, and when corrections are made for differences in wage

[1] OECD document DAC(68)14.

levels and population differences, the European R & D effort is not markedly less than that of the USA. Certainly, one cannot dismiss the political significance of defence and space research, nor its impact on civilian technology in, for example, aircraft, communications and electronics. But it is significant that industry in Switzerland and the Netherlands – and perhaps also in the UK and Germany – devotes a greater proportion of its own financial resources to R & D than does US industry; that these four countries, together with Sweden, all have strong competitive positions in world markets in high technology industries; and that Switzerland's export pattern is slightly more 'technology intensive' than even that of the USA.

Both technology and the multinational firm have been heavily influenced by conditions of industrial competition. As levels of education have risen, and the explanatory powers of science have grown, industry has come to recognize that organized knowledge and trained intelligence are an important competitive resource – in some sectors today more important than the cost and availability of conventional factors of production. In the USA, this recognition has taken place within the framework of a large, competitive, national market, and resulted in the growth of industrial R & D over a period extending roughly from 1910 to 1965, and the parallel growth of university-based business schools.

It is only over the past twenty years that US manufacturing industry and its technology have spilled over irreversibly into international operations. In many other countries, however, technology and international markets have been strongly interwoven from the beginning. To the extent that national markets have been recognized as too small, the exploitation of new technology in international markets has been very rapid: thus, the Swedish company S.K.F. was established early in the century on the basis of a ball-bearing invention, and had manufacturing subsidiaries in seven countries within ten years. And, to the extent that the pressure of international competition has been strong, firms have been forced to use knowledge and intelligence intensively: thus, in 1927, in the Netherlands, Philips and Shell gave an important endowment for the establishment of the Department of Technical Physics at the University of Delft.

Whether firms be multinational (i.e. with manufacturing subsidiaries in many countries) or not, the nature and the growing importance of the competitive advantage afforded by new technology, together with trade and capital liberalization and growing pressures of competition, are forcing firms to exploit both technological knowledge and markets on an international scale.

No country or firm can hope to be self-sufficient in generating all the scientific and technological knowledge necessary even for its own technological innovations. Indeed, one of the important functions of industrial R & D is to monitor, assess and absorb knowledge generated outside the firm. And since, apart from the USA, no country can hope to produce more than 10% of the world's scientific and technological knowledge, such monitoring must nearly always go beyond national boundaries if it is to be effective. In a recent study of more than fifty successful technological innovations in British industry, J. Langrish found that one-third of the knowledge inputs for these innovations came from outside the United Kingdom.[1] The proportion is probably much higher in smaller countries.

Furthermore, all firms are now under pressure to rapidly exploit the temporary monopoly afforded by technological advance in international markets, before foreign competitors redevelop or copy the technology. It is imperative for innovative European firms, for example, to penetrate the US market because of both its size and its technological sophistication. Some small, recently created, science-based firms in Europe go so far as to export their most sophisticated products to the USA *before* launching them on European markets.

However, for the industrial firm there are often important limitations to exporting as a channel for exploiting a technological advance in world markets.[2] They relate not only to wage costs, but also to transport costs, tariff and non-tariff barriers, and the advantages of having manufacturing close to the market. The other alternatives open to a firm for exploiting its technological advance are licensing, joint ventures, and fully controlled subsidiaries. There are numerous signs that firms increasingly prefer the last alternative to the other two: first, because licensing and joint ventures give other firms legal rights and technological knowledge which can later be used in competition against the licensor; second, because there are potentially greater financial returns from direct investment than from licensing, especially when the firm considering this alternative has a considerable technological lead over its competitors.

[1] J. Langrish, *Innovation in Industry: Some Results of the Queen's Award Study*, Research Report No. 15, Department of Liberal Studies in Science, University of Manchester, September 1969.

[2] For a discussion of the costs, benefits and risks involved in exploiting technology on foreign markets through exports, licensing and direct investment, see K. Pavitt, *Technological Innovation in European Industry: the Need for a World Perspective*, Long Range Planning, December 1969.

## PATTERNS OF INTERNATIONAL TECHNOLOGY-TRANSFER IN THE OECD AREA: THEIR NATURE

The channels open to the firm for exploiting its technological lead on foreign markets suggest the following framework for examining patterns of international technology-transfer and the role of multinational firms in them: namely, trade in producers' goods, licensing, investment and, coupled with these, personal contacts and personal mobility.

### 1 Trade in Producers' Goods

In the OECD area, a high proportion of new technology is embodied in producers' goods, and in particular in the products of the chemical, electrical, mechanical and aircraft industries, which perform most of the industrial R & D in the advanced countries, and which have relatively high rates of innovation in new products. Thus, international trade in producers' goods, together with the after-sales and training services which go with it, is an important vehicle for international technology-transfer. Trends in OECD trade patterns between 1962 and 1966 suggest that this form of international technology-transfer is increasing rapidly within the OECD area.[1] Over these five years, the share of intra-OECD exports has risen from 65% to 69% of total exports by OECD countries, and imports from 66% to 69%. OECD exports of manufactured products, which comprise high technology producers' goods, have increased annually by 11%, and from 67% to 72% of total OECD exports. The USA, Germany and the UK together accounted for about three-quarters of OECD exports in the high technology industries. In the main manufactured product groups, at least 80% – and sometimes more than 95% – of total OECD manufactured imports were from other OECD countries. The most intensive increase in trading relationships was amongst European countries, whilst a higher proportion of US trade was with Japan and Canada, the European share remaining roughly constant.

These trends suggest that international technology-transfer through producers' goods trade has increased rapidly amongst the Western European countries, on the one hand, and amongst the USA, Canada and Japan on the other. But the available data do not enable an assessment of the role of multinational firms in total producers' goods trade. Information for the USA and UK suggests that

---

[1] It would be more satisfactory to analyse trade patterns over a longer period, but the available statistical data do not permit it.

producers' goods exports from parent to overseas subsidiaries account for a very small proportion of total producers' goods trade, although the proportion varies considerably amongst industries, being higher in both motor cars and chemicals.[1]

## 2 Licensing and Foreign Investment

International technology-transfers through licensing agreements between independent firms, or between parent firms and their foreign subsidiaries, have grown more rapidly over the past ten to fifteen years. Data on monetary receipts and payments for patents, licences and knowhow suggest that US outflows and inflows of technology through these channels increased annually by 16% and 14% respectively between 1957 and 1965, those of France by 13% and 10% between 1955 and 1963, those of Germany both by 14% over the same period, and those of Japan by 80% and 26% between 1955 and 1964. These high rates of increase probably reflect both the growth of industrial R & D and of the consequent output of technology in the industrially advanced countries since World War II, and increasing technological specialization amongst them.

Between the mid-fifties and the mid-sixties, the same data suggest that the pattern of outflows of US technology through licensing and foreign investment changed significantly, with a relatively larger proportion going to Western Europe and, within this proportion, a larger share being transferred through direct foreign investment rather than through licensing agreements between independent firms. Between 1957 and 1965, the annual rate of increase of outflows of US technology to Europe was 18%, and the proportion of the total accounted for by foreign investment as against licensing increased from about 44% to 70%. This shift of emphasis was much less pronounced for US technology outflows to Canada and Japan. During the same period the relative weight of foreign investment increased from 75% to 90% in Canada, and from 15% to 25% in Japan.[2]

[1] M. T. Bradshaw, 'US Exports to Foreign Affiliates by US Firms' in *Survey of Current Business*, May 1969; W. Reddaway *et al.*, *Effects of UK Direct Investment Overseas: An Interim Report*, London, Cambridge University Press, 1967.
[2] The statistical data for receipts and payments for patents, licences and knowhow have many shortcomings. For example, in some countries they include management fees, in others authors' rights. Furthermore, international currency transfers under these headings can be influenced by tax considerations, and by the parent company's policy towards the charging of overheads to foreign subsidiaries, especially during the first few years of its existence.
Probably only the data for Japan are completely reliable. Nonetheless, the

The data suggest that about 64% of US outflows of technology through licensing and foreign investment were to the five medium-sized OECD countries – France, Germany, Italy, Japan and the United Kingdom. The total United Kingdom inflows of foreign technology through licensing and foreign investment were slightly lower than the average for all these countries, and the equivalent German inflows were about 40% more. This may simply reflect the wide margin of error in the data collected, but it may also reflect a greater past propensity in Germany than in the United Kingdom to import foreign technology, for example, related to the aircraft, nuclear and computer industries. But it would be altogether wrong to conclude that Germany has lived since World War II entirely on foreign technology. Research and development financed by German industry is nearly as high as in the United Kingdom, and its competitive position in world markets in the chemical, electrical and mechanical industries is very strong. Similar observations can be made about the Netherlands, Sweden and Switzerland. This point will be returned to later in this paper.

Finally, the data suggest that in the mid-1960s there were still considerable differences amongst the firms of the main technology-producing countries in the channels through which they exploited their technological lead on foreign markets. Whilst the USA accounted for only about 30% of OECD exports of high technology products, it accounted for about 55% of international technology flows through licensing and direct investment. Germany showed a vastly different pattern, accounting for more than 20% of the former, and only about 7% of the latter, thereby suggesting that German firms still exploited their technology on foreign markets predominantly through exports rather than licensing and/or investment. The United Kingdom came somewhere in between, with about 13% of total OECD exports of technology through licensing and foreign investment, and 14% of OECD exports of high technology products.

Furthermore, the relative weight in the OECD total and intra-European flows of technology through foreign investment and licensing was considerably less than in trade in goods: about 25% in the former case, as against about 60% in the latter. This suggests that transatlantic technology-transfers have relied mainly on foreign investment, whilst trade in producers' goods has played a relatively greater role in intra-European technology-transfers.

---

data collected by various governments are mutually consistent, and the above limitations are not of a nature to invalidate the broad conclusions drawn from them in this paper.

## 3 *The Industrial Pattern*

The available data on monetary receipts and payments for patents and licences show that a high proportion of international technology-transfers take place within the chemical, electrical, mechanical and aircraft industries. This is not altogether surprising, given that it is in precisely these industries that a high proportion of R & D is done, and new technology therefore created. This is not to say that new technology is not transferred, either nationally or internationally, to other sectors of the economy. On the contrary, such technology transfers take place continuously through transactions with firms in the high technology industries, either as a supplier or as a customer (e.g. computers in banking and administration, chemical fibres into textiles, machinery and chemical fertilizers into agriculture). These are the main channels through which technology contributes to overall productivity increases in the economy. Producers' goods trade, licensing and foreign investment all ensure the spread of this contribution internationally.

But to go beyond these general observations on patterns of international technology-transfer and the role of the multinational firm, more detailed information is required. Although such information is not as comprehensive as one would like, it does suggest that US direct investment in Europe has been strong in many high technology sectors, but that it has also been strong in other product areas where the market emerged earlier in the USA than in Europe (e.g. car hire, men's toilet products), and also in areas such as agricultural inputs like animal feed, where superior management technology has been an equal – if not more important – factor than superior hardware technology.

Furthermore, quite noticeable differences emerge *within* the high technology industries in the nature and importance of the international transfer of US technology. In computers and advanced electronic components, where the USA has had a very strong lead in invention and innovation, and where in consequence nearly all internationally diffused technology is of US origin, the OECD studies found that, about two years ago, half the component manufacturers in Europe and two-thirds of the main computer manufacturers were using US technology. In each of these two sectors, US technology was transferred to Europe in half the cases through licensing agreements, and in the other half through direct US investment, although the latter channel was considerably more important in value terms.

However, in the plastics and pharmaceutical industries the pattern was very different. In both these sectors, invention and innovation has been more evenly spread. US technological performance has been strong, but so has that of other countries – in particular, Switzerland in pharmaceutical products, and Germany in plastics. In the pharmaceutical industry, this pattern is reflected in the existence of multinational firms based on a number of OECD countries, a high volume of direct foreign investment, and important international flows of technology through this channel. In the plastics industry, competitively strong firms also exist in a number of countries but, although direct foreign investment is now increasing fast, the main channel for international technology-transfer in the past has been through licensing agreements and joint ventures.

These data on patterns of foreign investment and international technology-transfer are broadly consistent with Raymond Vernon's 'product cycle' thesis, namely that US firms tend to penetrate foreign markets through the export-licensing-investment cycle in product areas where they have a technological or other type of competitive edge due to the emergence of markets in the USA before they emerge in other countries.[1] However, they also suggest some important modifications to the thesis.

First, the 'lead time' between the US and European markets has depended not only on the higher level of GNP per head in the USA, and the consequent, earlier emergence of demand for labour-saving equipment and for new types of consumer goods. It has also depended on the scale and sophistication of demands emerging from the US defence and space programmes. Such demands played a very important role in advanced electronic components, and to a lesser extent in electronic computers. They played a very small role in pharmaceutical products and plastics.

Second, although the scale and sophistication of domestic demand may serve to 'explain' US competitive strength in high technology sectors, it certainly cannot 'explain' the similar strength of the Netherlands, Sweden and Switzerland, nor the differences in technological capabilities between countries of roughly equivalent size, such as France, Germany, Italy and the United Kingdom.

Third, the firm's 'mix' amongst exports, licensing and direct investment in penetrating foreign markets and exploiting its technology appears to vary considerably not only with the stage of

[1] R. Vernon, 'International Investment and International Trade in the Product Cycle' in *Quarterly Journal of Economics*, May 1966.

the 'product cycle'. We have seen that it varies amongst countries. It may also vary according to the characteristics of an industry and the relative strength of competitors within it. Thus, the reliance of US firms on direct investment rather than licensing in the computer and advanced components sectors probably resulted from a very strong technological and competitive lead, and the consequent possibility of high returns at relatively low risk through direct investment. In the aircraft industry, however, where the USA also has a strong technological lead, there is virtually no direct foreign investment, partly because of factors related to military security. In the plastics industry, the greater reliance on licensing and joint ventures may reflect the existence of a greater spread of competitive strength and of heavy capital requirements. In the pharmaceutical industry, in spite of a considerable spread of competitive strength, the greater reliance on direct investment than on licensing may reflect the highly differentiated nature of pharmaceutical products and the consequent specialization of drug firms in various product areas.

## 4 Personal Mobility and Personal Contacts

Any discussion of the international transfer of technology would be incomplete without some mention of the role played by the international mobility of scientists and engineers, and of personal contacts amongst them across national boundaries. Technological knowledge consists not only of access to scientific papers, formulae, blueprints and hardware. It consists also – and perhaps mainly – of what people know and what people can do. What happened to German rocket scientists after the World War II illustrates this point; the contemporary equivalent might be the ferocious competition for key scientists and engineers in the advanced electronic components industry in the USA.[1] This fact, coupled with the empirical observation that most technological knowledge is transferred through person-to-person contacts,[2] means that the international mobility – and contacts between – scientists and engineers plays an important role in the process of international technology-transfer.

Many of these contacts and flows take place naturally as part of the economic processes of international technology-transfer des-

[1] N. Lindgren, 'The Splintering of the Solid-State Electronic Industry' in *Innovation*, New York, No. 8, 1969.

[2] See, for example, W. Price and L. Bass, 'Scientific Research and the Innovative Process' in *Science*, May 16, 1969.

cribed above. Innovating firms have a network of personal contacts in foreign countries; the sale of producers' goods often implies the personal transmission of knowledge through technical and after-sales support; and international transfers of technology through licensing or foreign investment are often accompanied by the international mobility of scientists and engineers, personal contacts, and training and the upgrading of skills.

Unfortunately, there is virtually no empirical evidence on the scale, pattern and scope of these 'person-embodied' international flows of technology. Available statistics on the migration of scientists and engineers are incomplete – and often misleading – given that they are often for inflows, or for outflows, and rarely for both. Such data do, however, exist for the Netherlands and Switzerland in the early 1960s.[1] They suggest that inflows and out-flows of engineers, both national and foreign, were roughly in balance, and that incoming engineers had more experience than those leaving, between a quarter and a third coming from the USA. Thus, both countries appear to benefit from the international mobility of scientists and engineers. Both countries have large, multinational firms in technologically sophisticated industries. To ascertain whether these two factors are related would require more data from more countries.

## PATTERNS OF INTERNATIONAL TECHNOLOGY-TRANSFER IN THE OECD AREA: THEIR EFFECTS

### 1 *Economic Growth*

It is now widely accepted that the diffusion and effective exploitation of new technology is an important and essential source of produc-tivity and economic growth in the industrially advanced countries. And since no western country, apart from the USA, generates more than about 10% of the world's new technology, most countries' growth depends to a large extent on the importation and diffusion of foreign technology.[2] Thus, economic growth in the OECD area requires a well-developed system of international technology-

---

[1] *The International Movement of Scientists and Engineers*, OECD document STP(69)3, Part I, Tables 16 and 17.

[2] This explains why there is no correlation between the proportion of national resources that a country spends on R & D and its rate of growth of productivity. National R & D efforts are concentrated on invention and innovation rather than on diffusion. They therefore reflect only a small proportion of the total stock of technology available for diffusion, and hardly any of the factors that affect the rapidity of the diffusion process.

transfer. The data presented earlier in this paper suggest that the system has worked well. International technology-transfers have increased more rapidly than both economic growth and international trade. The methods of obtaining foreign technology may have varied considerably from country to country. At the two extremes, Canada has relied mainly on direct foreign investment, and Japan on licensing agreements coupled with a large, indigenous effort of absorptive R & D. Also, the methods of obtaining foreign technology may have changed over time, with inward foreign investment becoming a relatively more important channel. But with very few exceptions the results have been the same. The main technology-producing country (i.e. the USA) has not grown as rapidly as countries that have imported US technology. Although the level of use of advanced technology is higher in the USA, thereby reflecting higher living standards, the rate of increase in use of advanced technology has been higher in many other OECD countries, and (not surprisingly) very high in Japan.

## 2 *Trade Patterns*

Both the successful new application of technology (i.e. innovation), as well as the international diffusion of proven technology, have an important influence on trade patterns in manufacturing industry, and particularly in the high technology sectors. The data show a significant correlation between a country's ability to innovate and its performance in world markets in high technology industries. And the international diffusion of technology.has influenced the way in which trade patterns have moved over time.

Thus, countries exporting technology – either through licensing or direct foreign investment – at a higher rate than they are creating and applying new technology will tend to show their export shares diminishing in high technology industries. This has been most evidently the case for the USA over the past fifteen years. High technology products previously produced in the USA for export have been produced by subsidiaries of US firms in European countries, not only for the local market, but also for export to third countries.

At the same time, US imports of products of the high technology industries have increased rapidly. The degree to which this trend is linked to the international diffusion of US technology is difficult to determine. Certainly, in the case of Japan, the absorption through licensing agreements of US technology by independent Japanese firms, coupled with strong efforts in absorptive R & D by these

72

firms, has often led to Japanese exports to the USA in the same product areas – witness the remarkable success of Japanese electronic consumer-goods based on semi-conductor technology originally developed in the USA. In the case of Europe, however, the greatest proportion of US technology has been transferred through direct investment, a very small proportion of the production of which has been re-exported to the USA.

Thus, the reasons for increasing European exports to the USA of high technology products must be sought elsewhere. One possible explanation is that European firms are exporting in product areas which are at the second stage of the 'product cycle': in other words, product areas where the technology has become stabilized and widely known and available, and where conventional cost factors have become the key elements in competition. For example, Christopher Freeman has shown that Italian export performance in plastics can be explained within such a framework.[1]

However, there is one other possible explanation for Europe's increasing high technology exports to the USA, namely that European firms do have a strong capacity to create and apply technology (i.e. a strong position in technological innovation, or the first stage of the 'product cycle'), and that larger numbers of them have recognized that getting into the US market with such new technology is an essential condition for commercial success. If this explanation is at least partially valid, one can expect to see an increasing flow of European technology to the USA through direct investment, once European firms' market shares reach a level where such an investment is justified and not too risky.

Finally, it is worth noting that there is no single, discernible trend in European countries' export shares in high technology industries. Between 1962 and 1966, the trend in such countries' world market shares tended to follow the same trend as their shares for total manufacturing industry – that of Italy increasing and that of the UK decreasing – most rapidly. However, within the general trend in total manufacturing exports, the relative importance of exports of high technology products in the total increased for the United Kingdom (together with the Netherlands, Sweden and France), and decreased for Italy (together with Germany and Belgium). There are probably three sets of factors related to technology behind these trends, all of which have already been mentioned: patterns of production and exports of US subsidiaries in Europe, European firms' competitive

[1] C. Freeman, 'The Plastics Industry: A Comparative Study of Research and Innovation', *National Institute Economic Review*, London, November 1963.

performance in product areas at the second stage of the 'product cycle', and European firms' innovative performance and market horizons in product areas at the first stage of the 'product cycle'. John Dunning has estimated that one-third of the increase of Europe's exports in high technology industries between 1955 and 1964 was accounted for by US subsidiaries.[1] About the relative importance of the other two factors we know nothing.

## 3. *National Technological Capabilities*

'Technological capability' may well be an unfamiliar term to many economists, and indeed to many Europeans. It originated in American military jargon, and means essentially the ability to solve scientific and technological problems, and to follow, assess and exploit scientific and *technological* developments. To an increasing extent, technological capability is the basis of power in the advanced, industrialized countries, whether in terms of industrial competitiveness, defence, communications or prestige. In some ways it bears the same relationship to the advanced country today as a maritime power base to the United Kingdom in the past.

The activities of the multinational firms, together with the process of the international transfer of technology, have had an important impact on national technological capabilities. In particular, discussion has tended to focus on the policies of US multinational firms for the location of R & D laboratories in foreign countries, and for the exploitation of the results of these laboratories' work. But both the empirical evidence on this subject, together with the conclusions to be drawn from it, are not very clear, and sometimes even contradictory.

To begin with, it is not very clear how much R & D US firms actually perform outside the US. A survey by McGraw Hill estimated the total to be $400 million in 1966, of which about 60% was in the automobile and other transportation equipment sectors, just over 10% in both machinery and chemicals, and none at all in the aerospace sector.[2] This amounted to 2·6% of total R & D expenditure by US industry, a figure not very different from estimates made by Stanford Research Institute for R & D expenditures by 200 large US firms in Europe. If one assumes that most of the foreign R & D

---

[1] J. H. Dunning, *European and US Trade Patterns, US Foreign Investment and the Technological Gap*, in C. P. Kindleberger and A. Shonfield (eds) *North American and Western European Economic Policies*, MacMillan, 1971.

[2] McGraw-Hill, *Survey of Business Plans for Research and Development Expenditures*, 1967–70, May 12, 1967.

estimated by McGraw Hill is performed in Canada and Western Europe, then the percentage of sales devoted to R & D by foreign subsidiaries of US firms is roughly one-sixth of the equivalent percentage for firms operating in the USA (if one includes the US aerospace sector), and roughly one-quarter (if one excludes aerospace). In other words, the percentage of sales devoted by foreign subsidiaries of US firms to R & D would appear to be lower than the equivalent for industry generally in Canada and the industrially advanced countries of Western Europe, in being somewhat lower than the percentage in Italian industry.

But against this evidence must be set the results of other enquiries made in Canada and the United Kingdom. In Canada, in 1966, an enquiry by the Canadian Government found that, amongst the 100 largest firms in Canada, the R & D /sales ratio was higher in US-controlled than in Canadian firms. This may result from the relatively heavy concentration of US ownership in precisely those industrial sectors where the R & D/sales ratio is high. But John Dunning has found, for the United Kingdom in 1961, that US-controlled firms had a higher R & D/sales ratio than UK firms in seven out of the nine sectors that he examined.[1]

These apparently diverging sets of conclusions can be reconciled only if US firms do most of their foreign R & D in the UK and Canada. And one can advance two sets of factors which might cause this to be the case. The first is the relative greater period of time over which US firms have invested in these countries, thereby allowing greater possibilities for 'trouble shooting' activities related to current production to evolve to development activities and, eventually, fully-fledged R & D laboratories. The second is the fact that the Americans, Canadians and Englishmen all speak the same language. This is important in an activity like industrial R & D, where continuous and intense personal communication is so essential. It may have had an important influence on the American industrial research directors, when deciding where to extend their R & D programmes abroad. In some continental European laboratories of US firms, English is the working language.

But it may also be that the data we have on the geographical distribution of multinational firms' R & D is inaccurate, and that we need more and better. Similarly, we have no comprehensive information on the effects of new foreign investments on patterns of national R & D; for example, on the effects of takeovers on the

[1] J. H. Dunning, 'US subsidiaries in Britain and their UK competitors', *Business Ratios*, No. 1, Autumn 1966.

transfer of R & D knowledge and personnel between the newly acquired subsidiary and the parent firm, or on the degree to which the subsidiary's research programme is reoriented, or on the number of newly created subsidiaries which have R & D programmes.

Whatever the reality, however, opinions differ as to the desirability of having foreign-owned firms undertaking R & D. Some consider such activities as a hidden 'brain drain'. The Japanese Government, for instance, does not favour the establishment of R & D facilities by foreign-owned companies, and this attitude is perhaps understandable in a country which has spent the past hundred years creating and reinforcing a production and technological capability in nationally-owned firms. But it may not be the wisest policy in a country where scientists and engineers are in relatively abundant supply. Contrary to widely-held views, this may be the situation at least in certain European countries in certain fields. For example, Europe (and especially the UK) trains *per capita* more engineers than the USA, if one includes postsecondary, non-university training. And certain countries – such as the United Kingdom and, perhaps very soon, France – are cutting down R & D in sectors linked to what have been essentially defence or prestige activities, thereby releasing skilled manpower. When the alternative is between a 'hidden' and a 'real' brain drain, it is worth remembering that R & D undertaken in foreign-owned laboratories nonetheless forms part of a national technological capability.

The Canadian Government takes a more relaxed view of R & D in foreign-owned laboratories, and is instead trying to encourage foreign firms to concentrate units in Canada which are responsible, in specific product areas, for total company needs in R & D, production and marketing. It would be interesting to know more about the results of this policy.[1] But one difficulty that it probably does face is a tendency for some multinational firms' international division of labour in R & D to be different from their international division of labour in production and marketing. This, for example, is the case for IBM, whose European R & D laboratories form an

[1] Three examples can be cited. First, the United Aircraft of Canada Ltd. (a subsidiary of the US United Aircraft company) specialized in small gas-turbine engines, with annual sales of $136 million in 1969, of which $100 million was in US currency; second, Litton Systems (Canada) Ltd., specialized in inertial navigation systems; third, E. Leitz Canada Ltd. (with a German parent firm) specialized in high-precision optical equipment. See J. Lukasiewicz, 'A New Role for Canada: Warning Post Against Rampant Technology' in *Science Forum*, Toronto, February 1970.

integral part of IBM's total R & D effort, and where production in any specific European country is not necessarily based on the output of the IBM laboratory in that country.

Nonetheless, the R & D activities of both IBM and General Electric in computers appear to have led to a greater international division of labour and interdependence in technological development, to the benefit of the Europeans. IBM's German laboratory, for example, developed the 360–20, and the United Kingdom laboratory the 360–40. Whilst in 1962 100% of computer installations in the USA were US-designed, by 1967 the percentage was 94, the remaining 6% being nearly all computers designed in the European laboratories of these two US firms. And over the same time-period, the rate of increase in computer installations in six countries[1] was greater for computers designed in France, Germany and the UK than for those designed in the USA.

But the relationship between the multinational firm and the international transfer of technology, on the one hand, and national technological capabilities on the other, goes far beyond the problem of where multinational firms do their R & D. Both are intimately linked to national technological specialization – or an international division of labour in technology – brought about by growing R & D expenditures in all the industrially advanced countries, together with increased liberalization and international competition. Patterns of technological specialization are obviously more complex than conventional concepts of specialization. They involve differences not between wool and wine or electronics and agriculture but between, say, different branches of the electronics industry. Furthermore, they evolve over time as a consequence of new technological breakthroughs, and can be actively fostered through policies towards education, science and industry.

Nevertheless, the evidence shows that quite strong patterns of specialization in national technological capabilities do exist in certain advanced countries. This is the case for the Netherlands, Sweden and Switzerland, which are all highly specialized as a result of their small size and of their strong integration in international markets. So is Germany which, as a result of World War II, has been prohibited from R & D in sectors related to military technology. Yet all these countries have strong R & D efforts, and have had a strong performance in international competition in high-technology industries. And they have benefited fully from scientific and technological advances made in other countries through the published

[1] Belgium, France, Germany, the Netherlands, UK and USA.

77

literature, personal contacts and mobility, and through normal, international commercial transactions.

One argument often advanced against technological specialization is that there are certain 'key' technologies which have an important influence in a wide number of sectors of technological development, and in which it is therefore necessary to maintain a national technological capability. Various technologies have been advanced as being 'key' in the past: for example, aircraft, atomic energy, space, computers and advanced electronic components. All these fields have been subject to government support in various OECD countries, sometimes in relation to defence and space programmes, and sometimes as part of programmes to develop technology for civilian purposes.

This is not the place to examine the validity of the special claims made for these technological sectors, except to say that the four technologically specialized countries mentioned above have, in the past, given them far less support than the UK and France, without any harmful effects on their overall competitive position in high-technology product groups. But it is equally true that at least the computer and advanced electronic components sectors are 'key' technologies for the future. The ability to use the computer and to assess potential future developments in computer technology will be increasingly necessary in such areas as management and decision making, industrial processes, education and science, communications and government administration. And with the advent of the integrated circuit and large-scale integration, developments in component technology will have a growing impact on the design of all electronic equipment.

Thus, the ability to use and to deal with the consequences of technological developments in electronic computers and componentry will probably be essential elements in any national technological capability. But, without wishing to enter into a discussion on present national and company policies in these fields, it is nonetheless worth asking whether the maintenance of such a national capability necessarily requires the existence of nationally-owned R & D and production facilities.

In the computer field, for example, Switzerland is the European country with the largest number of computer installations per head of working population, yet it has virtually no computer-producing industry of its own. Certainly, national educational and research efforts related to computers are necessary for any effective national capability in computers, but this is not the same thing as spending much larger sums in order to convert the results of research into commercially viable products. And if one agrees that 'after growing wildly for years, the field of computing now appears to be approaching its infancy',[1] then many new and potentially profitable markets for comptuer application are likely to emerge in future, other than commercial EDP.

For advanced electronic components, some of the same applies. Sweden and Denmark, for example, have small and competitive computer industries which rely almost entirely on imported components, including integrated circuits. And any national capability must be based on an effort in education and research. There are, however, some additional complications. Standardized components can be readily obtained on world markets. But in this technologically very fast-moving field, the design of electronic equipment may often require knowledge of what components are likely to be available in three to five years from now, and close, personal contacts between component supplier and user. Can the European equipment makers emulate their US counterparts in maintaining themselves a capability to design and develop prototype components and circuits, and then contracting out large-scale production orders to the component makers? Can they establish effective contacts across national boundaries, or do they require a locally-based R & D effort belonging to the supplier? And how difficult is it for the user to obtain very important, custom-built components without the existence of a local R & D and design capability belonging to the supplier? These questions may seem rather detailed. Answers to them would illustrate what may – or may not – be a wider problem.

Thus, we can see that the industrial implications of national, technological specialization are complex. The implications for defence activities are much clearer. The growth of the multinational firm, of the international transfer of technology, and of specialization provide a greater potential of technology to be exploited. And some foreign subsidiaries of multinational firms have collaborated in defence research in host countries (e.g. Texas Instruments, Mullard/Philips and STC/ITT in the United Kingdom; IBM in France). But, at the same, time, it implies less government control over access to defence related technology.

## 4 Conclusions

Thus, the experience of the OECD countries suggests that the

---

[1] *Computers in Higher Education,* report of the President's Science Advisory Committee, Washington, DC, 1967.

multinational firm, although not the only agent for international technology-transfer, has become an increasingly – and perhaps the most – important one; that the rapid increase in international technology-transfer has had beneficial effects for economic growth, and complex though not harmful effects on trade patterns in high technology industries.

Europe's technological capability has not disappeared, will not do so in future, nor will it fall entirely into the hands of US companies. But the costs of certain sectors of modern technology, together with a more open and interdependent world, means that certain countries have already, or will have to, face the fact that they can no longer be at the forefront of all scientific and technological developments, and that technological specialization is an economic necessity. As the experience of the United Kingdom over the past six years has shown, this can pose difficult problems related to industrial, educational and science policies. France is now facing the same problem. Japan will soon. And so may even the USA, as R & D in other parts of the world increases, and if the trend continues in the USA to devote fewer resources to science and technology.

It is sometimes suggested that European countries could have done more in the past, or should do more in the future, to maintain a stronger and broader independent technological capability. Few would argue that this is still feasible in defence. But some suggest that Europe should follow the example and the experience of Japan in controlling foreign investment and getting foreign technology mainly through licences. For Europe, this would have been particularly difficult, given its commitment to liberalization and, for the Common Market countries, given the additional difficulty of agreeing on a common line of action amongst six countries. And in any event, the same policies in Europe may well have not produced the same effects as in Japan. Although protected against foreign firms, Japanese firms have tended to compete ferociously amongst themselves, once they have had the foreign technology. In Europe, lack of outside competition often led to cartels and sleepiness, which only the arrival of US firms changed. In any event, there are now strong pressures inside and outside Japan for a change in policy, and – as we have seen – firms are less and less willing to license their technology.

It would be foolish to deny that technology, like the multinational firm, has important political implications. Nonetheless, for European countries there are strong grounds for arguing that the main technological emphasis should be in relation to competition for world markets. The examples of post-war Germany and Japan show that, with such an emphasis, it is possible to create and maintain a strong technological capability, and the freedom to move in new directions. It would imply the strengthening and the creation of European multinational firms, and the international diffusion of European technology.

## THE LESS-DEVELOPED COUNTRIES

If the effects of science and technological progress have until now been largely beneficial to the economic development and welfare of the industrially-advanced countries, the same cannot be said with regard to the less-developed ones. If the production of science and technology is not an exclusively American phenomenon, it is nonetheless almost exclusively concentrated *within* the industrially-advanced countries, and equally exclusively related to *their own* requirements. As we have seen, most commercially successful industrial R & D is geared to ever more sophisticated and rich markets. And the governments of the industrially-advanced countries devote a very small proportion of their scientific and technological resources to the problems of the less-developed ones.

Futhermore, the very size and effectiveness of the industrially-advanced countries' science and technology have led to significant and harmful welfare effects in the less developed ones: for example, the development of synthetics replacing natural products; the orientation of educational structures in the less-developed countries to the skills required in the advanced countries, together with the 'draining' of these skills towards the advanced countries; the effects of health and sanitation technology on population growth in the less-developed countries.

In other words, much of the new science and technology being produced in the world today is irrelevant to the needs of the less-developed countries, and the effects of some of it have been positively harmful. In what is one of the realistic papers that have been written on science and the less-developed countries, C. Cooper concludes:

'. . . while 75% of the world lives on or below – and sometimes well below – the bread line, there is a certain irony in talking about the 'contribution' of science to social progress. I have intentionally avoided this phrase because it seems to me to misrepresent the state of the case. We would like to think that science contributes to human progress, but in the present conditions the realities don't really fit in with the wish. The blunt fact is that, for the mass of humanity, science has probably brought more trouble than gain.'[1]

This is not, of course, to suggest that all new science and technology has been harmful to the welfare of the less-developed countries: witness the 'green revolution' and the beginnings of the effects of birth-control programmes. But one can still argue that the harmful secondary effects of a very large quantity (i.e. science and technology oriented towards advanced countries' needs) have been greater than the beneficial, primary effects of a very small quantity (i.e. science and technology related specifically to the needs of the less-developed countries).

It goes beyond the terms of reference of this paper to discuss what welfare benefits could (or could not) be achieved by shifting a greater proportion of the advanced countries' science and technology towards the problems of the less developed ones, and how such a shift in orientation might be brought about. Nonetheless, it is worth asking here what contribution the multinational firm, in transferring technology to the less-developed countries, can make to the latter's welfare. If what follows is largely speculative and does not give satisfactory answers to this question, it is at least in part because there appears to have been very little empirically oriented research on the subject.[2]

The first point to make is that the 'key' technologies for the less-developed countries are very different from those for the advanced countries, and are not concentrated exclusively in multinational firms. For the moment access to, and the ability to use, computers and advanced electronic components are not critical to less-developed countries' development. Technologies related to tropical agriculture, public utilities and public works are. Furthermore, many of the industrial technologies required by the less-developed countries are relatively old ones, often not requiring sophisticated skills that only multinational firms have, and not involving problems of patent protection. This means that many technologies that are 'key' to the less-developed countries can (and often must) be obtained from sources other than the multinational firm, through indigenous development, through technical assistance from governments and private organizations in the advanced counties, through consultants, or the

[1] C. Cooper, 'Science and Underveloped Countries' in *Problems of Science Policy*, OECD, Paris, 1968.

[2] However, see A. Maddison, *Foreign Skills and Technical Assistance in Economic Development*, Development Centre of the OECD, Paris, 1965.

import of capital goods. Given that most of the multinational firms in the less-developed countries are in relatively old industries with relatively stable and widely-available technologies, the most critical contribution that they can make is probably through transferring 'software' technologies, in other words, skills related to management, accountancy, technicians, foremen, etc., by training and upgrading local nationals, and contributing to local educational programmes.

However, there are relatively sophisticated technologies that are largely controlled by multinational firms and that may be 'key' to the less-developed countries: for example, pharmaceutical products in relation to health programmes, communications technology in relation to broadcasting, and machinery in relation to agriculture. Since these firms are mainly focused on rich markets, the nature of their products, their marketing policies and their production methods may not be appropriate to the needs of the less-developed countries.

With regard to products, the luxury and comfort embodied in them may be completely inappropriate to the requirements of the less-developed countries: for example, do they need tractors with windscreen wipers and comfortable upholstered seats; large, architecturally impressive and expensive television sets? In such cases it is technologically feasible to make simpler and cheaper products.

With regard to marketing policies, pricing and selling methods used in urban and rich markets may be inappropriate in rural and poor markets: are, for example, methods of pricing and selling pharmaceutical products in the advanced countries appropriate to rural health programmes in poor countries?

Finally, the production methods of multinational firms have in general been developed to take advantage of economies of scale in serving large markets. But the national markets of many less-developed countries are too small to take advantage of such scale economies. Are these economies of scale technologically determined and inviolable? If they are, then the policy followed by many less-developed countries of simply inviting multinational firms to produce and sell their existing products on small protected markets is likely to compound social inefficiency with economic inefficiency. But, alternatively, do the economies of scale result not from any technological laws but simply from the habits of mind and work of production engineers in multinational firms? And, if so, how (if at all) can multinational firms be persuaded to develop economic production methods adapted to smaller scale requirements?

The production methods of multinational firms are also developed to economize on expensive and scarce labour, whereas labour is cheap and abundant in less-developed countries. Can equally economic, but more labour-saving, production technology be developed and used? Or does latest, 'best practice' production technology economize on all factors of production? This latter possibility often tends to be neglected, but may in fact be the case in many more instances than theoretical economists often seem to assume. It has been documented for the catalytical cracking of petroleum and steel making. And Japan in the 1950s, with very low-income levels at that time, imported most of its technology (more than 60% of the total), not from Southern Italy but from the USA. However, newer and more economic production technology generally requires greater skills and learning capacities, so that its effective use depends on the educational and skill level of the work force. Japan's skill levels in the 1950s were far above those existing in many less-developed countries today. All this suggests that the lack of labour skills may be as important a factor as low labour costs in making older, more labour-intensive production techniques, the most appropriate ones.

Thus, we can see that there will be cases where the normal behaviour of multinational firms may lead to products, marketing methods and production technologies which are not appropriate to the needs of the less-developed countries. And since the markets of these countries will often be only a very small part of the multinational firms' total market, these firms may be reluctant – indeed, it may never even occur to them – to adapt their policies and practices to local conditions. Less-developed countries clearly need to have at their disposal both the technical competence to identify, and methods of influence that can lead to, the necessary changes. Perhaps the past methods of work – though not necessarily the policies – of institutions such as the Japanese Development Bank and the Ministry of International Trade and Industry could, in this context, be studied with profit.[1]

Most of the above discussion has been about getting and adapting technologies to the local market requirements of the less-developed countries. But a problem of growing importance in the future will be the extent to which these countries can participate in the world-wide division of labour in production of multinational firms in high technology industries: examples of such participation are the pack-

[1] See N. Jéquier, *Stratégie Industrielle et Technologique du Japon*, Centre de Rechererches Européennes, Lausanne, 1970.

aging of integrated circuits in South-East Asia, and the manufacture of computer punch cards in Latin America. The advantages are that such multinational firms are in fast-growing sectors; and that participating in an international division of labour can mean export earnings and an efficient scale of production. But, as we have seen, the necessary efficiency for international competitiveness may often require a skilled labour force: the Japanese experience has shown that the combination of cheap skilled labour and good technology is a powerful one. This has obvious implications for training and educational activities, both by host governments and by the multinational firms.

Finally, there is the problem of the degree to which the less-developed countries will be able to maintain some degree of control over more sophisticated technologies developed by multinational firms, especially when these countries become richer and more skilled, so that the multinational firm can see both the promise of a sizeable market and the threat of local competition. It matters little that such control may be economically irrelevant. As some of the papers prepared for this conference point out, many countries will try to get it. But will they succeed in a period when a growing number of firms prefer to invest and maintain control rather than to license? In other words, will variations on the Japanese experience be repeatable?

# COMMENT ON THE CHAPTER BY
# MR PAVITT

## CHRISTOPHER FREEMAN

Keith Pavitt's chapter on the role of MPE in the transfer of technology suggests that their role has been positive in accelerating the diffusion of new techniques and improving the efficiency of their application.

However, as he recognizes, most of the data on which these conclusions are based relates to the experience of the OECD area, i.e. primarily to transactions within a group of developed countries. Economic theory has increasingly recognized that generalizations which may be valid for this group of countries are not necessarily valid, or even relevant, for the developing countries. Burenstam-Linder,[1] Prebisch and many others have demonstrated that free trade may have very different consequences for economic growth in the developing world, as compared with Europe. The same may well be true of the operations of the MPE.

Transfer of technology between North America and Europe and within Europe, whether between independents or through the medium of affiliates of MPEs, takes place between countries which have a relatively strong indigenous scientific and technical capacity, a highly-developed educational system and a strong infra-structure of supporting services. In these circumstances a new technology may be fairly rapidly absorbed by the importing country, modified to suit local circumstances where appropriate and, indeed, improved upon in second and subsequent 'generations'. Moreover there is often a reciprocal element in such transactions.

Circumstances are quite different in the case of the developing countries. These countries frequently lack the scientific and technical capacity even to imitate the foreign technology, let alone to modify it or improve upon it. The degree of *dependence* on the foreign source of technology tends to be very much greater, and this applies whether the source is an MPE or an independent company.

In such conditions, apart from the obvious danger of monopolistic

---

[1] S. B. Linder, *An Essay on Trade and Transformation*, Wiley, 1961.

power, there are several other dangers inherent in the MPE situation.

One is that a technology may be imported which is unsuited in various ways to the local environment although advantageous to the MPE. Economists have concentrated attention on the relative labour-intensity as one factor which is particularly relevant in this context, but there are many others. For example, the imported technology may be heavily dependent on imported spares, intermediates and components, and on imported maintenance or marketing skills. While the provision of these goods and services may bring net benefits to the MPE, it is by no means self-evident that it will lead to an optimal allocation of resources within particular developing countries.

So long as the capacity to generate and improve new techniques is largely concentrated in a few highly-industrialized countries, and the MPEs are largely based in these countries, the process of technology transfer is inevitably an extremely one-sided affair. The research and development which leads to technological change is necessarily based primarily on the market needs of the industrialized countries, and on their traditions and life styles. About 98 % of all the world's scientific research and experimental development is performed in the industrialized countries. Consequently the world stock of technology is not equally suitable for all comers, nor is it equally available to all comers.

The incentive to MPEs to apply scientific and technical resources to the peculiar and specific problems of the developing countries is not very great, so long as the market is so small, and the indigenous scientific skills are negligible. The costs to the MPE of internal transfer within the enterprise of technologies previously developed in industrialized countries are likely to be much lower. This may often be highly beneficial to the importing country in particular cases. But the long-term overall effect may be to stunt the capacity for self-sustaining growth and to heighten a dependent relationship. This situation can easily be self-reinforcing and self-perpetuating. It may lead to the maintenance of an international division of labour which is extremely uneven, and also reinforce political divisions and tensions.

In the long run, this problem can only be resolved by the development of an indigenous capacity to perform and to innovate within the developing countries themselves. This depends primarily of course on national policies within these countries in relation to education, science and industry. But international organizations may facilitate the process by various forms of support. Some of these have been discussed in a recent report for UNACAST.[1] The contribution of MPEs depends on the extent to which they may be willing to adapt their policy and their organization to the rather long-term and very specific requirements of the host countries. Some of them have given indications that they are capable of this.

However, it is notable that the two countries which have been most successful as late-comers to industrialization did not give much encouragement to MPEs. Both Japan and the USSR, each in their different ways, severely limited the freedom of foreign-owned companies to operate in their territories. In neither case was this attitude based on a rejection of foreign technology. On the contrary, both devoted great efforts to the import of technical knowhow and to licensing arrangements, and they continue to do so. But the relationship in both cases tended to be an 'arm's-length' one in which the main emphasis was placed on using the imported technology as a springboard rather than a mattress. In both cases also national policy placed very great emphasis on establishing a strong indigenous scientific and technical capacity as well as very heavy investment in education and training.

Neither the Japanese nor the Soviet experience is necessarily a model for other countries, and it is clear that size of national economy must be one of the elements which will lead to major variations in development strategy. Moreover, the MPE has shown great adaptability and may lend itself to various forms of 'internationalization', which would make it a more acceptable change agent. But its acceptability is likely to be strongly related to its capacity to respond to the efforts of poor countries to make their own contributions to the advance of world technology.

[1] United Nations Advisory Committee on the Application of Science and Technology to Development.

PART TWO. LABOUR AND THE
MULTINATIONAL ENTERPRISE

*Chapter 4*

# INDUSTRIAL RELATIONS, LABOUR
# DISPUTES AND LABOUR UTILIZATION
# IN FOREIGN-OWNED FIRMS IN
# THE UNITED KINGDOM*

MAX STEUER and JOHN GENNARD

## GENERAL INTRODUCTION

A number of studies appear to find that the foreign-owned subsidiaries of multinational firms are more efficient than comparable
domestic firms in the host country. This is true of American firms
operating in Britain, and of direct investment in other industrial
countries. Superior performance is thought of in terms of higher
profitability, greater output for the same total input, more advanced
technology, and sometimes simply as higher labour productivity.
This last, of course, need not in itself be a sign of either efficiency or
profitability. There is some literature, and the expressed opinions
of managers of foreign-owned firms, to the effect that managerial
skill, particularly in more careful and intelligent utilization of
labour, is largely responsible for better performance.

At the same time there is some general recognition that the presence of foreign-owned firms in host-country labour markets constitutes something of a problem. Oddly enough, this potential
problem area is not usually considered, or even mentioned, in the
direct investment literature as such.[1] Explicit discussion arises more

* This chapter is part of a wider study undertaken by M. D. Steuer and
colleagues of the effects of inward direct investment on the economy of the
United Kingdom. The authors are indebted to Miss E. Cope and Mr A. Osei for
able research assistance, and to Miss E. Atkins for helping us to use data collected
by the LSE Higher Education Research Unit. We also appreciate very much the
co-operation of the Unit itself, and the help given at Watford by the Department
of Employment and Productivity.
[1] For example, the industrial relations of multinational firms in host countries

in statements by governments, unions and the literature of labour economics.[1] However, the question is raised in the chapter by Jack N. Behrman for this volume. In listing the benefits and costs for host countries of direct investment, the opening remarks on costs note that, '. . . it [direct investment] alters competitive positions (though not necessarily the methods of competition); it alters wage rates and *labour relations, personnel practices*, advertising, etc. These disturbances are made more intense by the concentration of the large enterprises in a few industrial sectors – normally the technically advanced ones.'[2]

The purpose of the present chapter is primarily to marshal statistical and institutional information bearing on the industrial relations and labour utilization of foreign-owned firms in the United Kingdom. In subsequent work we hope to analyse the findings reported here, and to relate them to the phenomenon of direct investment generally. Our chapter is in three parts. The first part outlines the current pattern of British industrial relations, and the special situations which arise as a result of foreign firms coming into this environment. It emphasizes the contrasts between British and American industrial relations, trade union recognition, the nature of agreements between employers and unions, and plant personnel practices. We attempt to appraise the impact of the foreign firm on United Kingdom industrial relations. The second part examines the industrial disputes of foreign firms. A basic question is, are they more or less strike-prone than domestic firms, and are the stoppages which occur in them different in kind. In the third section the electrical engineering industry is taken as a case study to compare some aspects of labour utilization in domestic and foreign-owned firms. The emphasis here is on the use of more highly skilled labour.

## UNITED KINGDOM INDUSTRIAL RELATIONS AND THE FOREIGN-OWNED FIRMS

### 1 *Characteristics of Industrial Relations in the UK*

The foreign firm investing in the United Kingdom is coming into a

is not discussed with respect to any of the many countries examined in the recent volume edited by I. A. Litvak and C. J. Maule, *Foreign Investment: The Experience of Host Countries*, New York, Praeger, 1970. Nor does the topic occur in the well-known works of Brash, Dunning, Kindleberger, Safarian, and so on.

[1] See Barkin, Solomon, *et al.* (eds.), *International Labor*, New York, Harper & Row, 1967.

[2] Jack N. Behman, 'Governmental Policy Alternatives and the Problem of International Sharing', Chapter 11 in this volume.

country where there is already an established industrial relations system with its own structures and values which may differ radically from those of the parent company country. The foreign subsidiary has the option of accepting completely the main features of the British industrial relations system. Alternatively, it may attempt to adopt, by evolutionary means, some of the features of its home country. It is unlikely to totally reject the system here for fear of generating an intolerable level of industrial conflict. But the incentive to modify the system is strong, particularly in cases where its views on labour utilization differ markedly from those of domestic firms.

The prevailing ideology of the British industrial relations system is that of voluntarism, in that there is an absence of legal controls over the main features of collective bargaining. There is no legislation compelling employers to recognize and negotiate with trade unions; arbitration and state intervention are a minor mechanism in the system. Agreements made between trade unions and employers' organizations are not legally enforceable contracts and are considered to be binding in honour only. Such agreements tend to have no set termination date, and cover a small number of matters. Often these are only wages and hours in contrast to the American system where many aspects of employment are subject to formal agreement.

Apart from the voluntary nature of our system, which Allan Flanders[1] sees stemming from the value placed by the British on economic freedom (freedom of contract, freedom of association, freedom to strike and lock out and freedom of self government) and industrial peace, the foreign firm is faced with other peculiar features of our industrial relations system. There is a high degree of centralization of collective bargaining. This is centred at the national level and takes place between national trade union officials and national officials of employers' associations, and agreements reached are for the industry concerned and apply at the national level. In many industries a second tier of negotiation takes place at the workplace between shop stewards and individual management, although this is done on an informal basis. Some industries have formalized national negotiating machinery, which takes the form of National Joint Industrial Councils, or statutory wage-fixing bodies known as Wages Councils, while other industries have *ad hoc* negotiating arrangements. The Department of Employment and Productivity estimates that there are over 500 pieces of negotiating machinery at

---

[1] See A. Flanders, *Industrial Relations: What is wrong with the System*, London, Faber & Faber, 1965, Chapters 3 and 4.

the national level covering some 14 million manual workers out of 16 million in employment.[1] Collective bargaining machinery is increasing among non-manual workers, but at the present time less than 50% of such workers have their wages and conditions of employment settled through joint negotiating machinery.

There is also a high degree of unionization in this country. As can be seen in Table 4.1, apart from Sweden, the UK has the highest proportion of its labour force in trade unions. The British trade union structure is untidy, consisting of craft unions, general unions and industrial unions, and there has been little attempt until recently to rationalize the structure. This has led to problems of multi-unionism, bringing jurisdiction and demarcation problems. There is also the shop steward movement which has grown up outside the formal trade union structure of government. The Trades Union Congress is the central body of the unions but is a relatively weak organization only having the power which its affiliated unions are prepared to give it.

TABLE 4.1

*Trade Union Membership as a Percentage of the Labour Force*

| | |
|---|---|
| Sweden | 45 |
| Britain | 40 |
| Italy | 35 |
| Holland | 27 |
| West Germany | 26 |
| United States | 22 |
| Japan | 20 |
| France | 16 |

*Source: The Economist*, September 3, 1966, p. 927.

The industrial relations system of the United Kingdom, with its unique features, presents problems for foreign-owned companies operating in Britain. For the Western European companies the problem of adapting to the main features of our system are not too difficult since there are similar features in their parent countries; for example, industry-wide bargaining, a degree of organization among employers, and multi-unionism. (In France, Belgium, Holland and Italy there is the additional problem of religious and ideological splits in union movements which happily are not a feature here.) However, a major difference is that on the continent, in the

[1] Royal Commission on Trade Unions and Employers' Associations, written evidence of the Ministry of Labour, p. 19, para. 48, London, HMSO, 1965.

majority of countries, collective agreements between employers and unions are legally enforceable contracts.[1] For companies from the United States the acceptance of the British system requires a radical departure from the practices used in their parent companies.[2] American employers are used to dealing with unions that accept the 'free enterprise system' and which are mainly concerned with improving wages and working conditions rather than unions that want to make fundamental changes in society and in the structure and the role of the enterprise within it. In some ways this makes it easier for employers here. The American union expects to get virtually all improvements for its members from the company. The British union directs a much larger proportion of its pressure on the Government, particularly in the field of social security – for example, pensions, unemployment benefits and redundancy payments. USA firms at home have not had to face the jurisdictional and demarcation problems of multi-unionism because the National Labour Relations Act provides that the union selected by the majority of workers in a bargaining unit 'shall be the exclusive representative for all employees in such bargaining unit for the purposes of collective bargaining'. Collective agreements with unions are legal contracts and operate for a fixed time period. Disputes arising during the period of contract are usually settled through voluntary grievance procedures. Agreements made in the United States are much more comprehensive than the usual British agreements and the level of negotiation is at the place of work (the plant) and not the industry.

Lloyd Ulman has argued that the major characteristics of the British industrial relations system have a tendency to build in restrictive practices which have implications for the labour utilization of firms.[3] He considers the legal obligation of employers in the UK through the wage councils to observe terms and conditions of employment not less favourable than those which have been established by agreement as well as award to be a depressing influence on

[1] The notable exception is Belgium, but this country legislated in 1969 to enable agreements between unions and employers to be made legally enforceable if both sides desire it. In the present British Government's proposed Industrial Relations Bill agreements will be legally binding unless *both* parties state otherwise.

[2] For a discussion of the problems facing American companies investing in Europe and the UK see J. C. Shearer, 'Industrial Relations of American Corporations Abroad', in *International Labour, op. cit.*

[3] L. Ulman, 'Collective Bargaining and Industrial Efficiency' in *Britain's Economic Prospects*, edited by R. E. Caves, Brooking's Institution Study, London, Allen & Unwin, 1968.

productivity. In the United States, employers keep unions out by paying above the union rate and thus giving them complete managerial prerogative in the use of labour. This, in turn, influences efficiency levels in the plants of their unionized competitors. The British system gives less opportunity for the American types of trade-off between pay and labour efficiency. He considers the untidy trade union structure to have adversely affected labour utilization through its contribution to skill shortages through restriction of supply, inappropriate wage differentials, and overmanning and restrictive practices. The larger the proportion of the workforce segregated into craft unions, the more opportunity for duplication of work restrictions on work assignments and similar practices. National industry-wide bargaining has tended to weaken the ability of management to handle problems at plant level where the weapons in the hands of the shop stewards (for example the unconstitutional strike, the ban on overtime and the work to rule) can exercise a depressing influence on productivity because the uncertainty as to when unofficial action may take place can result in management delaying or refusing to install new capital equipment.

## 2 The Level of Negotiation

The level of negotiation in the UK has tended to be industry-wide rather than plant or company based. The employers in a particular industry combine together to form an association to negotiate with the unions and achieve a uniform basic wage rate for the industry. There are estimated to be 750 autonomous employers' associations.[1] National based bargaining resulted in industrial relations in the UK companies being seen as something outside plant management and an aspect of business to be hived off to an external body. However, there are clear signs that the picture is changing. Nationalized industries have always engaged in plant bargaining but in the private sector the number of domestic firms that have developed company bargainings is increasing.[2] A small number of privately-owned domestic firms, for example the Lancashire Cotton Corporation and ICI, have always undertaken company bargaining. The recent

[1] See the Evidence of the Ministry of Labour to the Royal Commission on Trades Unions and Employers' Associations, HMSO, 1965, p. 12. If one includes local employers' organizations affiliated to the nationals the figure is over 13,500.

[2] See In Place of Strife: a Policy for Industrial Relations, Cmnd. 3888, p. 10, para. 23, London, HMSO, 1969; and B. C. Roberts and John Gennard, 'Trends in Plant and Company Bargaining', Scottish Journal of Political Economy, June 1970.

trend to plant and company bargaining has not been the result of management initiative but has been a response to demands from shop stewards that companies engage in plant bargaining and from the Government that wage increases should only be given in return for productivity concessions, which by necessity involves the workplace.

A certain number of foreign-owned companies have always negotiated on a company basis with British unions. For these firms company bargaining has not been a response to trade union pressure but has been deliberate policy on the part of the management concerned. They have preferred to retain an autonomy over their industrial relations policies and practices. This fits in with the well-known reputation of the foreign firm to try to utilize labour more effectively. There are numerous examples of foreign-owned firms negotiating independently of employers associations, and this may or may not involve plant bargaining. These include in vehicles Chrysler (UK) Ltd. (Rootes), Fords and Vauxhalls; in oil refining Esso, Shell and Mobil Oil; in food manufacture Brown and Polsons, Heinz, and Kellogs; in engineering Alcan, Massey Ferguson, Kodak and International Nickel; and in retail distribution Woolworths., The foreign firms that have deliberately opted for plant bargaining are predominantly American owned. Massey Harris and Rootes are examples of British firms who, on being taken over by North American companies, withdrew from employers' associations to have autonomy in industrial relations. The foreign firms of Western European origin have tended to join employers' associations for their particular industry and have been partners to industry-wide agreements. This is to be expected since employers in Western Europe are highly organized into employers' associations. Although one Dutch company, Philips Industries, has questioned the usefulness of such associations, it has not withdrawn from the Engineering Employers' Federation. It has suggested that the Federation be broken down into smaller groups on an industrial basis.[1] However, a number of foreign companies from the continent have moved towards company bargaining under pressure from shop stewards and the Government's productivity, prices and incomes policy, for example British Olivetti and Electrolux.

Not all of the movement has been in the direction away from em-

[1] See Royal Commission on Trade Unions and Employers' Associations, Minutes of Evidence, 28, Philips Industries, HMSO, London, 1966. We are indebted to the Employers' Associations who have helped us with this part of the study.

ployers' associations. There are American-owned firms who have made a deliberate policy decision to join even in cases of takeover where the previously British firm was not a member. In March 1968 there were 186 American-owned firms, comprising 283 establishments, in membership of the Engineering Employers' Federation. The Census of Production (1963) showed 18 USA-owned rubber firms and all were in membership of the British Rubber Manufacturers Association. There have been no withdrawals since this date. In food manufacturing the Census revealed 57 American-owned firms of which about half were members of the Food Manufacturers Industrial Group. Within the jurisdiction of the Soap, Candle and Edible Fates Trades Joint Industrial Council there were 63 American-owned firms of which only two were members of the relevant employers' association. However, these two firms accounted for a very high percentage of the foreign output in the industry under the jurisdiction of this employers' association.

Domestic firms appear to deploy a smaller amount of management input into industrial relations than the foreign firm, especially the American ones. In the UK the role of personnel departments in top management is only just emerging. Such departments have traditionally been seen as performing a welfare function in industry and having little executive authority in industrial relations because such matters have been dealt with by the employers' association to which the company belongs. American firms have viewed the personnel manager as providing an essential service to management so that human resources can be used most effectively and thus help labour efficiency and cost stabilization. The personnel director is ranked in importance with other specialized management functions, e.g. production, research, sales and accountancy. The task of selection, training, promoting and servicing the personnel employed in a large enterprise is seen as one that can only be carried out by experts. American companies operating in the UK tend to employ more scientific methods of selection of personnel than domestic firms, e.g. the use of personality and intelligence tests.

Where the foreign firm conducts its own industrial relations it tends to appoint industrial relations directors, who in many cases are answerable to the parent headquarters. This may take the form of regular reports on labour matters in the plant and general industrial relations developments in the UK.

At the same time, many parent company headquarters send back periodic reports to the subsidiary showing the relative performance of its establishments on the basis of certain economic efficiency indicators, for example, labour productivity and work performance standards. The purpose of these reports is to 'shame' managements to improve their position in the league table. To do this may involve a review of existing labour utilization and in the light of such a review an improvement in labour productivity. Interplant comparison was important in the development of productivity bargaining in the UK, one of the results of which was hoped to be an improvement in labour utilization so that wage increases could be self-financing. We return to this later. It has not been possible for us to discover on a systematic basis to what extent the parent company interferes with personnel policy in the UK. The foreign-owned firms submitting written evidence to the Royal Commission argued that they had autonomy in labour matters, although they sometimes had to justify their actions to headquarters.[1] When there has been a dispute between British unions and a foreign-owned company the unions have often argued that the company has taken a particular course of action because of instruction from parent headquarters. In 1969 when the Ford Motor Company sued the Transport and General Workers' Union and Amalgamated Engineering and Foundry Workers some unionists argued that the company was acting on the instruction of Detroit, but this has never been substantiated.

## 3 *Trade Union Recognition Policy*

As indicated above, there are no means whereby a trade union can force any employer, whether British or foreign, to recognize and negotiate with it over the terms and conditions of employment for its members. This is in marked contrast to the situation in the United States, Canada, Australia and parts of Western Europe. The question of union recognition can be divided into two parts, manual workers and staff workers. The failure to recognize and negotiate with manual trade unions does not appear to be a problem with foreign firms from Western Europe. However, it has been suggested in some quarters that some USA-owned firms are anti-union and have refused to recognize British trade unions. One can point to examples of non-recognition. International Business Machines do not recognize unions, preferring instead to adopt a paternalistic approach to their employees and attempting to check demands for unionization by giving relatively high rates of pay and generous fringe benefits. In this company, communication with employees takes place through

[1] See Minutes of Evidence to Royal Commission on Trade Unions and Employers' Associations, Massey-Ferguson, Kodak, Esso, Mobil Oil and Philips Industries.

an Advisory Council elected from various levels and which has a chairman who is in turn elected by the representatives. There have been no demands at the company for union recognition.

An American company that has withstood demands for recognition of unions by its employees is Kodak. At its Hemel Hempstead factory there was a one-day stoppage for recognition. Ten unions have been attempting to get recognition from the company arguing that, although membership was not high in the company, this was the outcome of the anti-union attitude of the company. Kodak conducts relations with their employees through the Kodak workers' representative committees which the company claims have not expressed a desire for trade unionism. The usual anti-union devices of high pay and generous fringe benefits are used.[1] The TUC General Council has attempted to persuade the company to recognize the unions but has had little success, other than a suggestion from the firm that they would give serious consideration to any demand for recognition coming from the majority of their employees. Kodak does not recognize unions in the United States and has attempted and, so far, succeeded, in importing this policy into its British establishment.

The Amalgamated Engineering Union has complained of recognition problems from foreign-owned firms. In 1966 the union was refused recognition at the West of Scotland establishment of the Caterpillar Tractor Company, an American firm. Several approaches were made to the company but, when these proved fruitless, 1,200 employees came out on a strike which lasted for thirteen weeks. When the union withdrew 600 of its members from another factory of the same company where recognition has been granted, the company agreed to recognize and negotiate with the union. The AEF also had recognition difficulties at the Stockport factory of Roberts-Arundel. This was originally a British textile machinery firm that negotiated with the union, but when it was taken over by a USA company, recognition of the AEF was withdrawn, and union members were dismissed and replaced by female workers. There followed a twelve-month strike beginning in November 1967 for the reinstatement of the union members and the recognition of the union. Although the company conceded in 1968, in January 1969 it closed down and withdrew its capital to the United States.

These incidents of refusal to recognize British unions by foreign firms have resulted in two motions being debated on the matter at

[1] For some of the devices used, see *Report of Annual Trade Union Congress*, 1965, p. 405.

the TUC. In 1965 the Association of Cinematography, Television and Allied Technicians proposed:[1]

Congress can no longer tolerate foreign companies operating in Britain which deny their employees collective bargaining rights. . . . Meanwhile the General Council are instructed to mount a campaign to help affiliated unions experiencing difficulties with foreign companies operating in Britain and to draw public attention to the attitude of such companies who are guilty of anti-trade union behaviour.

In 1968 the AEF proposed and succeeded in getting carried the motion:

Congress calls upon the Government to make it a condition that foreign firms recognize the British trade union movement and the rights of organized workers before they are allowed to operate in this country.[2]

While there clearly is a problem of recognition with respect to foreign subsidiaries, the scale of this problem may not be very great. During 1967 the General Council of the TUC conducted an inquiry into the issue of trade union recognition and recruitment. Five hundred firms covering thirty-nine unions and six and half million trade unionists were surveyed, and although the majority were British there were a number of foreign firms The survey revealed that the areas in which trade union organization was noticeably difficult were characterized by:[3] (a) the prevalence of small firms; (b) a relatively high proportion of female employees; (c) a high incidence of labour turnover; (d) non manual employment. Attention was drawn to particular difficulties in firms under foreign ownership and control. These foreign firms were found to be larger than British companies in which similar difficulties were encountered, although there were several large British companies who were shown to refuse to recognize trade unions. The inquiry did not conclusively suggest that the foreign firm was more anti-union than the British-owned firm. Recognition problems are far greater amongst the small British firm with a paternalistic attitude. The TUC Economic Review for 1970 did suggest that with the foreign-owned firm there was a problem of determining where decisions were taken and how

---

[1] *Annual Trades Union Congress Report*, 1965, p. 405.
[2] See *Annual Trades Union Congress Report*, 1968, p. 429.
[3] See *Annual Trades Union Congress Report*, 1967, pp. 129–32.

attitudes were formed over such problems as trade union recognition.[1]

Esso provides an example of a company with an anti-union attitude in the United States, but who have accepted and recognized national unions in their British establishments. During the First World War the company installed an Industrial Representative Plan which became a model for other large employers wishing to avoid the recognition of trade unions. The employees were discouraged from joining unions by an elaborate welfare programme. This was challenged under the Wagner Act, but when the Act's constitutionality was upheld by the Supreme Court in 1937, a legalized version of much the same arrangement was produced whereby the companies negotiated with local, so-called independent unions. These arrangements have endured and have recently survived the onslaughts of large national unions.[2] In its UK establishments, however, the company has always accorded full negotiating rights to the appropriate British trade union, and those recognized include the Transport and General Workers Union, Amalgamated Engineering Union, the former Plumbing Trade Union and former Electrical Trades Union, the Boilermakers, and Amalgamated Society of Woodworkers and Carpenters.

The Commission on Industrial Relations, established in January 1969, is empowered to examine cases where a company is withholding recognition from trade unions. References to the Commission are made by the First Secretary of State for Employment and Productivity after consultation with the Confederation of British Industries and the TUC. By April 20, 1970 the Commission had issued seven reports, six of which were concerned with non-recognition, and of these two concerned non-manual workers. The four reports concerning non-recognition of manual unions covered domestic firms.[3] None of its pending references on recognition are concerned with foreign-owned firms. There are at present only four firms of foreign ownership that have been referred to the Commission and

[1] Trades Union Congress, *Economic Review*, 1970, Chapter 3, para. 85, p. 35, TUC 1970.

[2] See A. Flanders, *The Fawley Productivity Agreements*, London, Faber & Faber, 1964, Chapter 1, pp. 27, 28.

[3] See *W. Stevenson & Sons Suttons Cornwall Ltd*, Cmnd. 4248, Commission on Industrial Relations, Report No. 3, HMSO, London 1969; Commission on Industrial Relations, Report No. 5, *B.S.R. Ltd*, Cmnd. 4274, HMSO, 1970; Commission on Industrial Relations, Report No. 6, *Elliotts of Newbury Ltd*, Cmnd. 4311, HMSO, 1970; Commission on Industrial Relations, No. 7, *Brock's Firework's Ltd*, Cmnd. 4325, HMSO, 1970.

these are references covering the industrial relations procedure in the companies.[1]

The general conclusion is that non-recognition of manual worker trade unions by foreign-owned firms is no worse than amongst domestic firms. Where recognition is withheld the company tends to pay high rates of wages and give generous fringe benefits relative to the companies that recognize unions in their particular industry, e.g. Kodak, Mars and Heinz. Where trouble arises over non-recognition by an overseas company it tends to get a lot of trade union and press attention and gives the impression that foreign firms are more reluctant to recognize manual unions.

Information provided by five employers' associations indicates that the foreign firm, like the domestic firm, appears to have a fear of white-collar unionism, not only amongst middle and lower management, but also amongst clerical workers. In the UK in the public sector, staff unionism is widespread and encouraged. In local and national government, over 80% of white-collar employees are unionized. In the private sector, staff unionism is not very widespread but is nevertheless increasing. In the United States, unionism amongst staff employees in 1964 was about 11% and USA-owned companies have shown a reluctance to accept a demand for unionism amongst staff ranks here, even though they have been prepared to accept manual unions without much difficulty. The Ford Motor Company have recognized manual unions since the early 1940s, but are still reluctant to recognize unions for their supervisory staff, although they have recognized the clerical branch of the T&GWU for clerical staff. The policy of many of these companies is to speak with union officials but not to grant formal recognition. The Association of Scientific, Technical and Managerial Staffs complained in its evidence to the Royal Commission about such companies and argued that foreign-owned companies were hostile to white-collar unions.[2]

The first report of the Commission on Industrial Relations concerned non-recognition of staff unions at the foreign-owned Association Octel Company Ltd, which is also a firm with a history of satisfactory relations with the unions representing craft and process

[1] The companies concerned are International Harvester Company of Great Britain Ltd (Canada); the East Kilbride establishment of Standard Telephone & Cables Ltd (USA); the Merthyr Tydfil establishment of Hoover Ltd (USA) and Electrolux Ltd, Luton (Sweden).

[2] Royal Commission of Trade Unions and Employers' Associations, Minutes of Evidence No. 53, *Association of Supervisory Staffs, Executives and Technicians*. In 1968 this union amalgamated with the Association of Scientific Workers to form the Association of Scientific, Technical and Managerial Staffs.

workers on its payroll. The reasons given to the Commission for the withholding of recognition were those common to most firms, whether domestic or foreign, namely, unionism would destroy a direct relationship between management and employee and thus weaken loyalty and restrict the scope of management discretion.[1]

The attitudes of companies of West European origins to staff unionism are less well known than those of American firms. In rubber manufacture, Pirelli (Italian) and Michelin (France) are both reluctant to accept staff unionism, although they have always accorded negotiating rights to manual unions. In engineering, Philips Industries, a Dutch company, has been reluctant to concede recognition to staff members, but being members of the Engineering Employers' Federation they go along with that body's recognition of the draughtsmen union, Draughtsmen and Allied Technicians Association (DATA). In oil refining, all the well-known foreign-owned companies recognize manual worker unions, but they have shown a reluctance to accept claims for ASTMS to negotiate on behalf of technical and middle managerial staffs. The policy of Shell (UK) Ltd is to recognize a union for staff where the majority of staff in a common grade decide by ballot that they wish union representation. However, the common grades are so broad that it is difficult to get a majority. A ballot was held in two of the company's establishments for recognition of ASTMS but a majority was not secured. In companies where staff unions have been recognized, the attitude of management could be summed up as a grudging acceptance of an unavoidable but rather unpleasant necessity.[2] Some foreign companies have encouraged the formation of staff associations as an alternative to unionization.

4 *The Nature of Agreements*

Collective agreements in the UK are generally not legally binding contracts and are considered to be binding only in honour, though it has always been possible for an individual company and a trade union to conclude a legally binding contract if they both desire it. However, foreign companies in the UK negotiating on a company basis have not taken advantage of this legal provision, and have

---

[1] See Commission on Industrial Relations, Report No. 1, Associated Octel Company Ltd, Cmnd. 4246, HMSO, 1969.

[2] This is the general conclusion from a study of technicians in 14 plants in the UK, of which 7 were foreign owned (5 Dutch and 2 USA), undertaken by B. C. Roberts, J. Gennard, R. J. Loveridge and J. V. Eason of the *Industrial Relations Department*, London School of Economics, forthcoming.

only entered into 'morally' binding agreements. Agreements between employers' associations and trade unions are not legally binding because by legal definition they are both trade unions. Foreign firms who are members of employers' associations are thus voluntary partners to a 'gentlemen's agreement'. Hence the foreign firms in the UK can find themselves facing a problem of unconstitutional industrial action, that is, action in breach of an agreed procedure, without any form of legal redress. However, in 1968 and 1969 two foreign firms have attempted to achieve a revolutionary breakthrough. Henry Wiggins, a subsidiary of International Nickel, succeeded in 1968 in negotiating a legally binding agreement, and in 1969 the Ford Motor Company sued two British unions for allegedly breaking agreed procedural arrangements.

The Henry Wiggin agreement was made at the Hereford establishment and is unique in British industrial relations. Both the management and the union involved, the AEF, clearly intended on signature that the provisions of the agreement should bind them in law. The deal was to last for two years and there were to be no strikes or lockouts during the course of the agreement. However, the agreement has been concluded in an area where unemployment is high and little trade union tradition exists, and attempts by the company to secure a similar agreement at its Swansea establishment have resulted in a prolonged strike.

In February 1969 the Ford Motor Company succeeded in getting the majority of unions in its National Joint Negotiating Committee to accept a proposed settlement which would have given increases in basic rates, an incomes guarantee plan covering a holiday bonus and guaranteed pay for lay-off due to disputes in suppliers' establishments, and improved fringe benefits in return for which employees would lose some of the holiday and lay-off payments if they were involved in unconstitutional action. There was also a reform of the company's disputes procedure. When shop-floor pressures built up to oppose the deal, the T&GWU and the AEF declared the strike action official. The company insisted there was an agreement and, if there was a dispute about its terms, settlement should be through the company's procedure agreement of 1955 and the 1967 amendment. On February 27th the company sought and obtained injunctions against the two unions. Fords sued the unions, alleging that the calling of official action constituted a breach of the procedural agreements, which had laid down circumstances in which strikes could take place during the course of an agreement. The Judge concluded that the procedural agreements were not legal contracts because it

103

had not been the intention of the parties at the time to create legally binding contracts. On March 6th the injunctions were discharged and, when the strike action ended, the company dropped its intention to appeal against the decision or to take the matter to a full trial. The Court has thus upheld a tradition of the UK industrial system, that is, agreements were legally enforceable only if this was the intention of the parties.

Procedural agreements lay down a procedure to be followed where there is a dispute over the application and interpretation of any existing substantive agreement, i.e. the price list aspect of an agreement. In the UK industry-wide agreements generally have an industry-wide disputes procedure stating the number of stages in attempts to settle differences that have not been solved within establishments. Domestic firms tend to be parties to such procedures as do foreign firms that are members of employers' associations. British firms that negotiate on a company basis often follow industry-wide disputes procedures, but foreign-owned firms who are involved in company bargaining have their own domestic procedures which tend to be shorter and more speedy than industry-wide ones. Ford and Vauxhall are not members of the Engineering Employers Federation and have their own procedural agreements. Industry-wide procedures usually stipulate that there shall be no strike or other form of industrial action while a grievance is being processed. In return, employers pledge not to lock-out employees until all the stages of procedure are exhausted. The Royal Commission on Trades Union and Employers Association saw breach of procedures, and thus unconstitutional strikes, as a major problem in British industrial relations. The Commission suggested that before legal regulations were to be brought into our system to make procedural agreements legally binding there should be a reform of existing procedures. An examination of 160 agreements made between 1966 and 1969 indicates that some reform is in progress. In 1968, in twelve agreements, some kind of procedural reform was present as opposed to only three before 1968.[1] Of the twelve agreements, four concerned foreign-owned firms. For two the reform was of the plant procedure, but as members of the appropriate employers' association the industry-wide procedure operated in cases not settled at the plant. For another the reform was a modification to an existing company procedure, but for the fourth, which had just withdrawn from an employers' association, it amounted to a new company disputes procedure. The other eight were concerned with domestic companies and the main direction of change

[1] B. C. Roberts and John Gennard, *op. cit*

was a speeding up of the processing of grievances within the plant.

Although domestic firms are having to give more attention to procedural reform they have not been as inventive as some of the foreign-owned firms, two of whom have given their employees a financial incentive to observe an agreed procedure. Foreign firms have not attempted to obtain legally enforceable disputes procedures and have accepted the British system, and there have been few attempts to challenge it. The fact that foreign-owned firms operating in the UK and negotiating on a plant basis have not gone in for legally enforceable agreements illustrates the extent to which foreign firms abide by accepted customs and practices in industrial relations. It is nevertheless significant that a Canadian and United States firm have in the one case achieved a legally enforceable agreement and in the other tested the status of procedural agreements in the British Courts.

## 5 *The Duration of Agreements*

The typical UK industry-wide agreement has no set duration and negotiations for a new agreement can be started at any time. On a number of occasions unions have given notice of a new claim within a week or two of signing an agreement on the grounds of the length of time taken to negotiate the agreement just reached. For many foreign firms, and especially Canadian and United States companies, the pattern in their parent country is to negotiate fixed-term agreements which state clearly the number of years for which the agreement is to run, the period of notice required to terminate the agreement, and the circumstances that apply when a new agreement has not been negotiated at the expiry of the original agreement, and a commitment not to strike, or to engage in other forms of industrial action or lockouts during the term of the agreement. Fixed-term agreements alter the approach to bargaining since they carry with them the concept of exchanging peace and co-operation on specific terms for a definite period. This gives rise to two problems: (*a*) what to do if there is any major change which alters the basic assumptions on which the agreement has been made, and (*b*) resolving disputes over the application of the provision of an agreement during its term.

Since 1962 a number of UK industry-wide agreements have been concluded with set termination dates, lasting on the average about three years. Between 1962 and 1965 twenty-two such agreements were signed covering over seven million workers. The most important of these was the engineering agreement, and foreign firms who were members of the Engineering Employers' Federation were thus operat-

THE MULTINATIONAL ENTERPRISE

ing with a fixed-term agreement. Disputes over the agreement were to be resolved through the industry's disputes procedure, and the wage increase awarded was to be spread over the three-year period. However, fixed-term company agreements have been rare among UK firms, although by 1969 there were signs that under the influence of productivity, prices and incomes policy and the Royal Commission Report the position might be changing. Nationalized industries have concluded company agreements with fixed termination dates, e.g. the airlines, the electricity and gas supply, and railway sectors; but in 1968 some private British companies concluded agreements for a fixed duration, for example, Ilford and Parkinson-Cowan, and in 1969 it appears an even larger number were involved in such agreements, such as Ansell's Brewery, Swan Hunter and Tyne Shipbuilders Perkins Engines, the Scottish and Newcastle Breweries and GEC/AEI.

Foreign-owned companies have been involved in fixed-term company-wide agreements since the early 1960s, but as among domestic firms the trend appears to have accelerated in the last few years. In 1960 Esso, at its Fawley refinery, negotiated a two-year agreement with its employees. In 1962 Massey Ferguson concluded a four-year agreement; at the end of 1965 Alcan concluded an agreement with its production and service-workers to take effect in 1966, having concluded a similar agreement with its process workers in 1964, while in 1968 Henry Wiggins signed a two-year agreement. In 1969 a number of foreign-owned firms concluded company agreements with a termination date, for example, Chrysler (two years), Otis Elevator, International Harvester and Vauxhall.

Although company-wide fixed-term agreements are at present more prevalent among foreign firms than domestic, the former have not developed voluntary grievance arbitration for the settlement of disputes over the application and interpretation of the agreements during their duration. Such disputes are usually processed through the agreed company procedure and, should no agreement be reached, third-party intervention by the Department of Employment and Productivity is generally used only if specifically requested by one or both parties, or in some cases the matter may be referred to the Industrial Court. The Henry Wiggin agreements, however, come close to the typical USA type of fixed agreement. The 1970 agreement clearly states the length of the agreement; the circumstances in which negotiations can be restarted during the term of the agreement; the conditions in which industrial action is acceptable during the agreement, and provides a claims procedure as the means of

106

raising and resolving claims that the company has breached the provisions of the agreement. The procedure lays down time limits for each stage of the procedure and provides for a board of three arbitrators, and a separate board sits for each 'alleged' company breach. The union and company each appoint one arbitrator and if they cannot mutually agree a third, one or more of the parties may ask the Secretary of State for Employment and Productivity to submit lists of arbitrators and from this a third person will be selected. Any Arbitration Board is to deliver its decision in writing thirty days after the end of any hearing.

## 6 Productivity Bargaining

Productivity bargaining has probably been the major innovation in UK industrial relations during the last decade, and the foreign firms have had a large influence on this development. Among American-owned firms, comparison of performance between UK and US establishments is crucial. In engineering, rubber manufacturing, food processing, and soap making and chemicals, comparability appeared very influential. The personnel director of the UK foreign firm usually has to write monthly reports to the Vice-President of the parent company covering such matters as wages and conditions of employment, recruitment, and developments in industrial relations in the country as a whole. In return, the parent company sends reports showing how particular establishments compare with others and there are also visits from the Vice-President to see operations at first hand.

The first known productivity agreement in the UK was that signed at Esso's Fawley plant in 1960. However, the seeds of this agreement have been traced back to 1956 when its parent company, Standard Oil, showed a new interest in manpower utilization in an attempt to survive an intensification of competition in the United States and in international oil markets and so prevent falling profits.[1] The company introduced a new statistical basis for judging comparisons of manpower utilization and the Fawley plant made a comparatively poor showing. As a consequence, pressures built up on the Fawley management to do something about its use of manpower, and in particular the excessive amount of overtime worked. In 1960 an agreement was reached with the unions giving pay increases in return for which the elimination of overtime, flexibility between jobs, changed manning levels (in particular the ending of craftsmen's mates) and shift working were accepted.

[1] See A. Flanders, op. cit., Chapter 2.

It can be seen from the above that a productivity agreement is one in which workers agree to make a change, or a number of changes, in working practices that will lead to more efficient production. In return, the employer agrees to a higher level of pay or to other benefits. The idea is that the pay increase will be self-financing through the savings made by the workforce accepting and operating the agreed changes in the way in which a job is performed. Productivity agreements can be comprehensive or partial. The former cover a number of related changes in working practices and affect all, or nearly all, of the manual workers in an undertaking, whereas the latter normally affect only one practice and often only a single group of workers. Comprehensive productivity agreements are to be sharply distinguished from conventional wage settlements in the UK. These latter agreements generally relate pay to matters external to the plant, for example, changes in the cost of living, disturbances in comparative wages, profit levels and labour recruiting problems in the industry as a whole. Productivity agreements are related to the workplace itself.

It is difficult to discover the relative proportion of productivity agreements in domestic as against foreign firms because there is no register of such agreements before January 1967, and as firms submit the information in confidence there is no access to the register for non-governmental research workers. However, the first companies involved in the pre-1967 era were foreign owned. Table 4.2 below shows the dates when negotiation for a productivity agreement began, the degree of comprehensiveness and whether the company is foreign or domestic. Of the fourteen agreements, eight concerned foreign-owned establishments and six domestic firms.

The growth of productivity bargaining offers a challenge to the traditional British system of industrial relations. Since it is concerned with workplace matters, industry-wide negotiation is clearly being attacked as it would be impossible with this type of agreement to work out at national level the details for each individual plant. Although the 'pioneering' firms were mainly non-federated, they did represent a challenge since the rates of pay agreed upon were generally well above those for federated firms and there was a feeling that workers in such companies would demand parity with workers covered by productivity agreements but without the corresponding productivity concessions. Some of the companies involved in productivity agreements were at one time federated but felt it desirable to resign from employers' associations when they began to engage in productivity bargaining, and so free themselves from any need to observe industry level agreements. Esso withdrew from the Employers' Panel of the Oil Companies' Conciliation Committee after concluding its distribution workers agreement. Alcan, who concluded a productivity agreement, also withdrew from the local employers' association. Employers' associations were afraid that the supra-marginal firms might withdraw from association and conclude productivity agreements rather than be held back by the marginal firms

TABLE 4.2

*Productivity Agreements*

| Date of start of negotiations | Company | Comphrensive (C) or partial (P) | Ownership of company |
|---|---|---|---|
| 1960 | Esso (Fawley) | C | USA |
| April 1962 | Esso (Fawley) | C | USA |
| 1963 | Petrochemicals | P | Dutch |
| 1963 | Mobil Oil | P | USA |
| June 1964 | Esso (Milford) | C | USA |
| June 1964 | Alcan (Rogerstone) | C | Canada |
| July 1964 | Central Electricity Generating Board | C | British |
| July 1964 | British Oxygen | P | British |
| 1964 | Mobil Oil (Distribution) | C | USA |
| 1964 | BP (Kent) – Isle of Grain | P | British |
| Sept. 1964 | Esso (Distribution) | C | USA |
| May 1965 | Imperial Chemical Industries | C | British |
| 1965 | Co-operative Insurance Society | P | British |
| 1966 | Stanton and Stavely (Derbyshire) | C | British |

*Source:* National Board for Prices and Incomes, Report No. 36, Productivity Agreements, Cmnd. 3311, Appendices A to H inclusive.

in an association. However, the associations have dropped their initial opposition to productivity agreements, and the chemical, rubber and electrical contracting associations have taken steps to assist member firms in negotiation of such agreements. The rubber industry employers' association negotiates national minimum earnings levels which firms in membership can exceed through productivity bargaining. The Engineering Employers' Federation has also come to terms with productivity bargaining and has established a research department to assist its member firms.

On the trade union side the union officials, who are involved in nation-wide bargaining, opposed productivity bargaining because its concentration on the workplace might give more power to shop stewards. As stewards would become the main agents in the determination of pay, they might be able to undermine the authority of the full-time officials. However, trade union opposition has tended to subside as the realization of the benefits to be gained from such operations became clearer.

Between January 1, 1967 and December 31, 1969 the Department of Employment and Productivity considered nearly 4,200 productivity agreements, the majority of which were accepted. However, few of these agreements were of the type concluded pre-1967 and many were accepted although they were not genuine in the Fawley sense, with the result that the idea of productivity agreements has become somewhat weakened. Since January 1970 the incomes policy has become more flexible and the 'something for nothing agreement' appears to be re-establishing itself among the domestic firms. It is difficult to say at the moment whether the same trend is emerging among foreign-owned firms. The 1970 Ford Motor Company agreement was a 'no strings attached' agreement but is to some extent a special case because of the company's need to 'buy back' good faith with their unions following the court proceedings of 1969.

In summary one can say that the growth of productivity bargaining has been the biggest innovation in the British industrial relations system in the 1960s. A major impetus for this has come from foreign-owned firms, particularly Esso, Alcan, Mobil Oil and Shell. The British firms have followed, and the Government's productivity, prices and incomes policy has probably been an important factor in stimulating the growth of productivity agreements among domestic firms. Clearly this sort of innovation could have potential spillover effects beneficial to the UK economy generally. It is beyond the scope of this paper to quantify these.

## 7 Plant Personnel Practices

Inter-plant comparisons between parent and foreign establishments are important in wage payment schemes. In the UK the majority of firms employ workers on the conventional types of incentive payment schemes which in tight labour markets tend to become undermined. Few domestic firms employ schemes like measured daywork and cost reduction plans which require work measurement through the application of industrial engineering techniques, but the position is changing under the influences of the productivity, prices and incomes policy. American and some Dutch-owned firms in the UK have used inter-plant comparison within their own organization of worker performance and have demanded that comparatively poor UK establishments improve. The National Board for Prices and Incomes in Report 123 studied forty productivity agreements. A number of the agreements chosen for study tried to ensure, through tighter measurement of performance, that the increase in pay did not exceed the expected increase in productivity, and the Board argued that comparison with higher American performance was sometimes an influential factor getting subsidiaries to undertake reform in the case of firms with American parentage.[1]

There is a feeling among observers of industrial relations that measured daywork has been growing as a form of wage payment, but R. B. McKersie argues that a major trend to measure daywork is not under way at present and the impression has only been created because of the publicity given to the abandonment of piecework by a small number of firms, for example Vauxhall Motors, Pet Foods Limited and Glacier Metals.[2] The term 'measured daywork' covers many variations within the general theme of hourly wage payments accompanied by the use of performance standards. It would appear that in the motor-car industry there is a marked contrast between the payment systems used in the domestic company and those used in the foreign-owned companies.[3] There is now only one domestic motor-car firm, British Leyland Motor Corporation, and this employs its workers on conventional payment incentive schemes. The three foreign-owned motor-car firms, Ford, Vauxhall and Chrysler, have changed from piece rates to measured daywork. Vauxhall's abandoned piecework in favour of straight time in 1956, Fords in 1967 and Chrysler in 1968. It would be useful to see whether this has had any effect on the relative strike frequency and type of strike experienced in the domestic and foreign firm. One would expect there to be more wage issue strikes at the domestic firm than at the foreign one, and this appears to be the case.

Philips, a Dutch company, uses a measured daywork, system which has a very direct link between effort and earnings. Each employee works under a contract that enables him over a long-term period to generate more take-home pay by fulfilling the performance standards. The approach envisages the periodic adjustment of a

[1] See National Board for Prices and Incomes, Report 123 – Productivity Agreements, Cmnd. 4136, London, HMSO, 1969.

[2] R. B. McKersie, 'Changing Wage Payments System', *Royal Commission on Trade Unions and Employers' Associations*, Research Paper II, Two Studies in Industrial Relations, London, HMSO, 1968.

[3] But McKersie, *loc. cit.*, points out that outside the traditional automobile areas none of the new plants has been established on daywork.

worker's pay in accordance with his performance. It has been estimated that only 8% of the workers in the Philips plants have failed to fulfil their bargain with the company.[1] Successful results suggest that the practice will spread.

## 8 The Impact of the Foreign Firm on UK Industrial Relations

Writing in 1957 Allan Flanders remarked, 'The recent history of collective bargaining in post-war Britain is, perhaps, most remarkable for its lack of innovations. The traditional pattern has been extended – although this took place mainly during and immediately after the war – but it remains substantially the same in form and extent.[2] Since that date a number of innovations have taken place in the industrial relations system and the leaders in this respect have been foreign-owned firms. The majority of foreign firms have accepted the traditional features of the UK system and, while attempts at radical departure by importing practices from the parent country have been rare, one can point to clear innovations stemming from the foreign firm.

(a) Productivity bargaining, where workers are given wage increases in return for changes in working practices so that the increase is self-financing, is an example. Esso, a UK subsidiary of Standard Oil, USA, were the pioneers in this field, being followed by other foreign and British firms. Productivity bargaining, by concentrating on the plant, challenged the industry-wide basis of the industrial relations system and was opposed by employers' associations and trade union officials. However, the system has adjusted to the change and unions and employers now accept productivity bargaining. The idea of productivity bargaining has been a central plank in the Government's productivity, prices and incomes policy, and the Roberts and Gennard Study has shown that company bargaining is becoming more of a feature of the British system.

(b) Two foreign firms have made revolutionary attempts to overcome the unconstitutional strike problem by offering financial incentives to employees to honour the disputes procedure. Ford has offered payments into a lay-off and holiday bonus fund on the condition there is no unconstitutional action. Henry Wiggin has introduced a penalty of loss of premium rate if employees assist or take part in any industrial action that is in breach of agreement.

[1] R. B. McKersie, op. cit., p. 51, para. 103.
[2] A. Flanders, 'Great Britain', in Contemporary Collective Bargaining in Seven Countries, edited by A. Sturmthäl, Cornell University, 1957.

Employers' associations are beginning to reform industry-wide procedures, but an attempt by the Engineering Employers' Federation has met difficulties with the unions over the number of external plant stages to the procedure, and the *status quo* provisions.

(c) The foreign firm has been in the lead in the making of fixed-terms company agreements. This stems from the practice of some USA and Canadian firms in the conduct of their own industrial relations. In the early 1960s some industry-wide agreements were made with a fixed termination date. Some domestic firms are now beginning to make company agreements because of a more flexible approach to such agreements by employers' associations.

(d) Ford and Henry Wiggin have challenged the UK system in another way. The latter company have achieved a unique agreement in Britain with its legally binding agreement at its Hereford plant, backed with a voluntary grievance procedure to examine allegations of management's breach of the agreement. The Ford Company sued two unions in the Courts for breaching a dispute procedure. The suit was rejected by the Courts, but had it been successful it could have changed the whole environment of British industrial relations and seriously questioned the voluntary basis of the UK system.

(e) There are other areas where the foreign firms appear to have been innovators. International Business Machines and Shell (UK) Ltd have pioneered uniform fringe benefits for staff and manual workers. Philips Industries have been among the leaders in introducing work structuring and the application of industrial psychology to plant industrial relations. In the motor-car industry the foreign-owned firms have introduced stricter measures of performance of the workforce, by the use of measured daywork, than the domestic firm which still relies on the traditional conventional payment by results schemes.

## 9 Trade Union Response to the Foreign Firm in the UK

The British trade union movement has made surprisingly little response to the foreign-owned firm operating in the UK. This is largely due to the fact that some of the implications of such companies have not yet been realized and because the foreign companies have often accepted the main features of the British system. Anti-foreign feeling amongst some unions has been aroused on occasions through a failure of a small number of foreign companies to recognize and negotiate with manual trade unions. British unions are aware of the ability of the foreign-owned company

113

to withdraw its operations from Britain and continue business in another area, but up to the present they have suffered little from such moves. One example, however, is the AEF experiences with Roberts-Arundel when the company removed its operation back to the States following a twelve-month strike for union recognition. In addition, in February 1970, shop stewards at the Ford plant at Halewood, Liverpool, questioned Henry Ford, chairman of Ford of Detroit, about rumours of a possible build-up of car production in Germany at the expense of Britain. They were afraid that the company's replacement for their Escort model would be built at a new factory at Saarlouis, Germany. The unions were not afraid of a rundown in existing plants, but that a large proportion of future investment might be diverted to Germany at the expense of the UK. The American management of Ford, Detroit, is known to be shocked by the attitude to industrial relations in the UK, but the UK plants of the company have dismissed fears of a rundown in investments in the UK as nonsense. Unions have seen the power of the foreign firms in their ability to withstand strike action by supplying customers from establishments in the parent country or other countries of operation. American-owned rubber companies in the UK have used this tactic, but domestic companies have shown a similar inclination to satisfy customers' demands when involved in an industry-wide dispute with the unions. In 1959, during a six-week printing strike, many British printers attempted to get orders filled on the continent.

British trade unions have developed international contacts by affiliating to the International Confederation of Free Trade Unions, which is an umbrella for sixteen International Trade Secretariat (ITS), the biggest of which is the International Metalworkers' Federation. However, these contacts have not been the direct result of the upsurge of foreign-firm operations in the UK but rather spring from a desire for international trade union co-operation on all matters of interest to trade unionists. The contact between British unions in foreign-owned firms and unions in the firms' parent country or other countries of operation is small. Sid Harraway, for example, the shop-steward convenor at Ford's Dagenham plant, admits that there is too little contact with his European opposite numbers.[1]

[1] L. Turner, *Politics and the Multinational Company*, Fabian Research Series 279. However, on April 24, 1970, the *Financial Times* reported that convenors from Ford Motor's Plant in Britain were hoping in June 1970 to strengthen unofficial contacts made recently with Ford workers in Belgium and Germany.

Action to meet the threat of multinational companies is being instigated by the United Automobile workers, an American union. In 1969 it sent a delegation over to Britain to have talks with the Amalgamated Union of Engineering and Foundry Workers and the Transport and General Workers' Union. A conference of the three unions met to study each others' constitutions, problems and working methods, and to examine in considerable depth the agreements and negotiating procedures and timings as they stand at present and to see what sort of co-ordination might take place to bring progress and benefit to all three unions' members in the motor industry. At the end of the conference a statement acknowledged that there was a need for regular contact and an exchange of agreements and information on a consistent basis, and that it was likely that eventually there would be co-ordination of some aspects of agreements in the two countries, particularly so far as terminal dates for wage agreements were concerned.[1] Walter Reuther[2] (former UAW President) was a strong advocate of international co-operation and argued that in the negotiation of company agreements the unions should ensure that all agreements with supra-national car manufacturers end at the same time. This was seen as a precondition of international bargaining.

The British unions have not been as active, but as affiliates to the International Metal Workers Federation have joined its World Automobile Council, which was also the outcome of a UAW initiative. In December 1969 a Paris conference concerned with the development of the motor-car multi-nationals was attended by eleven British trade unions, including the AEF, the T&GWU and the Vehicle and Sheet Metal Workers. At the meeting, consideration was given to a study of wage rates and earnings paid by motor manufacturers to their employees in different countries. The union leaders in the Council Conference voted for a policy which aims to ensure that, for instance, all Ford workers in Europe earn the same in relation to their countries' cost-of-living levels, i.e. European parity of real wages. The object of this, apart from improving wages, is to ensure that international companies do not run down operations in one country and build them up in cheaper labour markets.

---

There are plans to hold a conference in Britain to discuss comparative Ford pay rates in the three countries and to examine whether 'parity' can become an international issue and a basis for wage demands.

[1] Transport and General Workers Union *Record*, October 1969, pp. 32–4.
[2] Walter Reuther was killed in an aeroplane disaster on May 10, 1970 in the USA.

However, the first priority in host countries is for the unions to get parity of earnings in their own factories, for example, the British unions in the motor-car industry are attempting to negotiate the same rates for all plants as those paid to the highest paid workers at Chrysler, Coventry.

At the Paris conference, the unions also agreed that they should try to stop companies transferring work from one country to another during strikes and that they should aim for a guaranteed annual wage, a forty-hour week (this has already been achieved in the UK) and security of employment. The union leaders set their sights on achieving equal pay for women without conditions, for example that women should now work shifts and that factory legislation giving certain protection to females should be withdrawn. Another example of British participation occurred on June 14th when a world conference of unions with workers employed in the Shell Oil Company was held in Istanbul. This conference noted that dwindling employment in the petroleum industry was one of the most disquieting aspects of recent developments. A study committee was appointed to examine the broad range of workers' relations with the Shell Company. The Sixth World Congress of the International Federation of Petroleum and Chemical Workers decided at its June 1970 meeting on important structural innovations to enable its member unions (which include British ones) in various countries to correlate for workers employed by the same international company wages, working hours, collective agreements and other issues. To this end the Congress recommended the convening of trade union council meetings covering Standard Oil, Du Pont, ICI and other world enterprises.

If the talk of a positive link between unions in the British plants of a foreign company and unions in the plants of the company in its own country were to materialize, then a number of problems would arise in negotiations. How, for example, would the relative cost of living be determined in each country? The Index of Retail Prices in the UK has a different basis to the Consumer Price Index in the States. Attempts to solve the problem by taking a basket of goods that constitute the major items in living costs runs into further difficulties since there may be no agreement in the two or more countries as to whether a commodity is necessary for everyday living. The countries that are more affluent may see as 'necessities' goods which are considered to be 'luxuries' in other countries. A second problem would arise over manpower utilization concessions. For example, how would one measure that workers in one country had made more concessions than those in another if the capital-labour ratios in the plants of the two or more countries were different?

The only action undertaken by British trade unions with respect to foreign firms has been in the form of demands that overseas companies should give an undertaking, as a condition of being allowed to operate in the country, that they will give recognition to British trade unions, and proposals to the Government that foreign companies should provide more information for collective bargaining purposes. The Trade Union Congresses of 1966 and 1968 debated motions concerned with foreign firms and union recognition, and these have been discussed elsewhere in this paper. The TUC *Economic Review* for 1970 called for more information on international companies, arguing:

'Trade unions thus have a common interest with governments in obtaining increased information about the activities of international companies, and defining guidelines for their operation. . . .'[1]

The Review said there was a clear need for obligations to be placed by governments on subsidiaries to provide information for collective bargaining purposes from companies' central accounts. More information was needed about how such companies worked and how they affected major questions like a country's balance of payments and how they paid or avoided paying tax. However, at a press conference on the Review, the General Secretary of the TUC discounted international trade union operations against international companies in the near future, feeling at the present time the most useful work to be done was the exchange of information between countries. In October 1970 the TUC held a conference on International Companies to consider what union action is needed to cope with the problems posed by the operation of such companies. The conference felt that more information was necessary about such companies, and the unions most active in the conference were those representing white-collar workers and those employed in the motor industry. It was suggested that the British Government should adopt a series of guidelines to regulate the activities of international companies operating in the UK.

To conclude this part, one can say that the British trade unions have made little response to the foreign firm because such companies have accepted the main tenets of the UK industrial relations system and because the ability of the foreign firms to

[1] Trades Union Congress, *Economic Review*, 1970, Chapter 3, para. 100, p. 39.

switch operations from one establshment to another has not been widely exercised. Foreign firms have on occasions refused to recognize trade unions and this has resulted in a number of motions at annual Trade Union Congresses calling for recognition of unions as a necessary condition of being allowed to operate in this country. The growth of policies to counter the foreign firms has come from the United Automobile Workers and the British unions have been approached by the union for co-operation. The result has been a conference with the AEF and T&GWU in July 1969 and a conference with European motor-car workers in December 1969. The TUC has shown an awareness of the problem by devoting a chapter of its 1970 *Economic Review* to the question of obtaining more information on the multinational firm to help restore the balance of power in collective bargaining. And as indicated above, the foreign-owned firm has been a significant influence in introducing innovations in UK industrial relations.

## INDUSTRIAL DISPUTES IN FOREIGN-OWNED FIRMS: 1963 AND 1968

There are four main reasons why we might expect the foreign subsidiaries of multinational firms to generate more disturbed industrial relations than is typical for a host country generally. One is the issue of ultimate decision-taking going on abroad. Power lies with people who are removed from the local host-country workforce and have no history of, or present experience of, involvement in the community. This could, in principle, give the multinational organization a lower sense of responsibility to its employees and a consequently greater willingness to risk a strike. At the same time, foreign ownership could generate greater suspicion and hostility on the part of the workers because of either actual or presumed callousness or insensitivity due to actual or presumed remoteness. The possibility of longer and more complex lines of communication opens up the potential for misunderstanding and protracted friction over differences that might be more directly resolved by domestic firms.

Greater distance, bearing in mind the *proviso* if it exists, is a source of difficulty in itself apart from the question of substantive, genuine economic conflict. That economic conflict might be heightened in the case of the foreign subsidiary is also a real possibility. Briefly, far wider economic factors impinge on the foreign subsidiary than on the domestic firm. It is not unreasonable to suppose that it would be experiencing swings in prosperity that would be less in step with the host-country economy than would be true of most domestic firms. Doing well when other firms were doing less well would not be a problem, but the converse could be a source of extra tension bearing on its industrial relations.

In the previous section of this chapter we have discussed some ways in which the industrial relations traditions and practices of foreign parent companies, particularly United States companies, differ from those of the United Kingdom, and the general tendency for inward-investing firms to import at least a part of the labour relations structure of the source country to the host country. Particularly in the initial phases of direct investment, but indeed all the way along, there is a potential source of conflict due to the imposition, or the attempted imposition, of a different system of industrial relations which could lead to more and more intense industrial disputes. Of course, there is nothing necessary about this. The foreign system may be a better system in the sense of leading to fewer strikes.

Finally, there is the related factor that the foreign subsidiary, again particularly the American-owned firm, is alleged to utilize labour more effectively, which could be a nice way of saying work people harder. Here also this need not lead to industrial disputes. Better motivated workers, whose special talents are more quickly recognized and productively employed may not only be paid more, but may find the work itself more satisfying and identify more closely with the interests of the employer. More and more intelligent supervision, including more flexibility in promotion, can contribute to industrial peace. However, different standards of work intensity can be a disruptive factor.

The four factors we outline above, viz. distance, economic conflict, different industrial relations traditions, more intense labour utilization, establish some plausibility for adding in labour relations tension on the cost side of direct investment. However, the latter two factors have at least the potential of operating in the other direction on balance, that is, towards industrial peace. The primary purpose of this section is to determine if stormier industrial relations in the United Kingdom are, in fact, a cost for this country of inward investment.

We direct our attention to strikes because of a lack of other kinds of data on industrial unrest. This is a limitation. Industrial tension can exist without reaching the stage of strike action. Indeed, in isolated cases, the foreign firm may have an effective policy which does not allow unions in the subsidiary. This could raise tension without leading to strikes. Even with unions it may be possible to avoid strikes while paying a higher price in terms of other forms of conflict. Ideally, one would like to examine a spectrum of discontent in which actual strikes were one important element. Analysis of turn-over figures and of absenteeism would be relevant, but it was not practical to obtain such information. Similarly, large-scale inter-views of managers and employees could provide important informa-tion. But while strike figures are not the whole story, they do have certain advantages. They are relatively hard information and they are an important index of personal and social cost.

We do not want to imply that the optimum amount of industrial disputes in the form of strikes is zero. There certainly are worse things, such as passive acceptance of a sustained work environment which is dangerous, unjust, arbitrary and spiritually debilitating. The national cost of strikes generally is often overestimated. But it is interesting in itself to know if foreign-owned firms have more or less of them than domestic firms, and it sheds some light on the four propositions discussed above.

In appraising whether or not inward investment entails extra industrial disputes we make two simple assumptions. The first is that industrial unrest due to foreign subsidiaries is not external to the firms themselves. In other words, setting aside for the moment the question of how to quantify strike activity, we assume that the relative amount of striking to peaceful relations in domestic firms would be the same whether the foreign firms were in the United Kingdom or not. The second assumption is that the relevant comparison is the norm for the industry rather than, say, the region, size of firm, age of firm or some other category. As it happens, the results are quite strong and the conclusions would tend to stand up under considerable relaxing of these assumptions.

Information on stoppages is given to the Department of Employ-ment and Productivity through its regional offices. No distinction is drawn between strikes and lock-outs, though the latter are held to be very few in number. The coverage of the data is believed to be excellent, affording a virtually complete picture of industrial disputes. Very small stoppages, that is those involving less than ten workers and those lasting less than one day, are excluded from the statistics, unless the aggregate number of days lost exceed one hundred.[1] The figures include the workers indirectly involved,

[1] The total strike statistics, drawing no distinction between domestic and foreign, are reported and discussed annually in the May number of the *Employ-ment and Productivity Gazette*.

i.e. those out of work at the establishment where the strike is going on who may not themselves be party to the dispute, but workers laid off at establishments outside the one in which the stoppage takes place are excluded. This can lead to an understating of the costs of a strike.

In principle it would be possible to extract the strike figures for foreign firms for a large number of years, but given the sheer volume of material we settled for two years, 1963 and 1968.[1] The choice of years followed fairly naturally from three considerations. We wanted a pair of reasonably recent years; the general consensus is that these two are rather 'normal' years, apart from a special one-day stoppage in 1968; being Census years the strike figures can be related to other industrial information.[2]

TABLE 4.3

*Aggregate Comparison*

|  | Number of stoppages | Workers involved | Working days lost |
|---|---|---|---|
| 1963 |  |  |  |
| 1 Foreign owned | 70 | 21,046 | 58,077 |
| 2 Domestic | 1,998 | 434,154 | 1,938,923 |
| 3 Total | 2,068 | 455,200 | 1,997,000 |
| 4 Ratio of (1) to (3) | 0·033 | 0·046 | 0·029 |
| 5 Ratio of foreign to total sales | 0·104 | 0·104 | 0·104 |
| 1968 |  |  |  |
| 6 Foreign owned | 208 | 75,532 | 454,437 |
| 7 Domestic | 2,170 | 1,998,468 | 4,264,563 |
| 8 Total | 2,378 | 2,074,000 | 4,719,000 |
| 9 Ratio of (6) to (8) | 0·087 | 0·036 | 0·096 |

The choice of 1968 does, however, entail a potential problem which requires comment. On May 15th of that year there was a one-day stoppage involving 1,500,000 workers in the engineering and several related industries. This was a token stoppage in support of a claim for an all-round pay increase. From the data, no foreign subsidiaries appear to have reported being involved in that dispute.

[1] We are much indebted to the DEP at Watford for making the annual volumes available, and the considerate help provided.

[2] At the time of publication, the 1968 Census showing proportion of foreign ownership by Minimum List Headings is not available, and it appears that it will not be available for some time. This forces us to use the 1963 sales figures as a rough guide for 1968 as well.

As the total number of working days lost in the year was 4,690,000, the 1,500,000 days lost through this single action is very significant in the total, being 32%. One can make a reasonable case for either keeping it in or for taking it out of the figures; where possible, we try to indicate the role of this dispute in the strike picture which emerges.

Table 4.3 shows the overall proportions of foreign-firm disputes to the total, with the surprising result that the foreign subsidiaries are less subject to strikes than the domestic firms.

While the results are much stronger for 1963 than for 1968, for both years the contribution of foreign-owned firms to total stoppages, whether measured by number of stoppages, number of workers involved, or working days lost is less than their proportionate contribution to total output.[1]

Inevitably, this result calls for some qualification. Our list of foreign-owned firms may not be complete.[2] Errors in extraction would be more likely to misclassify a foreign firm as domestic than the other way around. However, it is reasonable to expect that errors, if they occur, would be confined to the small firms. This means that the effect on the number of stoppages might be significant, but it would be less on the number of workers involved and working days lost. As to row 5, the ratio of foreign to total sales, there are two reasons to regard this figure too high. One is that certain service and transport categories are included in the strike figures but missing from the output figures, and these are ones where foreign participation is very small or non-existent.[3]

Secondly, an employment comparison, unfortunately not possible on a comparable basis, would be more appropriate and would lead

---

[1] Removing the one day token engineering stoppage alters Table 4.3 as follows:

|  | Workers involved | Working days lost |
|---|---|---|
| 1968 |  |  |
| (6) Foreign owned | 75,532 | 454,437 |
| (7) Domestic | 682,068 | 2,735,523 |
| (8) Total | 757,600 | 3,189,960 |
| (9) Ratio of (6) to (8) | 0·10 | 0·14 |

While removing the token stoppage reverses the above conclusion with respect to working days lost, there are two points to bear in mind. The main one is that the proportion of foreign to total sales in 1968 may well have risen 5% over the five years. And secondly, of course, there is no clear reason to remove this stoppage.

[2] It is the official Board of Trade List and, while no doubt the best available, it is also generally regarded as quite reliable.

[3] See note to Table 4.4 for industries where we lack figures on foreign-owned proportion.

to a smaller foreign proportion. For 1963 these changes could conceivably raise row 4 to the order of 6% and lower row 5 to the order of 8%. This still supports the conclusion that on aggregate, the foreign-owned subsidiaries are more peaceful. For 1968 we lack, at the moment, firm figures for foreign participation, but are safe in presuming that it was higher than for 1963. The foreign strike proportion is also higher for 1968, except in terms of workers involved, but still supports the conclusion that foreign subsidiaries generally are equally or more peaceful compared to domestic firms.

The aggregate comparison of quantity of disputes in foreign-owned and domestic firms is not the most searching one. It is well known that some industries are more strike-prone than others, this persistent differential tendency to strike activity showing up in both international comparison and in examining a single country over time.[1] As foreign investment is not evenly distributed across sectors, a better comparison could be made holding the industry mix equal. The available data do not allow us to normalize for other factors such as region and firm size, but the industry factor is by far the most important one. For example, coal-mining is very strike-prone and, of course, in the United Kingdom there is no foreign investment in that industry. The procedure we have adopted to deal with this problem is, for each industry, to multiply the domestic quantity of strike activity by the ratio of foreign to domestic sales, and sum.[2] This figure can be compared to the total foreign strike activity directly, as it gives the volume of domestic strike activity, with given propensities, that would occur if the domestic sector was the same size as the foreign-owned sector in each industry. The results are shown in Table 4.4.

This more appropriate comparison suggests very strongly that the foreign-owned firm is less strike-prone than its domestic counterpart. For both years there was less of a difference in number of stoppages compared to the other measures, but still a very marked one. In

[1] C. Kerr and A. Segal, 'The Inter-industry Propensity to Strike – an International Comparison', in A. Kornhauser, R. Dubin and A. Ross (eds.), *Industrial Conflict*, New York, McGraw-Hill, 1954, Chapter 14, pp. 189–204; K. G. J. C. Knowles, *Strikes, A Study in Industrial Conflict*, Oxford, Institute of Statistics Monograph No. 3, Blackwell, 1952.

[2] Where: $S_{Di}$, volume of strikes in domestic firms in the $i^{th}$ industry

$S_{Fi}$, volume of strikes in foreign-owned firms in the $i^{th}$ industry.

$O_{Di}$, sales of domestic firms in the $i^{th}$ industry.

$O_{Fi}$, sales of foreign-owned firms in the $i^{th}$ industry

We compare: $\sum_i \dfrac{O_{Fi}}{O_{Di}} \cdot S_{Di} \gtrless \sum_i S_{Fi}$

1968 total strikes were well up over 1963, and the foreign proportion rose. But, broadly put, there was in excess of twice as much strike activity in domestic firms compared to foreign-owned firms, after allowing for differences in the distribution of foreign to domestic proportions across industries.

TABLE 4.4

*Disputes Comparison Normalized by Industry*

|  | Number of stoppages | Workers involved | Working days lost |
|---|---|---|---|
| 1963 |  |  |  |
| 1 Foreign owned (actual)* | 55 | 19,905 | 48,855 |
| 2 Domestic (normalized) | 152 | 106,494 | 271,357 |
| 3 Ratio of (1) to (2) | 0·36 | 0·19 | 0·18 |
| 1968 |  |  |  |
| 4 Foreign owned (actual)* | 175 | 97,368 | 385,003 |
| 5 Domestic (normalized) | 276 | 420,815 | 821,018 |
| 6 Ratio of (4) to (5) | 0·63 | 0·23 | 0·47 |

\* Rows (1) and (4) in this Table show smaller numbers than rows (1) and (6) in Table 4.3 because certain industries had to be excluded from the comparison here for lack of industry breakdown on foreign and domestic proportions. The excluded industries are: construction; gas, electricity and water; railways; road passenger; road haulage; sea transport; port and inland water; other transport and communication; distributive trades; insurance, banking and finance; professional and scientific services; miscellaneous services; public administration and defence. Most of these have no foreign component and the exclusions do not bias the results.

For the above comparison, in our view the critical one, we are working with thirty-three industrial categories. In fact, most industries make only insignificant contributions to the total volume of disputes, however measured. Taking only those eight or so industries making the biggest contribution in either year (usually an industry is big in both years if it is in one year), gives a very large proportion of the total. Motor vehicles and non-electrical engineering are important contributors to total strikes as are certain heterogeneous categories such as 'Other manufacturing industries', 'All other metal manufacture' and 'Metal goods not elsewhere specified'. It is only in these last three categories that, on a normalized comparison, the foreign subsidiaries tend to be more strike-prone than the domestic-owned counterparts.

Because of the heterogeneous nature of the industries where the foreigners are more strike-prone, it is difficult to generalize about them. One point can be made, however. The 'Other manufacturing industries' category includes rubber, and it is this sub-sector which accounts for all the foreign strike contribution. It is interesting to note that in this case the foreign firms are all members of the employers' association.

There is some interest in comparing the magnitudes of the stoppages in foreign-owned and domestic firms, as well as the aggregates and their industrial distribution. Totals, of course, may be made up of lots of little strikes, strikes involving few workers and of short duration, or the opposite. This comparison is made in Table 4.5. To economize on time and effort, only proportions are given. (The absolutes are readily calculated from Tables 4.2 and 4.5.) The comparison is a little faulty on three counts. The foreign proportions are compared to the total, not the pure domestic contribution (again, to save on computation effort); there is no normalization as to the size distribution of the foreign owned compared to the domestic firms, particularly in 1963, with the small total number of strikes in foreign firms, the categories of the distributions tend to be a little fine, which introduces some meaningless variation. None of these points appears to be of great significance.[1]

The comparison suggests that very big and very small strikes are more important in the domestic total. The foreign-owned firms are given to nice, medium-sized disputes. To highlight some of the aspects, many more of the domestic strikes than foreign involve

[1] We can readily correct part of Table 4.5 for the token one-day stoppage. The duration percentages, taking out this dispute are as follows:

| | | Per cent of workers involved – domestic (total) | Per cent of working days lost – domestic (total) |
|---|---|---|---|
| Not more than one day | | 28·1 | 5·0 |
| 1 < | ⩽2 | 15·0 | 4·8 |
| 2 < | ⩽3 | 13·3 | 6·9 |
| 3 < | ⩽4 | 9·6 | 5·5 |
| 4 < | ⩽5 | 6·2 | 5·7 |
| 5 < | ⩽6 | 4·0 | 4·3 |
| 6 < | ⩽12 | 10·2 | 15·7 |
| 12 < | ⩽18 | 5·9 | 13·6 |
| 18 < | ⩽24 | 3·7 | 11·8 |
| 24 < | ⩽36 | 2·0 | 7·5 |
| 36 < | ⩽60 | 0·5 | 4·2 |
| 60 < | | 1·5 | 15·0 |

Again, this does not appear to seriously alter the conclusion in the text.

TABLE 4.5

*Comparison by Magnitude of Domestic and Foreign Stoppages*

1963

*Duration in working days*

| | | Per cent of total number of stoppages | | Per cent of number of workers involved | | Per cent of total working days lost | |
|---|---|---|---|---|---|---|---|
| | | Domestic (total) | Foreign | Domestic (total) | Foreign | Domestic (total) | Foreign |
| Not more than one day | | 38·9 | 27·1 | 25·1 | 34·3 | 5·8 | 8·8 |
| 1 < | ⩽2 | 23·0 | 20·0 | 22·1 | 14·4 | 10·0 | 8·8 |
| 2 < | ⩽3 | 13·4 | 8·6 | 10·9 | 3·1 | 6·6 | 2·3 |
| 3 < | ⩽4 | 7·2 | 12·9 | 9·8 | 8·1 | 7·9 | 7·0 |
| 4 < | ⩽5 | 4·2 | 8·6 | 7·2 | 4·2 | 7·0 | 7·2 |
| 5 < | ⩽6 | 2·7 | 4·3 | 13·2 | 2·4 | 19·5 | 2·4 |
| 6 < | <12 | 5·6 | 10·0 | 5·9 | 17·3 | 10·5 | 42·6 |
| 12 < | <18 | 1·8 | 2·9 | 0·8 | 1·5 | 2·9 | 3·2 |
| 18 < | ⩽24 | 0·8 | 2·9 | 1·2 | 14·0 | 5·1 | 10·8 |
| 24 < | ⩽36 | 1·7 | 1·4 | 3·4 | 0·1 | 22·5 | 0·9 |
| 36 < | ⩽60 | 0·4 | 1·4 | 0·3 | 0·6 | 1·5 | 6·2 |
| 60 < | | 0·3 | 0·0 | 0·1 | 0·0 | 0·7 | 0·0 |

*Number of workers directly and indirectly involved*

| | | | | | | | |
|---|---|---|---|---|---|---|---|
| Under 25 | Workers | 25·7 | 5·7 | 1·5 | 0·4 | 1·5 | 1·3 |
| 25 ⩽ | < 50 | 19·4 | 11·4 | 2·3 | 1·4 | 2·2 | 1·2 |
| 50 ⩽ | < 100 | 15·7 | 21·4 | 3·8 | 4·7 | 3·6 | 5·4 |
| 100 ⩽ | < 250 | 16·5 | 28·6 | 9·1 | 12·9 | 9·0 | 22·6 |
| 250 ⩽ | < 500 | 11·0 | 12·9 | 13·6 | 13·5 | 10·4 | 11·8 |
| 500 ⩽ | < 1,000 | 6·3 | 14·3 | 14·8 | 29·1 | 11·4 | 26·7 |
| 1,000 ⩽ | < 2,500 | 4·0 | 4·3 | 20·0 | 24·8 | 17·4 | 26·5 |
| 2,500 ⩽ | < 5,000 | 0·8 | 1·4 | 10·1 | 13·2 | 5·1 | 4·7 |
| 5,000 ⩽ | < 10,000 | 0·4 | 0·0 | 10·4 | 0·0 | 6·9 | 0·0 |
| 10,000 ⩽ | | 0·2 | 0·0 | 14·4 | 0·0 | 32·5 | 0·0 |

*Number of working days lost*

| | | | | | | | |
|---|---|---|---|---|---|---|---|
| Under 250 | Days | | | | | | |
| | 250 | 64·9 | 44·3 | 12·9 | 9·6 | 5·2 | 6·1 |
| 250 ⩽ | < 500 | 11·4 | 20·0 | 10·2 | 20·8 | 4·2 | 8·3 |
| 500 ⩽ | < 1,000 | 9·8 | 17·1 | 11·7 | 17·8 | 6·9 | 13·8 |
| 1,000 ⩽ | < 5,000 | 11·7 | 17·1 | 31·1 | 43·0 | 24·8 | 47·6 |
| 5,000 ⩽ | < 25,000 | 1·8 | 1·4 | 15·9 | 8·9 | 16·6 | 24·1 |
| 25,000 ⩽ | < 50,000 | 0·3 | 0·0 | 6·2 | 0·0 | 11·8 | 0·0 |
| 50,000 ⩽ | | 0·1 | 0·0 | 12·0 | 0·0 | 30·5 | 0·0 |

TABLE 4.5 (cont.)

### 1968

### Duration in working days

| | | Per cent of total number of stoppages | | Per cent of number of workers involved | | Per cent of total working days lost | |
|---|---|---|---|---|---|---|---|
| | | Domestic (total) | Foreign | Domestic (total) | Foreign | Domestic (total) | Foreign |
| Not more than one day | | 28·6 | 18·3 | 75·9 | 23·7 | 35·2 | 4·9 |
| 1 < | ≤2 | 20·5 | 21·2 | 5·0 | 15·9 | 3·3 | 4·5 |
| 2 < | ≤3 | 11·9 | 13·9 | 4·5 | 15·2 | 4·8 | 7·6 |
| 3 < | ≤4 | 8·0 | 8·7 | 3·2 | 8·8 | 3·7 | 6·7 |
| 4 < | ≤5 | 6·0 | 8·2 | 2·1 | 8·7 | 3·9 | 9·1 |
| 5 < | ≤6 | 4·3 | 3·4 | 1·3 | 4·9 | 2·9 | 5·0 |
| 6 < | ≤12 | 11·1 | 18·3 | 3·4 | 14·1 | 10·7 | 27·0 |
| 12 < | ≤18 | 4·0 | 2·9 | 2·0 | 2·0 | 9·2 | 3·8 |
| 18 < | ≤24 | 2·0 | 3·4 | 1·2 | 5·3 | 8·1 | 21·3 |
| 24 < | ≤36 | 1·7 | 1·9 | 0·7 | 1·6 | 5·1 | 10·2 |
| 36 < | ≤60 | 1·1 | 0·0 | 0·2 | 0·0 | 2·9 | 0·0 |
| 60 < | | 0·8 | 0·0 | 0·5 | 0·0 | 10·2 | 0·0 |

### Number of workers directly and indirectly involved

| | | | | | | | |
|---|---|---|---|---|---|---|---|
| Under 25 | Workers | 15·8 | 6·25 | 0·3 | 0·2 | 1·0 | 0·4 |
| 25 ≤ | < 50 | 15·8 | 12·0 | 0·6 | 0·8 | 1·2 | 1·0 |
| 50 ≤ | < 100 | 17·4 | 15·9 | 1·3 | 2·1 | 3·1 | 2·0 |
| 100 ≤ | < 250 | 23·4 | 24·0 | 3·9 | 7·2 | 7·5 | 8·9 |
| 250 ≤ | < 500 | 12·3 | 12·0 | 4·4 | 7·4 | 7·7 | 6·7 |
| 500 ≤ | < 1,000 | 9·2 | 17·8 | 6·5 | 23·6 | 11·9 | 21·7 |
| 1,000 ≤ | < 2,500 | 4·1 | 7·2 | 6·6 | 21·4 | 17·4 | 25·5 |
| 2,500 ≤ | < 5,000 | 1·3 | 4·3 | 4·7 | 28·8 | 10·7 | 31·9 |
| 5,000 ≤ | < 10,000 | 0·5 | 0·5 | 3·5 | 8·5 | 7·6 | 2·0 |
| 10,000 ≤ | | 0·2 | 0·0 | 68·2 | 0·0 | 31·9 | 0·0 |

### Number of working days lost

| | | | | | | | |
|---|---|---|---|---|---|---|---|
| Under 250 | Days 25 | 50·4 | 31·7 | 3·9 | 4·7 | 2·6 | 1·5 |
| 250 ≤ | < 500 | 16·2 | 18·3 | 3·4 | 6·6 | 2·9 | 3·1 |
| 500 ≤ | < 1,000 | 13·2 | 16·8 | 5·2 | 12·8 | 4·6 | 5·2 |
| 1,000 ≤ | < 5,000 | 15·4 | 21·6 | 9·6 | 27·9 | 15·8 | 19·9 |
| 5,000 ≤ | < 25,000 | 4·2 | 10·6 | 9·0 | 42·7 | 21·0 | 45·7 |
| 25,000 ≤ | < 50,000 | 0·3 | 0·5 | 0·8 | 1·1 | 5·1 | 7·2 |
| 50,000 ≤ | | 0·3 | 0·5 | 68·1 | 4·3 | 48·0 | 17·4 |

less than two days, under twenty-five workers, and less than two hundred and fifty man days lost. At the other end, 68% of the domestic workers involved in any strikes were in strikes where over fifty thousand man days were lost. This is true of less than 5% of the 'foreign' workers. Nearly half the man days lost by domestic firms were in these big strikes, with less than a fifth for foreign-owned firms. Again, for 1968, three-quarters of the workers were involved in one-day disputes, with only a quarter for foreign-owned firms. That did not hold for 1963, but if we compare the biggest and smallest categories, for the three by three classification, for both years, that makes thirty-six comparisons. Of these, in thirty-one the domestic component is bigger than the foreign at the extremes of size, big and small.

The difference in strike patterns between domestic and foreign firms may be related to the bargaining structures and procedures in these firms. Domestic firms tend to be involved in national bargaining for increases in basic wages and conditions of employment: as a result, any, stoppage will involve large numbers since all firms in the employers association will be involved. Procedures for dealing with grievances involve a large number of stages, and employees become frustrated that their grievances are not being dealt with quickly enough and unconstitutional action takes place in order to force the issue. The foreign firms, on the other hand, are most engaged with plant and company bargaining and have shorter and quicker procedures for negotiating new agreements and settling grievances. This encourages a greater adherence to procedures, but it must not be thought that the unconstitutional strike is not a problem to the foreign firm, although it would appear less so than to the domestic firm.

The different pattern of strikes in the foreign-owned firms suggests they have personal policies and industrial relations procedures that somehow avoid a large number of small unforeseeable strikes and terminate large strikes before either too many people are involved or the stoppages go on too long. There is a body of opinion that considers the short, small unplanned-for strike is more damaging than the longer, larger, but more predictable strike in the sense that the former type of strike may result in management failing or delaying to introduce new working methods and capital machinery for the fear that employees may down tools without warning. If this argument has any validity, then the different strike pattern in the domestic and foreign firms may account for some of the greater efficiency in the latter firms over the former. The foreign firm appears to be less affected by the problem of the continuous unscheduled interruption of production lines through stoppages and may therefore be less inhibited in introducing new capital investment.

Apart from industrial relations, the differences in strike magnitudes may have to do with the causes of the strikes, and it is to these that we now turn. Any student of industrial relations is familiar with the problem of determining the major cause of an industrial dispute and the possible difference between stated and actual causes. While being aware of this, it would be a mistake to go to the other extreme and regard the official classification of disputes according to causes as meaningless. The official figures use a broad, eight-way, industrial classification. For our purposes we have eliminated Mining and Quarrying, which has no foreign component, and two other sectors, Shipbuilding and Marine Engineering, and Transport and Communication, all of which have tiny foreign contributions to total strikes. We then divide the causes into two groups, wage and non-wage. The wage category includes claims for increases and other wage disputes. The non-wage category consists of hours, demarcation, employment or discharge, personnel questions, other working arrangements, union status and sympathetic action. It is possible that hours would be better classified with wages, but the numbers are so small as not to affect the overall result. Table 4.6 compares foreign and domestic proportions of total disputes.

Without formal significance testing, one nevertheless feels some confidence that there is no difference as to causes of disputes between domestic and foreign-owned firms when we look at the number of stoppages. But in terms of workers involved and man days lost, three generalizations seem well supported. In general, wage disputes are quantitively more important than non-wage. This is

TABLE 4.6

*Comparison of Causes of Disputes (Wage and Non-wage) in Foreign-owned and Domestic Firms*

|  |  | 1963 | | 1968 | |
|---|---|---|---|---|---|
|  |  | Wage | Non-wage | Wage | Non-wage |
| Number of stoppages | Domestic | 47·6 | 52·4 | 52·0 | 48·0 |
|  | Foreign | 43·5 | 56·5 | 56·8 | 43·2 |
| Workers involved | Domestic | 61·6 | 38·4 | 90·4 | 9·6 |
|  | Foreign | 52·7 | 47·3 | 57·9 | 42·1 |
| Man days lost | Domestic | 76·0 | 24·0 | 80·6 | 19·4 |
|  | Foreign | 53·4 | 46·6 | 68·3 | 31·7 |

more marked in 1968 than in 1963. And the difference is bigger in domestic firms than foreign-owned firms. None of this need be too surprising. The points raised at the beginning of this section suggest a relatively greater involvement of foreign-owned firms in disputes over such things as union status and working arrangements.

With respect to the above comparison, the removal of the one-day token stoppage in the engineering industries (broadly constructed), now does seriously affect the results. It will be recalled that this action was over wages. Table 4.7 sets out the relevant wage–non-wage information taking out the national one-day stoppage.

TABLE 4.7

*Comparison of Causes of Disputes (Wage and Non-wage) in Foreign Owned and Domestic Firms, Taking Out the One Day (May 15, 1968) National Engineering Stoppage*

|  |  | 1968 | |
|---|---|---|---|
|  |  | *Wage* | *Non-wage* |
| Workers Involved | Domestic | 43·5 | 56·5 |
|  | Foreign | 57·9 | 42·1 |
| Man days lost | Domestic | 64·1 | 35·9 |
|  | Foreign | 68·3 | 31·7 |

With this one strike removed there is now nothing to choose between domestic and foreign-owned firms. Indeed, there is a slightly greater tendency of the domestic firms towards the non-wage dispute. More detailed examination in terms of industry mix may be revealing. But pending this one must conclude that the issue of causes sheds little light on the relative number or magnitude of domestic and foreign disputes.

To summarize the statistical findings, we conclude that foreign-owned firms have fewer disputes than domestic firms, especially after allowing for differences in industry mix. There are only one or two industries where this is not true. Disputes in the foreign firms tend to be in the middle-size range, without either many of the very small strikes or the very big ones. And finally, disputes in foreign subsidiaries are hard to distinguish as to cause from domestic firms. These findings relate to, and are broadly consistent with, other aspects of the labour market, the industrial relations structure which was outlined earlier, and the question of labour utilization to which we now turn.

## LABOUR UTILIZATION IN DOMESTIC AND FOREIGN-OWNED FIRMS IN THE ELECTRICAL ENGINEERING INDUSTRY

The industrial relations and strike experience of foreign-owned firms can differ from those of domestically-owned firms for reasons to do with foreignness as such. Several of these reasons have been discussed in the earlier sections of this chapter. In addition, it may be the case, and is often alleged to be the case, that foreign subsidiaries generally have a different labour policy compared to their domestic counterparts. The most popularly held views as to the differences may be summarized as follows. The foreign firm uses relatively (a) more capital, (b) more people in the higher skill categories, (c) better qualified people in comparable categories, and (d) pays higher wages per man hour. As indicated above, this may or may not be the same thing as paying more for labour services. One rational reason for paying more for comparable labour services might be a greater reluctance on the part of the foreign-owned firm to experience an industrial dispute. If the foreign firm is more efficient in the utilization of labour services it can afford to pay more for them. And a subsidiary which is a part of an integrated multinational complex may be reluctant to interrupt production when that could harm the whole complex. However, in cases where the firm is producing duplicate, or near duplicate, items in more than one country, it may be a stronger bargainer, being able to play one union off against another. Along with these views it is often suggested that the management of a foreign subsidiary devotes relatively more resources to labour management and utilization, employing and deploying its labour with considerably greater expertise and care.

This set of views is interesting on several counts. One of them is that collectively they are often offered as an explanation of the superior performance of the foreign-owned firm. Of course, they constitute an explanation of better performance which is flattering to the subsidiary management, in contrast to some alternative explanations such as exclusive access to technical advances undertaken by the parent organization, or the exploitation of a monopoly position. Secondly, this set of views implies different behaviour in the labour market on the part of foreign-owned firms which has implications for the appraisal of the impact of inward direct investment on host countries.

The purpose of this last section is to present some data which will afford us no more than a glimpse into these labour utilization propositions. A glimpse into a significant and little explored area may

131

be better than nothing, but at the same time we should be cautious in attaching too much importance to the results. Rather, the familiar rubric of treating them as suggestive must reluctantly be applied.

We are indeed fortunate that the Higher Education Research Unit at the London School of Economics has for some time been engaged in a research project on the effect of educational experience on industrial productivity, and that an unintended consequence of their remarkable effort at data collection is to provide some figures which shed light on our problem. That project, which is nearing completion, is based on unusually solid statistical information, most of it generated by the project itself. Though intended for other purposes, the detailed information generated on sixty-eight firms in the electrical engineering industry, some of whom are foreign owned, can be reworked in an effort to get some insight into our particular concerns. Do the foreign-owned firms get more output from their labour? Do they pay more? Do they use more skilled people? Do they use trained people in different ways? The Unit, while maintaining complete confidentiality of the data, has extended some analysis for us so that we can at least make a start on these intriguing questions. The choice of the electrical engineering industry is a particularly appropriate one from the point of view of direct investment. Foreign-owned firms are important in it, and it is a science-based industry. As such it is an important employer of highly qualified labour. Where just over 1% of workers in British industry are qualified scientists and engineers, the proportion is two-and-a-half times as high for this industry.[1]

TABLE 4.8

*Electrical Engineering Factories (England and Wales, 1968)*

| Numbers Employed | | Electrical machinery | | Cables | | Telephone apparatus | |
|---|---|---|---|---|---|---|---|
| | | Foreign | Domestic | Foreign | Domestic | Foreign | Domestic |
| 2,000 and above | In sample | — | 7 | 1 | 2 | 1 | 2 |
| | Population | 17 | | 9 | | 9 | |
| 1,000 to 1,999 | In sample | — | 2 | — | 1 | — | — |
| | Population | 21 | | 7 | | 7 | |
| 500 to 999 | In sample | — | 7 | — | 2 | — | — |
| | Population | 29 | | 14 | | 7 | |
| 200 to 499 | In sample | — | 5 | — | 1 | — | — |
| | Population | 70 | | 10 | | 14 | |
| TOTAL | In sample | — | 21 | 1 | 6 | 1 | 2 |
| | Population | 137 | | 40 | | 37 | |

[1] Committee on Manpower Resources for Science and Technology, 1966.

A complete description of the data would extend a lengthy chapter beyond reasonable bounds.[1] Briefly, the industry can be divided into six categories: electrical machinery (mainly for electricity generation and related activities); cables; telephone apparatus; electronics (a very heterogeneous category covering radio, radar, cathode ray tubes, computers, television transmitters and receivers and much else); domestic appliances (all the more simple electrical home equipment); other goods (obviously a catch all, but mainly 'car electrics', sparking plugs, batteries, lamps and so on). The data refer largely to 1968, the unit of analysis being the factory rather than the firm. A stratified random sample, with replacement for non-responders, was adopted for all factories employing over two hundred men. This resulted in a sample of about 12% of all factories. The foreign factories are not proportionately distributed across activities within the industry, as can be seen from Table 4.8, which gives a cross-categorization by size, and shows the foreign and domestic contributions to the sample. There are other ways than the distribution across activities that the question of the comparability of domestic and foreign factories arises, and we will be turning to some of these.

Taking no account of the fact that foreign-owned and domestic factories may be making very different types of products, and in general be in rather different economic circumstances, Table 4.9 gives an overall view of the basic economic data describing the sample factories. On average, the foreign and domestic factories turn out to have broadly similar sizes of output, the foreigner having

| Electronics | | Domestic appliances | | Other goods | | Total | |
|---|---|---|---|---|---|---|---|
| Foreign | Domestic | Foreign | Domestic | Foreign | Domestic | Foreign | Domestic |
| 1 | 5 | 1 | 1 | — | 2 | 4 | 19 |
| | 26 | | 6 | | 10 | | 77 |
| — | 7 | — | — | — | 1 | — | 11 |
| | 46 | | 9 | | 15 | | 105 |
| 1 | 3 | 1 | 1 | 1 | 3 | 3 | 16 |
| | 65 | | 15 | | 26 | | 156 |
| 1 | 3 | 1 | 1 | 1 | 2 | 3 | 12 |
| | 116 | | 15 | | 77 | | 302 |
| 3 | 18 | 3 | 3 | 2 | 8 | 10 | 58 |
| | 253 | | 45 | | 128 | | 640 |

[1] Interested readers will, of course, be able to get this information from the published report of the Higher Education Research Unit, forthcoming.

a somewhat higher value added as a proportion of output. The data lend some support for some of the views expressed above. The foreign factories have more capital per head, with the difference being in fixed rather than working capital. In fact, the domestic firms appear to use relatively more working capital. We also see a higher net output per head in the foreign-owned factories, and a higher labour cost per head. Total factor productivity appears to be almost identical.[1] With the figures also indicating a nearly equal rate of return on capital, the domestic and foreign-owned factories give the impression of being equally efficient, with the latter using relatively smaller amounts of labour, and paying its workforce relatively more. If we look just at the highly-trained part of the workforce, either by education, i.e. Higher National Certificate and above, etc., or by occupation, i.e. technicians and technologists, the foreign-owned and the domestically-owned firms appear to be paying roughly the same annual salaries. It is interesting, however, that in the same category the foreign-owned factory is inclined to employ a significantly younger man. This, of course, is the same thing as being on a generally higher pay schedule for less trained workers. The fact that the foreigners pay better, in the sense of promoting more quickly, in income terms keeps their wage bill in the higher training and occupational categories the same as for domestic factories. They may even have the advantage of having more recently, and hopefully therefore better, trained people. And maybe the trade-off between experience on the one hand and more drive, flexibility and so on is also in their favour. At the lower levels of the employment structure they simply pay more. As yet we cannot say whether this higher pay has to do with hiring a different kind of workforce, or paying more for the same man. The sales of the foreign factories are growing faster than those of domestic factories, with the numbers employed in each growing equally quickly.

So, as is indicated above, the general picture to emerge is one that lends some support to many of the widely-held views, namely, that the foreigners go in for a more expensive labour force and a more capital-intensive operation. These greater costs, compared to domestically-owned operations, are offset by higher productivity.

---

[1] This is value of output per unit cost. Labour cost is the wage, and capital cost was calculated by amortizing machinery at 12·5% over ten years, and buildings and land at 10% in perpetuity. Clearly this method may introduce a bias in evaluating the domestic and foreign capital input, though we have no *a priori* reason to assume it goes one way or the other due to systematic differences in capital structure.

What these figures seem to reject is the view sometimes put forward by managers of foreign-owned firms themselves that they achieve higher labour productivity *solely* through better labour utilization and not through a larger capital input.

TABLE 4.9

*Basic Economic Data on Domestic and Foreign Factories in sample, 1968* (£000s – means)

| | Domestic | Foreign |
|---|---|---|
| Gross output | 6,648 | 6,324 |
| Net output | 2,714 | 2,912 |
| Numbers employed (000s) | 2,074 | 1,640 |
| Labour cost | 2,003 | 1,943 |
| Total capital | 4,795 | 5,929 |
| Fixed capital | 2,642 | 4,301 |
| Working capital | 2,153 | 1,629 |
| Total capital per head | 2·37 | 3·48 |
| Fixed capital per head | 1·34 | 2·32 |
| Net output per head | 1·43 | 1·86 |
| Labour cost per head | 0·98 | 1·12 |
| (Pure Numbers) | | |
| Total factor productivity | 1·11 | 1·12 |
| Rate of return on capital | 0·20 | 0·21 |
| Growth of sales 1964/1967, per annum | 1·06 | 1·15 |
| Growth of numbers employed 1964/1967 per annum | 1·03 | 1·03 |
| (£s) | | |
| Mean salary of Higher National Certificate employees and above | 1,682 | 1,646 |
| Mean salary of Ordinary National Certificate employees and above | 1,510 | 1,516 |
| Mean salary of technologists | 1,841 | 1,854 |
| Mean salary of technicians and above | 1,522 | 1,581 |
| (Years) | | |
| Mean age of HNC and above | 38 | 34 |
| Mean age of ONC and above | 37 | 34 |
| Mean age of technologists | 40 | 38 |
| Mean age of technicians and above | 37 | 37 |

On all these conclusions a warning must be emphasized on the question of the comparability of the domestic and foreign-owned factories. Take the question of the larger capital input per man and per unit output on the part of foreign-owned factories. It could be that this reflects more than anything else a difference in the mix of type of product, or line of activity, and that the domestic factory is like the foreign-owned one when they are doing the same things, but in our sample of factories there is a significant difference, on average, in what they are doing. The heterogeneity of the industry is, after all, very great. Some of the products are very new, others have long histories. The industry ranges from mass production to large once-off jobs. It produces simple and complex capital goods, as well as simple and complex consumer goods.

TABLE 4.10

*Breakdown of Economic Data by Age of Product*
(Units as in Table 4.9 for 1968)

|  | Age of Product | | | |
|  | Pre-1955 | | Post-1955 | |
|  | Domestic | Foreign | Domestic | Foreign |
|---|---|---|---|---|
| Net output | 2,559 | 3,813 | 4,103 | 809 |
| Net output per head | 1·44 | 1·67 | 1·25 | 2·28 |
| Capital per head | 2·40 | 3·49 | 2·07 | 3·46 |
| Fixed capital per head | 1·43 | 2·59 | 1·10 | 1·69 |
| Total factor productivity | 1·10 | 1·01 | 1·06 | 1·56 |
| Rate of return on capital | 0·21 | 0·14 | 0·18 | 0·36 |

Table 4.10 gives a further breakdown of some of the information contained in Table 4.9 on the basis of whether the factory is producing newer or older products, taking 1955 as the cut-off year. This is the most practical breakdown for the sake of checking on general economic comparability, and it does yield some interesting extra information. While the general impression from the above material is confirmed, we note that the foreigners have a markedly higher total factor productivity and rate of return on capital when it comes to the newer products, and the position is reversed with the older ones. Also, the domestic factories are smaller than the foreign-owned factories when it comes to the older products, the situation being reversed on the newer ones. On the basis of these numbers, however, one would not be wise to infer decreasing returns to scale. What holds up nicely under this breakdown is the higher net output per head of the foreign-owned factories along with a greater input of fixed capital.

Without dwelling too long on the point we should mention again the problem of intrafirm pricing in these, and indeed other comparisons, and even with perfectly accurate pricing the foreign-owned subsidiary is more likely to be a specialist link in an integrated production process than the domestic factory. One might, for this reason, want to compare foreign multinationals to domestic multinationals. But again, this would be a comparison of parent operations to subsidiary operations. The key point is, of course, that without more theory, no particular comparison is the right one and the interpretation of any observed difference is very open-ended. At best, some new and possibly suggestive information is made available, and some popular myths, rather than theories, are exposed to a limited range of data.

TABLE 4.11

*Proportion of Educated Employees in the Total Electrical Engineering Workforce, 1968*

|  | Domestic | Foreign owned |
|---|---|---|
| Graduates | 1·26 | 0·67 |
| Professional | 0·99 | 0·93 |
| Higher National Certificate | 2·13 | 2·84 |
| Ordinary National Certificate | 2·03 | 2·05 |
| Professional and above | 2·25 | 1·60 |
| HNC and above | 4·38 | 4·44 |
| ONC and above | 6·41 | 6·49 |

It is still interesting and significant in appraising the effect on host countries of inward direct investment, and especially the industrial relations aspect, to enquire if the foreign-owned subsidiary uses a more highly-educated workforce. The Higher Education Unit data enables us to examine this question only at the top end of the training scale. The figures are grouped in terms of four education categories. First come Graduates with university training. The next is called Professional, which consists of training as an engineer. And then comes Higher National Certificate and Ordinary National Certificate. Table 4.11 gives the broad picture, without taking account of how these trained workers are used, or how the aggregates are affected by the industry mix in the foreign-owned or the domestic sectors.

Overall, the proportion of educated employees in the total electrical engineering workforce is remarkably similar, 6·4 as against 6·5% in the domestic compared to the foreign-owned factories. The overall equality masks the tendency for the foreigners to use fewer Graduates and more Higher National Certificate trained employees, with very close similarity, domestic and foreign, in the other two categories. There is a suggestion in these numbers that the foreign-owned subsidiary gets some of its required input of knowledge from being a member of the international network as such, without embodying that input in labour in the subsidiary factory. But below the two highest levels, it uses correspondingly more people who have the Higher National Certificate. Overall, the figures certainly question rather strongly the view that foreign-owned firms employ a markedly better educated workforce.

TABLE 4.12

*Proportions of Educated Employees in Total Workforce in 'Heavy and Electronic' and 'Other' Electrical Engineering Sectors, 1968*

|  | Heavy and Electronic | | Other | |
|  | Domestic (27) | Foreign (4) | Domestic (23) | Foreign (6) |
|---|---|---|---|---|
| Graduate | 1·89 | 1·17 | 0·49 | 0·34 |
| Professional | 1·36 | 1·10 | 0·56 | 0·82 |
| HNC | 2·87 | 3·02 | 1·26 | 2·72 |
| ONC | 2·77 | 2·58 | 1·22 | 1·44 |
| Prof. plus | 3·25 | 2·27 | 1·05 | 1·16 |
| HNC plus | 6·12 | 5·29 | 2·31 | 3·88 |
| ONC plus | 8·89 | 7·87 | 3·53 | 5·32 |

This last conclusion rests very critically, of course, on the comparability in terms of activity, or product mix, of the foreign-owned and domestic factories. Ideally one might want to compare product and process, only grouping closely similar enterprises. Even here there would remain the problem of the efficiency factor in multi-product factories. But given the small number of foreign firms it does not pay to do a very detailed breakdown. Most of the cells would be empty, and one would really be asking about the performance of individual factories rather than about the characteristics of foreigners generally. It is, however, of some interest to try a two-way split into Heavy and Electronic as against the rest, the former tending to represent the more technically advanced sectors of the electrical engineering industry.

The main conclusions with respect to use of highly educated labour hold up under the normalization set out in Table 4.12. In addition, we see, as might be expected, that both domestic and foreign-owned factories employ more educated people in the more complex and advanced activities. What appears also to be the case, and certainly is in line with widely-held views, is that the foreigners use a significantly more educated input, comparatively, into what are presumably the more prosaic activities. Some further check on this possibility may be made by regrouping the above figures along product lines.

TABLE 4.13

*Proportion of Educated Employees in the Total Workforce in Electrical Engineering by Product Groups, 1968*

| | Machinery and cables | | Telephone and electronics | | Domestic appliances and other | |
|---|---|---|---|---|---|---|
| | Domestic | Foreign | Domestic | Foreign | Domestic | Foreign |
| Graduate | 0·84 | 0·70 | 2·13 | 0·36 | 0·56 | 0·36 |
| Professional | 1·10 | 0·68 | 1·14 | 0·89 | 0·57 | 1·05 |
| HNC | 2·05 | 1·55 | 2·83 | 2·71 | 1·57 | 3·32 |
| ONC | 2·15 | 1·50 | 2·58 | 2·50 | 1·09 | 1·26 |
| Prof. plus | 1·94 | 1·38 | 3·27 | 1·25 | 1·13 | 1·41 |
| HNC plus | 3·99 | 2·93 | 6·10 | 3·96 | 2·70 | 4·73 |
| ONC plus | 6·14 | 4·43 | 8·68 | 6·46 | 3·79 | 5·99 |

Table 4.13 gives interesting support to the possibility that the domestic firm is less aware than the foreign subsidiary of the potential use and economic benefit of employing educated labour in what might be termed ordinary economic activity, as against the obvious need to employ such people in the technically more advanced and more rapidly advancing sectors. Where it is possible, rather than optimal, to make a product in a more traditional way using a less skilled imput, the domestic firm may be inclined to do so. The data are consistent with the view that the foreign-owned subsidiary is more alert to opportunities for employing more educated labour. This leads naturally to our final topic, namely how, or in what jobs, the more educated workers are being used. Before going on to this question we should note that taken together, Tables 4.11, 4.12 and 4.13 suggest that overall, and in some detail, the differences between the domestic and the foreign-owned factories on the score of proportion of educated input are not very great, if we look at workplaces themselves. Unfortunately, our information is restricted to the very upper end of the education scale.

The remaining tables are intended to provide information on two points: how the foreign and domestic factories deploy educated labour in different activities, namely research and design, production, and sales, and what is the comparative education input into broad occupational categories. The collection of data bearing on these questions involved considerable discretion and on-the-spot judgment on the part of individual researchers. Using rather broad categories avoids some of the problems and does afford an indication of broad tendencies. The general criteria applied were that if a job involved the skills and knowledge typical of a pass degree in science or engineering, or passing the examinations for the main professional institutions, it was classified as a 'technologist' occupation. At a lower level, if the job involved substantial scientific or engineering knowledge, at least of the 'A' level or ONC curricula, but not as high as the technologist requirements, then it was classified as a 'technician' occupation.

TABLE 4.14

*Educational Input into Selected Occupations: Proportions of People with Given Qualifications, 1968*

|  | Technologists | | Technicians | | Management | |
|  | Domestic | Foreign | Domestic | Foreign | Domestic | Foreign |
|---|---|---|---|---|---|---|
| Graduates | 22·3 | 22·6 | 2·1 | 2·1 | 15·3 | 12·4 |
| Professional | 21·6 | 18·8 | 4·9 | 5·7 | 13·1 | 11·9 |
| HNC | 24·7 | 31·8 | 20·4 | 22·1 | 18·4 | 26·2 |
| ONC | 9·9 | 14·5 | 22·8 | 26·2 | 8·9 | 5·6 |
| Prof. plus | 43·9 | 41·4 | 7·0 | 7·8 | 28·4 | 24·3 |
| HNC plus | 68·6 | 73·2 | 27·4 | 29·9 | 46·8 | 50·5 |
| ONC plus | 78·5 | 87·7 | 50·2 | 56·1 | 55·7 | 56·1 |

Table 4.14 shows the education input into the occupational categories of technologists, technicians and management. The figures show some tendency for the foreign-owned factories to employ roughly 10% more formally qualified people in the technologist and technician categories than the domestic factories. This difference does not emerge at the Graduate and Professional levels, but at the National Certificate levels. It is an interesting finding, in line with the view of a number of observers, that British industry tends to play down the importance of education below the university level. A similar tendency can be seen in the figures with respect to management, that is, slightly smaller proportions in the foreign factories at the upper levels, offset by a larger proportion at the Higher National Certificate level. But this is slight. What is striking with respect to management is the very equal education input in the domestic and foreign factories. This challenges the idea that management in foreign subsidiaries is better educated, and again raises the point that the knowledge input into the subsidiary of a foreign parent company need not all be embodied in men on the spot.

Our final table takes up the question of where the highly educated labour is being used. It is often emphasized that British industry would benefit from greater use of more qualified people in the less obvious areas, such as sales. This raises the question of whether the existing qualified workforce is optimally deployed, as against the need for greater numbers of educated employees. The present paper, of course, cannot contribute in that area, being only concerned with comparing practices in foreign-owned and domestic-owned factories. And especially on this last topic, even that comparison reveals very little.

TABLE 4.15

*Proportion of Educated Employees in Total Workforce in Electrical Engineering by Activities, 1968*

|  |  | Research and design | Production | Sales |
|---|---|---|---|---|
| Machinery and cables | Domestic | 3·05 | 1·30 | 1·52 |
|  | Foreign | 0·89 | 1·43 | 0·82 |
| Telephone and electronics | Domestic | 5·22 | 2·03 | 0·71 |
|  | Foreign | 2·23 | 4·65 | 1·32 |
| Domestic and other | Domestic | 1·56 | 1·46 | 0·56 |
|  | Foreign | 2·67 | 3·13 | 0·57 |

Clearly the comparison in Table 4.15 would be meaningless without an industry, or product, breakdown. Even so, the usual caveat of significant product differences across firms within a category applies strongly here. More interestingly, the comparison with respect to research and sales calls for particular comment. For both of these activities are likely to be very different for a link in a multinational complex compared to a more self-contained business unit. This is probably why, for both of these activities, the foreign proportions are strikingly low. Once again, the point that the foreigners do not employ more educated people in sales in this country is being made. The production comparison is probably the most meaningful. It supports the finding discussed earlier of greater use of knowledge in more prosaic activities.

### SUMMARY AND CONCLUSIONS

The impact of the inward investing foreign firm on the economy of the host country may have important components due to indirect, or spillover effects. We have examined one locale of such effects, namely the labour market in the United Kingdom. The emphasis is on United States direct investment because it is quantitatively larger, and because industrial relations practices in that country differ more from British practices than do those of most European countries. This chapter has undertaken a three-pronged attack on the topic by looking at foreign subsidiary industrial relations as such, labour disputes in foreign subsidiaries, and labour utilization in foreign firms in the electrical engineering industry (taken as a case study). This work is at an early stage, and while some effort will be made here to briefly draw the threads together, we will also indicate gaps in understanding and further areas for investigation.

On the issue of union recognition by employers, our investigation suggests that though there are foreign subsidiaries who display a markedly anti-union policy, such an attitude is no more character-istic of foreign firms generally than domestic firms generally. How-ever, there is a difference in the two situations. When the foreign firms comes here, backed by a powerful parent company organiza-tion, it is not like a domestic company starting from scratch. And the balance of power could well be such as to make organization of the workers and subsequent recognition more difficult to achieve. This suggests a possible need for legislation.

The main innovation stimulated by foreign subsidiaries here is productivity bargaining. This practice, and other considerations, raise the general issue of the impact of foreign firms on wage move-ments in this country. In the case of duplicates, where the foreigner is capable of producing in many countries, the subsidiary could be a tougher bargainer than its domestic counterpart. Conversely, where the subsidiary is a link in an integrated international produc-tion complex, it might be especially unwilling to risk a strike that could damage the whole complex. So we have reasons to expect de-partures in both directions. As to the spread of productivity agree-ments, the inflationary danger is that parity considerations could force wage increases without the full accompanying changes in output per man taking place. Earlier work suggesting that the foreign firm, while often paying higher wages, has not been an important stimulus to domestic firms paying more, tends to be questioned by some recent unpublished work. At this stage we can only point to this interesting question in the transmission of inflation without pro-viding any answer.

There is a clear indication in our work that the foreign subsidiary in the UK is an innovator in industrial relations in ways that can lead to greater flexibility and higher productivity. Casual evidence would suggest that the general extent of such an impact through spillover has not been large. However, it remains an important possibility for the future. In the short run, concern with general legislation on industrial relations is likely to take precedence.

We have pointed out in the text a number of responses on the part of trade unions to the multinational firm. At the moment the emphasis seems to be on better exchange of information. There is, however, some discussion of the question of international parity. Apart from the practical difficulties of implementing this policy, it should be noted that it receives its major support from high-wage areas. This is natural, of course, as the burden of such a policy is likely to fall on the lower-wage areas and keep capital in the areas where productivity and wages are currently higher.

An interesting finding of our study is that foreign subsidiaries do not appear to suffer more labour disputes than domestic firms, particularly on the basis of a comparison normalized by industry mix. There are *a priori* reasons to expect more strikes in foreign firms, and the opposite outcome is probably due to a combination of factors. Among them may be more and better management input into personnel problems, a high wage and high productivity policy, less willingness to risk strikes, and in some cases a stronger and more successful anti-union policy. Perhaps the most important factor is less use of industry-wide bargaining.

Claims that foreign management achieve higher productivity solely through better utilization of labour are not supported in our data, which, on the contrary, suggest larger fixed capital inputs as playing a major role. Nor do the figures suggest that the foreign subsidiaries employ a significantly better educated workforce, at least at the upper end of the scale. Two points immediately suggest themselves. One is that differences in the quality of labour need not necessarily be readily measurable in terms of formal qualifications. The other is that the knowledge input of a multinational company in host-country production need not be entirely embodied in the workforce in the host country.

Our work suggests that inward investment in the United Kingdom has a tendency to bring the source country (which is primarily the United States) industrial relations practices with it. The foreign firms have been, on the whole, cautious with respect to introducing change, and flexible with respect to adjusting to British conditions. Some subsidiary firms have enviable records in their dealings with British trade unions while refusing to recognize unions in the United States. Apparently this caution and flexibility has been rewarded. While organized American workers are markedly more strike-prone than their British counterparts, foreign subsidiaries here are less troubled by disputes than domestic firms. This is not to suggest the absence of problems, and in particular there remains the issue of the balance of power between labour and management which is raised by the multinational firm. In the future, trade unions and governments are likely to direct increasing attention to this area.

# COMMENT ON THE CHAPTER BY
# MR STEUER AND MR GENNARD

### RICHARD E. CAVES

Evidence from numerous sources suggests that foreign subsidiaries earn higher rates of return and attain higher productivity than the domestic firms with which they compete. This superiority could be due to a number of causes, and which of these prevail in practice has a considerable effect on our assessment of the size and distribution of the welfare benefits and costs that foreign direct investment may create. Since the effective management of labour relations is one way to increase (or protect) productive efficiency, it is desirable to know whether this is a significant source of the subsidiaries' productivity advantages and, if so, how it arises. The chapter at hand offers a valuable contribution in what has been a factual void, and the following remarks will aim mostly at exploring the significance of its conclusions.

Various commentators have noted that the features of the British industrial relations system summarized by the authors at the outset conspire to amplify workers' preferences for restrictive practices, channel industrial strife into forms costly to efficiency, and thus impair the level and probably constrict the growth rate of industrial productivity. Thus there is scope for gain to British industry generally from any innovations that break away from this pattern. The authors show that foreign firms have been disproportionate innovators in seeking to escape from some of the features of this system through productivity bargaining, enforceable contracts of fixed durations, and reforms of piecework pay methods and the two-tier bargaining system. Furthermore, most of these innovations seem to have succeeded to some degree, and to have been copied elsewhere in the economy. The evidence then suggests, strongly, if in a general way, that superior labour relations (implemented in part through greater commitments of managerial talent) have been one source of the subsidiaries' superior performance. To put this in full perspective, however, would require further evidence on two points. Can the subsidiaries' performance be tied *specifically* to their labour-relations practices, or do these merely reflect a high level of managerial ability generally? Is the foreign firm adroit at labour relations because it brings the experience of operating in other national systems, or merely because it is efficient? (The market tends, after all, to deny international status to inefficient firms.)

One possible cost to set against real gains of this sort would be any increase of industrial strife and associated political discontent due to the international corporation. Steuer and Gennard show, first, that the foreign firm has not been a bone in the throat of the British trade unions. I am not fully convinced by their argument concerning the unimportance in this context of the unwillingness of some firms to recognize trade unions as bargaining agents. But the fact remains that this has not provided a divisive issue, probably (as they say) because most foreign firms have been willing to accept the principal features of the British industrial-relations system as they find it.

For the reasons they suggest one would surely expect the extent of labour disputes in the foreign firms to be no less than in domestic firms, especially since British managements have often been accused of taking a short-run view of the costs of a strike that stems from resisting or seeking to abolish restrictive work rules. Quite strong confirmation of the superiority of foreign firms' labour-relations practices arises therefore in their findings that the time lost through industrial disputes in foreign firms is less than proportional to their share of output, after allowance is made for their distribution among industries. (As the authors imply, a better comparison would be to their share of labour input, because of their putatively higher efficiency and capital intensity; but this re-basing of the comparison would probably not change the conclusions.) The evidence also suggests, less clearly, that foreign firms tend to avoid continuing plagues of minor and 'unofficial' stoppages. These seem likely to extract a disproportionate cost in overall industrial efficiency because of their effects on production scheduling, inventory holding, and the like.

The chapter's final section addresses another hypothesis about the sources of superior productivity in foreign firms: that it is furthered by recruiting employees with higher levels of education. Their findings for the electrical engineering industry, which should afford a good test case, provide no support for the hypothesis. These data could stand further inspection, especially since they may be dominated by a few long-established subsidiaries making standardized domestic appliances. In any case, they can be related to the finding, reported in other studies, that any superiority in the labour force employed by foreign firms may lie in their recruitment of the best-quality workers locally available possessing any given level of education.

## Chapter 5

# MULTINATIONAL COMPANIES AND TRADE UNION INTERESTS

### DAVID LEA

#### INTRODUCTION

A resolution of the 1969 Trades Union Congress drew attention to the transformation of major British companies into multinational corporations 'which, if not controlled by the extension of social ownership and/or a system of public accountability would create new problems of job security and economic difficulties, both now and for the future of the British economy'.[1]

Trade unions at a national and international level are carefully considering their response to the new form of economic power which is represented by the phenomenal growth of giant enterprises operating across national frontiers. This chapter is a preliminary review, from the perspective of British trade unionists, of the problems and opportunities created by these enterprises – be they UK or foreign owned. It orginated as part of the TUCs Economic Review 1970 and was designed to initiate discussion within the British trade union movement.

The primary task of trade unions everywhere is to advance and protect the interests of their members. This being so, it is understandable that the British trade union movement is concerned, in the first instance, with the impact of the growth of multinational companies on the situation in the UK labour market; its effects on pay and conditions, on job security, on communications within the enterprise and plant; on the relative bargaining strength of labour and management, and on the attitudes of international companies to industrial relations. But secondly, trade unions are interested in examining the scope for international co-operation amongst their members, so that the managements of multinational companies may be faced with a 'countervailing power' of trade unions co-ordinating strategies across national frontiers.

[1] This resolution was moved by the Chemical Workers' Union.

Thirdly, the trade union movement – like other sectors of the UK economy – are concerned with the impact of the multinational enterprise on the national economy as a whole which will, in turn, have its effects on the long-term labour market. The spread of international companies, in fact, represents a shift of economic power away from national governments. Trade unionists are anxious lest the activities of these enterprises, British and foreign owned, should conflict with the achievement of national economic and social objectives, e.g. a faster rate of economic growth and a more equitable distribution of income and wealth.

This chapter, therefore, discusses certain problems which face governments, but which concern also trade unions. Foremost amongst these are the balance of payments and real income effects, on the UK, of inward and outward investment, intra-company transfers and internal financial and pricing arrangements, and the domination by international companies of key sectors of the UK economy.

While recognizing the very real advantages of inward investment in terms of technology, employment and trade, the case is put for more information to be made available, and for a greater measure of accountability, by international companies, both to the people whom they employ and to the national governments in whose territory they operate. Unlike many countries where international companies operate, the UK has a stake both as parent country and host country to a large number of multinational companies. Much of this chapter is concerned with the operation of foreign-owned companies in Britain, but we also touch briefly on the some of the possible implications of uncontrolled outward investment – drawing upon both UK and US experience.

## GROWTH OF INTERNATIONAL COMPANIES

As previous chapters in this volume have shown, the vast majority of multinational companies are of a kind whose headquarters and ownership are based in a particular country, but which operate subsidiaries in other countries. While there are very few examples of companies in which ownership and control are dispersed between different countries, there are several thousand companies based in Europe, North America and the Far East which operate subsidiaries in several other countries, and an increasing number of these plan their investment globally, and integrate their production as well as marketing on a global basis. Some companies have developed far more of the characteristics of the geocentric MPE than others, and they vary in the degree to which decision-making is decentralized to subsidiaries.

An estimate by one US economist of the value of *output abroad* resulting from 'direct investment' in plant and equipment of the ten loading capital exporting nations[1] put the value of the output of these companies at $240,000 million in 1967 (which is two and a half times as big as Britain's gross national product). The combined exports of these same nations amounted to $130,000 million. Moreover, 'foreign' production is currently growing faster than exports. About four-fifths of international direct investment is accounted for by US and UK firms. Britain is *par excellence* a two-way international investor; at the end of 1968, UK enterprises owned foreign assets worth nearly £8,000 million and about a third of all corporate profits were derived from overseas operations. At the same time, the foreign direct stake in the UK amounted to £3,500 million. Probably as much as 15% of the manufacturing output is now produced by foreign (mostly US) subsidiaries, although the latest published figure relates to 1963, when it was 11%.[2]

## PROBLEMS FOR TRADE UNIONS

### 1 *The Locus of Decision Taking*

From a trade union point of view, one of the factors which is of special significance, in connection with negotiation and consultation with foreign-owned companies, is that it is often difficult to determine where the *locus* of authority in multinational companies really lies. Subsidiary companies may say that decisions are taken at the centre, while parent companies claim that they are taken by their subsidiaries. Given the widely different types of international ventures, it is difficult to generalize about where, in fact, decisions are made. International companies go through a process of development whereby, at one stage, crucial investment decisions, for example, may be centralized in the parent company and country, whereas decisions about industrial relations may be decentralized. Later, a policy on industrial relations and wages may be adopted in the parent

[1] USA, UK, Canada, France, West Germany, Italy, Japan, Netherlands, Sweden and Switzerland. See J. Polk, 'The New World Economy', in *Columbia Journal of World Business*, January/February 1968.

[2] *Census of Production*, 1963. For further details of the foreign capital stake in the UK see J. H. Dunning, 'Foreign direct investment in the United Kingdom economy', in I. A. Litvak and C. J. Maule, *Foreign Investment: the Experience of Host Countries*, New York, Praeger, 1969.

company's headquarters which will then be applied in subsidiaries overseas.

Most empirical research confirms this diversity of practice, with the degree of decentralization being based on the parent company's appraisal of the most commercially advantageous method of operation, subject to a variety of political and other constraints.

Centralized control over decision-taking does not necessarily mean the same as uniformity. Decisions may be reached on industrial relations without a uniform pattern of application in different countries: for instance, differences in the laws of different countries will inevitably affect local industrial relations practices. But some broad generalizations can be made: one is that American-owned companies tend to place a greater emphasis on managerial prerogatives than companies of other nationalities, although even here it may be necessary to distinguish the American pattern of behaviour from the behaviour of international corporations as such.

With regard to collective bargaining, wage negotiations in international companies are invariably conducted on a country-by-country basis. But the decentralization does not necessarily apply to company guidelines on procedure agreements and wages systems, where there may be a strong degree of policy centralization.

## 2 Collective Bargaining

Although some foreign-owned subsidiaries in Britain belong to employers' associations, the proportion who do is smaller than for British companies. In the case of American companies this may arise from assumptions about the best system of industrial relations and collective bargaining which stem from normal US practice to concentrate on negotiations within a company, and often at plant level; or their reluctance to accept the industry-wide disputes procedure, which gives other employers the right to a view and, to some degree, the right to arbitrate, on matters within member companies. The US-owned motor companies, for example, Ford, Vauxhall, and Rootes, are not members of the Engineering Employers' Federation; in fact, Rootes withdrew on being taken over by Chrysler.

The problem which foreign direction presents for trade unions is that where the power centre of a corporation cannot be properly identified, it cannot be easily dealt with. It is also difficult to determine where decisions are taken and how attitudes are formed over such problems as trade union recognition. Two factors influence this. One is the set of assumptions made in the parent company about trade union recognition, and the other is the prevailing convention in the host country. Thus a foreign company beginning operations in Britain – whether by takeover or by the establishment of a new enterprise – may recognize the strength of trade unionism in Britain and agree to use traditional bargaining methods, but might take quite a different attitude in another country where workpeople are less well organized. On the other hand, these same considerations may influence the company's decision about where to expand its operations.

Problems certainly have been encountered in the UK as a result of differing concepts of industrial relations practices. There have been several instances of foreign subsidiaries in Britain refusing to recognize trade unions. Partly this may be because some American firms also resist union organization in the US; some take the line that their method of personnel management dispenses with the need for unions. Another part of the explanation may be that all American firms are familiar with the National Labour Relations Board procedure (laid down in the National Labour Relations Act) for making recognition mandatory after a ballot. This procedure does not, of course, apply in Britain and some companies may assume incorrectly that the absence of legislative pressure means the absence of established industrial obligation. This is a key source of misunderstanding. It applies to Kodak and IBM, for example. It often applies particularly strongly to any attempt to organize white-collar workers.

Some of these kinds of problems are also encountered by British-owned companies. However, a TUC survey carried out in 1967[1] concluded that the foreign-owned firms involved in such difficulties tended to be significantly *larger* than their UK counterparts. Foreign subsidiaries in the UK vary in the extent to which they attempt to import foreign US labour practices. In a sample of ninety-eight large US subsidiaries in Britain, Professor Dunning found that only four stated they were 'strongly influenced' in their wages and industrial relations policies by their parent companies. Nineteen were 'moderately' influenced, and seventy-eight 'negligibly' influenced. Moreover, only in three cases did the parent companies strongly influence decision-taking in this field.[2] Periodically, however, it does seem that a subsidiary attempts to unilaterally transplant American practice. For example, it is not clear whether the Ford management were influenced by their American parent in their attempts to sue unions

[1] TUC Report 1967.
[2] 'US subsidiaries in Britain and their UK competitors', *Business Ratios*, Vol. 1, No. 1, 1966.

for breach of contract in March 1969, but this was certainly a widespread impression among Ford workers. There are, of course, firms which have resisted unions in the United States who have recognized them in the United Kingdom. One such is the Esso Petroleum Company, who pioneered a new approach to productivity bargaining at Fawley. In general, however, foreign-owned firms are *not* more prone to industrial disputes and strikes than their UK equivalents, though a slightly higher proportion of strikes are on non-wage questions.[1]

There is no general rule as to whether foreign-owned companies pay higher wages than domestically-owned companies. In Britain, for example, the American-owned motor companies do not pay higher wages than the British Leyland Motor Corporation, but in some industries, e.g. food products, detergents and pharmaceuticals, they tend to do so. Part of the reason for this is probably higher productivity, and part a more selective labour recruitment policy. Foreign-owned companies also tend to pay higher than average wages when establishing a new venture, sometimes to the disruption of local labour markets. These comparisons may be further complicated by the fact that multinational companies often have large plants, and to some extent, earnings are related to size of plant.

It is believed that the salaries of executives in US subsidiaries in the UK are generally higher than their counterparts in UK firms, and this may reflect opposition to the growth of trade unionism in the executive field. There is also some evidence that American companies generally give better fringe benefits, and this may be a spillover from American practice. Direct payment-by-results would appear to be uncommon for American-owned companies, reflecting their style of management control.

### 3 Special Factors Affecting Bargaining Power

In the last resort, companies operating in more than one national economy are able to switch their operations elsewhere. This flexibility is a powerful force on the side of management in any bargaining situation with nationally-based trade unions. In the course of wage negotiations, management may claim that unless the settlement is below a certain figure, the corporation will be forced to reduce production or expand in a different country. This type of threat is quite common as a bargaining tactic, in the UK motor industry for example, but it is difficult to trace a case where a MPE has closed down or cut back its UK operations for this reason alone. Certainly,

[1] See Chapter 4.

foreign firms have been attracted to low-wage areas, but not necessarily as a result of specific wage negotiations. There are cases of UK-owned MPEs setting up component manufacturing facilities abroad both to supply the overseas market and as part of an integrated global process (e.g. GEC in India and Plessey in Portugal).

Likewise, elsewhere for example, it has been a major preoccupation of United States unions that differences in wage levels led to US-owned MPEs establishing 'runaway' companies over the Mexican border and in Formosa, Norway, Italy and Singapore;[1] cheap labour and taxation incentives both provide the attraction to these locations. Again, it is impossible to trace these locational decisions to particular collective bargaining tactics. Nevertheless, the cumulative result of effective trade union organization and bargaining in gaining higher wages can be undermined by the power of MPEs to switch resources to less well organized, more poorly-paid areas. This, of course, applies particularly to horizontally integrated companies where parallel plants already exist or parallel markets are already being supplied.

Even if a long-term re-location of resources is not carried out, the possibility of diverting short-term production between countries is itself a powerful weapon when industrial action is threatened or carried out. A MPE, when faced with a strike in one country, may be able to compensate for this by expanding production in another. However, where its international operations are vertically integrated, its bargaining position is less strong, as for example in such industries as motors (including components), earth-moving equipment, computers and chemicals. In these areas the trade union response can be a realistic countervailing force to the international company, and there are examples of action being taken by unions in different countries to stop overtime being worked, e.g. the Pirelli dispute[2] in 1969, or to stop extra shipments to a particular country where strike action is being taken. This kind of response is dealt with more fully below.

## 4 Foreign Takeovers

From the viewpoint of workpeople whose firms are acquired by foreign-owned copanies, there is inevitably an element of concern about management motives following a foreign takeover. This is not

[1] See, for example, P. Jennings, Testimony to the Foreign Economic Affairs Sub-Committee of US Congress, July 1970, and AEC-C10 Federationist, May 1970.
[2] See ICF (International Federation of Chemical and General Workers) Bulletin, December 1969–January 1970.

just a matter of xenophobia. There is a real feeling of diminution of job security when it is known that decisions on jobs are taken much further away. Moreover, there may be anxiety that the new management may introduce new methods of work and/or a new and less acceptable basis for determining wages and conditions. Because of this, there is sometimes a negative attitude to management proposals, partly in order to establish the bargaining position of workpeople in the new situation.

The problem of mergers and takeovers is not solely one of the MPE, but the special feature of foreign takeovers and mergers as far as domestic employment is concerned was that it can be difficult for unions to get prior guarantees on such matters as trade union recognition and job security from the firm taking over the existing establishment. Where a domestic takeover was promoted through the Industrial Re-organization Corporation (IRC) for example, the TUC could ensure that the IRC discussed, with the potential owner, guarantees on negotiation affecting such issues as recognition and job security. This type of discussion necessarily has to devolve on government where there is a foreign takeover, unless unions can negotiate directly with the head office of the MPE.

Foreign takeovers often cause anxiety among executives, scientists and technologists about the location of future research and development, and the recruitment of future top management. The actual numbers of foreigners employed as top managers in foreign-owned subsidiaries in Britain is probably not very large. According to a survey carried out by the American Chamber of Commerce in 1969, only about half of the American firms in British manufacturing industry employed resident American personnel in a managerial capacity.[1] Of a total work force of 402,000 in 211 companies surveyed, 368 Americans were employed in management, 155 in production and 105 in sales. This would appear to support the contention of Professor V. Perlmutter who argues that there is a trend towards a global strategy of the larger American corporation, which is geocentric in character as opposed to ethnocentric. The geocentric company is one in which local nationals take the top jobs in the foreign subsidiaries as part of an international team. The ethnocentric company, by contrast, is one where the parent companies exert a rigid control over subsidiaries and do not employ local personnel in senior management positions.

The International Metal Workers' Federation quotes an example of a union in response to a foreign takeover of a Belgian company,

[1] *Anglo-American Trade News*, September 1969.

successfully insisting that national management was not replaced. In other cases there have been demands that there should be no shift in the location of production without union consultation, security against downgrading of jobs and guarantees against displacement of research.

## 5 'Runaway' Companies

We end this section with a brief review of the attitude of unions in investing countries to the development of overseas investment in subsidiaries. The AFL–CIO cities union demands in the United States to guard against the possible adverse effects of runaway companies or foreign sub-contracting: some unions are attempting to get it written into collective bargaining agreements that there should be no overseas sub-contracting (which is a growing practice in Europe). Up to now, the concern of British trade unions at the level of outward investment by British-owned international companies has been directed primarily at its impact on the balance of payments. The effect on employment in the UK is likely to be less direct or obvious than in the US since it is not often economic to transfer production to cheap labour areas to supply the UK market. However, there is some evidence that UK companies are switching to supply export markets by production overseas, and this could have a distinct, though as yet an unquantifiable effect on UK employment.

### INTERNATIONAL TRADE UNION ACTION

In order to redress the balance of collective bargaining strength arising from the growth of the international company, much more co-operation and co-ordination would appear to be needed between trade unions in different countries. The scope for international trade union action is necessarily limited – there is, for example, not much likelihood, in the near future, of international collective bargaining over wages and conditions, but there are certain fields in which progress may be possible. The need for unions nationally to know about corporate investment plans and their implications for employment is reinforced when the company has the capacity to expand faster in one country than another. This points to the advantage of unions meeting internationally and forming joint consultative committees with international companies.

In Britain recently, the Transport and General Workers' Union and the Amalgamated Engineering and Foundry Workers held the

155

first of (what is hoped to be) a series of discussions with the United Auto Workers of the US to talk about problems of common interest arising from the operation of multinational motor corporations. A meeting held in Paris in December 1969 of trade unions in the European motor industry agreed to strongly oppose any move by manufacturers to move work from one country to another in the event of a strike. The American Steelworkers Union is now inviting German trade unionists to attend the annual conference at which the International Canning Corporation gives advance notice of its investment plans. An example of consultation at an international board level is the series of recent meetings held by the Philips organization with the EEC countries.[1] This kind of development is likely to progress further in the EEC countries, where discussions on the 'European company' formula will probably result in trade unions from different countries being given the legal right to participate in discussions at international level.

In other respects, International Trade Secretariats are developing their work along traditional lines, concentrating on research, and on giving advice and assistance to unions in difficulties. A recent example of a strike against an international company was that by Fiat workers in Turin in connection with dismissals of union members in Fiat in Argentina. The International Chemical Workers' Federation (ICF) has been responsible for co-ordinated international trade union activity in disputes for example with the French-owned St Gobain glass company. Trade Unions affiliated to the ICF from France, Italy, Germany and the USA agreed in March 1969 on a six-point programme for a Standing Committee to co-ordinate wage demands made to St Gobain and its affiliates and help any national union in the event of strike action in a St Gobain plant in one country. This help would be in terms of information, financial assistance, prevention of transferred production and bans on overtime, but not of sympathy strikes, though this, in the last resort, was not ruled out. As a result, favourable settlements were reached with St Gobain by the German union (IG Chemie) without a strike, in Italy by Federchimici (CISL) and (UILSID) after the threat of a strike, and in the USA (Glass and Ceramic Workers) after a bitter twenty-six-day strike.[2]

[1] In October 1967, June 1969 and September 1970.

[2] The French situation is less clear because the union affiliated to the national centre which is in turn affiliated to ICF (CFDT) is a minority union in the French plant, and the major union centre, the communist, CGT, and the other minority unions signed separate and less favourable agreements with the company.

Other examples of pressure brought through the ICF include joint action against a German multinational company, which was trying to defeat a strike by the Turkish Chemical Workers Federation, and against the Swiss-owned General Superintendence Company, which was attempting to break a strike in Japan by the Federation of Chemical Industry Workers against their Far Eastern subsidiary Fesco.[1]

It is premature to discuss co-ordination of wage demands in most industries on an international basis, but one way in which unions may counter the use of balance of payments arguments in wage negotiations is by synchronized applications in different countries. This does not mean that the same claim is made in different countries, but that there may be co-ordinated timing of claims: some trade union internationals, in particular the metal workers in relation to the automobile industry, are examining this in the context of how they can develop a strategy for bargaining with international companies.

## PROBLEMS OF COMMON INTEREST TO GOVERNMENTS AND UNIONS

### 1 *Information*

One of the problems facing unions, which also faces governments, is the difficulty of understanding the financial accounts of international companies. Trade unions are clearly interested in these in so far as they reflect economic strength and weakness: governments are also concerned with questions of tax liability.

### 2 *Balance of Payments Effects*

Trade unions not only have a common concern with governments in obtaining increased information about the activities of international companies, and defining guidelines for their operations. They feel also that there is a clear need for obligations to be placed by governments on subsidiaries to provide information for collective bargaining purposes from companies central accounts. This should extend to such factors as their international patterns of trade and investment.

A number of studies have demonstrated the importance of 'internal' trading patterns of international companies (i.e. between subsidiaries) which account for a rapidly rising proportion of British exports. But there are serious gaps in the information which is avail-

[1] *ICF Bulletin*, June–July 1969.

able, in particular about the imports of such companies, either generally or from the parent company and fellow-subsidiaries. American studies have shown that American parent companies have positive trade surpluses with their subsidiaries. This must mean that overseas subsidiaries, taken together, buy more from American parents than they supply to them, though the main part of the explanation may be large US surpluses *vis-à-vis* developing countries.

The only information which is published by the Board of Trade on the export performance of international companies relates to a special survey for 1966 of direct exports (i.e. those which take place in the name of the manufacturer rather than in the name of a wholesaler). The results of the Board of Trade[1] 1966 survey are given in Table 5.1:

TABLE 5.1

*UK Exports and International Companies*

| Analysis of returns received Exports by: | 1 Total exports £ million | 2 Exports to related to companies £ million | 3 Column 2 as % of column 1 |
|---|---|---|---|
| UK subsidiaries of US companies | 701 | 392 | 56 |
| UK subsidiaries of other overseas companies | 299 | 109 | 36 |
| UK associates of overseas companies | 180 | 22 | 12 |
| UK parent companies having overseas affiliates | 2,248 | 610 | 27 |
| UK companies, having no overseas affiliates | 343 | — | — |
| TOTAL (returns received) | 3,771 | 1,133 | 30 |

*Source: Board of Trade Journal, May 16, 1968.*

The overall percentage of exports going to related companies shown in the Board of Trade's table is 30%.[2] This makes 'the inter-

[1] *Board of Trade Journal*, May 16, 1968.

[2] The Board of Trade believe that to ascertain the percentage of *total* UK exports, this figure should be reduced to about 22% to take account of indirect exports, exports by oil companies and by small companies (broadly those not exporting more than £100,000 a year) which were not included in the table.

nal transfer price' at which these goods were traded a matter of supreme importance in the balance of payments performance of the UK economy.[1]

## 3 *Currency Markets*

Another problem arising is that if an international company takes the view that a particular currency (e.g. the £) is over valued, it is clearly in its interests to switch production to, or to expand production more rapidly in, a country where the currency is relatively undervalued. Also, many international companies maintain Eurodollar accounts, the great advantage to them being freedom of quick convertibility between currencies. This process can, in the short run, intensify any tendency to international monetary instability: in the long run it can have a significant effect on the determination of rates of exchange. Such monetary movements can, of course, be exaggerated, but there is no question of the potential importance of this factor. National governments are, in fact, extremely circumscribed in dealing with this sort of situation because there is no way in which international control can be exercised over these companies.

## 4 *Investment Incentives*

Whereas governments tend to have misgivings about foreign *takeovers* of domestic industry, and sometimes make attempts to restrict foreign control (the policy of the de Gaulle administration being the best example),[2] they usually adopt a much more favourable policy towards investment in *new ventures*, particularly as these can often be steered to high unemployment areas.

Much is heard about the quality of American management and the contribution of inward investment to improving standards of management in Britain generally. Hard evidence of this kind of is, however, difficult to find, and it is hoped that the current Board of Trade study on inward investment will be able to throw some light on this area of debate.

At the present time, governments tend to compete with each other to attract inward investment in a sort of auction of incentives to MPEs. The companies concerned obviously find this very much to their advantage, and as British companies are the beneficiaries of this sort of favourable treatment abroad, it is unlikely that industry itself will press for greater international control. It is therefore in the

[1] For further details of the balance of payments effects of outward investment, see Chapter 6.
[2] See Economist Intelligence Unit, *The Growth and Spread of International Companies*, 1971.

common interest of trade unions internationally to encourage governments to take joint action in order to strike a fair balance between the interests of MPEs and those of governments, consumers and employees.

## 5 Outward Investment

Incentives to inward investment need to be considered alongside policies towards outward investment. In 1969, direct outward investment by UK companies amounted to £500 million, nearly twice the level of inward investment.[1] This represented a rise of 20% over the previous year. It is recognized that some of this is financed out of reinvested profits, but a substantial amount still consists of a real transfer of resources out of this country. The implications of this outflow need to be examined carefully from two viewpoints – firstly the direct balance of payment effects of overseas investment and earnings, and secondly its direct or indirect impact on domestic investment. The balance of payments effect has been covered in chapter 6 of this volume, and it is not intended to go into it in any detail here. Trade unions are concerned that failure to control such investment flow adequately could lead to further balance of payments crises with detrimental effects on the domestic economy.

The effect on domestic investment of overseas investment by UK-owned firms is both direct and indirect through the balance of payments. Professor Reddaway[2] and others have argued that the cases of overseas investment being a direct alternative to domestic investment are rare. Clearly the choice for the corporation is more complex than this, and involves assessment of the relative growth and profitability of the UK and overseas markets, and the relative availability of funds. Trade unionists need to be convinced that the social opportunity costs of investing abroad are fully taken into account in granting Treasury permission for direct overseas investment. At present, we seem to be in a vicious circle: low growth due to balance of payment difficulties leads to low domestic investment and high overseas investment which, in turn, lead to further balance of payments problems and necessitate further deflationary policies. Clearly, high overseas investment is not the only mechanism operating this circle, but failure to control it certainly exacerbates our economic difficulties. Comparison of purely financial returns on investment at home and abroad is insufficient to assess the real cost.

[1] *Board of Trade Journal*, April 8, 1970.
[2] W. B. Reddaway *et al.*, *The Effects of UK Direct Investment Overseas*, Final Report, London, Cambridge University Press, 1968.

The Government has stated as an objective that inward investment and outward investment should balance 'at a high level'. There is reason to doubt whether it is in the national interest to allow any general move to a higher level of investment in both directions until a new system of relationships has been established.

## 6 Taxation

One incentive to governments to enquire further into this matter is the problem of corporate taxation. The establishment of many holding companies or 'group finance' companies in Switzerland is believed to have arisen from the advantage of low corporate tax rates and anomalous disclosure requirements in that country. Thus an international company with subsidiaries of the Swiss holding company in countries such as the UK, France and Germany, where corporate taxes are relatively high, can sell to the holding company at very low 'transfer prices' making very low profits, and declare a high profit in Switzerland. Several studies[1] have given examples of this type of operation, but none have been able to estimate its total magnitude, for the reason that governments have not agreed on a system of collecting information. The relation of this factor to location decisions underlines its importance.

## 7 National Economic Planning

The fact that large modern international companies can increasingly plan production, location and trading patterns across national boundaries points to the increased need for governmental planning to be linked to corporate planning. In a speech in December 1969 Lord Stokes referred to the fact that 'the loyalties of the transnational company are not to the country within which it is operating, but to the country of ownership'.[2] Other observers take the view that the distinction is not as sharp as this: it is argued that the loyalty to the country of ownership is not so crucial a factor as the degree to which any particular country is a dominant market. On this view, it is precisely when a company's exports have expanded to the point that world markets are as important as the domestic market that a company can no longer afford to be too 'national' in its orientation. The situation is then judged on commercial criteria – long term as well as short term – in relation to the development of

[1] For instance, *Transfer Pricing in Multi-National Business*, James A. Schulman, Ph.D. thesis, Harvard University, 1966.
[2] *Financial Times* and *The Times*, December 4, 1969.

the economy and the arrangements which can be negotiated with the national government.

In the UK context, this suggests that the TUCs demand in the 1968 and 1969 Economic Reviews for discussion on export targets and import levels with large companies is an important one, given the degree of corporate planning which already exists. This is one way in which some measure – albeit a small measure – of national economic interest can be exercised; public ownership would very rarely be as advantageous as a mutually agreed solution. With key sectors increasingly in the hands of foreign or British-owned MPEs it is essential that the corporate plans of these concerns are integrated and synchronized with the Government's own national economic planning process.

## INTERNATIONAL GOVERNMENTAL ACTION

On the level of international governmental co-operation and control, this problem can be examined at the level of industrial countries generally, in OECD, or in the context of trading blocs, such as EEC and EFTA.

The first step for organizations such as these must be to collect information, which is very sparse indeed. For example, there is no authoritative information on employment in international companies, and no standardized information on trading patterns, accounting procedures, capital flows, tax payments and many other matters. It is only when such information is available that it will be possible to determine proper guidelines of good practice.

This raises what might be regarded as a political problem, given the special importance of the United States in this field. The USA accounts for over 50% of the GNP of all OECD countries, and also for about two-thirds of the foreign operations of international companies. The main role of the United States is in the role of the parent country rather than the host country, whereas most European countries play the role of host country rather than parent country.

Demands for investigations of the role of MPEs should not be regarded as anti-American. There is an equal need for investigation of the economics of foreign investment from the point of view of host countries, such as was carried out by Professor Reddaway in relation to UK overseas investment. Both inward and outward flows have to be considered, and in relation to the formulation of trades union policy it is quite consistent to be considering guidelines for both outward and inward investment. Indeed, there are advantages in having guidelines for both, in order to respond to the argument that controls over outward investment may lead to retaliation by other countries restricting their investment in Britain. A rational policy suggests the need for guidelines in both directions to be set by governments collectively.

It is in the long-run self-interest of investing, as well as host, countries that these problems should be discussed by both types of country, rather than that restrictive attitudes should be struck by host countries acting in isolation. From a trade union point of view, governments should be encouraged to begin early discussions on formulating guidelines, and they should be reminded of the very considerable trade union interest in this subject.

# COMMENT ON THE CHAPTER BY
# MR LEA: A BUSINESSMAN'S
# VIEWPOINT

DAVID BARRAN*

Mr Lea's chapter reflects, fairly accurately, some common misunderstandings about the nature of multinational enterprises and their possible effects upon industrial relations systems that have been built up within national jurisdictions.

Essentially, these views turn on the assertion that the 'centre of power' has passed to a 'foreign head office' with whom trade unions have no channels of communication. Those who hold them are buttressed by the fear that multinational enterprises can and will switch employment opportunities from a country in which trade unionism is aggressive to one where it is not. The scope for international trade union action – multinational unions to match multinational companies – is taken to be necessarily limited. A more effective ripost lies in pressure through government to get multinational enterprises to reveal their investment and employment plans. A legislative requirement for companies to admit worker representation on their boards is one route. Government also have need of more information about the plans of multinational enterprises and it is implied that this common requirement will adduce governments to act as the trade unions wish.

I believe these views are based on a misunderstanding of how multinational enterprises work; and of the economic forces which have brought them into being and to which they must respond. In practice, the multilateral enterprise is simply the latest phase in the development of commercial mechanisms to handle the international movement of goods and services. It has evolved from the exporter who established overseas branches to handle business that was previously handled by agents. From that point, a logical step in the development of the framework for international trading lies in the formation of overseas subsidiaries.

* Some of the views expressed in this contribution were also presented at a conference of the British–North American Committee at Palm Beach in December 1970.

164

The concept of an enterprise located in the form of separate companies in different countries is now a familiar feature of the international economic scene. But this does not mean that MPEs are able to ride rough-shod over the laws and practices of the countries in which the constituent companies do business.

In many of these enterprises, and certainly in the Royal Dutch Shell Group, a prime objective is to extend maximum autonomy to the management of the companies on the periphery. The aim is to achieve optimum results from the enterprise, as a whole, but reconciling decisions made at the periphery, one with the other. This is the role of the centre, wherever it may be located, and it is a role that seeks to ensure that all companies in the enterprise get their appropriate share of the resources of the enterprise, whether these be in the form of manpower, technology, materials or money.

Many benefits accrue to countries where MPEs operate and these are particularly evident in the field of personnel management. Such enterprises attach importance to their reputation and this generally reflects itself in the quality of their personnel policies. In the case of Shell, the general philosophy is that people are individuals with unique attributes who should be able to give of their best in the work environment for their own benefit as well as for the benefit of the enterprise as a whole. All the Company's personnel policies are directed to this end: whether they are concerned with the negotiation or establishment of rates of pay and other incentives, or are directed towards the more subtle process of inducing fundamental change in the styles of management and supervision. The discipline of maintaining a good international reputation is a compelling one and, while management must exercise its proper office and accept the duties to manage, this must be combined with an awareness that the better part of management is exercised through consent and co-operation.

Industrial relations' policies and procedures are usually left entirely for local management to determine, but in multinational enterprises there is a vast accumulation of experience and knowledge available to the local manager. This may be exemplified in Shell's attitude to trade unionism. The company's broad view is that an employer may be expected to have some interest in the sort of unions that his employees join: but, subject to the usual limitations, it must be accepted that if employees wish to join unions that is their business.

Although unions have a legitimate part to play as representatives of unionized employees, the management of Shell companies are much more concerned with individual employee participation, which is often lacking in the individual to some degree in his role as employee and is undoubtedly lacking to a greater degree in his role as a member of a union. There is a contradiction between full recognition of the individual (i.e. the only real unit in society) and the apparent desire of large representative organizations such as unions to become in a sense the new bosses for their members. In practical terms this is currently reflected in the move towards plant-level bargaining and is contradicted by a trend that may be artificially stimulated by union leaders towards 'multinational bargaining'.

I would suggest that the trend has instead been in the opposite direction, to meet the ever-growing demand (applicable to many sectors of the community) for greater direct participation and hence for decentralization of power. In the field of labour relations this is to be seen in the movement away from industry negotiated agreements and even, at least in the case of many larger companies, from company agreements towards plant-level bargaining.

In the light of considerable variations in local conditions, with the emphasis increasingly on productivity, and also with the growth of conglomerates embracing a great variety of activities which do not necessarily fall within one particular industry, this trend towards plant bargaining is likely to intensify. Here again, therefore, this is essentially an issue for local managements.

Good employee communications must always be a feature of progressive enterprise, whether national or multinational. There is no reason why trade unions should not know as much about a company as its employees and there is no dearth of information, in Shell's case at least. But unions have no case for special treatment in this respect. To this extent union representation at board level is based on a false and unnecessary premise. The right of employees to know does not require such representation.

As economic (and other) forces bind the nations into an even closer whole, people – as well as money and materials – will move with increasing freedom across national frontiers. Moreover, rise in educational attainments, skills and income expectations, will encourage broader personal horizons. While these may never result in a 'mobility of labour' on a scale comparable to the 'mobility of capital' it will be a factor which unions will need to take into account, the more as they aim to include in their membership categories of employees that have hitherto not been unionized. Practices which raise costs and restrict employment opportunities in one country *vis-à-vis* another will not only deter investors, they will divert the stream of skills. The consequence can only be to bring unionism into disrepute, not merely with employers but with potential and actual members and ultimately with governments. There is, however, a constructive alternative open to them which is essentially to act as a further spur on management to efficiency. Such a role is compatible with many of the traditional functions of unions, e.g. in determining the levels of remuneration, conditions of work, and so on. Nor need it imply the abandonment of the strike, though this will more and more, one hopes, be seen to be ultimately self-defeating. However, it will call for fresh attitudes and approaches on the part of the unions – and on management's part also. If these are forthcoming, management and unions can help to educate each other. As influential members of the national and international community they will have it in their power to do much to ensure the prosperity alike of the enterprise, of the community and of the individual employee. But for this to happen each will need to accept their social responsibilities and to acknowledge the inevitable limitations on the action and powers of the other.

*Chapter 6*

# THE MULTINATIONAL ENTERPRISE:
# TRADE FLOWS AND TRADE POLICY

### DAVID ROBERTSON

## INTRODUCTION

Historical observation establishes that there are irrefutable links between trade flows and overseas investment. What is more difficult to determine is the nature of the relationships between different types of foreign direct investment and international trade flows. With the rapid proliferation of transnational operations by large companies, where investment decisions become interwoven with transfers of technical knowledge, management expertise and skilled labour, relationships between investment and trade have become even more complex.

Until quite recently foreign direct investment was closely associated with trade interests.[1] Early merchants were concerned with obtaining supplies of essential raw materials and primary products to sell in their home country and with establishing new outlets for domestic production. The former often led to investments in plantations or mines, although in many cases this trade originated without such direct control over harvesting or extraction, for example tea and spices from the orient. Subsequently the search for new outlets for home produce frequently led to investments, too, in selling organizations and agencies.

These early overseas investments engendered trade which was founded on absolute advantage in production. When overseas investment extended to cover overseas assembly plants or the manufacture of products that competed with exports from the

---

[1] Frequently, portfolio investment was also associated with trading interests, for example, the investment of British capital in the nineteenth century in pioneering railways in North and South America.

investing country, then trade displacement resulted; products assembled or fabricated locally were substituted for imports. A further stage has been reached with the rapid development of the operations of multinational enterprises (MPEs) in recent years. Multinational enterprises are concerned with control over production rather than flows of direct investment, which represent only one of the many instruments available to implement their aims.[1] New overseas projects may be financed by an outflow of capital from the parent company or by retentions of profits by a subsidiary. But with increasing frequency they are financed also by drawing on local savings. The measure of the operations of a MPE, therefore, is the extent of the assets it controls. (Determinants of the proportions of equity and debt capital are not the concern of this chapter.)

The way in which a MPE exercises its control over overseas subsidiaries can have substantial effects on trade flows in addition to the traditional links associated with international investment flows. Multinational operation can involve international planning of production, of purchasing policies for materials and components and of marketing strategy in order that the enterprise operating as an entity is able to optimize its objective function. The extent of the control exercised by the management of the parent company and the amount of control retained by local management varies from one enterprise to another, and it often differs even between subsidiaries of the same enterprise. The degrees of centralization and integration of functions such as production, finance and marketing depend on many considerations, including the equity structures of subsidiaries, the bargaining power or boardroom skills of directors at different levels, the nature of the industry, the market situation of the subsidiaries and even the attitude of host countries' governments. To a greater or lesser extent all large multinationals are anxious to show good citizenship in all countries where they operate, which has some influence on management decisions. Nevertheless, the fact that decisions taken within multinational enterprise lead to international flows of materials, components, finished goods, production resources, technical knowhow, etc. means that the external economic positions of countries where these enterprises have operations are influenced and altered, both directly and indirectly.

Intuitively it is clear that decisions taken by MPEs involving allocations of resources in several countries must be influenced by the economic environment in different countries, which includes the

[1] C. P. Kindleberger, *American Investment Abroad*, New Haven, Yale University Press, 1969.

mixture of policies on trade, investment, taxation, employment, etc. adopted by national governments. More especially, perhaps, their interests concentrate on differences between national policies and ways in which these differences may be exploited. At the same time, of course, the decisions of multinational enterprises affect output, real incomes and their distribution in the countries where they operate.

Under these circumstances, some commentators consider a conflict between MPEs and national interests as inevitable, and in some cases already evident. Yet the economic consequences of the operation of multinational enterprises have received little analysis. This chapter surveys some of the evidence on the effects of multinational enterprises on trade flows, and discusses what the operations of multinational enterprises may mean for traditional trade policy measures.

## THE BALANCE OF PAYMENTS APPROACH

Until recently attention has been focused principally on the effects of foreign direct investment on a country's balance of payments, either as the investing country or as the recipient country. Perhaps the overriding concern with this aspect of the subject is a consequence of the external payments difficulties in recent years of the most important overseas investors, the United States and Britain. (These two countries also happen to be the only ones that publish detailed statistics on investments suitable for analysis!)

The usefulness and, indeed, the validity of isolating one section of a country's balance of payments for investigation appears questionable. The balance of payments represents the outcome from an aggregation of the net external effects from all types of internal and external transactions involving residents of the reporting country. It is not possible to isolate the external consequences for an economy of a particular item as its balance of payments. To say that certain changes would have occurred in the absence of a particular outflow or inflow of capital necessitates assumptions about the alternative position and the net effects on production, employment, prices, etc. – in fact, all economic variables. Moreover, national economies are interdependent through trade so that the consequences for other countries also have feed-back effects on the reporting country.

The net effect of a foreign investment flow on the balance of payments should be considered in the same way as the balance of payment effects of any other disturbance affecting economic equilibrium. This section discounts any 'loss' of community well-being associated with nationalistic feelings about the increase in foreign ownership or control of production. An inflow of foreign investment creates a flow of incomes in the future, which accrues to owners of domestic factors of production and to foreigners, in the same way as a stimulation of domestic output through lower taxes or increased government expenditure. The incomes generated lead to higher imports and, assuming sufficient unemployed resources are available in the recipient country, higher domestic output and employment too.

The magnitudes of these increments depend on the nature as well as the size of the initial changes. If the foreign investment simply replaced an investment that would have been undertaken by a resident firm anyway, then the increments in total output, employment, etc. depend on how the domestic funds it releases are utilized. If they are not employed elsewhere, a net increase in output only occurs in as far as the foreign investor achieves higher productivity than the domestic competitor would have shown, through better organization or superior production methods. If the released funds are invested elsewhere, there is a larger increase in the value of output, even though the return on the domestic investment would be less in this alternative use compared with the preferred use. If the foreign investment represents additional resources, then the whole value of output, employment, etc., represents an increment.

The foreign investment may also be a takeover of existing plant. In this case, as above, the outcome depends on how the released capital resources are employed and how much more efficient the foreign company proves to be.

The changes induced by the foreign investment inflow differ from a shift in a purely domestic variable only because the foreign investment brings a net addition to the recipient country's foreign exchange reserves, equivalent to the inflow of capital funds less any expenditure on imported capital equipment. Over time the flow of repatriated profits, fees, etc. to the parent company will affect the current account position too, but so will flows of imported inputs for production and exports from the foreign-owned plant. Whether the postulated change involves foreign investment or a domestic change affecting incomes, output, etc., it involves adjustments in economic policy if the original economic objectives are maintained. The net effects of either type of change for the balance of payments can be compensated by policy adjustments, even within the present system of fixed exchange rates and limited foreign exchange reserves.

Similarly, an outflow of investment has repercussions for domestic

172

incomes, employment, etc., over time. Assuming the outflow results in a reduction in investment at home, the initial effect is a decline in the flow of expected incomes; unless full employment existed already, in which case it would help to maintain an acceptable level of aggregate demand in the investing country, acting from a balance of payments point of view in the same way as a disinflationary policy of increased taxation or tighter credit. Future repatriations of profits, fees, etc., and export displacements or import increases resulting from the project, also affect future incomes. Again, adequate economic management can resolve the net balance of payments effects within the normal operation of the economic system.

The balance of payments is a residual and it cannot be treated as an end in itself. In so far as inward or outward investment affects the balance of payments, therefore, it must be interpreted within the framework of economic policy adjustments necessary to achieve basic objectives on employment, prices, economic growth, social equity in income distribution and so forth. It remains necessary, though, to determine the types of effect that can be expected to result from overseas investment flows and the operation of multinational enterprises. To operate effective national policies the impact of existing policies on decisions by MPEs and the impact of the growing presence of these organizations on the general environment needs to be understood. The interdependence of separate national policies in these circumstances must also be recognized.

## TRADE CONSIDERATIONS

Although balance of payments considerations have dominated much of the debate on national policies with regard to the impact of foreign investment by multinational enterprises, there are several more fundamental aspects of transnational operating that deserve attention.

In the first place, a MPE is concerned with the allocation of resources between different countries. In the case of a multi-product or a vertically integrated enterprise there is also the question of distributing resources among the different stages of production in order to optimize its objective function. International trade seeks to extend specialization in production by enlarging the sizes of markets and by widening the choices available to consumers. Under conditions of free trade, resources are employed such that the value of world output is maximized; this situation does not prevail in practice. When a MPE invests in an overseas plant and introduces new methods of organization and production, it affects the allocation of resources between countries in a variety of ways. In consequence, it also affects potential trade and the maximum value of world output under conditions of free trade. In assessing the implications for international trade flows of the operations of MPEs, therefore, it is necessary to employ an adequate analytical model of international trade and investment. Only if the model allows the types of change in resource allocations between countries that are affected by multinational enterprises can it help to explain their consequences for real output and consumption.

The situation is more complicated in practice because it is not possible to achieve a first best allocation of resources owing to distortion. Free trade does not exist. The many distortions that prevent the attainment of optimum welfare, even in the theoretical model, mean that only second-best solutions are possible.[1] Restrictions on trade and factor movements exist for natural reasons, such as geographical distance and non-tradeability, or for reasons of national economic policy. These interferences mean that the activities of MPEs may improve, or worsen, the allocations of available resources within or between some countries and achieve an increase, or decrease, in real outputs and incomes. But, because we are dealing with second-best solutions where resource allocations are subject to distortions, it is not possible to state with certainty whether the reallocations brought about by the activities of MPEs will raise or lower real outputs and incomes in a given situation. Equally the effects on trade among countries cannot be specified. Furthermore, trade policy and other aspects of national economic policy affect not only resource allocations within countries but also decisions made by MPEs about allocations between countries of resources under their control. In other words, the policies of MPEs are influenced by both the overall effect of national economic policies on the world-wide allocation of resources and the differences between these policies with regard to their own specific activities.

Little attention has been given to the effects of MPEs on international trade, or to the manner in which they take account of national economic policies. Basically, these are questions concerned with the effects of the operations of MPEs on the international allocation of resources. Is the MPE an instrument which extends the international division of labour?

[1] See, R. G. Lipsey and K. J. Lancaster, 'The General Theory of Second Best', *Review of Economic Studies*, 1956.

A THEORY OF TRADE AND INVESTMENT FOR A
CHANGING WORLD

The operations of MPEs cannot be examined or discussed within
the framework of a static theory of international trade. According
to conventional theory, differences in comparative costs between
countries are caused by differences in relative factor endowments,
which are fostered by social and cultural differences between
nations, and augmented by deliberate government policies. In
addition, differences in the relative economic sizes of national
markets create differential opportunities to exploit economies of
scale in certain industries. Comparative advantage founded on these
differences is maintained by the many natural and government-
designed barriers to trade, and the fundamental assumption that
factors of production are not free to move among countries.

MPEs seek to grow and earn profits by transferring the means of
production from one location to another. This requires a dynamic
theory of trade in which productive resources of all forms are mobile.
Several major contributions to a theory of trade for a changing world
have evolved in recent years from attempts to verify or extend the
scope of certain aspects of neo-classical theory. Harry Johnson has
attempted a synthesis of these contributions into a comprehensive
theory of comparative advantage in a changing world.[1]

Barriers to trade which emphasize comparative advantage among
countries provide the basis for a dynamic theory. Johnson specifies
three broad categories of trade barriers:

(a) the influence of geographic distance and the transport costs of
overcoming it;
(b) differences of political and legal systems, culture and language
which divide the world into separate national markets;
(c) the obstacles to international trade created by governments, such
as tariffs and other trade policy instruments, exchange rate policies,
taxation policies, etc.

These barriers create a *raison d'être* for MPEs. On the one hand,
barriers to trade promote the location of production in the country
where the market exists for the product. On the other hand, they
inhibit producers from transferring production from a high-cost
location to a lower-cost location in another country. MPEs seek to
take an advantage possessed in one country and to transfer it to

[1] H. G. Johnson, *Comparative Cost and Commercial Policy Theory for a Developing World Economy*, Wicksell Lectures, 1969.

THE MULTINATIONAL ENTERPRISE

other lower-cost locations by overcoming barriers to trade and barriers against movement of productive resources. In the case of backward vertical investments the motive is still to overcome trade barriers but of a rather different or potential kind. Uncertainty about supplies means producers feel it necessary to invest in the highly capital-intensive processing of raw materials which are often located in remote and poor countries.[1]

The differences which give rise to comparative advantage in the first place – natural endowments of various factor inputs, geographical location, etc., and acquired differences such as differences in the stock of physical capital, the stock of production and technical knowledge, skills embodied in labour, management, etc. – also provide the basis for change. A comparative advantage is vested in a nation's industry. Individual firms or groups of producers discover new types of product and new techniques of production to meet the needs of their insulated domestic markets. As income levels rise, consumption patterns become more capital-intensive and less time-intensive. New products are created to meet new wants; washing-machines, dish-washers and easily maintained furniture become available at prices consumers can pay. Labour resources become more expensive relative to capital as incomes rise and this stimulates industry to find less labour-intensive methods. Labour-saving machinery is developed; tractors and combine harvesters for extensive farming methods, fork-lift trucks and conveyor belts to facilitate in-plant movements of materials, components, etc. Past investments in the acquisition of highly specialized human knowledge can obviously facilitate the rate of innovation to meet new wants, which is again a reflection of the wealth of a country since education is an expensive process in terms of short-term opportunity costs.[2]

The strongest incentives to introduce new products and new techniques are felt in the largest and richest countries where new wants manifest themselves most obviously. This largely accounts for the technological lead of the United States in the past hundred years. But innovation is not the prerogative of the largest and richest. Each country's producers in responding to their own market situations may discover innovations that can be marketed in other countries. S. B. Linder[3] has observed that such innovations are

[1] See H. G. Johnson, *op. cit.*, and J. H. Dunning, Chapter 1.
[2] G. C. Hufbauer, *Synthetic Materials and the Theory of International Trade*, London, Duckworth, 1965.
[3] S. B. Linder, *An Essay in Trade and Transformation*, New York, Wiley, 1961.

most likely to be exported to countries with similar demand patterns, as represented by average income levels. Moreover, smaller countries cannot provide economies of scale from their own markets, so that these countries tend to specialize in internationally traded goods whereas larger countries can specialize in nationally differentiated products, because their large home markets give the opportunity to achieve low unit costs of output.

Once a competitive advantage is procured over local producers, or a new market has been created for an innovated product, it is possible for the innovator to gain further benefits by selling it abroad. In terms of Raymond Vernon's theory of the product cycle[1] the first stage of expansion into overseas markets is by means of exports. This has been referred to as 'technological gap' trade.[2] Because countries are at different stages of economic development, new markets are readily available to receive new products through the demonstration effect from richer countries. And more important perhaps for MPEs, the value of labour time differs between countries so that by shifting production towards lower-cost locations they may manufacture at lower costs and extend their markets further.

During the development stage the production of the innovated product is likely to remain within the market for which it was designed, according to Vernon. In the early stages, costs of production are probably relatively unimportant because of the monopoly position of the producer. Another reason for early immobility is that while commercial production is being developed the innovator needs close contacts with both customers and suppliers of components, machinery, etc., for as the product's market expands the methods of production employed and possibly the materials and components may be adapted and improved. When the product stabilizes into a standard form, production costs become more important as competing products are evolved and because expansion of sales is likely to depend on price reductions. It is at this stage that the innovator may look overseas for lower-cost locations and for new markets. This is particularly the case for American companies. Innovators from smaller, European countries may first look towards higher-cost locations in the large and rich United States' market in order to raise sales volume for a new product and thereby reduce unit costs.

In the classical and neo-classical theories of international trade,

---

[1] Raymond Vernon, 'International Investment and International Trade in the Product Cycle', *Quarterly Journal of Economics*, Vol. LXXX, May 1966.
[2] M. V. Posner, 'International Trade and Technical Change', *Oxford Economic Papers*, 1961; and G. C. Hufbauer, *op. cit.*

the innovatory advantage once acquired remains as a permanent source of exports to other countries; factors of production are not transferable between countries. In practice, however, production is eventually transferred from the country of innovation. It may occur only in the long run when the proprietary knowledge giving the advantage becomes generally available; for example, if a patent lapses, or if the commercial value of the knowledge disappears through competition or it is superseded. Competing firms at home and abroad may decide to invest resources in acquiring the knowledge to imitate the innovator.[1] This is likely to be expensive and some guarantee against the risk is probably required in the form of protection of the home market or the prospect of lower labour costs. Both these forms of transfer involve substantial time lags during which the gap will be filled by trade.

The role of MPEs in the transfer of production is expounded in Vernon's theory of the product cycle. In this case, the technology is retained under the control of the innovating firm. Its first option is to sell or lease the productive knowledge to overseas producers. In this way the innovating firm achieves additional income from its invention without having to bear the risks attached to producing and marketing in a foreign country, where it may be unfamiliar with the legal system and accepted business practices. Moreover, it avoids the uncertainty of whether a profitable volume of sales can be achieved. The disadvantage of this approach is that a competitive advantage is given up either permanently or temporarily. Even when a licence lapses the foreign licensee is usually aware of the necessary knowledge and he may even have so improved on the original that the innovator is at a competitive disadvantage. If the innovator considers his real advantage is in research and development rather than production and marketing, then, of course, lease or sale of proprietary knowledge may be the most profitable course to follow, since he expects to retain a technical lead over his rivals.[2]

The second option is to invest in an overseas subsidiary. When

[1] See Hufbauer and Posner references; *op. cit.*

[2] Technological lead depends on research and development effort, which in turn usually depends on sales and profit performance of an enterprise. The importance of R & D to United States trade and investment has been shown by W. Gruber, D. Mehta and R. Vernon, 'The R & D Factor in International Trade and International Investment of United States Industries', *The Journal of Political Economy*, Vol. LXXV, 1967. Also, J. H. Dunning, 'European and US Trade Patterns, US Foreign Investment and the Technological Gap', in C. P. Kindleberger and A. Shonfield (eds), *North American and Western European Economic Polices*, MacMillan, 1971

exports reach a sufficient level, the first concern is likely to be for support services, such as a distribution network and after-sales servicing. This may later extend to an assembly plant. If new capacity is required the decision may be taken to invest in an overseas plant close to major markets or potential markets. The decision may be encouraged by trends in competition at home or abroad. Lower production costs may be available abroad, both because factor inputs are less expensive and because additional economies of scale may be obtained by allocating production of components to different plants, permitting longer production runs. International programming of production of components and assembly plants can offer substantial economies of scale for some products.

In general, horizontal investment abroad can be justified for any unique asset or advantage possessed by an enterprise that differentiates it, or its product, from competitors. Typically multinational enterprises operate in oligopolistic market situations where product differentiation is characteristic.[1] Differentiation may be derived from the nature of the product, the methods employed in its production, or special attributes of the producing firm, such as marketing ability, management or research and development strength. Any attribute that differentiates its position on the home market may be exploited by a firm on foreign markets. In the first place this is likely to be by means of exports. Investment in overseas production will be undertaken only when the investor is convinced it is possible to earn higher profits than local competitors on that market; the differential must compensate for extra expenses and inconvenience of operating in an unfamiliar environment, and the greater risk that implies.

The mechanisms for the transfer of production, in which the multinational enterprise plays an important role, provide a basis for a dynamic theory of comparative cost. Technical improvements generated in response to rising living standards and changing relative costs of capital and labour yield initial comparative advantage which is lost by diffusion through the world economy in response to economic incentives provided by differences, ultimately, in relative costs of human labour time, themselves the result of international differences in capital accumulated per unit of labour time availability, and the immobility especially of labour.[2]

Thus, except for trade in primary commodities which depends

[1] See Chapter 1 and R. E. Caves, 'International Corporations; the Industrial Economics of Foreign Investment', *Economica*, Vol. 38, February 1971.
[2] H. G. Johnson, *op. cit.*, p. 37.

primarily on natural resource endowments, most trade depends on comparative advantage, that is, international differences. But comparative advantage is temporary and after a time it is likely to be eroded away. Multinational enterprises, therefore, may be able to contribute to general world welfare and to raise real incomes by accelerating the diffusion of more efficient processes of production and more advanced types of products. That is, they extend the international division of labour within the economic system in as far as they are able to overcome barriers to trade and factor movements.

## TRADE POLICY

One of the reasons for the development of comparative advantage in the manufacture of certain products among countries is difference in national economic policies. Taxation redistributes income within the community and government expenditure policies affect the nation's stock of physical capital and the level of human skills (embodied capital) according to the resources directed towards education and capital investment. Even the rate of increase in the labour force can be controlled through policies in migration and encouraging or discouraging large families. Similarly, barriers to trade and the movement of resources between nations prevent the diffusion of the benefits of technological or organizational advances across frontiers. One function of MPEs is to overcome these barriers as a means of furthering their own growth and profits. The question is whether by overcoming these barriers they are benefiting or harming the community at large.

Obviously it is not possible to consider all aspects of national economic policies. But since this survey is concerned with the effects of multinational enterprises on trade flows, national trade policies are immediately relevant. The interaction of their effects on problems of resource allocation has been mentioned already. Moreover, the adequacy and the impact of national trade policy within the broad context of national economic objectives is an aspect of the international economy in need of reconsideration, in view of the many changes that have occurred in the international economic environment in recent years.

Because it transcends national boundaries a MPE is able to treat national trade policy as internal to its operations and incorporate into its decision-structure any differences in trade policies between countries, or any changes in trade policy by a country. A fully integrated MPE can then locate production or assembly plants, or

180

component and material supplier, in a way that minimizes the cost impositions of these policies on its overall operation, within the limits imposed by other parameters. It can also divide markets so that the effects on profits are minimized too. One device that can be employed is adjustments in internal transfer prices, which permits the enterprise to determine profits at different stages of production and, therefore, to decide in which country the profits shall be taken. If integrated enterprises adopt this device it affects the value of goods transferred between subsidiaries in different countries, which appear in the balance of payments accounts of those countries.

In reaching decisions using this additional information on trade policies, it is possible that a MPE may even be able to exploit differences between national trade policies to earn additional profits or a margin of advantage over its competitors. For example, a decision may be taken to introduce modern capital equipment into one subsidiary in order to manufacture components at low cost in a country with low-wage rates. These cheap components may then be imported by another subsidiary into a high-wage economy, which has a high tariff on finished goods but which has a much lower tariff on imports of components. The components could be assembled in the second country and the finished products sold with high profits behind the protective tariff wall. It may even be profitable to assemble all completed units in the high-tariff country and export assembled units back to the first country, especially, say, if there are economies of scale in assembly or comparatively low tariffs are levied on finished goods. In this case, the tariff structures would result in a two-way flow of trade and it would have substantial effects on production and consumption of the products of this MPE in both countries. Clearly more complex situations along the same lines could be devised, and doubtless exist.

Whereas as in this simple example a MPE is able to exploit differences in tariff structures, the purely national company has to submit to the effects of trade policy. A company in the low-wage economy faces a high-tariff wall when exporting to the high-wage economy, while in the reverse case a competing company in the high-wage economy would be unable to export at a competitive price to the first country (*ceteris paribus*). In this hypothetical case, a MPE with careful planning could sell in both markets competitively. If the main impact of trade policy is likely to be felt by national companies relying on exports for overseas sales, this must bring into question whether this frustrates the achievement of the objectives for which the trade policy is designed.

The theoretical basis for the trade policy measures adopted by a particular country must be sought in terms of optimizing some kind of collective preference function for the community. Harry Johnson has developed a theory for the selection of a trade policy in terms of an elementary economic theory of democracy.[1] This theory accepts the relevance of non-economic objectives, such as nationalist aspirations, in the collective preference function that trade policy is intended to optimize. In most cases, trade policy is probably directed towards achieving a higher volume of industrial production and employment than would be the case without an active commercial policy; that is, it is a problem of resource allocation. There is a wide variety of measures available to governments in the field of trade policy, notwithstanding the constraints imposed by international agreements, such as the GATT and the IMF. In developed countries, import tariffs, export subsidies, quotas, discriminatory taxes and other devices are employed primarily to protect the interests of domestic producers against foreign competition.[2] (An even greater variety of restrictions and incentives are applied to agricultural production and trade, but we are concerned predominantly with manufactures.)

In practice, a particular trade policy represents a compromise between many internal and external pressures, past and present. They often represent the amount of political leverage a group of producers has been able to exert at different times on the policy-making authority in a country. If the resultant policy fabric appears to make little economic sense on examination, it is extremely doubtful whether it would ever be possible to demonstrate this adequately for such a complex structure. Often trade measures continue in effect long after the reasons for them have vanished. Furthermore, the process of tariff bargaining that has been used in GATT to obtain more liberal conditions for industrial trade in the last twenty years has probably created many additional inconsistencies in national tariff structures.

Instruments of trade policy may be used intentionally to attract foreign investment, or they may be introduced for other reasons yet have unintended consequences for trade flows and investment

[1] H. G. Johnson, 'An Economic Theory of Protectionism, Tariff Bargaining, and the Formation of Customs Unions', *Journal of Political Economy*, Vol. LXXIII, 1965.

[2] In some less-developed countries import duties may be used as the most efficient way to collect taxes, with less emphasis on the protective element; for example, taxed products may not be produced locally.

decisions through the activities of MPEs. Some effects of trade policies can be specified.

The opportunities afforded to MPEs by differences in tariff structures have already been discussed in a hypothetical example. Many examples exist of MPEs shifting manufacturing plant to take advantage of such opportunities. When Japanese producers of transistor radios were forced to accept 'voluntary' quotas on their imports into the United States, several companies established assembly plants in Hong Kong or Taiwan where such restrictions did not exist. The effect was a substantial increase in trade flows. Components were exported to Hong Kong, assembled – using cheap but efficient labour – and then exported to the United States. Imports of transistors into the United States increased although imports direct from Japan were held constant or may have declined. In addition, exports were created between Japan and Hong Kong, and some trade in the reverse direction probably developed as a secondary effect too in order to enable Hong Kong to pay for the imports of components. As a tertiary effect, transistors assembled in Hong Kong may have found new outlets in other countries because of the trade Hong Kong merchants already had with countries where Japanese firms may have been unable to sell their products. The overall effect is a very substantial increase in trade flows following an investment of possibly modest resources.[1]

Changes in tariffs may also have important effects on the activities of multinational enterprises. Experience in EEC offers some support for the view that tariff protection may be exploited effectively by outsiders if they establish subsidiaries behind the tariff wall. When the Treaty of Rome was adopted in 1957, it was evident that the implementation of the common external tariff would discriminate against exports of third countries and in favour of competing producers in the member countries. Thus, the profitability of exporting to EEC from the United States would be reduced, for instance, while the returns to be expected from direct investments in production plants within EEC would become relatively more profitable. Following the inauguration of EEC there was a substantial increase in the absolute value and in the relative share

---

[1] Similar developments occurred when textiles and clothing imports from Japan, Hong Kong, etc. faced 'voluntary' quota restrictions in developed countries' markets; new materials were employed such as woollens or synthetics to by-pass the controls; this resulted in a continuation of exports of a slightly different product; but also an increase in trade owing to the need to import wool and synthetic yarns.

of United States direct foreign investment going to the six member countries. The observed increase, however, cannot be attributed entirely to the tariff adjustments. Studies by Balassa[1] and Krause[2] show that although the common external tariff appears to have had some influence on decisions by American corporations to invest in EEC, many other factors are involved. These two studies, and various others cited therein, found tariffs less important than other developments arising from the implementation of the Treaty of Rome; namely, expectations of rapid economic growth in EEC and the prospect of potential cost savings from large scale production as a result of the removal of national trade barriers. In addition, they established that other considerations, such as comparative rates of return on investments in the same industries in EEC and the United States and fewer uncertainties associated with larger markets, were equally significant. Thus it was the broader economic effects of EEC and the general psychological impact of the publicity given to economic integration in Western Europe on American businessmen that made companies more aware of the opportunities in European markets. Nevertheless, the creation of the common market benefited outsiders as well as producers in the member countries, so that the discriminatory effect in favour of producers within the Common Market was turned to the advantage of outsiders by means of direct investments.[3]

The inflow of American direct investment into EEC has been greeted with mixed feelings and considerable ambivalence. But in other parts of the world, tariffs have been used to attract foreign investors. In some less-developed countries the potential size of the domestic market does not warrant a MPE to construct a plant. Governments committed to development using import substitution policies, though, are prepared to offer incentives to attract investments by international giants, including tax concessions, subsidized factories, and a guaranteed home market by introducing tariffs or quotas. At some stage these less-developed countries may even offer export incentives to these same enterprises to export. In some less-developed countries the strong competition among leading world producers led several of them to invest in uneconomic plants in

[1] Bela Balassa, *Trade Liberalisation Among Industrial Countries*, London, McGraw-Hill, 1967, Chapter VI.

[2] L. B. Krause, *European Economic Integration and the United States*, Brookings Institute, Washington, 1968, Chapter IV.

[3] R. D'Arge, 'Note on Customs Unions and Direct Foreign Investment', *Economic Journal*, Vol. LXXIX, June 1969; this study gives formal statistical support for this conclusion.

order not to lose potential future markets; this occurred in the motor-car industry in Argentina and Brazil. Under these circumstances trade policy had been used actively to encourage foreign investment.

The reverse effect is achieved by *the provision for United States goods returned.* This provision in the United States Tariff Schedules[1] states that articles assembled abroad using components made in the United States when imported into the United States shall only be charged duty on the value added abroad; that is the f.o.b. import value less the value of United States components. In a country with high-wage labour this is a clear incentive for large companies to invest in overseas assembly plants where low-wage but efficient labour is available in ample supply. Such plants have been established, or the work contracted out to foreign companies, in Japan, Taiwan and Mexico, for products such as transistor radios, electrical equipment, chocolate bars, motor-car components and various types of clothing. Whether this is profitable or not depends on the differential in the value of the labour-content in the process between the United States and the foreign country, less the additional transport costs, etc. To be profitable it requires a high volume of production. Nevertheless, the provision encourages enterprises to operate certain types of plant in foreign countries and to become multinational in their operations. It generates trade flows between the United States and other countries. It encourages international specialization according to the labour-intensity of a process rather than by product. The consumer in the United States benefits from lower priced goods. Economic development is advanced in the countries where the assembly is undertaken. And if labour for the assembly line is scarce in the United States it has no adverse effect on real incomes or employment there.

These represent some of the ways in which differences in national trade policies or changes in trade policy can affect the operations of MPEs and trade flows. The examples given are not intended to be comprehensive and, as mentioned above, trade policy has a complex structure which no doubt hides many subtle influences on trade and investments. These examples show, however, the way in which trade policy can influence the operations of MPEs. They also indicate the way in which the investment and production policies they adopt affect international trade flows. What cannot be established from their evidence is whether MPEs in taking acount of trade policy are serving the interests of more efficient production and higher real

[1] Tariff Schedules of the United States items 806.30 and 87.00.

incomes, or whether their actions, in as far as they frustrate national economic objectives by by-passing the chosen policy instruments, are against the interests of some or all countries.

One thing is, however, clear. Trade policy and the operations of MPEs are interdependent over areas of mutual interest because both are concerned with resource allocations. The one cannot be determined without reference to the other. Whereas MPEs appear to take account of trade policies in reaching their decisions on investment, production programmes, supply arrangements of different inputs, distribution policies, etc., there is little evidence that national authorities have considered how MPEs influence the efficacy of different trade measures, or the overall efficiency of an existing trade policy structure.

## THE NATURE OF TRADE EFFECTS

The specific effects on merchandise trade flows of the operations of MPEs are complex. Discussion is usually restricted to the effects caused by foreign direct investments. Yet not all overseas direct investment is undertaken by MPEs, neither is all the foreign investment undertaken by multinationals recorded as international flows. The latter is probably the more serious qualification because local savings are being increasingly employed by multinationals, whereas the proportion of total foreign direct investments not undertaken by companies with transnational activities is quite small. Other decisions by MPEs have a bearing on trade flows too, such as production programming on an international scale and the allocation of export markets among particular subsidiaries. No attempt has been made to measure these less quantifiable influences, as the trade effects discussed in this survey are restricted to those derived from investments by MPEs.

Direct investment flows concerned with manufacturing are of principal interest because the expansion of the activities of MPEs in this area has had most influence on trade patterns. Investment in the production of primary products and raw materials is less relevant to the present interest.[1] Although such investments may be important for vertical integration within the large company and in some cases they may cause changes in trade flows, especially substitutions between sources, they are not greatly affected by considerations of trade policy; most advanced industrial countries have low

[1] For a full discussion of different types of overseas investments by multinational enterprises, see Chapter 1 in this volume.

or zero tariffs and few other restrictions on raw material imports.

Following the formal theoretical sequence of investment decisions for an enterprise's overseas expansion, set out by Vernon and described in a previous section, it is evident that effects on trade flows vary in intensity according to the nature of the product and the form of the investment; for example, whether a complete production plant is established or only a sales and servicing organization to promote export sales. It is possible, however, to specify certain general trade effects that can be associated with overseas direct investments.

*Export generating effects* result from additional sales of finished goods, components, raw materials or capital equipment from the investing country. These may be direct exports from the parent or other subsidiaries. They may also be indirect exports from other suppliers in the investing country to the new subsidiary, resulting from established links fostered by the parent company. After a time lag similar exports may arise as competitors in the foreign market learn of superior or cheaper techniques, components, machines or materials which they decide to adopt.

*Import generation* results if the foreign subsidiary begins to export components or finished products back to the market of the parent company. Increases of imports into the investing country in this manner are in accordance with the product cycle theory. There are several reasons why such trade flows may occur. It may be a management decision to specialize production in plants in several countries which would involve flows of materials, components and finished goods between countries. Or, lower labour costs or other factor inputs may enable the subsidiary to manufacture at lower costs once a particular scale of output has been achieved. These reasons may be present together in such trade flows. If a company is interested in maximizing its profits internationally it is rational that it should place its sources of supply in the most efficient locations and programme its production in such a way as to obtain all cost reductions available from economies of scale and from minimizing transport costs, tax payments, tariffs, etc.

*Export displacement effects* result if output from an overseas subsidiary replaces exports from the parent company's factories, or exports from a competitor in the investing country, or exports from another affiliated company, either in the local market or in a third country market. Such changes do not increase international trade flows necessarily, but by affecting the pattern of trade there are, of course, further induced effects on national income levels and trade flows.

187

These three effects – export generating, import generating and export displacement – constitute what one might call a net trade balance effect for the investing country. The net trade balance effect together with other income remittances, from profits, licence fees, royalties, service charges, etc. represent the flow of incomes to the investing country resulting from the initial investment decision.

For the recipient country, the net trade balance effect is composed of the same effects, but they are reversed. Imports are generated by the capital inflow to provide necessary materials and components; these may be supplied by the parent company or other affiliates, or suppliers with whom the parent has close association or from independent producers in third countries. In addition, the presence of the local plant may attract to the market imports of other finished products from the parent company and affiliates. Local production also replaces purchases of similar products previously imported. And if the new plant also exports its output, either back to the country of the parent company or to third country markets, new exports are generated for the recipient country. On the other side of the ledger, the local subsidiary would have to make various external payments profits, licence fees, service charges, etc., to the parent and dividends to other foreign creditors.

Having established the three types of trade effects of international investment flows – export generating, imports generating and export/import displacement – it must be pointed out that these are direct trade effects.[1] These changes in trade flows also alter income levels in the countries involved which induce further changes in trade flows according to the multiplier; changes that eventually dissipate themselves throughout all international trade. (This reverts back to the basic problem of balance of payments effects of foreign investment flows.)

Measuring even the direct trade effects of foreign investment flows is very difficult, and the multiplier effects have so far received little attention.[2] One basic problem of measurement concerns time. When an investment decision is taken several time lags influence developments. If the investment is to create new plant there is a delay before production commences; and a further delay before

---

[1] The system of valuation may distort the effects. Intra-firm transfers may not be made at arm's-length prices, if another system of valuation could benefit the company can obtain some advantage in terms of lower taxes or as a means of transferring liquid funds between countries; the issue of transfer pricing.

[2] The multiplier effects are examined rather unsuccessfully in the Hufbauer-Adler Report; see below.

full-capacity output is achieved. Furthermore, even if the parent company has been exporting to the local market it is likely to take some time before sales in the local market can be expanded to absorb a substantial proportion of potential output from the new plant. Similarly, breaking into overseas markets with exports only occurs after a time lag. All these lags in developing markets also influence imports of materials and components, and up to a point even imports of capital equipment will be affected by output requirements.

## EMPIRICAL EVIDENCE

The only evidence available on the effects of MPEs on international allocation of resources and trade flows is restricted to empirical studies on the effects of overseas investment flows on particular countries balances of payments. The two most detailed studies of the effects of direct overseas investment are the Hufbauer–Adler Report[1] for the United States and the Reddaway Report[2] for the United Kingdom. Work on the effects of inward investment has been done by Safarian[3] for Canada, Brash[4] for Australia and Dunning[5] for the United Kingdom. Although these studies provide useful indications of the trade effects of direct overseas investment, even they do not show the full impact on trade flows. They are concerned with the bilateral effects of direct investment flows between the investing country and the recipient; exports of capital equipment, components and parts and finished products from the former to support the investment project, and the reverse flow of imports of finished goods from the new overseas plant to the investing country. In order to understand the full trade effects of an investment flow, it is necessary also to examine the consequences for third countries; the extent to which their exports of finished products and components to the investment-receiving country might be curtailed or increased by the construction in a new plant; or the extent to which imports into the recipient country of materials and components might be

[1] G. C. Hufbauer and F. M. Adler, *Overseas Manufacturing Investment and the Balance of Payments*, Tax Policy Research Study No. 1, US Treasury Dept.

[2] W. B. Reddaway (Director), *Effects of UK Direct Investment Overseas: Final Report*, Department of Applied Economics, Cambridge University.

[3] A. E. Safarian, *The Performance of Foreign-owned Firms in Canada*, Canadian-American Committee, Washington and Montreal, 1969.

[4] D. T. Brash, *American Investment in Australian Industry*, Australian National University Press, Canberra, 1966.

[5] J. H. Dunning, *The Role of American Investment in the British Economy*, PEP Broadsheet No. 507, February 1969.

increased; or the impact of exports from the new plant on other countries exports to third markets or the investing country.

The Hufbauer–Adler and Reddaway reports show that the results of such studies are highly dependent on the specific assumptions adopted. Comparisons between the results of these studies are difficult because of the different assumptions, the different basic approaches to the empirical investigations (the Reddaway report relying principally on information collected from firms while the Hufbauer–Adler study used published statistics), and differences in the time-periods covered.

Studies of this kind are concerned with comparing what actually happened with what might have happened in alternative circumstances. It is necessary, therefore, to make an assumption about the alternative position. The Reddaway report works from a reverse classical assumption that a given foreign investment substitutes for investment in the host country without decreasing the capital formation in the investing country. Another possibility is a classical assumption which postulates that a given foreign investment causes a net addition to capital formation in the host country but an equal decline in capital formation in the investing country. Both these involve no change in total capital formation for the world as a whole. The third alternative is the anti-classical assumption that foreign investment leads to an increase in capital formation abroad without reducing capital investment in the investing country. The Hufbauer–Adler report investigates all three alternatives.

For practical purposes the best alternative will depend on other assumptions. For example, if full employment exists in the host country an inflow of foreign investment must substitute for local investment (anti-classical assumption or reverse classical) or equilibrium in that economy will be disturbed, bringing structural changes. Which of these two assumptions is most suitable will then depend on the position in the investing country. If full employment equilibrium is maintained there, then an anti-classical assumption is most suitable. A reverse classical assumption would disturb the investment-saving relationship in the investing country. If the full-employment assumption is released, of course, then an increase in capital formation in the recipient country would stimulate economic growth through the multiplier. This latter possibility is not followed in either the Hufbauer–Adler or Reddaway studies.[1]

[1] For a fuller discussion of the different implications of the altnernative assumptions, see a review of the two reports by J. H. Dunning, 'The Foreign Investment Controversy' in *Bankers' Magazine*, May and June 1969.

The concern in this chapter is to examine the trade effects revealed by these studies without going into their full conclusions. For this reason the results following the reverse classical assumption are used for direct comparison of the two reports. Two types of trade effect can be distinguished: the initial effect, which will not be repeated, and the continuing effect over time once the investment has been implemented. In discussing the estimates from these studies it must be understood that the figures refer to average global figures and that wide differences exist between the results for particular industries and particular countries. Details about the range of results given in each study can be obtained in the references given below.

The initial effect is concerned principally with the exportation of suitable plant and machinery for the investment project from the investing country. For Britain this was estimated at an average of 11 % of the value of the overseas direct investment in manufacturing. Wide variations were revealed between industries; estimates as high as 21 % were found for the vehicle industry compared with 1 % for the paper industry.[1] An important consideration, of course, is the suitability and availability of the right kind of equipment in different countries. Higher estimates of the initial effect were made for the United States in the Hufbauer–Adler report, an average estimate of 27 % of the value of overseas direct investment in manufacturing. Account must be taken, though, of the potential exports of plant and equipment to independent foreign producers. Hufbauer and Adler show that the United States is a much more important supplier of machinery to world markets than Britain. They go on to show that the direct effects on British exports of capital equipment are more favourable than for the United States;[2] that is, if the investment were made by a non-British company, very little equipment would be likely to be purchased from Britain. On the other hand, the high level of American exports of capital equipment probably includes an indirect benefit from the size of American overseas investment through a 'demonstration effect'. Facing competition from American overseas subsidiaries, local companies may be forced to buy American equipment if it is more efficient.

In addition to the once-for-all effect of initially equipping a new plant, there are continuing trade effects. Established overseas subsidiaries may continue to import components and parts from the parent company, or from independent suppliers in the investing

[1] Reddaway, op. cit., Table XIV 1, p. 374.
[2] Hufbauer–Adler, op. cit., Appendix B.

191

country. Again the estimated purchases of input items from Britain by British overseas manufacturing subsidiaries were lower than for American companies; 3·2% of total subsidiary sales compared with 4·2% for the United States.[1] Yet, as in connection with exports of capital equipment, British exports appear to be more favourably influenced by direct overseas investment than American exports, because United States industry is a more important supplier of these items anyway to independent foreign companies.

Establishing an overseas subsidiary can affect existing production patterns in the investing enterprise in a variety of ways too. A foreign assembly or production plant may stimulate exports of finished products or components from the parent company. In the former case the goods of the parent company become identified with the local branch, and there is probably an improvement in sales effort and servicing. If components or semi-manufactures are available from the parent company (or another subsidiary for that matter) there is a profit incentive for the vertically integrated international company to buy through its own facilities, thereby retaining the profit element in the cost of components, as well as the obvious advantages of direct control over stocks, quality, etc.

Evidence on the expansion of exports in this way is incomplete. The Reddaway report[2] found that purchases of goods from Britain for resale by overseas subsidiaries represented around 6% of their total sales; possibly 10% if transport costs are added. A large proportion of these purchases for resale were reported as being from the parent group. What was also clear, however, was that the importance of this business declined over the period of the study, 1955–64. The Hufbauer–Adler study found a similar proportion for 'associated exports', 4·5% of subsidiary sales.[3] A later survey by the Office of Business Economics suggested a somewhat higher figure of 5·3% in 1965. In that year $4·5 billion of exports by American parent companies were channelled through foreign affiliates, and $2·5 billion consisted of goods exported and sold without further processing. On the other hand, the same group of international companies covered in this survey also exported $4 billion to independent purchasers. The total of $8·5 billion exported by these companies represented one-third of total United States merchandise exports; 45% of non-agricultural merchandise exports.

Assigning the importance of overseas direct investment to these

[1] Reddaway, *op. cit.*, Table VI 2, p. 365; Hufbauer–Adler, *op. cit.*, Table 3.7.
[2] Reddaway, *op. cit.*, p. 367 and Interim Report.
[3] Hufbauer–Adler, *op. cit.*, p. 30.

exports of finished goods is a difficult task. Given the large volumes of exports by the parent companies to non-affiliated buyers, it is likely that a substantial share of these exports would have taken place anyway, without the investment flow. That is, they could be marketed through normal marketing channels. Hence, by no means all these exports could be considered as a trade effect of the investment flows. It is questionable, too, how long such exports will continue. In many cases they may be used to 'fill a gap' until local production is expanded to cover the full range of products marketed by the company. When a suitable market has been created locally by means of imports from the parent local manufacture will be initiated.

Parent company exports are also displaced by overseas production. The extent to which this occurs depends largely on the assumptions about the alternative position. Following the reverse classical assumption, overseas direct investment causes little export displacement because in the absence of the investment flow from one country a competitor, either local or from another country, would have made a similar decision and displaced the exports of the first country. Supporters of foreign investment as competing with exports adopt a classical assumption; that the investment flow creates capital plant in a country where it would never have existed while it deprives the investing country of that investment. The Hufbauer–Adler report after some complex regression analysis concludes, under a reverse classical thesis, that increased output by an overseas subsidiary causes the output of local competing firms to be reduced.[1] Reddaway, on the same assumption, asserts that displacement of British exports of finished goods by overseas direct investment would be small; around $2\frac{1}{2}\%$ per additional £100 of operating assets. Export displacement appears to be greater for Britain, however, than the United States, and it greatly reduces the net effects on continuing exports.[2] The explanation given for this is that British production abroad frequently involves models and brands identical to those exported from Britain.

Following direct overseas investment it is possible also that the new subsidiary may be able to export is output back to the investing country. Given that investment in overseas manufacturing plant may be stimulated by relative cost advantages, it is distinctly possible that the subsidiary's output of finished goods or components may be imported. The Reddaway Report 'found virtually no trace . . . of

---

[1] Hufbauer–Adler, *op. cit.*, pp. 33–43.

[2] Reddaway, *op. cit.*, p. 299; and Interim Report, p. 110.

imports into the UK of manufactured goods produced by overseas subsidiaries.[1] The Hufbauer–Adler report, on the other hand, found substantial effects: 4·3% of sales by subsidiaries. The explanation of this probably rests with the size and value of the American market, which has encouraged investment in lower-wage countries where American techniques are used to produce at low cost for export throughout the world. For Britain, imports from subsidiaries are mainly materials which would have had to be imported anyway.

Countries receiving an investment inflow experience additional trade effects. Apart from trade flows generated by the close association with the country of the parent company, there are also likely to be new trade flows created with third countries. In the first place there may be imports of capital equipment from third countries if the items required are not available in the host country or from the country of the parent, or if suitable equipment is only available at higher delivered prices. More significant, however, may be the continuing effects on trade with third countries. Imports of materials or components from independent suppliers may be essential inputs for the manufacturing process, or the finished products may substitute for some items previously imported from third countries. Similarly, exported output may create new trade or displace exports from competitors in third countries, or from an affiliated company, if lower production costs, lower transport costs or preferential trading arrangements, such as the European Economic Community, enable the subsidiary to penetrate new markets.

For an integrated MPE new trade flows may evolve directly from policy decisions. International programming of production to obtain maximum economies of scale from long production runs may lead to substantial movements of component, semi-processed goods and finished goods between manufacturing and assembly centres and markets. Equally, if particular markets are allocated to specific subsidiaries, the potential trade flows may be curtailed, although if profit maximization is the assumed objective for the company as a whole this is only likely in the short-run.

It is difficult to arrive at reasonable estimates of these potential trade flows. Figures for 'associated exports' in the Reddaway and Hufbauer–Adler reports do not cover intra-company transfers between overseas subsidiaries. They are concerned only with transactions with the parent company. A Board of Trade survey[2] has

[1] Reddaway, op. cit., p. 345.
[2] Board of Trade Journal, August 16, 1968.

estimated that in 1966 around 22% of Britain's merchandise exports were accounted for by transactions between related concerns. Out of this total, approximately 12% were exports by British-owned companies to their overseas affiliates. Of the remaining 10% which were controlled from outside Britain, 7% was from American-owned companies. Unfortunately, the survey does not indicate the proportion of those intra-company transfers[1] that are for resale by the affiliates, which may be high as they include selling organizations; neither does it show what proportion is for further processing. Wide variations in the values of those transfers were indicated between different industries. Exports by the motor vehicles industry to affiliates were particularly important, representing one-third of the total value of those related exports and more than half of total motor vehicle exports from Britain; the proportion for subsidiaries of American companies was 80%, compared with 37% for exports of British companies to overseas affiliates. Other industries showing a high proportion of exports to affiliates included chemicals and electrical engineering.

More detailed figures are available for exports from United States parent companies to overseas affiliates in a survey by the Office of Business Economics of the US Department of Commerce.[2] The basic figures from this study were mentioned earlier (see page 192 above). A somewhat smaller proportion of total American exports than Britain's exports went to overseas affiliates in 1965; around 17%. (Figures are not available, though, for exports of companies controlled by non-residents of the United States. These are probably small but would raise the total figure closer to the British estimate.) Out of these intra-company transfers, just over half were finished goods for resale and the remainder were for further processing. Variations between industries were again significant. Approximately 68% of exports of motor vehicles were channelled through foreign affiliates; around 55% were exports for further processing. Other industries showing a high proportion of exports to foreign affiliates included chemicals, rubber products, non-electrical machinery and professional and scientific instruments.

These estimates indicate the importance of intra-company transfers across frontiers, and these flows have probably increased greatly since these surveys were carried out. It must be recognized, of

[1] The article does not consider the valuations placed on these intra-firm shipments and it accepts the declarations.

[2] Marie T. Bradshaw, 'US Exports to Foreign Affiliates of US Firms', *Survey of Current Business*, May 1969.

course, that in the absence of MPEs a substantial proportion of this trade would have occurred between independent companies in those countries, simply on a basis of relative cost differences. Hence, the whole of this trade cannot be treated simply as an effect of the operation of the multinationals.

Some investment receiving countries have become worried about the effects on their economies of the performances of foreign-owned firms; that is, whether foreign ownership inhibits exports and stimulates excessive imports. Safarian found that there was little evidence to suggest this was true for Canada.[1] American-owned enterprises in Canada exported around 20% of their output in 1965, about the same proportion as for American subsidiaries in Europe. This represented 48% of manufactured exports from Canada in that year, while residents of the United States controlled 46% of capital invested in Canadian manufacturing investment. Safarian found, too, that there was no tendency for firms to export less as the number of overseas affiliates increased. Some foreign-owned subsidiaries exported through their parent company's sales organization. In many cases this assisted exports, but in a few cases, where markets were allocated among the affiliates, some limitation might occur; usually, however, relative production costs were thought to be the major constraint on exports. Imports into Canada by foreign-owned subsidiaries were found to be smaller in value than their exports. The proportion of imported inputs used by these firms varied widely from one industry to another; the impact of the Canadian–American Automotive agreement is mentioned specifically. In general, Safarian found that subsidiaries established abroad commenced as partial alternatives to imports, but it was a common experience that once a subsidiary became established it tended to raise the domestic content of production. This was supported by evidence that, of the firms under foreign control, the largest firms had the lowest import content in their production. Statistical investigation showed that foreign-owned subsidiaries in Canada were more import-oriented than purely domestically controlled firms; in part Safarian considered this was due to Canadian tariffs, and for the remainder it reflected the opportunities for improved specialization within the MPE.

Australian experience indicates a much smaller share for exports of manufactures for American-owned companies than in Canada or Britain. Brash[2] considers this not surprising because many direct

[1] Safarian, *op. cit.*, Chapter 4.
[2] Brash, *op. cit.*, pp. 203–40.

investments in manufacturing in Australia were made to get behind high-tariff barriers. The need for the tariff indicates that the industries are not competitive by world standards; a view supported by the statements from export companies that Australian production costs are high. In general, Brash arrives at the same conclusions as Safarian. Foreign affiliation often aids the export activities of subsidiary companies and, although market allocation by the parent company may limit exports, the main consideration in exports appears to be the inability of the Australian subsidiary to compete abroad. The import content of production by American-owned subsidiaries in Australia has declined in recent years under the influence of tariff policy.

## IMPLICATIONS FOR TRADE POLICY

A review of recent investigations into the effects of foreign direct investment yields some guidance as to the magnitude of the changes in merchandise trade flows that result from the rapidly expanding activities of MPEs. But this is only part of the picture. No measurement has so far been attempted of the consequences of overseas direct investment for the trade of third countries, although these effects could cause significant changes in trade patterns. Similarly, feed-back effects through the various multipliers have received only cursory treatment. Furthermore, it must be emphasized that investment is only one aspect of the activities of the MPE that affects trade flows. The location of production plants, the planning of output and the allocation of specified markets to subsidiaries must also alter trade patterns.

Even the evidence gleaned from studies not intended specifically to measure trade effects, however, indicates the powerful influence that the activities of MPEs can have on trade flows. United States overseas direct investment represents around two-thirds of the total overseas investment stake; at the end of 1968, this was valued at $65 billion.[1] Hence, figures relating to United States output and exports may be used to provide a crude estimate of the relationships for all overseas investments. For 1965, it was estimated that exports accounted for over 18% of total sales by foreign manufacturing affiliates of United States companies;[2] this export/sales ratio was

[1] D. T. Devlin and F. Cutler, 'The International Investment Position of the United States; Developments in 1968', *Survey of Current Business*, October 1969.
[2] Safarian, *op. cit.*, p. 25; derived from *Survey of Current Business*, November 1966.

higher for Europe (23·5%) and Canada (19%) than for less-developed countries; there were also wide variations in this ratio between different industries. In addition, it has been established that in the same year around 17% of total United States merchandise exports (and more than a quarter of manufactured exports) were directed through foreign affiliates.[1] Unfortunately, similar figures are not available for other countries. The importance of the operations of the multinationals, however, can be illustrated by Dunning's estimate that, by 1981, 25% of British exports will be controlled by American companies.[2] He also shows that American subsidiaries in Britain tend to export a higher proportion of their output than competing domestic companies, which corroborates the conclusions drawn by Safarian and Brash (see previous section). This suggests a general interpretation that multinational companies are more interested in international trade than national companies, although this may also be a function of size.

Some commentators conclude from such estimates that the influence that foreign-controlled companies can exert on a country's trade balance through their subsidiaries can be harmful to the interests of the host country, and they often recommend that government supervision is necessary. There appear to be two origins to this line of argument. First, the common nationalistic approach to international transactions. Fortunately, this is under attack from several quarters, yet it persists in attitudes towards trade in spite of the rapid extension of international co-operation in the economic sphere. Second, a misunderstanding of the underlying economic model within which the activities of MPEs should be considered. Too often because MPEs cannot be comprehended within the static neo-classical theory of international trade, their activities are condemned as necessarily being contrary to the interests of the community.

The problem of nationalism extends far beyond the present area of discussion. Johnson and others have indicated how nationalistic goals can be included in an assessment of trade policy, but at an economic cost. Some aspects of the activities of MPEs are principally political, however, and fall outside the economic field altogether. Problems of extra-territorality, for example, are clearly a political issue. In this case, policy decisions made by one national govern-

[1] M. T. Bradshaw, 'US Exports to Foreign Affiliates of US Firms', *Survey of Current Business*, May 1969.

[2] J. H. Dunning, *The Role of American Investment in the British Economy*, PEP Broadsheet, 1969.

ment may be insidiously imposed on another country through the commercial links between a parent and its overseas subsidiaries.[1]

Within the context of trade and investment flows, however, critics of the development of MPEs are prepared to accept the national benefits derived from the operations of foreign-owned subsidiaries; the financial aspect of a capital inflow, the extra employment and incomes generated within the country, the availability of superior technology and management, the increased exports for the trade balance, and so forth. Offsetting increases in imports of materials and components, and remission of profits, fees, dividends, etc. to the parent company are reluctantly accepted. National rivalry really comes to the forefront, though, in connection with the allocation of a new investment or a division of overseas markets between different national subsidiaries of a MPE. Then the claim is that a national company would have acted differently. It would have expanded its production at home, or it would have successfully penetrated an overseas market with exports, regardless of competition. The implication is that the foreign-owned subsidiary has in some way acted against the national interest; some kind of 'loss' is involved.

Much of this discussion proceeds in a balance of payments context without reference to the general equilibrium of the national economy; and, moreover, without questioning whether if the foreign-owned subsidiary had been a national company it would have achieved the same degrees of success to have warranted expansion anyway. The international aspect of resource allocation is ignored in this neo-mercantilist approach. In the case of the division of overseas markets, reference is not usually made to whether the local subsidiary has sufficient capacity to sell in the bespoken market. In the case of investment in new capacity, the aggregate demand position in the economy, the likely pressure it would create on existing resources – labour, capital goods industries, etc. – is not considered. A MPE makes its decision in its own best interests, but these need not diverge from the national interests. If investment in one country would create inflationary pressures, then it would not be in the interest of a MPE to invest there, where it would have to compete for scarce resources in order to operate the new plant. Similarly, such investment would be against the interests of the national economy if it created inflationary pressures.

It is possible that in some circumstances a MPE may act in a

[1] United States regulations on supplying strategic materials to Cuba and China are direct examples; the impact of United States Anti-trust Laws may have direct consequences also.

manner that is discordant with the best interests of a particular country, as defined by its government. But this cannot be asserted generally in economic terms. Within a multinational enterprise it can be assumed that economic resources are allocated rationally. Non-economic factors may influence decisions, such as political stability or the record of industrial disputes. But within the framework of its objectives a MPE can be expected to allocate its resources according to economic criteria.

A fundamental problem, therefore, is the adoption of an economic theory that permits analysis of the impact of the activities of MPEs on international flows of trade and investment. An outline of a dynamic theory of comparative advantage is sketched in this survey. It is within this type of framework that the problems of resource allocation induced by MPEs, within and between nations, must be considered.

Trade theory is usually couched in terms of exchanges of final goods, embodying primary factors of production, between a buyer in one country and a seller in another. In practice, trade involves transfers of goods at all stages of fabrication; that is, raw materials, components, intermediate goods and finished products. Some components may pass across frontiers many times before they reach the final consumer. MPEs are specifically concerned with this kind of trade at many stages of processing. This has given cause for concern about the values attached to intra-enterprise transfers across national frontiers.

Transfer prices for goods passing between affiliated companies in different countries can be adjusted in a manner that permits financial resources to be shifted from one country to another. It may suit a MPE to take its profits in a country with low taxes and, therefore, to invoice exports of components to that country at manufactured cost without a normal profit element, and possibly to invoice exports from that country at inflated prices to reduce profit margins earned in other markets. Motives for this kind of manipulation include exploiting differences between tax regimes, avoiding exchange controls, or simply a method of transferring funds. (Inter-affiliate credit or unusually long delays in payments for goods received – leads and lags – have similar effects on international monetary movements.)

Whatever the motive, the effect will be to distort the values of trade flows between countries involved in such transactions; one country's exports may be undervalued, hence another country's imports will be undervalued; alternatively, the value of a trade flow may be overvalued. If this device is employed to maximize profits in one country, then a subsidiary there may have its imports undervalued and its exports overvalued. In terms of interest in national trade balances this country benefits at the expense of its trading partners.

In theory this device appears to offer considerable opportunities, especially as inter-affiliate transfers become more intricate. But, in practice, the opportunities are probably more limited. Customs officials are aware of import and export values of invoiced items, either because similar products pass in trade between other independent companies, or because the supplying subsidiary also calls to non-affiliated companies at full commercial prices. Moreover, the managements of subsidiaries of multinationals are generally anxious to achieve the best possible financial results for presentation to the parent company's board. Rivalry between subsidiaries will tend to establish transfer prices at commercial rates. The only case where this may not provide a safeguard would be in a highly integrated and centrally controlled multinational, and few of these exist so far.

The stratification of trade over many stages of production towards the final good has also introduced special problems in trade policy. Following the same lines as traditional trade theory, tariffs were considered as protection for final goods. But, in fact, goods passing in international trade depend on inputs of raw materials and components that may themselves be imported. It is necessary, therefore, to differentiate *nominal* tariffs from *effective* rates of protection afforded to specific processes; that is, rates of protection on value added in a process, which takes into account tariffs on inputs.[1] Effective rates of protection may differ greatly from nominal rates contained in national tariff schedules.[2] It is assumed throughout the discussions on trade policy in this paper that MPEs are aware of effective rates of protection and act on these. This seems to be the most realistic assumption since by definition MPEs are concerned with the distribution of different stages of production in relation to markets. The issues raised by effective rates of protection are all part of the same problem of resource allocation in a changing world.

A simple reading of the position would suggest that national trade policy, especially tariffs, have a far greater impact on national-based companies, relying on exports for overseas sales, than on

[1] W. M. Corden, 'The Structure of a Tariff System and the Effective Protective Rate', *Journal of Political Economy*, 1966.

[2] Bela Balassa, 'Tariff Protection in Industrial Countries; an Evaluation', *Journal of Political Economy*, 1965.

MPEs which can allow for differences in national trade policies. If this is the case, it must bring into question whether the principal aims of national trade policies are being thwarted. The trade effects of decisions taken by MPEs have a direct bearing on the effectiveness of trade policy instruments because both are concerned with the international allocation of resources. In these changed circumstances, the selection of policy instruments designed to achieve a particular objective must be re-examined and probably altered. A more fundamental problem is whether the objectives of a national trade policy should be adjusted, and how one country's policy selection is influenced by another's choice.

Altready the development of MPEs has raised questions about certain aspects of traditional international economic policy and helped to bring change. Exchange control regulations intended to isolate national money markets have been exploited by international enterprises. Control over capital movements was conceived as a means of insulating financial markets from external influences. A MPE, however, has access to several capital markets and, in many cases, it is able to transfer funds, directly or indirectly, between subsidiaries, or between subsidiaries and the parent company. Through a system of fixed exchange rates this acts as a link between capital markets, which weakens the impact of monetary policy as a domestic economic instrument. A tight credit policy in one country can be overcome by a suitable strategy of borrowing and transferring funds between subsidiaries, or between subsidiaries and the parent company. The insulation sought through exchange controls can be overcome by selective borrowing and transferring of funds because the enterprise operates within the segregated national parts of the economic system. Taken a stage further, of course, this same mechanism of financial control by MPEs can be used for speculative purposes during times of exchange rate uncertainty.

The managed exchange rate system, which involves large discreet adjustments at infrequent intervals, plays into the hands of the MPEs because they are able to benefit from the actions of separate decision-taking segments of the system, that is national monetary authorities. Governments show increasing recognition of the weaknesses of the managed exchange rate system in the presence of MPEs and they seek to overcome difficulties with greater co-operation in monetary policy and by changing the system. This is witnessed by the open discussion and growing support for a change towards greater flexibility of exchange rates.

International monetary relations could be cited, therefore, as one area of policy in which the operations of MPEs have helped to elicit changes. Perhaps the growing international economic interdependence, of which the development of MPEs is one aspect, will also induce national authorities to review and reassess the effects of present trade policy measures in the light of revised policy objectives for the changed environment.

## FURTHER RESEARCH

The present paper is intended as a preliminary survey of how the activities of MPEs may have affected international trading relations. Within this changed environment the traditional instruments of trade policy may not have the effects expected, in view of the special nature of the decision-structure in a transnational organization. Clearly, much more research is necessary within the framework of a dynamic theory of trade and investment before the relationships between the activities of MPEs and international trade flows can be established.

Two basic approaches can be adopted towards the gathering of further information on trade relations. A broadly-based econometric study might be undertaken in an attempt to establish functional relationships between types of direct investment and trade flows. The United States Bureau of Economic Research has embarked on an ambitious project of this kind, using Department of Commerce data.

Alternatively, a narrower approach based on a specific industrial sector may yield clearer behavioural relationships. A breakdown of American investment in the chemical industry in Western Europe, for example, might be studied over a period of years. An attempt could be made to relate investment to plant, and the output from those plants might be traced to particular changes in trade flows into and from the recipient country. Such a study would be assisted by technical knowledge of production methods and market potential for products. It would require detailed breakdown of commodity trade flows. Co-operation from international companies would greatly assist this kind of study.

Only when more is known about the trade effects will it be possible to deduce whether trade policy is an important consideration of MPEs. Perhaps more important, the effectiveness of traditional trade policy instruments can only be tested when more is known about the trading relations of the multinationals.

203

## Chapter 7

# THE CHEMICAL INDUSTRY:
# A CASE STUDY

### J. F. SUDWORTH

### INTRODUCTION

The range of products supplied by the chemical industry extends from basic chemicals, such as caustic soda and ammonia, through intermediate products, like nylon salt, to sophisticated end products, such as pharmaceuticals. Most of the world's largest chemical companies also manufacture synthetic fibres, in addition to the polymers from which they are derived, although in many countries these fibres are not classified as products of the chemical industry. ICI, with little or no involvement in some of the industry's sectors, has many thousands of products on its range.

The chemical industry is one of the most capital intensive of all industries. The statistics of fixed capital formation by UK industry show that, over the period 1963 to 1968, the average annual fixed capital investment per employee in the chemical industry was £426, compared with £185 in Mineral Oil Refining, about £200 in Food and Drink, and Iron and Steel, and an average for all manufacturing industry of £150.[1] The trend is towards ever-larger plants which need to be operated at or near maximum capacity in order to earn acceptable rates of return on the very large sums of capital invested.

The industry's record of technological advance is a strong one, both in respect of processes and products, and the industry sustains a high level of spending on research and development. An international comparison covering several major industrial countries has shown that, although there were considerable variations in the distribution of their national research and development expenditures across industries, the chemical industry ranked amongst the first

[1] Fixed Capital Formation: *National Income and Expenditure Blue Book,* 1969; Employment: *Ministry of Labour and Department of Employment and Productivity Gazette.*

three industries, or groups, in each country.[1] The available data for 1969 suggests that the research and development expenditures of at least six of the world's main chemical groups, including the ICI Group, exceeded £30 million in that year.[2]

## INTERNATIONAL TRADE IN CHEMICALS

The international involvement of a majority of the world's leading chemical companies both as exporters from, and as producers outside, their national markets stems largely from the basic characteristics of the industry. In particular, there is the need to achieve large sales volumes from intensively-operated plants and the need to generate a total sales turnover which is large enough to support the heavy research and development costs. A strong international organization is also essential for the rapid, broadly-based exploitation of innovations, whether new products, new processes or improvements in existing products.

The main producing countries (i.e. West Germany, France, Japan, the US and the UK) together supply almost 70% of world exports of chemicals and the figure is raised to 85% if all EEC producers are included. Their respective shares of world exports of chemical products (excluding synthetic fibres) in 1968 are shown below in Table 7.1. In recent years, the exports from the EEC countries and Japan have grown markedly faster than those of the UK and US.

The figures in this table represent varying proportions of the total sales turnovers of the chemical industries of the countries concerned. Although no precise figures are available, exports of Belgium and the Netherlands in 1968 accounted for at least 55% of their total turnover of chemicals in that year. The corresponding minimum proportions for the other countries were 34% for W. Germany, 21% for the UK and France, 13% for Italy and 7% for the US.[3]

A main feature of world trade in chemicals is that the chief producing countries are also major importers of chemicals. For example, the US, UK, West Germany and France together account for about one-quarter of the world total of chemical imports. Their imported supplies consist of, first, materials and intermediates for use in the manufacture of finished chemical products and, second, finished

---

[1] UK, USA, France, Germany and Canada. See *Technological Innovation in Britain*, HMSO, July 1968.

[2] Annual reports of major chemical companies.

[3] Based on OECD statistics.

chemical products such as plastics and fibres. In this second category, the imports usually enter over a substantial tariff either directly to consumers, in competition with local producers, or to a subsidiary or affiliated company in order to supplement its product range and/ or offset a temporary shortage of the product.

TABLE 7.1

'*World*' *Exports of Chemicals (SITC5) by Major Exporting Countries, 1968*\*

| Exporting country | £ million | To world<br>% Share |
|---|---|---|
| Belgium | 265 | 4·3 |
| France | 567 | 9·3 |
| W. Germany | 1,297 | 21·2 |
| Italy | 325 | 5·3 |
| Netherlands | 462 | 7·5 |
| Total EEC | 2,916 | 47·6 |
| UK | 599 | 9·8 |
| USA | 1,370 | 22·4 |
| Japan | 336 | 5·5 |
| Others | 903 | 14·7 |
| Total 'World' | 6,124 | 100·0 |

\* Excludes exports of the Sino-Soviet bloc, Australia and Latin America.

*Source: OECD Foreign Trade Statistics.*

Another main trade flow is in finished chemical products from the largest producing countries to markets in the developing countries. These markets, which usually have little or no indigenous manufacture of the products involved, account for about one-third of the chemical exports of the industrialized countries.

Although foreign investment by chemical companies has increased sharply over the last ten years, the value of international trade in chemicals has continued to expand at about 12% per annum. Some of this trade represents intra-company transactions *within* the MPE. In 1966 for example, one-third of the exports of the leading UK chemical companies were 'sold' to their affiliates or associated companies overseas.[1] The UK, West Germany, the US and nearly all the other main exporting countries increased their favourable chemical trade balances between 1960 and 1968.

[1] *Board of Trade Journal*, August 16, 1968.

## DIRECT FOREIGN INVESTMENT BY CHEMICAL COMPANIES

A very large part of direct foreign investment in chemical plant and equipment over the last ten years has been undertaken by US, UK and West German companies. The expenditure of subsidiaries of US companies on plant and equipment outside the US in 1968 was five times the 1960 value at £1,200 million and this spending represented 29% of all US manufacturing investment abroad compared with 17% in 1960. Investment has been increasingly channelled to the EEC as an area of growing economic and market integration with a large share (20% in 1968) of world consumption of chemical products and a high rate of economic expansion.[1] The EEC's share of US chemical companies' foreign investment in 1968 was 25%. The other main recipient areas in 1968 were Canada, Latin America and the UK.[2] In that year US companies in the UK accounted for one-fifth of the total production of chemical products.[3] There are no comprehensive figures published on the investment of UK chemical companies overseas, though the Reddaway study gave a figure of net assets of £269 million for four of the leading chemical firms, at the end of 1964.[4] In 1968–9, the direct sales of the foreign subsidiaries of a rather different group of chemical firms[5] amounted to £742 milion, 37% of the total home and overseas sales of these companies.

ICI Group investment in fixed assets outside the UK was £50 million in 1969 against £10 million in 1960. About 30% of the 1969 expenditure was in Western Europe, mainly within the EEC, and North America accounted for nearly 25%. Virtually all overseas capital spending in 1960 was in the Commonwealth countries. The 1969 expenditure of £50 million compared with an expenditure of about £110 million on fixed assets in the UK.

The foreign capital spending of the West German chemical companies in recent years has been concentrated in North and South

[1] Economic growth in the EEC over the years 1960–8 averaged 5% p.a. in terms of Gross National Product at constant prices and the average annual increase in the output of chemicals was 11%. This contrasts with average GNP and chemical industry output growth rates of 3% and 5½% p.a. respectively in the UK over the same period. See, *Quarterly Survey* of the EEC Commission; *National Income Blue Book*, 1970; OECD Industrial Production.

[2] *Survey of Current Business.*

[3] *Survey of Current Business*, October 1970, and *Board of Trade Journal*, December 3, 1969.

[4] ICI, Beecham, British Oxygen and Fisons.

[5] ICI, Beecham, Fisons, Glaxo, and Reckitt and Coleman.

America and in Western Europe. Although much of their foreign European investment has been in countries outside the EEC, each of the three main chemical companies has sited a major new chemical plant in Benelux, which will serve West Germany, other EEC countries and world export markets. This development stems from the evolution of the EEC in the sense that companies can now choose between possible locations for new plants in any member country without having to consider the incidence of internal tariffs.

### EFFECTS OF FOREIGN INVESTMENTS ON TRADE FLOWS

The objectives and strategies of the major chemical companies are among the main determinants of the size and geographical pattern of foreign investment in chemical plant and equipment. They provide a framework for the individual investment decisons which, in turn, involve assessment of the hard commercial facts of a situation and of relative profitabilities and risks.

Investments by chemical companies which are concerned with the establishment of new production units outside their national markets can conveniently be classified according to the underlying market circumstances. First, there are investments, mainly in countries which are not highly industrialized, which stem from the existence of such restrictions on imports into a market that there is no alternative to local manufacture as a route to major sales development. Second, investment frequently follows the development of an overseas market by exports from a company's national plants to a point where local manufacture becomes viable. The investing company may stand to gain protection for its new plant, either in the form of a tariff or import controls, or both. The timing of such investment is sometimes influenced by the date of expiry of the company's main product patents in the market concerned. Third, there are the foreign investments in plants in major industrial markets such as the US, UK and EEC. In these circumstances, the company may have a genuine choice between production in the country concerned and supplying the market with exports from its national plants. The market motivation for such investments is usually the sheer size of product consumption, the growth potential for the product and the effect of import duties on the profitability of supplying the market from external sources. Since the existing capacities of plants located within these markets are often sufficient to satisfy the national demand for the product, the investing company tends to select high

208

growth-potential products in respect of which it has some particular advantage, either technical or marketing. The position of the investing company is strongest where it is seeking to exploit an innovation or a product in which it has a major lead over its competitors.

Although this list of investment categories for new plants is not comprehensive, it does cover many of the investments made by chemical companies outside their national markets over the last ten years. The third category in particular has assumed increasing importance for US and British companies. Products chosen for such investments have notably included synthetic fibres, sophisticated organic chemicals and plastics. Examples of ICI Group investments which are representative of each of the types mentioned above are given in the following sections, together with an indication of their significance in respect of trade flows:

## 1 Dyestuffs in India

India has a large textile industry which produces a high volume and wide variety of textiles, mainly cotton. In the first half of the 1950s, the industry was substantially dependent on imports for its supplies of synthetic organic dyestuffs. Imports from all sources had risen to about 7,000 tons by 1954–5. However, with the growth of the Indian dyestuffs industry and with India's shortage of foreign exchange, restrictions on imports were tightened in subsequent years. In 1958–9 imports from all sources were only about half the 1954–5 level. The Indian Government's Third Five-Year Plan included a 1965–6 target for the further expansion of dyestuffs manufacturing capacity and ICI judged that the growth of local capacity, and the pressures of India's development plans on foreign exchange resources, would be such that no major relaxation of import restrictions should be expected.

A main implication of this assessment was that sales in India of ICI's newer types of dyestuffs, such as Procions and Alcians, at best might only reach a small part of their potential value if they were dependent on supplies from UK plants. ICI had developed these reactive dyestuffs, in brighter shades than those of the traditional products, during the 1960s. It was expected that they would be well accepted in the Indian market.

A study of the viability of production in India of the newer dyestuffs was undertaken and the findings were favourable. ICI had an existing investment in the manufacture of traditional types of dyestuffs through a 50% shareholding, jointly with Atul Products Limi-

o

ted, in Atic Industries Limited. The investment plan which received the approval of the Indian Government was for the construction of plant at Bulsar by Atic Industries Limited to produce both Procions and Alcians. The plant is now in operation.

The Procion and Alcian dyestuffs project in India is an example of an investment decision which was substantially influenced by restrictions on imports into an important market. In this instance, the capacity of the plant is such that it can have no large effect on trade flows. The investment has, however, given rise to imports of intermediates from ICI's UK plants and to some linked exports of finished products from the Indian plant. Imports of dyestuffs into India have remained subject to licensing arrangements. The investment, in the prevailing conditions, has strengthened ICI's position as a supplier of dyestuffs to the Indian market to an extent which would not otherwise have been possible.

### 2. Polythene in Australia

Polythene, which was invented by ICI in the 1930s, was produced only on a small scale until the end of the second World War, early usage being largely confined to defence applications. A broad range of new end-uses was developed in the 1950s and UK capacity was rapidly expanded to meet the rising demand. A major export business was also developed. Australia, as one of the markets in which ICI held basic patents, had a high development and sales priority, and the value of exports to Australia increased from an average £55,000 a year in 1950–1 to an average of £1·25 million a year in 1957–8.

The pace of market development in Australia, and the future growth potential, led to a decision to start local manufacture of low-density polythene before the expiry of ICI's basic patents in 1960. The decision was influenced by the Australian Government's policy on the development of secondary industry. Investment was encouraged by a system of investment allowances and research and development grants. In particular, however, investing companies knew that they were likely to be given tariff protection against imports provided that certain conditions were satisfied.

The capacity of ICI's initial unit, which started production in 1957, was 4,000 tons per annum, and this has subsequently been increased several times. Two developments followed the expiry of ICI's basic patents in 1960. First, another producer (one of the major US chemical companies) commenced local production of low-density polythene and second, the British Preferential Tariff rate on imports was raised from nil to 25% and the Most Favoured Nation rate from 12½% to 35%. The rates have been subsequently increased.

The two local plants have been expanded to match the growth of market requirements over the last ten years and, aided by the tariff, imports have been contained. Australian consumption of low-density polythene is now several times the 1957 level, partly due to the development efforts of the local producers. There is, nevertheless, no doubt that imports into Australia would have been many times their current level in the absence of domestic production.

For these reasons, the low-density polythene plants in Australia provide a good example of overseas investment decisions that have had a substantial effect on trade flow in the product concerned. The effect on British exports of polythene to Australia has been appreciable. ICI's exports, which reached their peak over the period 1957–8, declined sharply in subsequent years. On the other hand, there have been associated exports of catalysts and capital equipment from the UK. It is questionable, also whether the value of ICI's exports to Australia would have been substantially larger if the investment had not been made. The nature of the investment opportunity made it virtually certain that one of the other international polythene producers would have built a plant or that the US producer now concerned would have built a larger plant. ICI's polythene capacity in the UK has continued to expand rapidly in spite of this investment in Australia.

## 3 Nylon in West Germany

In 1963, nylon was manufactured at three UK plants by ICI's then joint subsidiary, British Nylon Spinners.[1] About 85% of their combined output was sold in the UK and the balance was shipped mainly to Scandinavia and Commonwealth markets. Sales to EEC countries were small.

The distribution of West European nylon consumption in 1963 was roughly as follows:

TABLE 7.2

*West European Consumption of Nylon in 1963 m.lb.*

| UK | Other EFTA | EEC | Total |
|----|-----------|-----|-------|
| 125 | 50 | 310 | 485 |

[1] British Nylon Spinners was acquired by ICI in 1964 and merged with ICI Fibres Division to form ICI Fibres Limited.

Germany and France were the largest national markets within the EEC, each with a consumption of over 100 million lb. per annum. It was expected that consumption in all the EEC countries would rise rapidly over the following ten years.

For several reasons ICI has had as a main long-term objective the achievement of a substantial share of the total market in continental West Europe. In 1963, import duties on shipments to EEC countries from British plants ranged up to 17%, according to destination. It was expected that, with EEC tariff harmonization, there would be a common external tariff of the order of 12% by 1967. The failure of Britain's application to join the EEC in January 1963 meant that the possibility of competing in EEC markets with supplies from UK plants on terms of equal access with the major Common Market producers was removed for some years at least.

One of the main findings of a study of the feasibility of manufacturing within the EEC was that sales in the EEC from a local plant were likely by 1970 to be nearly three times the volume which might at best be achieved with exports from UK plants The difference between the estimates stemmed mainly from three considerations. First, there was the significance of the Common External Tariff. This would depress the returns from selling from UK plants and reduce the attractiveness of EEC sales in relation to sales in the UK and in export markets with tariff-free access. Second, there was a limit to the volume of product which could be shipped to EEC markets from the UK plants without becoming exposed to the possibility of anti-dumping action. It was expected that this uncertainty would inhibit the sales effort. Third, it was recognized that potential EEC customers would accept a produc tmanufactured in, say, Germany or Belgium more readily than they would accept a product exported from the UK. Remoteness from the customer, longer deliveries and possible delays through shipping strikes, etc., would be important considerations at a time when EEC users were benefiting from a wider choice of products through the withdrawal of internal EEC duties.

The decision to build in the EEC was taken in 1963. A site at Oestringen in Germany was chosen, and the new plant started operating on a commercial basis in 1965 with an initial capacity of 50 million lb. per annum.

The investment has had a complex effect on nylon trade flows. First, it has made an important contribution to the rapid growth of intra-EEC trade in nylon over the last five years. The sales

212

base was gradually expanded to include all national markets within the EEC and, whereas sales were initially concentrated in the German market, other EEC countries now account for a large proportion of total output. Second, the consequent increase in the self-sufficiency of the EEC in nylon and the stimulus to competition provided by a new producer added to the difficulties experienced by most outside producers in selling in EEC markets. In this way, the investment acted to restrain total EEC imports of nylon.

ICI's exports of nylon fibre to the EEC have probably not reached the level that would have been achieved had the Company not been producing locally. In our judgment, however, the difference has not been large in value terms. This is partly because production at the Oestringen plant has been supplemented by shipments, *inter alia*, of product variants from UK plants. The substantial sales of such variants, which have commanded a higher price than standard products, have largely resulted from the scale of EEC sales of standard products supplied from Oestringen. Virtually all its output has been sold within the markets of the Six so that UK plants have not been deprived of exports to third markets.

The investment has had a favourable effect on ICI's exports from the UK to the EEC of products other than nylon fibre. Although part of Oestringen's requirements for nylon intermediates is now satisfied from an ICI plant in the EEC (at Rozenburg), there is still a substantial consumption of intermediates shipped from UK plants. In our judgment the value of these exports more than compensates for the somewhat smaller value of exports of nylon fibre caused by the existence of the Oestringen plant.

## SOME BALANCE OF PAYMENTS ASPECTS

An internal study was made by ICI in 1965 of the inflow of funds into the UK which resulted from the overseas capital spending by the ICI Group over the years 1950 to 1964. The main contribution to the inflow, representing about half the total, came from exports of raw materials and intermediates from ICI's plants in the UK to the new overseas manufacturing units. The remission of dividends, interest, and technical aid fees, resulting from the investments, and the contribution arising from associated exports of UK capital equipment, accounted for the remainder of the inflow. Although the capital equipment was not an ICI export, the ICI involvement in the investments in question was highly relevant. The complexity of the processes and the knowhow involved is such that a strong tendency exists among chemical companies to prefer equipment supplied by firms of which they have experience.

A main conclusion of the study was that the total value of the inflow of funds, after making a large allowance for the import content of the exports of both plant and raw materials/intermediates, was at least three times the value of that part of the capital spending which involved an outflow of funds from the UK.

The overseas investments made by the ICI Group over the period of the survey had a dual, but immeasurable, effect on exports of finished products from ICI's UK plants. In some instances, the investments gave rise to exports of finished products which would not otherwise have been made. In other cases, the commissioning of new overseas plants caused a decline in exports from UK plants to the markets concerned. The continuity of the extra exports if such investments had not been made, however, was usually in question since attractive investment opportunities would probably not have been disregarded indefinitely by other chemical companies.

Increases in overseas manufacturing capacity and in exports from UK plants have both contributed to the rapid expansion in the overseas sales of the ICI Group over the last ten years. In 1969, the value of Group sales overseas was about £700 million, over £80 million more than the 1968 figure and £50 million more than sales in the UK. Sales of products manufactured in UK plants accounted for more than one-third of total overseas sales.

The 1969 distribution of ICI exports (f.o.b. values) is shown in Table 7.3. Sales to Europe represented nearly half the total value of exports, and sales to North America amounted to about 10%.

Local manufacture by subsidiaries in Australia, Canada and India provided the major part of Group sales in those markets and in continental Europe a growing proportion of goods sold was locally manufactured in subsidiaries' plants, mainly in the EEC. Local manufacture also contributed significantly to Group sales in the United States, Argentina, Malaysia and Pakistan.

In varying degrees, exports from the parent country plants of chemical companies are constrained by tariffs, import restrictions, transport costs and the natural supply advantages of local producers in foreign markets. Circumvention of these constraints by direct foreign investment helped, in the case of the ICI Group, to raise total Group sales to £1,355 million in 1969. Total sales were higher than those of any other chemical group, except for the largest of the US groups, and they exceeded those of most of the other major US and EEC groups by substantial margins. The comparative posi-

THE CHEMICAL INDUSTRY: A CASE STUDY

tions of the major groups in respect of their research and development efforts followed a similar pattern. ICI Group expenditure on research and development at about £40 million in 1969 exceeded the individual expenditures of nearly all the other large chemical groups.[1] The strength of the ICI Group's international marketing capability, and the level of the research and development effort which the scale of Group sales supports, are both relevant to the UK balance of payments in the sense that they have a strong bearing on the competitive effectiveness of ICI at an international level.

TABLE 7.3

*ICI Exports in 1969*

| | *F.o.b. value of exports* £ million | % |
|---|---|---|
| EEC | 50·0 | 20·5 |
| EFTA | 40·7 | 16·7 |
| Africa | 27·4 | 11·2 |
| N. America | 23·5 | 9·6 |
| Rest of W. Europe | 19·9 | 8·1 |
| Australasia | 18·6 | 7·6 |
| Far East | 16·7 | 6·8 |
| Central and S. America | 16·0 | 6·6 |
| Soviet Union and countries in E. Europe | 14·1 | 5·8 |
| India, Pakistan, Ceylon | 8·2 | 3·4 |
| Other countries | 9·0 | 3·7 |
| TOTAL | 244·1 | 100·0 |

[1] See annual reports of chemical companies.

215

# COMMENT ON THE CHAPTERS BY
# MR ROBERTSON AND MR SUDWORTH

## LIONEL NEEDLEMAN

Mr Robertson's chapter is a fairly non-controversial and extensive introduction to the subject. He discusses how the trade policies of nations can affect the flow of foreign investment – the most important effects probably being governmental restrictions on imports encouraging investment within the protected area by foreign companies previously supplying those imports – and he also examines how foreign investment can affect trade flows through import and export generation and displacement.

Mr Sudworth, in his chapter, discusses with examples the reasons for investment abroad by the major chemical companies as well as examining some of the effects of ICI's overseas investment on the balance of payments of the United Kingdom.

Both chapters stress the importance of attempting to measure the effects of foreign investment on the trade flows and the balance of payments of the investing and the recipient countries, and both bear witness to the difficulty, in principle and in practice, of actually measuring these effects. Thus Mr Sudworth mentions on page 213 that in 1965 ICI did a study of the effects of overseas investment by the ICI group on the UK's balance of payments over the period 1950 to 1964. The effects measured included exports of UK capital plant, materials and intermediate goods purchased by the overseas subsidiary, the import content of those exports, and the invisible exports of dividends, royalties and fees. On this basis it was calculated that over the period examined the overseas investment had resulted in a balance of payments inflow into the UK of at least three times the original outflow of funds.

It is not clear what assumptions were made about what would have happened if ICI had not made its investments abroad, but Mr Sudworth, like the authors of the Reddaway report,[1] seems to be making the 'reverse classical' assumption,[2] that is, that ICI invest-

[1] W. B. Reddaway et al., *Effects of UK Direct Investment Overseas*, Interim and Final Reports, 1967 and 1968.

[2] See G. C. Hufbauer and F. M. Adler, *Overseas Manufacturing Investment and the Balance of Payments*, US Treasury Dept., 1968, p. 6.

ment abroad did not reduce total investment in the UK, nor did it increase investment in the recipient country. The assumption is that if ICI had not set up a plant, either a local firm or another foreign firm would have done so. But in that case, would one not expect that the non-ICI firm to have bought some of its capital equipment and materials from the UK? If so, then Mr Sudworth's estimates of the beneficial effects of ICI's foreign investment on the UK's balance of payments would need to be reduced.

The Reddaway team, in fact, did attempt to estimate what pro-portions of purchases of capital and current items from the UK would still have been made if the investment in the host country had been made by a non-UK firm. For their sample of chemical firms, their best guess was that, in the alternative situation, UK exports of capital good to UK subsidiaries over the period 1955–64 would have been reduced by about 80% that there would have been no effect on UK exports of current services,[2] but that UK exports of current goods would have increased by about 10%.[3]

Over the period 1955–64, purchases of non-capital goods, includ-ing finished goods for resale by overseas subsidiaries of UK chemical companies, were over ten times as great as purchases of capital goods. If ICI were representative of the six firms in the Reddaway sample of chemical firms (which included ICI), and if the nine or ten years of the Reddaway observations were comparable with the fifteen-year period of the ICI observations, and if one accepts the Reddaway team's 'best guesses' of what would have happened in the alternative situation, then instead of the ICI investment bringin back a balance of payments inflow of 300%, there would have been a small net out-flow of funds!

There are, of course, lots of 'ifs' in this chain of inferences, but the huge discrepancy between the estimates based on the Reddaway assumptions and those of the ICI illustrate vividly just how sensitive findings on balance of payments effects can be to the precise choice of assumptions made.

Mr Sudworth does not describe the time path of the inflows into the UK as a consequence of ICI investment overseas, but it is reasonable to suppose that a net outflow preceded a net inflow. If so, then the net flow will need to be adjusted to correct for the effects of inflation as well as discounted to allow for time preference. Again, these adjustments would reduce any favourable effect of

[1] Reddaway *et al.*, *op. cit.*, Table X.1, p. 370.
[2] *Ibid.*, Table XII.4, p. 373.
[3] *Ibid.*, Table XII.1, p. 371.

ICI foreign investment on the UK balance of payments but, given the great uncertainty of the alternative situation, the net effects could still be positive.

There seems to be a tendency for companies to exaggerate the favourable effects of overseas investment on the balance of payments of both the investing and the recipient country. But even allowing for the element of overestimation, the more general question then arises: is there a conflict of interest between investing and recipient countries as far as the effects on the balance of payments are concerned? It is, of course, possible, though unlikely, that the balance of payments of both countries could improve entirely at the expense of the third world: as Mr Robertson emphasizes, our ignorance of the effects of foreign investment on the rest of the world is profound. But even if a given investment had no net effect on the balance of payments of the rest of the world, the investment could still be in the interests of both the investing and the host countries, even if one only considers balance of payments effects. Where the investing country is rich and the recipient country poor, which is the standard case for investment in underdeveloped countries, one would expect the social time preference rate to be higher in the poor country than in the rich one. In such a case, the 'present value' of the net flow of payments in and out of the investing country discounted at the rich country's low rate might be positive, while the same flow with the signs reversed discounted at the poor country's high rate could also be positive.

Conflict of interest between the investing firms and the recipient country can also arise as the proportion of industry in the host country owned by foreigners increases. Foreign capital tends both to be attracted to, and to stimulate, the more profitable and rapidly-growing sections of the host-country's economy. The dilemma then arises that, if the profits of the foreign investment are largely remitted, there are complaints of adverse effects on the host-country's balance of payments. If, alternatively, the profit are reinvested, then it is objected that the host-country's industry is being increasingly dominated by foreigners.

Many foreign companies operating in developing countries have been encouraged by host governments to sell shares to the local public. This, however, can have strongly adverse effects on the balance of payments as it involves the replacement by local funds of foreign capital, which is then repatriated. Local participation through the purchase of shares is similar in its effects to the local community directly investing abroad in the industry of a Western country.

218

The unfavourable effects on the balance of payments would, of course be lessened if the local funds were diverted from investment abroad rather than from other indigenous investment projects, or if the foreign capital released when the local participation occurred were reinvested in the host country. But these qualifications will only rarely be applicable.

The problem of reconciling the requirement of the foreign investor to get a reasonable return on his investment, with the need of the host country to avoid having its industry largely under foreign control, is a thorny one. One possible approach is for both sides to accept from the initiation of the investment that the ownership of the foreign firm would eventually be transferred, not sold, to the indigenous people, but that the transfer of ownership should not begin until the firm had been operating for, say, fifteen or twenty years. This would allow the firm to have obtained a satisfactory return on its investment and should then proceed gradually so as to avoid disruption of the firm's operations. Obviously, any such scheme that was to be fair to both sides would have to be fairly complicated, but if the basic principles were acceptable the details of the arrangement could be worked out.

PART FOUR. DIRECT FOREIGN INVESTMENT
AND THE LESS-DEVELOPED COUNTRIES

*Chapter 8*

# THE STATE AND MULTINATIONAL
# ENTERPRISES IN LESS-DEVELOPED
# COUNTRIES

EDITH PENROSE

## INTRODUCTION

In a recent series of lectures an eminent American economist predicted, rather hopefully, that the 'nation state is just about through
as an economic unit'.[1] This prediction comes just at the moment
when large numbers of countries in the Afro-Asian world have become politically independent for the first time – members in their
own right of the society of nations, and under the impression that
the era of the independent 'nation state' has, for them, just begun.
Professor Kindleberger's prediction implies that the peoples of these
countries are under a grave illusion if they think that their newly-won
independence will include any real influence over their economic
affairs. Nevertheless, within Asia and Africa, which after all includes
China, reside the majority of the world's population, and it is of
some interest to enquire whether this 'cosmopolitan'[2] point of view,
so vigorously put forward in different contexts by a number of North
American economists, seems likely to prevail in the near future.

[1] 'The nation state is just about through as an economic unit. General de
Gaulle is unaware of it as yet, and so are the Congress of the United States and
Right-wing know-nothings in all countries.' C. P. Kindleberger, *American
Business Abroad: Six Lectures on Direct Investment*, New Haven and London,
Yale University Press, 1969, p. 207.
[2] Cosmopolitan: 'Belonging to all parts of the world. Free from national
limitations or attachments' (OED). The selection of the term 'cosmopolitan' by
those holding the views analysed in this paper to describe their position clearly
has persuasive value and seems on the surface to be accurate. Whether it accurately describes the likely outcome of the events predicted is another question.

221

True, Kindleberger does not specify the time horizon of his prediction, but one has the impression that he is not peering into far-distant historical vistas but into the foreseeable future. Already, he says, 'Tariff policy is virtually useless. . . . Monetary policy is in the process of being internationalized. The world is too small. It is too easy to get about. Two-hundred-thousand-ton tank and ore carriers and containerization . . . airbuses, and the like will not permit sovereign independence of the nation state in economic affairs.'[1]

True also, there is no hint that the 'nation state' is 'through' as a political unit, which may be of some comfort for those countries under the illusion that their time had just begun. But historically political independence – like political dependence – has had very important implications for economic policy. No one, of course, assumes that any state can, by virtue of its political independence, be completely independent of the rest of the world in its economic affairs. Sharp limits to the power of governments to shape the economic life of their countries as they would wish if no other country existed, are imposed by many types of circumstance, including the possibility of war, and are very different for countries of different sizes, with different endowments and in different locations. Such limits have always existed, but have not called into question the importance of the modern state as a significant economic unit.[2] Hence, the issue must turn on the extent to which contemporary developments are imposing such extensive new limits on the power of the state to adopt and implement independent economic policies that one will soon be unable to consider it as an important 'unit' from an economic point of view.

In this chapter I shall deal with the question only so far as it relates to the countries of the third world. First, I shall briefly recapitulate the contemporary developments that have led to the so-called 'nation state controversy' and to conclusions which, from almost any standpoint outside North America, seem bordering on the absurd. Secondly, I shall examine the way in which the countries of the world are to become so closely 'integrated' into the international economy that they lose their economic identity; I shall then look at the relation of this process to conditions widely prevalent in the less-developed countries. Finally, I shall suggest what seems to me a more likely course of events.

[1] Kindleberger, *op. cit.*, pp. 207–8.
[2] See, for example, the discussion by Simon Kuznets, 'The State as a Unit in the Study of Economic Growth', *Journal of Economic History*, Vol. 11, Winter 1951.

## THE LARGE ENTERPRISE AND ECONOMIC INTEGRATION

The new developments in the modern world that are to bring about the economic obsolescence of the state relate to technology and (or including) techniques of organization. These have reached the highest stages in their evolution so far in the United States and have enabled the large business corporations of that country not only to dominate or, if you like, 'integrate' the US economy, but also to reach abroad on a hitherto unimagined scale and directly to organize economic activity in other countries. It is not surprising, therefore, that American economists should take the lead in drawing attention to the prospect that these corporations (aided perhaps by some from other countries) will now proceed to accomplish in the international economy what they have accomplished at home. The emergence and spread of the large national corporation in the United States is held to provide a pattern, or prototype, not only for the evolution of the international corporation, but of the international economy as well.

The future economic organization of the world under the aegis of the large corporation is seen, therefore, as the culmination on a global scale of an evolutionary process that has been long in the making. Kuznets has looked at economic history in terms of 'economic epochs', the distinctive features of an epoch being determined by 'epochal innovations'.[1] He finds that the innovation distinguishing the modern economic epoch is 'the extended application of science to problems of economic production'.[2] It is within this framework that the modern corporation has developed. From small beginnings in the introduction of simple technology, the basic economic units in the organization of production, – the factory and the firm – have grown steadily in size and in complexity.

This growth has been characterized by increasing division of labour, increasing use of capital, and continuous innovation in the techniques of both production and organization and in the nature of output. The potentialities of the corporate form of organization have been progressively developed as a means of raising capital, spreading risk and expanding the scope of the enterprise through merger and acquisition. It became possible for one firm to integrate vertically entire industries within its scope and to spread horizontally over wide geographical areas. Because the potentialities for the growth

[1] S. Kuznets, *Modern Economic Growth: Rate, Structure and Spread.* New Haven and London, Yale University Press, 1966, pp. 2 ff.
[2] *Ibid.*, p. 9.

of the firm tend to exceed the growth of demand for a given product after a point, the aggressive enterprise will for ever be seeking new fields of activity, devising new products, and developing new markets.[1] This process has been especially prominent in the United States where 'product development and marketing replaced production as a dominant problem of business enterprise'.[2]

Such diversification brought with it an appropriate internal structure of organization, for it was found desirable to create separate central divisions to deal with the several activities of the firm, although the activities themselves were often carried on in separately incorporated subsidiaries. The 'multidivisional' form of organization is extremely flexible, for new activities can be taken on and old ones thrown off with relative ease, while the central activities of planning and directing overall corporate development and strategy can be concentrated in head offices with a very long view and a very wide horizon, which even curves round the earth. In these circumstances, and given the scope for profitable expansion abroad, the international spread of US corporations, as well as of corporations in similar positions in other countries, is easily explicable. The chief older incentives to direct foreign investment – the development of new sources of supply of raw materials or control over old ones – were increasingly supplemented by the need to secure and control markets.[3] New methods of organization supported and induced by new technology in office machinery and data processing seem to have greatly extended the limits to size which had previously been imposed by the requirements of administrative co-ordination. Extensive decentralization of responsibility and authority are characteristic of the new forms of organization, but do not seem to have prevented the central planning of strategy and control.

Galbraith's vision of the emerging American society is relevant to the argument we shall be discussing, although it is possible that its adherents would vigorously reject any association of their views with those of Galbraith.[4] Nevertheless, it must be remembered that implicit in the discussion is the presumption that it is in the American image that the international corporation will reshape the world, and Galbraith's picture is in broad outline plausible. It is of a society

[1] See my *Theory of the Growth of the Firm*, especially Chapters V and VII.

[2] See S. Hymer, 'The Multinational Corporation and the Law of Uneven Development', in J. N. Bhagwati (ed.), *Economics and World Order*, New York, World Law Fund, 1970.

[3] Hymer, *op. cit.*

[4] Kenneth Galbraith, *The New Industrial State*, London, Hamish Hamilton, 1967.

ruled – or rather managed – by the 'technostructure' of the large corporations. The members of this class – if it can be so called – are responsible for the profitable management of the vast resources of capital, skilled manpower and technology at the disposal of the one or two hundred leading corporations which dominate the modern industrial economy. Successful management of resources on such a scale requires long-range planning. Successful planning requires, in turn, a high degree of control over the environment in order to reduce to a minimum unpredictable reactions to the corporations' activities.

This environmental control must be far-reaching: it requires extensive vertical and horizontal integration to establish and maintain control over sources of supply and of markets; effective use of advertising and other techniques of managing consumers' demand; the maintenance of close relations with government to achieve the necessary support for capital-intensive technological research and to ensure the required demand from the government as a consumer; the cultivation of close relations with academic institutions to ensure certain types of research and the required sources of technological recruitment; and the promotion of appropriate adaptations in the labour force and in the trade unions. The corporate 'technostructure' is thus the pervasive and effective power through the society.

As I understand the argument of those who predict that the economic future of the world lies in the hands of the large corporation, it is by an extension abroad of the same type of managerial control now exercised by the 'technostructure' in the United States, that the big corporations are supposed to integrate the world and reduce to insignificance the economic importance of 'nation states'.[1] We now turn to a discussion of the way in which this state of affairs might be achieved.

## A NEW STRUCTURE FOR THE WORLD ECONOMY

I have seen very little concrete discussion of the process by which the world economy is to be integrated under the impact of the international corporations. The analysis seems to consist mostly of draw-

[1] 'The multinational corporation, if it succeeds, will reproduce on a world-level the centralization of control found in its internal administrative structure.' – S. Hymer and S. A. Resnick, 'International Trade and Uneven Development', to appear in Kindleberger, *Festschrift*, 1970.

ing analogies with the United States and sometimes with US/Canadian relations. In the United States the large corporations have not had to contend with independent states and national boundaries, for the local states have never had the type of power which could seriously interfere with interstate investment, trade, money flows, or migration. On the other hand, in spite of national boundaries, there has been considerable integration of the Canadian and US economies through the agency of the international corporations. I shall return to this later.

It is true, as Kindleberger has emphasized, that the national corporation raised capital in those parts of the United States where funds could be obtained most cheaply and invested where labour was relatively cheap, thus helping to equalize wages and the cost of capital throughout the country,[1] and that through national advertising it created the same wants and brand attachments from coast to coast, thus creating a national market. In addition, its managerial and technical personnel (the 'technostructure') are highly mobile, further reducing regional attachments within the corporation. On all this type of thing is hung the generic label 'integration' which, as the opposite of disintegration, is supposed to be a very good thing indeed. It is easy to see in broad terms that a similar process may take place internationally – in fact, that it already is taking place in some degree. But how is it to reduce the economic significance of the state?

A vivid picture of a possible structure for the emerging international economy matched against the structure of the international corporations that shape it has been painted by Stephen Hymer, so far as I know the only economist to go into much concrete detail.[2] Ingeniously combining location theory with Chandler and Redlich's 'three-level' scheme for the analysis of corporate structure, Hymer sketches a model of a world in which the international corporations dominate great industries on a global scale. Their head offices, on which the framework of control is centred and where global strategy is determined, are located in the great major cities of the world, to which the best men of all countries are attracted and which become the true centres of world power. Below these cities are arranged a hierarchy of lesser, though still large cities, where the activities requiring white-collar workers and technicians of all kinds are concentrated. These are concerned with communications, information, and all other functions involved in co-ordinating and supervising the managers of the production and distribution activities that take

[1] C. P. Kindleberger, *op. cit.*, pp. 187–8.
[2] Hymer, *op. cit.*

place at the next level below. The 'level III' activities are devoted to managing the day-to-day operations of the enterprise and are spread widely over the earth, their location being determined by 'the pull of manpower, markets, and raw materials'.

Thus the structure of the world economy itself reflects the corporate structure – cosmopolitan and truly international: a few great cities containing the richest and the most powerful who make the long-range plans and exercise overall control, lesser cities, flourishing with lesser functions of co-ordination and supervision, and finally a hinterland of on-the-ground production and distribution personnel, and presumably even manual workers, in the smaller cities and towns below. All are 'integrated' within the hierarchical structure of the few hundred international corporations, and their development is shaped in accordance with corporate plans. Investment and production are spread widely over the world, but the centre of attention is on international *industries*, not on the development and growth of national economies.[1]

It is not very clear from Hymer's exposition how far he really believes in his own model, and certainly he is not convinced of its desirability. But if the type of development outlined is to 'integrate' the world economy so successfully that national frontiers become relatively insignificant, the international corporations will have to be able to carry on their activities – and especially those relating to their investment, trade, financial affairs and labour and recruitment policies – with minimal interference from individual governments. It is envisaged, at least by Kindleberger, that the national interests of the countries involved would be protected by independent international bodies or through international agreements. The international arrangements would presumably be established partly as a result of free negotiations, such as those of the European Common Market, and partly also because the force of circumstances left little alternative to the governments concerned.[2] The truly international cor-

---

[1] It should be noted that, in spite of the terminology commonly adopted in these discussions, the 'world' referred to in fact excludes over a third of the population of the earth, for all of Eastern Europe and the largest country in Asia are presumably not expected to be amenable to integration by the international capitalist corporation. One might have thought that Kindleberger should have included 'left-wing know-nothings' among the ignorant. (See footnote 1, p. 221.)

[2] Both Kindleberger and Hymer suggest that the activities of international corporations have placed significant limitations on the freedom of action of even the United States Government in the conduct of its foreign economic affairs.

poration, without national attachments, with no 'citizenship' and therefore indifferent to all national considerations, would attempt to equalize return on assets at the margin subject only to 'the discount for risk which applies realistically at home as well as abroad',[1] and would be free to do so within the internationally agreed constraints.

According to this 'cosmopolitan', or 'international' thesis, such corporations would do for the world economy what national corporations have allegedly already done for the United States economy: their capital would flow to raw materials and the cheaper sources of labour, with the result that the benefits of modern technology would reach the poorer and backward areas of the world, opportunities for all peoples, both at home and abroad, especially as internationally mobile employees of the large corporations would be widened, and consumption standards would rise everywhere. In short, the classical advantages of the international division of labour and free international trade would bring about greater world output and greater efficiency in the allocation of world resources.

It is not my purpose here to discuss the merits of this argument. Rather I now want to turn to an examination of the relationship that is envisaged between the international corporation and the state in the light of conditions and attitudes now widely prevalent among the less-developed countries.

## ATTITUDES TOWARD INWARD INVESTMENT

In discussing the problem from the point of view of the less-developed countries, I shall deal with three broad interrelated considerations: first, the emphasis that the new states place on 'nation-building', an integral part of which is the economic development of their own countries with a view to increasing the opportunities and standard of living of their own peoples in their own lands; second, the emphasis commonly placed on national economic 'planning' and the role of the so-called public sector, sometimes referred to loosely as 'socialism'; and finally, the ambivalent attitude toward foreign enterprise and the widely-expressed fear of foreign 'exploitation', again loosely referred to as 'imperialism'.

There is no doubt whatsoever that the less-developed countries in general take a 'narrowly-nationalistic' view of their situation. Economists from the industrialized countries, the riches of which are spilling over the frontiers may, with impeccable theoretical

[1] Kindleberger, *op. cit.*, p. 183.

credentials and considerable practical force, point out to the poorer countries the folly of their ways, but one must deal with the world as it is. And the fact is that these countries are obsessed with their own economic problems and care not a bean for 'world allocative efficiency'. It follows, therefore, that their leaders must be convinced that the economic development of their own countries will be hastened if they give reasonably free rein to foreign corporations, or else they must be forced to do so by a variety of economic or political pressures to 'liberalize' their policies.

There are very great differences in the attitudes of the countries of the third world in this respect, but even in countries where foreign firms are reasonably welcome, restrictions are usually placed on their freedom of action, and these restrictions are often of a kind that force the foreign corporations to pay as much attention to national development needs as to international efficiency, if not more. There must be few underdeveloped countries in which foreign companies feel really secure and at ease, for suspicion of them is very widespread indeed.[1] Are such attitudes likely to change in the foreseeable future? I think not, for three reasons.

My first reason (not necessarily the most important) relates to the inconclusiveness of the relevant economic analysis. That I should suggest such a consideration as an important influence on the attitudes of the leaders in less-developed countries may cause many to doubt my sanity, let alone my experience of these countries. Nevertheless, I submit that if all Western economists were agreed that direct private foreign investment always brought important net benefits to developing countries, benefits that were maximized when foreign companies were allowed to operate as freely as they chose, and if all the students from the developing countries studying economics in the Western world were firmly taught these propositions, it would be very much easier to persuade their economic ministers of the truth of this point of view. In practice, all relevant economic theory places much emphasis on the possible conflict between social and private benefit and on the dangers of monopoly, and some of it emphasizes the wastes of competition. In certain fields of international economics, special stress is laid on the specific problems raised for national economies by the operations of foreign firms. Considerable attention is paid in modern theory to the role of 'learning by doing' (which, of course, suggests that one does not gain by allowing foreigners to do too much). The list could be lengthened. My

[1] The exceptions will be found primarily in countries which are straightforward political dependents of industrialized countries such as, for example, Taiwan.

229

point is that serious and competent economists can make a strong case against a permissive attitude toward private foreign investment and thus bring respectability even to attitudes originally based upon an unthinking, emotional reaction.

My second reason for thinking that the role of the international corporation will be limited by the state in the third world for a long time to come is in a sense a continuation of the first. Economic planning, one of the most outstanding characteristics of the large corporation itself, is now widely accepted as an important function of the state in the interest of the development and stability of its national economy. The term 'planning' is only a generic one, covering many qualitatively different species of activity, but it carries with it the notion of establishing priorities among objectives, of setting targets and then of attempting systematically to achieve these targets.

Development planning is almost universal in the less-developed countries, aided and supported by international organizations and by developed countries of all political shades. In my view, development planning is not necessarily inconsistent with a large and growing private sector, nor with a high degree of autonomy for both private and public enterprises. But this is by the way; the fact is that many developing countries have conceived of planning as the antithesis of private-enterprise capitalism responding to the profit motive. Attributing much of their present lack of development to colonialist exploitation or capitalist imperialism, and with an eye on the alternative modes of economic organization seen in the communist world, many of them enthusiastically adopted – at least formally – a centralized type of planning, nationalizing their major industries and creating in the process a large 'public sector'. For the most part their reach exceeded their grasp, and their first enthusiasm has given way to much disillusion. A public commitment to 'socialism' usually remains, but in many countries reappraisal and retrenchment is the order of the day.

It would be a very grave mistake, however, to interpret retrenchment as a return to the older system, as a complete reversal of policy. More freedom and autonomy for enterprises there may be, and more sympathy and encouragement for the private sector, but governments will continue to be concerned with priorities, and will continue to intervene in attempts to ensure that the private sector, including foreign enterprises, will operate in ways consistent with overall government objectives. The priorities and objectives will differ for countries in different economic positions, but there is no reason to think that they will be consistent with the objectives of international corporations, were the latter free from state interference. They will continue to find that the state will remain a powerful and difficult economic unit. This is not to say that international corporations will become less important than they are now; on the contrary, their contribution should increase as countries develop, but this contribution will have to fit in with national priorities.

Finally, I come to my third reason why governments in the third world can be expected to continue to assert their economic independence *vis-à-vis* foreign corporations – a widespread dislike of foreign domination, ranging from obsessive fears of 'imperialist exploitation' to simple political pride in the ability to maintain a high degree of independence. These attitudes will tend to persist as long as there are really glaring disparities in the economic position of the peoples of different countries.

As noted above, some countries trace many of their present problems to imperialist exploitation in the past, and their governments make great political play with anti-imperialist slogans in attempts to rally their people to support their policies. This is particularly common among governments which consider themselves 'revolutionary'. But even when governments are relatively conservative, there are always vocal groups which use such slogans in appealing to the people for support, and which governments can rarely afford to ignore. The roots of these attitudes, and the justifications for them, are far too complicated to explore here. They lie deep in grievances, real or imagined, inherited from the past, and in bitter feelings of inferiority directly traceable to the wide disparities in standards of living, technology and education that exist between the rich and the poor areas of the world. These feelings are exacerbated by sheer frustration and a sense of helplessness in the face of the overwhelmingly difficult problems inherent in attempts to force economic development and political progress at anywhere near the pace considered essential. They therefore become a potent political force in internal political struggles, and can be used to arouse class antagonism when conservative or 'reasonable' governments come too close to foreign business interests.

Because xenophobia is often used as a scapegoat for domestic troubles, there is a tendency among Western observers to put this entire complex of attitudes and behaviour into the box labelled 'irrationality' with no further attempt at analysis, or else to assume that the source of the trouble lies with 'communists' and the cold war. No one can deny that there is often much stupidity, illogicallity and unthinking emotionalism to contend with, as well as genuine ideological controversy, but I think that there is a real problem underneath the froth worthy of serious attention – and this apart from the seriousness with which one must examine the ideological basis of conflicting views.

It is, of course, irrational of economists to label other people's preferences 'irrational', provided that these preferences are consistent and that their implications are appreciated by those who express them. It has always been understood that welfare encompasses much more than objectively measurable economic goods and services – workers (and businessmen) may prefer leisure to income after a point without being thought irrational, 'psychic utility' lies at the basis of the theory of consumers' choice. Even the notion of 'community preferences' is respectable in much welfare theory, in spite of the obvious difficulties, and surely it is not unreasonable to postulate that some peoples may prefer to run their own affairs as far as possible rather than have them run by foreigners. In other words, extensive and dominant foreign control of economic activities may in itself be a positive disutility to a community, and the community may be willing to incur a cost to avoid it.[1]

If 'disutility' of this kind exists, it may take the form of complaints that the country is being 'exploited' by foreign companies, who may then be accused of 'neo-imperialism'. It is very difficult to give a concrete meaning to such terms as 'exploitation',[2] but there can be no doubt that a feeling of being exploited is one of the compelling forces behind much of the hostility directed toward large foreign firms. Their size, international scope, political, managerial and technological expertise, and in general the apparently wider 'options' open to them in determining their policies, all give rise to a feeling in their less well-endowed host countries that bargaining power is grossly unequal, with the result that the foreigner obtains a disproportionate gain from his activities in the country. The notion of *disproportionality* rather than the notion that the country necessarily loses *absolutely* is, in my view, the important consideration on which to focus in explaining the prevalence of the belief that foreign in-

[1] I have developed this argument in more detail in an essay, 'International Economic Relations and the Large International Firm', in *New Orientations: Essays in International Relations*, Peter Lyon and E. F. Penrose (eds.), Cass, 1970, pp. 114–22.

[2] See my attempts to do this in 'Profit Sharing between Producing Countries and Oil Companies in the Middle East', *Economic Journal*, June 1959, pp. 251–2; Professor Kindleberger's criticism in *Economic Development*, New York, 2nd ed., p. 334, and my further attempt in the article cited in the previous footnote.

vestment tends to be exploitative.[1] The larger and more internationally powerful a foreign firm becomes, the greater may be its need to demonstrate its value to the host countries by contributing even more extensively to their development in terms of their own objectives.

Resentment, and difficulties, are sometimes intensified by attempts of dominant industrial countries to put pressure on less-developed countries in order to force them to admit private investment more freely. There is a certain analogy here with what has been called the 'imperialism of free trade' in the nineteenth century. Britain was committed to free trade and she sometimes forced it on other areas under her political domination. It may be that she did so in the firm belief that, for all of the classical economic reasons, it was economically advantageous to the colonies as well as to the mother country. Nevertheless, one consequence was the destruction of some local industries with nothing to take their place. Today, infant industry (or infant country) arguments are almost universally accepted as grounds for making exceptions to free trade. But as Robinson and Gallagher have pointed out, the function of imperialism was to integrate new regions into an expanding economy, and it did so for a variety of agricultural and mining activities in an earlier period, but probably at an unnecessary cost to local development.

Today we have what might be called the 'imperialism of free investment', with precisely the same function, supported by arguments similar to those advanced for free trade, and enforced where possible by the dominant industrial power. From the point of view of the regions peripheral to the industrially advanced economies, however, 'free private investment' may have disadvantages similar to those attaching to free trade. Indeed, it is for this reason that even the most enthusiastic supporters of it admit the necessity for some sort of international controls.

It seems to me that these are powerful obstacles in the way of the new organization of the world under the aegis of the international corporation. Few will deny their importance, and the only question is whether or not the almost mystical forces of modern technology

[1] 'The notion is that the foreign company is obtaining a *disproportionate* gain – a gain greater than he ought in some sense to get when it is compared with the gain accruing to the receiving country. In other words, it is a feeling of 'unfair' treatment, and this is what makes the notion so extremely difficult to analyse from an economic point of view, for it does not depend on any objective measurement of the absolute gain received by either side, but on their *relative* positions in the light of what seems fair to one side only', Edith Penrose, 'International Economic Relations and the Large International Firm', *op. cit.*, p. 119.

and organization are even more powerful. The vision of the American economists of an 'integrated' world may to some extent be shaped by their experience with Latin America and Canada, where the big American corporations are indeed making great strides in integrating many industries across national frontiers without serious opposition from governments. In Latin America, the organization of the bauxite-aluminium industry between the Caribbean, North America and Latin America is a case in point:

> The resources of each region reach the other in a more finished form *via* processing plants in the United States. For example, in 1962 Latin America imported 60,000 tons of aluminium, the bulk of its requirements, from the United States and Canada. But the United States and Canada in turn import nine-tenths of the raw materials needed to make aluminium (bauxite and alumina) from the Caribbean. That is to say, North American-based multinational corporations, four in number, mine and treat bauxite in the Caribbean and transfer the material to processing plants in the United States and Canada. Part of the output of aluminium and semi-finished aluminium products is then exported to Latin America. . . . What is . . . important to bear in mind is that the product and commodity flows are not so much between economies as between one plant and another within the multinational corporations and their own marketing agencies. Thus, intracorporate commodity transfers between plants located within different countries may satisfy the formal criteria of international trade, but so far as resource allocation is concerned the flows are of an internal character, within frontiers which are institutionally, not politically defined.[1]

---

[1] Norman Girvan and Owen Jefferson, 'Institutional Arrangements and the Economic Integration of the Caribbean and Latin America', University of the West Indies (mimeo), pp. 13–15. The authors go on to say: 'The converse of the high degree of mobility within the company is a certain degree of rigidity so far as intra-regional product and capital flows between companies are concerned. For example, the [multinational corporation] with raw material facilities and processing capacity will not normally purchase raw materials from another producer. . . . Thus corporate integration can, and often does, result in regional fragmentation. This fragmentation does not only occur between the two regions, as already suggested. The experience of the Caribbean with its bauxite industry suggests that fragmentation can take place within a given region and even within one country. Thus that part of the bauxite output of Jamaica and Guyana which is produced by Reynolds Metals, the US aluminium producer, reaches the fledgling aluminium smelting industry of Venezuela after being shipped to the US and manufactured into alumina at Reynolds' plants and then re-exported to the South

It is possible, therefore, that the present position in Latin America gives much support to the American vision. I am not competent, however, to judge how stable this position is, nor how much harmony there exists in the relations between governments and peoples in Latin America on the one hand and between both and their great northern imperial neighbour on the other. On this may depend whether or not experience with Latin America will contradict my thesis. The case of Latin America, however, must be distinguished from that of Canada. The essential difference lies in the fact that the peoples to the south are much less well-off by and large than are the Canadians. Here I have been concerned with the problem only with reference to the unindustrialized, undeveloped, poor countries of the world. The problems – and perhaps also the outcome – are very different when the relationships involved are less unequal and the sensitivities and needs less acute.

It is also possible, however, that my views are excessively coloured by my own experience in the Middle East and certain parts of Asia, and with the international petroleum industry in all areas, including South America. In this industry, the necessity of international integrated planning has been put forward as persuasively as anywhere, yet events have been moving in a rather different direction since the war. The industry points to its own history in support of its arguments regarding the advantages of integration for there is, and has been, a very high degree of international integration within the framework of a few large multinational enterprises. This integration includes a large part of the world, but excludes the Communist countries, as well as the United States, which has an independent and highly nationalistic policy of its own. Although from the point of view of overall economic efficiency the development of the industry has been seriously distorted in several important respects because of its oligopolistic and vertically integrated structure, very large supplies of oil have been brought to the consumers of the world at a really remarkable pace, and very large revenues have accrued to the less-developed countries where crude oil is produced.

Before the war the international companies did not have much to contend with from the governments of the several countries in which they operated. It is probably fair to say that their greatest difficulties

American mainland, in spite of the fact that Guyana borders on Venezuela, and Jamaica is also nearer to that country than the United States. Conversely, Reynolds' bauxite output in Guyana and Jamaica has not so far been available to the existing processing capacity in both countries because this capacity is owned by a different company.' (Pp. 15–16.)

arose from the rivalries among their own home governments. Since the war there have been substantial changes and, in addition to their increasingly effective demands for greater tax revenues, governments have interfered in a wide variety of matters, including transfer prices, product prices, production programmes and policies, exploration and exploitation arrangements, refinery locations, and a host of minor matters. Nevertheless, the unit of planning is still the international industry and, strictly speaking, the crude-oil producing countries are still largely receivers of revenues, not exporters of oil.

Nevertheless, national enterprises in both exporting and consuming countries are becoming more important, and the international companies are finding their task of integrating and organizing the industry on a world scale (always excluding the US and the Communist countries) increasingly complicated by government pressures. In my opinion, a process of international disintegration has begun in this industry, and among the major reasons for it are those I have discussed above. But I do not believe that this will be disastrous, or even a serious setback, to most of the international companies, or that it will be unfavourable to the development of the exporting countries, or disadvantageous to consuming countries. 'Adjustment problems' there will be but, with the technical help of the oil companies, the exporting countries can find and produce oil. With co-operative arrangements between the companies and these countries, there is no reason why exports should not find their way in appropriate quantities, qualities and at appropriate times to refining centres and, if international refining arrangements are required for particular markets, they will be worked out at least as efficiently as they are now. Arguments that integrated control by a few big western firms is essential for efficient operation of this industry are little more than assertions based on very flimsy assumptions. In a far less integrated and more open industry, the international companies could (and will) continue to grow, earn profits in a variety of ways, and in general adapt themselves to changing environments and diverse government policies.

\* \* \*

To summarize this section, I suggest that the state will remain an overwhelmingly important economic unit in the less-developed world, at least so long as that world is poor and technologically backward: (1) because the arguments designed to persuade it that its welfare would be increased by rapid and comprehensive 'integration' with the advanced countries via the international firm are inconclusive and unconvincing; (2) because their peoples seem to want to demonstrate their competence and independence and to establish their own economic priorities – and insist on doing so; and (3) because inequality breeds fear of the more powerful. Where foreign domination has been extensive, as it has apparently been, and still is in Latin America, it seems to raise political problems consistent with these considerations. It has even been suggested that some Latin American regimes are maintained in power only with the help of the great capital-exporting country whose firms have achieved dominant positions. In other instances there are signs that national governments are attempting to assert their economic autonomy against international firms.

## THE FUTURE ROLE OF THE MULTINATIONAL ENTERPRISE

What, then, is the role of the multinational enterprise *vis-à-vis* the state? In spite of all the difficulties and attitudes outlined above, the less-developed countries, by and large, are prepared to accept – even to welcome – foreign enterprise and foreign help on their own terms where they believe it is clearly advantageous. 'Social-istically' inclined governments tend to insist on partnership arrange-ments; countries more sympathetic to private enterprise may also do so in less restrictive ways. For their part, the great international en-terprises are likely to invest wherever they consider it profitable to do so, without worrying overmuch about ideological considerations if only they feel reasonably secure – which means if expected profit will compensate for any additional risk. These enterprises have a great contribution to make to the less-developed countries, but it is very different from what it is in the developed countries.

It has been persuasively argued that continual innovation in tech-nology, and in methods of stimulating and sustaining consumers' demand with new products, new designs, new methods of marketing are necessary to maintain the momentum of the great industrial economies. Even if this is true, however, innovation and change of the kind that is characteristic of the United States economy, for example, is not the need, nor the popular demand, of the poor world. Many of their governments are aware of this, as are many inter-national firms, some of whom devote special efforts to research into the ways of meeting their real needs – agricultural development, the provision of water supplies, special health or nutritional problems, etc. Moreover, much of the nascent industry of many countries has been established with the help of the great international corporations, which have provided technical advice, granted licences and help under their own patents, given managerial assistance and even made training facilities of various kinds available for local technical people. If attention were focused on this kind of thing instead of on the more sweeping and spectacular generalizations about the 'integration of the world' through the multinational enterprise and the economic absorption of the 'nation state', I wonder which type of activity would really turn out to be generally the most important in the developing countries?

A firm is a pool of managerial and technological expertise. It is also an efficient operating machine for both production and distribution. It can enter areas of inefficiency and set up and operate efficient units. It can also train others to do so, making much of its own expertise available in the process. Both of these are important activities, but I have not yet understood why the former will take precedence, or why world-wide planning on an industry level is the most efficient way to raise the standards of living of all peoples.

The notion that firms will integrate the industries, and thus the economies, of the world within their own administrative framework, and that this will maximize world welfare, rests basically on the notion that planning on a world-wide scale is not only the inevitable outcome of present trends and United States economic power, but is also the most effective way of bringing the peoples of the world closer to the United States levels of living. It seems to me equally likely that they will continue to function as important international organizations, complementing and aiding the economic efforts of independent countries to develop their economies, and that such enterprises will have an important independent role in all sorts of international economic relations, but will also have to conduct continuous negotiations with states whose economic sovereignty they must respect as they try to 'harmonize' their own interests with those of the countries in which they operate.

I have not tried to discuss 'welfare' considerations here or the extent to which integration by firms would advance the development of any particular country, both economically and politically. My primary thesis has been that so long as the inequalities among the nations of the world are so great that a large proportion of the peoples of some are in real poverty, the governments of these peoples will be unwilling to give the rich and favoured foreign economic interests a dominating position in their economies. I also think it probable that, for as long as we can conveniently foresee, governments must insist on a high degree of sovereignty over their

238

economic affairs in order to provide a national economic framework for the activities of their people on the one hand, and on the other to ensure that their economic needs are represented as identifiable claimants for international consideration. If the basic economic unit for planning is the independent country – or a group of countries where some of the national units are very small – it may be less likely that pockets of backwardness in the world will be forgotten and left to rot. It is argued that the existence of the economic sovereignty of the state leads to economic cleavages along national lines, but if national differences were eliminated through integration, would not cleavages of an even more intractable nature along class (or even colour) lines tend to be accentuated?

The concern of a government for the economic welfare of its country must inevitably encompass a variety of considerations which would not be important to a great international enterprise. Indeed, I suspect that multinational enterprises as we know them today would find their life intolerable if the 'state as an economic unit' really did disappear!

*Chapter 9*

# COSTS AND BENEFITS OF MULTINATIONAL ENTERPRISES IN LESS-DEVELOPED COUNTRIES

PAUL STREETEN

## ADVOCATES AND OPPONENTS OF THE MULTINATIONAL ENTERPRISE

The multinational producing enterprise (MPE)[1] has been acclaimed as an agent of development and has been condemned as a weapon of exploitation. Those who have acclaimed it have argued that what they believe to be the likely future decline of official aid makes it even more advisable than before to switch attention to direct private foreign investment as an external source of development finance. Those who have condemned it point to the small or negative resource transfer and some advocate expropriation.

Most advocates and opponents agree that the MPE can be a most potent agent of innovation, a ruthless cutter of costs and a wily harnesser of resources. Attention has recently shifted from the contribution that it makes through the transfer of capital to the contribution that it makes through its ability to draw on a fund of not freely available knowledge, subject to economies of size, on a network of information, on managerial and technical skills, including those of marketing the product (again subject to scale economies), and on the institutionally built-in propensity to adapt and

---

[1] The term is used in this paper in the widest sense. It comprises in the loaded terminology of the Task Force *Foreign Ownership and the Structure of Canadian Industry*, the national company with foreign operations, the multinational corporation in the narrow sense, which is sensitive to the local needs of the countries in which it operates and the international (or the transnational) corporation, which is guided largely by standards transcending those of any particular nation state (cf. C. P. Kindleberger, *American Business Abroad*, New Haven, Yale University Press, 1969, p. 179, fn.). I am grateful to Mrs Frances Stewart, Mr Vijay Joshi, Mr J. P. Hayes and Mr F. B. Rampersad for helpful comments.

innovate.[1] In the current jargon, it is the software as much as the hardware that counts.

The knowledge that goes with the investment may relate to production or to marketing. *Production* knowledge may refer to a specific and stable process of production or to a *changing* flow of varying processes. Specific and *stable* processes can again be sub-divided into stable and *simple* recipes and stable and *complex* processes. The former can be patented or sold through licences. The latter require experts to go along with the process, at least initially and possibly continually. Access to a flow of changing knowledge is less easily bought.

*Marketing* knowledge may refer to (1) access to an existing network of outlets, or (2) quality guarantee or goodwill attached to a brand name, or (3) access to economies of scale through a marketing organization.

These distinctions are relevant to three questions: can the knowledge be purchased separately? what is the value of the knowledge? how are any gains distributed between different countries and the world as a whole?[2] The ability to purchase the information separately will depend upon its separate transferability. Where the advantage lies not in any specific formula, but in a complex network of information gathering, filtering, processing, feedback and application, a separate transfer may be impossible. When parting with the knowledge would be detrimental to the company, a separate transfer would be possible but will not occur. And there are numerous intermediate cases.

If advantages of information shade, on the one hand, into advantages of institutional relations, mutual trust and co-operation, they shade, on the other, into monopoly power. The line between the efficient network of communication and the old boys' network becomes blurred. Where does 'knowing' markets end and carving up markets begin? Where does a brand name advertise special

[1] Cf. Jack N. Behrman, 'Promoting Free World Economic Development through Direct Investment', *American Economic Review*, May 1960, pp. 271–81.

[2] Several people have made to me the fairly obvious point that one should distinguish between international firms operating in extractive industries, in production for the domestic market, for exports and in services. While these distinctions are clearly important for many purposes, I did not find them useful for the purpose of this paper. Much more useful would be a typology along the lines suggested above, for it is these categories which determine how the components of the private foreign investment 'package' should best be bought and assembled, what the benefits from buying them are and how these benefits are distributed between countries and throughout the world.

characteristics and where does it prey on ignorance or anxieties? Where are only private risks reduced and where social risks? Whatever the reasons, the MPE has a special advantage over the local firm in producing and selling.

It may then be true of certain cases, but it is irrelevant – the advocates argue – that capital could be borrowed more cheaply and information bought separately. The higher returns earned by foreign subsidiaries reflect exploitation, not of the country, but of the opportunities which the firm itself discovers or creates. In spite of declarations of public relations men to the contrary, the proponents of the MPE admit, indeed boast, that the creation of profitable opportunities pays little heed to social considerations; to justice, to equality, to even or balanced progress or to national sentiments. The profit-motivated approach, the tougher proponents of the MPE say, is incompatible with an approach emphasizing social planning. The operations of international companies will accentuate inequalities in the distribution of income because rewards will go to the most productive. They will increase unemployment of the unskilled, for the technology which they use has been developed in societies where labour is scarce and capital abundant. They will aggravate regional inequalities, for location of plant in the service of efficiency will conflict with regional, provincial or state claims for fair shares. They will accentuate sectoral inequalities and reinforce dualism, for modern technology is suited only for certain types of industrial activity. They will draw on outside resources and men, and will draw resources and men outside, guided only by costs and returns, without regard to national sentiments or social needs.

Between the Schumpeterian protagonists and the socialist–nationalist antagonists of the MPE there are those who advise the developing host governments to harness its beneficial effects and to control or curtail its damaging effects. Three sets of problems arise here. First, even if the will and the political power to control were present, to what extent is it feasible for a host government to control the MPE effectively (i.e. to what extent has it the necessary expertise and non-political power)? Second, even if it had the political power, does it have the will? Third, even if it had the will, the knowledge and expertise and the non-political power, does it have the *political* power?

### ABILITY TO CONTROL

If the centre of decision-making is located in the parent country, while subsidiaries and branches are located in many overseas countries, the technical ability of a host government to control is greatly reduced. The MPE will be less responsive to exhortations and requests. There may be doubts about which legal system applies. It will be less responsive to monetary policy, for it can draw on alternative sources of funds, both from abroad and from internal accumulation. While this ability to draw on funds from outside may in some respects be an advantage, it, together with its reputation and size, also increases the firm's borrowing power in the host country, with consequential effects on the allocation of domestic resources and on the balance of payments. Fiscal policy can be circumvented by adjusting prices charged between stages of a vertically integrated firm, by the allocation of overhead and other joint costs, by the conversion of what should be regarded as profits to management fees, royalties or other 'costs'. Trade policy may be determined by marketing considerations of the parent firm or by political conditions imposed upon it by the parent government, such as the prohibition of American firms to trade with Cuba and China.

Against this, it is sometimes argued that because the foreign firm is large and visible and its accounts published and accessible, it has less scope to evade the law than smaller domestic firms. It has also been said that in granting concessions, or generally permitting entry, the host government can exercise more influence on the decisions of foreign firms, say, with respect to where the plant should be located. In Britain, for example, it was easier to steer foreign than domestic firms into depressed areas, possibly because they were more responsive to financial incentives.

In spite of these considerations, the balance of the argument for less-developed countries seems to be on the other side. Economic control will tend to be less feasible and therefore less effective. While illegal evasion of the law is more difficult for the foreign firm, it has more scope for legal avoidance. It is larger and more powerful than the domestic firm, it is less dependent on the goodwill of the government and it can always go elsewhere.

## WILL TO CONTROL

There is a wide area of policies, supported by entrenched vested interests including, ironically, many of which both the host government and the foreign firm are most proud, which are hostile to development. This unholy harmony of interests is reinforced by the high prestige which institutions, practices and ideas in advanced industrial countries enjoy and by the inertia which makes their transfer to societies with utterly different conditions and problems so tempting.

The transfer of trade union objectives from industrial to under-developed countries, the introduction of collective bargaining, the setting of high labour standards, minimum wage legislation, short working hours, resistance to multiple-shift working and the adoption of expensive social welfare services are a potent source preventing the beneficial effects of foreign direct investment from spreading. The principles which these practices reflect are enshrined in declarations of human rights, in international conventions and in the sermons of officials and managers. The foreign firms pride them-selves on the high labour standards which they introduce into less-developed countries, the high wages they pay, the short hours their workers work and the generous welfare services which they provide. In fact, all these are detractions from, not contributions to, the development effort. It is precisely in the area where host government and foreign firm seem to pursue common interests, where the profit motive and national aspirations seem to coincide, that most damage is done, particularly if these benevolent activities are accompanied by tax concessions.

In the acceptance of wage-increasing union activity, the foreign firm does not necessarily sacrifice profits. Where it can pass on wage increases in higher prices, inflationary pressures are communicated to the rest of the economy. Even where it absorbs wage increases, it benefits from improved labour relations and ability to attach a more contented and privileged labour force to the firm. The small domestic competitor, who is unable to match the higher wages, is squeezed out or is not given an opportunity to set up in business. The differentials between the privileged labour aristocracy attached to the MPE and average incomes are very large. In Jamaica, an un-skilled worker earns at least three times as much in the bauxite industry as in the sugar industry, and a fraction of this in indigenous rural employment. The same differentials exist in Zambian copper mines and in Mauritian and Guyanan sugar plantations. The practices reduce the incentive to develop unskilled-labour-intensive methods of production and management and they aggravate unemployment and social inequality. While there was a case for a high wage policy in colonial times, when the foreign company was not taxed, the payment of higher wages was the only method of transferring some of its profits to the indigenous population, and higher wages were a condition of an efficient labour force, today it would be more sensible to tax profits directly, rather than indirectly by imposing conditions on the use of local supplies, local labour, local share capital or by imposing on it welfare costs for the benefit of a small labour aristocracy. If it is decided to admit foreign firms, the host government does best to encourage them to lower costs by drawing resources from wherever in the world they are cheapest. It is here that its particular virtue lies. It is not sensible to transfer income by attempting to transform the MPE from what it is – a profit-seeking animal – into something it is not – a public servie.

## AUTONOMY OF POLICIES

Anglo-Saxon welfare economics tends to be conducted on the assumption that the government of a country is the custodian of the social interest (which is sometimes tacitly or explicitly equated with the national interest) and has supreme and autonomous power (although not perfect knowledge) to implement policies in pursuit of this objective. In fact governments everywhere, and particularly the governments of less-developed countries, are neither monolithic nor fully autonomous. They represent a conglomeration of ideals and interests, usually susceptible to outside pressures, which may reinforce some local interest. A proper theory of foreign investment must therefore be integrated into a political theory of the sources of policy. The point has become increasingly important. For in the nineteenth century a host of small and anonymous lenders and businesses confronted a handful of large governments. Today, a handful of powerful, large companies confront a host of small, competing, weak and not always single-minded governments. The large and powerful MPE can draw on a pool of skilled and experienced manpower and, on occasion, on the support of the government of the parent company. The officials of the host government, by contrast, are typically inexperienced. The foreign firm will tend to demand privileges with regard to taxation, relief from duties on imported products necessary for its investment and production (sometimes at overvalued exchange rates), low bank interest rates and protection against foreign competition. If these concessions are granted, there is no longer a presumption that the foreign investment will contribute to the resources of the host country.

Consider a protective tariff. In conditions of free trade, the international firm sells its product at world prices – say at $100. If imported inputs cost $50 and local costs amount to $30, the remaining $20 profit is a net contribution to production, which can be divided between foreign shareholders, ploughed back profits and taxes. But assume a 100% tariff enables the firm to sell the product at $200. Private profits no longer are an indication of gains in production, for imported inputs may now swallow up more than what is added to social product. Even 100% taxation of profits would not reduce this loss to the host country and any tax concession would increase it. An allowance could be made for a shadow wage rate below actual wages, but the danger often remains. Moreover, as Harry Johnson has shown,[1] technical progress or the accumulation of factors of production in the protected industry may further reduce the country's real income.

Tax concessions to foreign investment not only deprive the host government of development revenue; they also encourage methods of production which are less capital-saving than if the concession took the form of a wage subsidy. Such a subsidy may be justified if the shadow wage is lower than the money wage and if there is a choice of technique. Arguments have been advanced that labour may be an inferior good and that such subsidies would then reduce the demand for labour.[2] They are based on fallacious reasoning, for it is always possible to tax directly the extra income, generated by the wage subsidy, and thus restore the pre-subsidy real income level, leaving the firm only with the substitution effect in favour of more employment.

However great the contribution of the international enterprise to development, which stems from its advanced techniques in production and marketing, its training of local labour, of suppliers and of purchasers and its encouragement of ancillary business through subcontracting, its operations require a number of complementary or compensating activities to which it does not normally contribute. Above all, there are the necessary complementary investments in physical and social overhead capital: roads, harbours, utilities, education, health, nutrition. The foreign firm has normally no reason to make a substantial direct contribution to these. Then, finance is needed to conduct pre-investment, design and feasibility studies which prepare the ground for the private foreign investment. Third, where a transfer problem exists, finance is needed to service the payment of remittances and possibly repatriation of capital across the exchanges. Fourth, a country may wish to finance a

---

[1] H. G. Johnson, 'The Possibility of Income Losses from Increased Efficiency or Factor Accumulation in the Presence of Tariffs', *Economic Journal*, March 1967, pp. 151–4.

[2] Michael P. Todaro, 'A Theoretical Note on Labour as an "Inferior" Factor in Less Developed Countries', *The Journal of Development Studies*, July 1969.

gradual and agreed transfer of equity to indigenous (public or private) ownership.

But more important than any of these reasons for complementary sources of finance is the desire of a country to correct some of the violations of social objectives inflicted by the MPE. Wherever it operates unchecked, it perpetuates and aggravates inequalities of income and wealth, it creates new oligarchies and it destroys a sense of participation of the less-productive masses. Its operations are also liable to sudden and large changes over time. The host country may therefore wish to restore balance in the face of this uneven impact by reducing extreme inequalities, as between income by size, or between regions, even when these do not give the unproductive groups or regions a better opportunity to become productive.

For any, or all, these reasons, complementary sources of finance will be required when the green light is given to the multinational enterprise. These might take the form of aid funds contributed on soft terms or of tax revenue. The deficiences of aid are by now well known and adequate collection of tax on company profits is essential if the MPE is to be used as an agent for development. I have argued that political and economic pressures weaken the political and administrative power to tax adequately. Lack of information about taxable capacity further reduces the bargaining power of the host government. In conditions of bilateral oligopoly or bilateral monopoly, the maximum tax that can be levied without deterring investment and the minimum tax that will still make it appear worth while to the host country to attract the investment will be some distance apart, sometimes quite far apart. The pressures to reduce taxation and to grant concessions do not come only from the foreign firm but also from competing developing countries trying to attract the investment. The elasticity of supply of total direct overseas investment is probably low, so that competitive tax concessions lead to beggar-my-neighbour policies. Companies often declare that concessions, though welcome, do not make much difference to their decisions to invest if expected profits are adequate (or threatened losses from not investing are serious), if the continuation of the concessions is uncertain and if the company expects to be subjected to other forms of restriction. The study carried out by the Institute of Development Studies and Queen Elizabeth House on private overseas investment has shown that few of the twenty-nine foreign firms interviewed in Kenya and Jamaica considered inducements offered by host governments to be of major importance in their decisions to invest. The size of the tax concessions and the height of protective tariffs appeared to be in most cases excessive.

It is difficult to interpret these declarations in the light of rational behaviour, attempting to equate continuously varying marginal revenues to marginal costs. But it must be remembered that the relation between companies and host governments is often one of bilateral oligopoly. The firms would be prepared to carry out the same investment even with smaller concessions, while the countries would be willing to attract the investment even at the cost of granting larger concessions. This situation creates an area of bargaining within which concessions can vary without affecting any decisions.

Assistance is therefore required in enabling a host country to identify the bargaining area and to determine the range of optimum taxation. One set of obstacles to the imposition of the optimum tax would be removed if several host countries combined in eliminating competitive concessions. Although gains from such co-operation could be substantial, they face the danger of all such agreements that an outsider can damage the scheme. Benefits to individuals from corruption would also remove their incentives to co-operate. Another possibility would be an expert advisory service, either in the form of an international agency or of an independent group of consultants. What is needed is information and technical assistance in negotiation.[1] There would be several considerable advantages in more expert handling of the taxation of international firms. A greater contribution through tax revenues would reduce the need for development aid. At the moment, taxpayers in donor countries subsidise, to some extent, the operations of MPEs by providing aid for infrastructure projects which make these operations profitable. It would also make for the quiet style in resource transfer for which some have pleaded. It would remove international co-operation for development from the noisy arena of annual budgetary appropriations, performance criteria, confrontations and recriminations, and assure a fairly regular flow of resources on which recipients could rely in their forward planning.

A more radical solution has been proposed by Professor Edith Penrose.[2] Her proposal is that international firms should be incorporated under international law and subject to a single international income tax. In this way all distortions and conflicts which arise from different income tax rates would be eliminated, as well as the incen-

---

[1] See Dudley Seers, 'Big Companies and Small Countries: A Practical Proposal', *Kyklos*, Vol. XVI, 1963, Fasc. 4.

[2] Edith T. Penrose, *The Large International Firm in Developing Countries*, London, Allen & Unwin, 1968, p. 273.

tives to grant competitive tax concessions. Information and expertise could be concentrated in the international tax authority. While Professor Penrose does not propose this, an obvious next step would be to use the tax revenue for development aid. It could take the form of grants, thus avoiding the laborious stage performance of loan agreements, debt relief, rescheduling, etc. The distribution of the revenue could be guided by genuine criteria of development, rather than by the accident of the geographical distribution of oil resources.

The conclusion of this part of the argument is that those who hope for a substantial contribution to development by foreign direct investment, particularly if they are also pessimistic about soft aid prospects, should emphasize the importance of strengthening the power and willingness of host governments to tax. This involves detailed research into optimum tax levels, which should take into account both ability and incentive of the international firms to continue investment; it involves co-operation between less-developed countries; and it involves strengthening the basis of information on which decisions are made. A rational system of company taxation might go a long way to save the tax-payers in rich countries money for aid programmes and at the same time make the expenditure more effective.

## THE ALTERNATIVES BEFORE THE HOST GOVERNMENT

The characteristic feature of foreign direct investment is that it transfers a whole complex set of productive factors, some amenable to conventional economic analysis like capital and technical skills, others less easily comprehended by it, like executive capacity, management, knowhow, goodwill and a network of relationships giving access to supplies or markets and feeding back information gleaned. From the point of view of the host country the question is whether, assuming the investment is wanted, these factors and conditions can be assembled more cheaply in some other way.[1] What matters for a correct assessment by a host government of the potential contribution to development of the MPE is not what historically preceded the direct foreign investment, but what the next best alternative would be. Any operational assessment of its potential contribution must start from an assumption about this alternative. If a country wishes to evaluate the costs and benefits to be derived from setting up an additional plant, it is irrelevant to compare the

[1] See also Chapter 1 in this volume, p. 42.

established plant with the situation before its establishment. What is relevant is a comparison between the following possibilities:

(a) to raise the capital and other resources domestically and set up an indigenous plant;

(b) to borrow money abroad, hire engineers and managers and buy the knowhow through a licensing arrangement;

(c) any partial combination between (a) and (b), including management contracts;

(d) joint ventures between, on the one hand, direct foreign investors and, on the other hand, private or public local capital, management, etc.;

(e) to import the finished product;

(f) not to carry out the investment now, nor to import the product, but to do without it for the time being or altogether.

A clear formulation of the alternatives is an essential prerequisite to the proper appraisal of the value of foreign enterprise. The important point for analysis and policy is to envisage the various alternatives, against which any operational assessment has to be made and to assess the benefits and the costs of each, measuring what is measurable and judging what is not.

This formulation of the problem has come under considerable attack, both from academic colleagues and businessmen. It is said that administrative talent is scarce and it is quite unrealistic to hope that such investigations can be conducted; that no lessons can be learned from a particular evaluation in one country at one period for other countries or other periods; that the best alternative may be impossible and hence irrelevant.

My reply is that the opposite view leads to no conclusions. From complete ignorance, nothing follows. I should certainly not wish only first-best alternatives to be considered, but should be content with either second-best possible or first-best feasible alternatives. I have more faith in the profitability of investigating case studies of similar industries put up in different ways in similar countries, subject to the costs of administering the investigation. The typology suggested on p. 241 will be a help. No one proposes today to use direct foreign investment for railways or public utilities. Many would agree that it might be suited for petrochemicals. Intermediate cases, like fertilizer or cement plant, do not seem to raise impossibly difficult problems.

Once the problem is viewed in this manner, new possibilities arise. Foreign or international development corporations may be invited or created, domestic development corporations may be created or expanded, an indigenous base for research and development may be built up, an altogether different pattern of final consumption or of productive techniques may be adopted, etc.

Here again, as in the formulation of tax policies, technical assistance in assessing the alternatives and in creating and providing the alternative institutions will be necessary.

### AREAS OF CONFLICT AND HARMONY

Conflict between the multinational enterprise and the host government may derive from four sources: from the fact that it is *private* and hence may clash with the social and national goals; that it is *large* and oligopolistic and hence possesses market and bargaining power which may be used against the interest of the host country; that it is *foreign*, particularly if it is American, and hence may be serving the national interests of a foreign nation; and that it is *'western'* and hence may transfer inappropriate knowhow, technology or management practices, or products, designed with characteristics not needed in less-developed countries.

Foreign companies are sometimes accused of sacrificing the national development of the country to its desire for profits. It would be both unreasonable and possibly undesirable to expect them to act altruistically in promoting local development. Within the constraints set by competition, legislation, morality and public opinion, there is a presumption that it is best employed in seeking profits, as long as it takes a long-term view, not giving excessive weight to quick profits at the expense of future profits and as long as it assesses correctly the constraints set by political action and public opinion.

More serious is the charge that the foreign subsidiary sacrifices its own profits to the interests of the parent company or sister companies in an advanced industrial country or indeed to the interest of the group of companies as a whole, and that this, rather than any lack of nationalism, charity or altruism, damages local development. Such restrictions on local profit maximization can have different reasons. The company may charge higher prices for its products in order to prevent the elimination of inefficient sister or parent companies in the investing country. But the reverse may also be true: the parent company pricing its products so as to keep an inefficient subsidiary in business. In the former case the high prices of primary products may lead to faster innovation in synthetic substitutes, in which the parent company may be engaged. The

251

problem here is not monopoly pricing by the subsidiary, for price reductions would increase local profits, but the foreign locus of ownership and control. Or again, local 'profits' may be minimized rather than maximized, by underpricing output and overpricing inputs, if by this device tax liabilities can be shifted from a high-tax country to a low-tax country, or losses can be set off against highly-taxed gains. Another cause of conflict is to be found, as we have seen, in the high wages and fringe benefits which the foreign company can offer to local workers and which do not reflect the cost of alternative uses of the labour forgone. While this policy ensures that some of the profits of foreign enterprise are retained by citizens of the host country, it can play havoc with the wage structure in the rest of the economy, aggravate social inequality, perpetuate unemployment and encourage the wasteful use of capital.

Conflicts may arise, as I have suggested, between profit-seeking and social objectives, between the uneven progress imposed by the profit-orientation of the MPE and the balanced progress desired by the country, between the dualism created and deepened by it and the need for spread effects.

First, the impact of the MPE will be strongest in those sectors in which the knowhow of the foreign firm can be applied. Sectors like tropical agriculture, small-scale production, traditional crafts, the processing of local raw materials, the use of local by-products and subsistence farming have no parallels in advanced industrial countries and will therefore remain untouched by foreign investment, or may be destroyed by it, except in so far as their transformation feeds the activities of the international firms.

Second, the MPE will use not only the capital-intensive, often inappropriate technology which it transfers from its parent company, but it will also employ labour-saving management techniques and practices. Its interests lie in minimizing industrial relations with a foreign labour force, which may be unskilled, underfed, unhealthy, unreliable, undisciplined and perhaps hostile, and dealings with which may give rise to political difficulties. How much easier to rationalize this reluctance behind a 'decent wages' and generous industrial welfare policy, where the standards of decency and generosity are taken from the economic and social conditions prevailing in the parent country.[1]

Third, while the MPE will have an incentive to borrow locally, it

---

[1] For evidence of limited local training, see J. N. Behrman, 'Foreign Investment and the Transfer of Knowledge and Skills' in R. Mikesell (ed.), *US Private and Government Investment Abroad*, University of Oregon Books, 1962.

will prefer fixed interest loans to equity and will tolerate local equity participation only to the point where the parent company maintains control. This means that a high proportion of earnings will accrue to foreign equity holders. If ploughed back, they will further raise the foreign stake; if remitted abroad, they will burden the balance of payments.

A conflict of a different kind arises for a developing country when it has to choose between benefiting from the power of the MPE by gaining stable and monopolistic outlets for the products whose raw materials are extracted from its soil but at the same time sacrifice national control and, on the other hand, gain national control through indigenous operation or joint ventures, but sacrifice the advantages of market outlets which only the MPE can offer.

Political risks, such as expropriation without adequate compensation, restrictions on remittance of profits and repatriation of capital, multiple currency practices or devaluation are often cited as factors which make it necessary to earn high rates of profit to compensate for these risks. The high rates earned then cause suspicion and hostility in the host country, which feels that the firm is taking out much more than it puts in, and tend to lead to those dreaded events which the high profits seek to compensate for. This leads to the demand for even higher profits and the vicious spiral is given another twist. High profits, required because of risks, also impose a heavy balance of payments burden, tending to lead to restrictions on remittances and repatriation, and once again strengthen the demand for higher profits to compensate for the risk of the imposition of such restrictions.

There are other vicious circles of a similar nature. If, for instance, the firm estimates the risks as high and anticipates leaving the country before very long, it will have no incentive to train local labour. But the absence of such training schemes reinforces the desire on the part of the host government and local opinion to push out the company, because it contributes little to long-term development. Once again, these sentiments reinforce the company's desire to quit soon.

It is clear that mutual gains could be derived from measures which lower these risks, lighten the balance of payments burden, reduce the rate of profit required by the company, increase the time horizon and the incentive to train local labour, and dispel fear and suspicion. Private investment in uncertain conditions is not a zero-sum game[1]

[1] The expression is applied to a different state of affairs from that envisaged by C. P. Kindleberger in *American Business Abroad*, pp. 150 ff.

and both investor and host country can gain from such mutually agreed 'disarmament'.

Against these conflicts between the aims of the MPE and national and social objectives must be set the benefits that flow from the urge to make profits. This primary urge can have a number of incidental spread effects, beneficial to development in the host country. We have already discussed the need to avoid tax concessions, to gather full information about profits and about the range within which bargaining power can be used and to make tax revenue contribute fully to development expenditure.

Apart from taxation, the firm itself may have incentives to generate spread effects. It has an incentive to train and improve the performance of local suppliers and to spread information and skills among its potential customers. A firm processing or tinning fruit may teach fruit growers to grow and supply the required kinds of fruit (although firms are known to have imported fruit and even sugar from their parent country, on the ground that it could not be grown or be properly refined in the host country). A firm may have an interest in encouraging the growth of efficient local repair shops or supplies of components and spare parts. A firm producing for the domestic market fertilizers or farm equipment will have an interest in training farmers in their proper use, as Esso in the Philippines and Shell and Standard Oil of California in India are doing. To the extent to which it pays the firm to employ local labour, it will be in its interest to train it. It will also wish to train local managers and technicians, if its time horizon is sufficiently long. The cost of trained labour transferred from the parent country is substantially higher than training local labour, because both investment in teachers and earnings forgone by the taught are much greater in a rich country. This diffusion of incentives, knowledge and skills amongst suppliers, users and employees will be beneficial to indigenous development.

There are clearly limits to these spread effects and there are, as we have seen, backwash effects, such as the possible discouragement to indigenous production, skills and entrepreneurship. The power of the foreign firm to increase competition and to force cost reductions on hitherto inert local competitors has sometimes been a beneficent force in old-established advanced industrial countries. The arrival of the American subsidiary in Western Europe has often shaken up a sleepy entrepreneurial clique. But in underdeveloped countries the bracing effect of the cold wind of competition may be so harsh as to kill or prevent indigenous growth.

## NATIONAL INTEGRATION AND INTERNATIONAL DISINTEGRATION

So far we have discussed the relations between the MPE and the host governments. Different problems arise in the relations between host government and government of the country in which the parent company is located over their different attitudes to the international firm.

The growth of the integrated nation state has created problems for the developing countries which the now industrialized countries did not face in their pre-industrial phase. Advance has meant national progress and national consolidation in the industrial countries. But the benefits of the welfare state are largely confined to its citizens. National consolidation in rich countries has tended to lead to international disintegration.[1] Attempts to maintain full employment in rich industrial countries, particularly if interpreted to apply to all regions and occupations, to avoid the costs of disruption through low-cost imports and to insulate the national economy from outside influences, have strengthened the forces of protection and reduced the opportunities for trade and migration. Export of capital and scarce skills, and immigration that threatens to upset industrial peace or national prejudices, are restricted by the rich countries.

In the early enthusiasm about full employment and welfare policies after the last war, it was thought that the achievement and maintenance of full employment would reduce the need for protectionist policies and would restore the era of free international trade. In the event, full employment has created its own strong motivation for restrictions on trade, payments and immigration. First, full employment tended to cause inflationary pressures and balance of payments difficulties to those who inflated faster than others. These led to restrictions, including restrictions on the free flow of foreign investment. Second, full employment tended to be interpreted as applying to particular regions and occupations and the structural unemployment which some low-cost imports would have entailed was disliked. This makes it difficult for the MPE to exploit the cost advantages of producing labour-intensive, low technology products in less-developed countries for export to developed countries. Third, full employment brought with it the desire to make the fullest use of resources and brought the terms of trade argument for trade restrictions to the fore. In particular, it became important to keep

[1] Gunnar Myrdal, *An International Economy*, London, Routledge, 1956.

255

the prices of imported food and raw materials as low as possible. Fourth, the desire to maintain and raise wages constituted a powerful argument against immigration of workers who would weaken the bargaining power of trade unions, while encouraging the immigration of people with scarce skills. Fifth, the need to mobilize savings for domestic objectives set a limit to the outflow of aid and private capital. For these and similar reasons, the national welfare state has turned out to be a not very good neighbour to poorer countries, which depended on trade, migration and capital. By its general welfare policies, it inhibits or frustrates the internationally integrating power the MPE would have in conditions of free trade and free movement of men. In the absence of these restrictions, the MPE, recruiting wherever it can, irrespective of colour, nationality, creed or caste, and selling wherever it can, might be guided by the invisible hand to promote something not too different from the cosmopolitan interest. What, then, should be the response of the less-developed countries?

One way is that suggested by Gunnar Myrdal. Though by conviction an internationalist, he says:

> The road to international integration must go over national integration; nationalistic policies by the poor countries and an increase of their bargaining power, won through these policies and through increased co-operation between them as a group, is a necessary stage towards a more effective world-wide international co-operation.[1]

The thesis has to be negated by an antithesis before a synthesis is reached. Option for the nationalist solution is not necessarily motivated by nationalistic or xenophobic ideals. It is quite consistent for a genuine internationalist to argue that national consolidation is a necessary stage in progress towards internationalism in our present world economy. The other option for the developing countries is to lay themselves open to what integrating forces prevail in the world economy, adopting free trade, free migration, and a welcome to investment from abroad, accepting the policies of the rich like natural obstacles.

It may be said that the international economy offers benefits which a small, weak developing country cannot afford to forgo and that the way to national strength and consolidation is through full participation in the international division of labour, by adopting

[1] *Reshaping the World Economy*, edited by John A. Pincus, Prentice-Hall, p. 90.

free trade and unrestricted investment policies. Just as the internationalist can advocate national policies as a step towards the ultimate goal, so the nationalist can advocate outward-looking policies. Little can be inferred about ultimate ideology from the path proposed, or about the path from ideology. It may well be that either path is possible. History has certainly shown that successful development can be achieved by both types of policy. But history's lessons are of limited value here. For it makes a crucial difference to the development prospects what happens in countries in the lead. Coexistence of rich and poor, for good and ill, has made a vital difference to the efforts of the poor.

CONCLUSIONS

A main theme of this chapter is that we should not contrast the multinational enterprise and the nation state, but that the important alignments cut across this distinction. Firstly, the nation state is not monolithic. Different interests within it align themselves differently with the foreign-owned firm. Among those who will side with it are bribed officials, the small employed aristocracy of workers who enjoy high wages and security, the satellite bourgeoisie to whom world-wide mobility and prospects are opened and the domestic industries producing complementary goods who benefit from the concessions which the MPE has achieved for itself. On the other side of the fence are the masses of unemployed, non-employed and underemployed, those who suffer from the higher costs, the competitors, actual and potential, and those who dislike foreigners. In view of this division, it is misleading to speak of the interest of the nation state.

Secondly, the interest of the ruling élite in the nation state should be viewed in relation to the interests of other élites in competing or neighbouring developing countries. Many policies damaging to a particular country and its interest groups result from competitive concessions, ignorance and weak bargaining power. The gathering and dissemination of information, the pursuit of joint policies and similar forms of co-operation promise gains for the developing countries as a group. On the other hand, the existence of such co-operation gives a premium to any one country staying outside, or breaking away; and the fear of such break-away may reduce the cohesion of the alliance. Sanctions may be required to enforce participation. What institutional forms these alliances should take is not under discussion here. It may be that a separate UN agency is desirable or that inter-governmental co-operation suffices. The main point is that with the expansion of international direct investment and with the possibility of trade union action becoming international, the nation state must look beyond its boundaries if it is to match the new forces.

Thirdly, MPEs pursue different objectives which sometimes clash. To group them together as a single force for world integration or world domination, undermining the nation state, is misleading. Exciting generalizations, often a symptom of the infancy of research, are intoxicating but they share some of the after-effects of intoxication.

# COMMENTS ON THE CHAPTERS BY PROFESSOR PENROSE AND MR STREETEN

## J. P. HAYES

This part of the discussion concentrates on the effects of multi-national enterprises specifically on the poorer countries.

Professor Penrose does not agree that the 'nation state is just about through as an economic unit'. Listening to the discussion in the past day and a half, I have the impression that Professor Kindleberger has been convicted, by an almost unanimous majority, of the misdemeanour of arguing by exaggeration. It is within the power of governments not to let in foreign investment. When they have permitted such investments, they still retain the power to nationalize them if they see sufficient cause.

Professor Penrose correctly reminds us that a country can be interested in other things besides maximizing GNP and/or employment. Preferences cannot be branded as 'irrational' '. . . provided that [they] are consistent and that their implications are appreciated by those who express them'. I will just note the fascinating range of questions (further developed in Mr Streeten's paper) about who expresses the preferences, who agrees and disagrees with them, and what those of us should conclude who have any part in trying to influence the course of events.

I would agree that *laissez faire*, with MPEs like whales among the minnows, would leave pockets of backwardness to rot. I would not suppose that national governments or even providers of aid are about to be put out of business. But it may or may not follow from this that developing countries ought to exclude whales which are willing to swim in. This is one of the questions which have to be invesitagted.

Professor Penrose considers that developing countries will tend to resist invasion by foreign firms – even, by implication, when these operations would in fact contribute to maximization of national product and/or employment. Mr Streeten, on the other hand, appears to be concerned that developing countries may let in foreign firms when their operations are not the best way towards national economic objectives.

Mr Streeten also refers to various 'vicious spirals' whereby fear of expropriation or restrictions of various kinds lead foreign-owned firms into policies inimical to the interests of the host countries, so increasing the likelihood of expropriation, etc.

Mr Streeten would like to see developing countries carefully reviewing each proposal for foreign investment and considering the relative advantages of all possible alternatives before deciding whether to let the foreign investor in. This is, of course, a counsel of perfection, the more so in view of the shortage of administrative and other skills in many developing countries. Professor Penrose comments on – should I say, regrets? – 'the inconclusiveness of the relevant economic analyses'. One may fear that the behaviour of governments will be influenced by general conclusions that the MPE is bad for their countries (or good, as the case may be), without regard to the particular merits or demerits of individual cases. It would be useful to the developing countries if they could have some valid rules of thumb, or an appraisal manual, to help them to decide what foreign investments to admit, and how far to go when they are negotiating terms and conditions with foreign investors.

I gather that Mr Streeten would say that there cannot be simple but nevertheless valid rules of thumb. To quote from another article which he wrote jointly with Lord Balogh: 'Once the assumptions of perfect competition, divisibility of factors and products, diminishing marginal productivity of capital, constant terms of trade and adjustment to equilibrium positions, are abandoned, it is impossible to say with certainty whether, from a national point of view . . . foreign capital should be attracted into or kept out of a country. Much depends on the industries and the conditions in which the investment takes place.'[1] Given his conclusions on the difficulties of generalizing, it seems odd that Mr Streeten has not found it useful to distinguish between MPEs operating in extractive industries, in production for the domestic market, in services or in agriculture or manufacturing for export; activities in these various sectors would seem to raise different types of issue. Some of Mr Streeten's comments appear highly specific to one type of activity, some to another.

Various efforts are now being made to investigate empirically what the effect of foreign private investment has in fact been on developing countries. But it is not clear how successfully these investigations are succeeding in coping with four types of difficulty. First, there is the difficulty of deciding what should be counted as

---

[1] 'Domestic versus Foreign Investment', *Bulletin of the Institute of Statistics*, Vol. 22, August, 1960.

consequences of the private investment, rather than of *any* enlargement of economic activity or of host government policies. For example, it would seem invalid to attribute to foreign investment the increase of imports due to multiplier effects started by increase of domestic incomes due to the foreign investment. Second, identification of all consequences which should have an important effect on the conclusions. Third, when we ask whether a foreign investment (or foreign investment in general) has left the host country better or worse off, this raises the awkward question – better or worse off than what; what would have been the alternative state of affairs if the foreign investment had not taken place? Fourth, there is the question of project appraisal technique; for example, for an investment producing for the domestic market, it is necessary to be able to weigh together the value of the product, the opportunity cost of domestic factors of production and the cost to the economy of any imported inputs and of factor income payments to the foreigner. This raises the problem of the shadow price of foreign exchange – or, Little and Mirrlees would say, the prices of specifically domestic factors in terms of foreign exchange. Mr Streeten lists the alternatives which developing countries ought, ideally, to take into account. But this raises the problem of how the alternatives are to be compared. Importing the goods in question involves, other things being equal, increasing export earnings to pay for them. Use of domestic capital presumably has its opportunity cost. The first essential is to clear up the remaining disagreements about appraisal technique.

I am not quite clear whether Mr Streeten's main purpose is to advise developing countries on how to deal with foreign companies in their midst. Or is he saying they will have difficulty in harnessing inward direct investment to their advantage, and so had better be wary of it? This could reinforce the attitude which Professor Penrose says they are likely to take in any case, out of concern for independence and proportional sharing of benefits. But I think that we ought to look very carefully at the question of how developing countries should behave to their own advantage, given any limitations in their capacity to appraise individual investment proposals and to strike appropriate bargains as to the conditions of foreign investment. I mentioned the snag that the question, does foreign investment leave the host country better or worse off, raises the prior question, better or worse off than what? Whether he intended it or not, Mr Streeten's paper appears to me to suggest an unfavourable comparison between the operations of foreign firms and the best possible way of getting hold of the goods in question (or, presumably, other

261

goods of equivalent value). Now, while it is good advice to developing countries to do all that they reasonably can to seek out the best alternative, I feel that to judge foreign investment *as if the best alternative would, in fact, always be found* gives a biased view of where the balance of advantage lies to all practical intents and purposes. We cannot assume that the range of possibilities that is in fact open to many developing countries is very broad. To say that something is not the best that was *theoretically* possible is not necessarily to say, in any practical sense, that it is disadvantageous.

It has been suggested that direct foreign investment has an inherently anti-competitive effect. This is an important assertion calling for further investigation. The vision may be of a foreign firm coming into a protected local market which is none too big for it. If the point is really excessive protection, then this is important. But whose fault is it? Governments of many developing countries have been all too prone to fall into the trap of excessive protection of domestically financed as well as foreign investments. Is it not, indeed, the main incentive to the MPE to produce inside a developing country for the domestic market that there is already high protection against imports? The foreign investor may ask for excessive protection. But surely the host country need not concede it?

Some commentators imply that governments of developing countries tend to act weakly, foolishly, even corruptly, in their dealings with foreign investors, and go on to draw a contrast with an alternative state of affairs in which an all-wise government will plan all things for the best. Here again, the vision of the hypothetical alternative may be unrealistic. In practice, the powers of organization of an international firm may bring in something valuable which would not otherwise be there.

The possibility of tax avoidance by MPEs has already been discussed. Mr Streeten rightly emphasizes that developing countries should not be afraid to tax foreign investors. But it is not clear whether he considers that taxation determines whether the foreign investment is or is not advantageous to the host country.

The question of excessive wages and fringe benefits may merit some consideration. High wages would seem to be, in themselves, a benefit to the host country, except in so far as inequality is considered undesirable *per se*. However, it does appear to be the case that trade unions in developing countries follow the curious policy of demanding wages for all occupations comparable with the wages in the highest-paid occupations, and would rather keep people out of work than allow them to work for less. How far, I wonder, can this type of conduct survive the pressures of massive urban unemployment and underemployment? If a foreign subsidiary producing for the domestic market secures unduly high returns, allowing it to pay exceptionally high wages, why does this not provoke competition? Will the distorting effect on the labour market be serious if MPEs are only relatively small employers? Will not the advantages of high wages outweigh the disadvantages if these firms come to employ a pretty substantial proportion of the urban labour force?

At the end of his chapter, Mr Streeten raises the question of how to create conditions which will enable foreign investors to take a long view in the interests of themselves and of the host country alike. I imagine that several of their spokesmen would claim that they are so well established, and have spread their risks so widely, that they are better able to take a long view than smaller firms. Beyond that, it is difficult to see how a foreign investor can ever entirely banish from his mind the risk of expropriation after some future change of government. Here again, the general impressions of developing countries as to where their interests lie may be very important.

Is it possible to simplify the task of developing countries in dealing with foreign investors by offering them rules of thumb? In the case of extractive operations, they will obviously seek the highest possible royalties for the use of the natural resource. May I suggest that the most important single rule of thumb should be that the host country should never allow protection for production for the home market of more than, say, 20% of domestic value added? I suspect that the one clear case where foreign private investment is disadvantageous to the host country is when it goes into excessively protected production for the home market, thus diverting local resources which would be better employed in production of exports or in import-substituting production requiring less protection.

Finally, some commentators have had the vision of MPEs reaching out into developing countries for the more labour-intensive parts of their total activities. It is, of course, a commonplace that labour in developing countries may not be cheap when its quality is taken into account. But foreign firms might consider it worthwhile to undertake the necessary training, thus making a valuable contribution to the employment situations in developing countries. It would be particularly useful to explore whether this is already happening, to what extent it is likely to happen in the future, and whether there is any way in which developments of this kind could conceivably be encouraged.

*Chapter 10*

# THE INTERNATIONALIZATION OF CAPITAL AND THE NATION STATE

ROBIN MURRAY

## INTRODUCTION

Nation states have always had a primary status in classical and neo-classical models of the international economy. International economic relations have been discussed in terms of the operation by each state of some notional utilitarian calculus. In these models, corporations are subordinate structures. They are entirely included in the various national entities of the system. Their utility is part of the national utility, their actions are national actions. While the corporation is included in the concept of the nation the reverse is not true, for the nation is a unitary authority co-ordinating the interests and activities of all its component elements.

Two assumptions are involved here as far as the relationship between the firm and the state are concerned: first that there is an identity of interest between the firm and its state; second that the state has the power to control the economic activities of its firms in order to maximize national utility. The growth of international firms has brought both these assumptions into question.

To begin with, the development of international operations has destroyed the evident national identity that a firm possessed when its main productive units and/or markets were situated in a country, which was also its country of incorporation, and the country of origin of its main shareholders and managers. When these features of a firm and its activity no longer coincide, the question arises as to what are the criteria for deciding a firm's nationality. Clearly the legal criteria of the country of incorporation is inadequate for economic analysis. Yet there is no commonly accepted alternative. Economists have used the concept of corporate nationality (and its

265

obverse, internationality) in the spirit of Humpty Dumpty, to mean what they want it to mean. There is no common definition because there is no common question. The only thing on which there seems to be a greater measure of agreement is that the internationalization of corporate activity has at least brought into question the necessary identity of interest between a firm and its domestic state, just as it has brought into question the necessary non-identity of interest between a state and a foreign-owned subsidiary located within its borders.

Whatever the outcome of this debate, it is clear that there is an important economic relationship between a state and private capital, whether we define this capital in terms of national location, national ownership, or both. The second assumption now becomes relevant, and recent evidence suggests that this assumption (that the nation state has the power to control the activities of national firms in the light of national utility maximization) must also be questioned.

If, then, the two basic assumptions implicit in the traditional model of international economics about corporate/national state relations are brought into question so, too, is the basic model. An alternative model where the primary analytical units were international firms with nation states as merely subordinate structures is suggestive and makes more sense of certain international economic data than does the traditional nation-state model. Nevertheless this would be reacting too symmetrically. One needs a model which contains international firms, nation states and international institutions as primary units, and discusses the international distribution of production and income in terms of their interrelations and not merely the interrelations of nation states.

One might summarize the point in this way. The study of the international firm, albeit a somewhat jejune branch of economic study, has brought into question the traditional model of the international economy. It has found itself working in an area which has been somewhat peripheral to economics, namely the dynamics of firm/state relations, and in which there is only a thin body of literature on which to build. However, as Kuhn has argued in the case of new scientific paradigms, it is common for the central issues of the new paradigm to be peripheral issues in the old.

I would argue that the core of any new model which seeks to explain the dynamics of the international economy will indeed come from peripheral areas: (a) the theory of the growth of the international firm; (b) the theory of international firm/state relations. These are suggestions whose worth can only be tested when a new model is fashioned. All I would argue at this point is that the economist's study of the international firm has suffered from the lack of a general theory of the international economy which assigns to the international corporation an importance which the empirical research on the subject already strongly suggests.

I have accordingly interpreted the subject matter of this session in the more general terms of the questions raised above rather than on those of empirical studies of particular national policies towards incoming or outflowing investment. In the sections which follow I want to outline one possible framework for a theory of international firm/state relations. The approach falls into two parts: the first discusses the relationship of the state and private capital in economic space; the second develops this discussion in terms of the relationship of the state and private capital in territorial space. In a concluding section I outline some of the more general points that are suggested by the analysis.

## STATE AND PRIVATE CAPITAL IN ECONOMIC SPACE

In this section I want to suggest that in any capitalist economic system the state has certain economic functions which it will always perform, though in different forms and to different extents.[1] If it is possible to establish that there are certain public functions of this kind, we will then be in a position to ask what bodies will perform these functions when private capital expands territorially outside the boundaries of the nation state to which it has been historically allied. For if the performance of certain economic functions by a public body is a *sine qua non* for any capitalist system, the territorial expansion of the private elements of that system will imply the need for the performance of state economic functions in the expanded territory.

Two points should be made immediately clear. First, state economic functions for any given capital or coherent body of capitals need not be exercised by a single authority, though commonly there will be a dominant authority. Second, the body or bodies which perform these functions are not necessarily the governing authorities of nation states. For when we talk of 'state' economic functions we refer to what may most aptly be called 'economic *res publica*', those economic matters which are public,

[1] I have throughout this chapter specified that we are discussing the relation of state and capital in a capitalist system, since this is a quite distinct matter from their relationship in other forms of economic system.

267

external to individual private capitals. These public economic matters may be dealt with by a grouping of private capitals, by national governments, or by international public bodies. For the moment we are more concerned with the character of these public matters than with the bodies that deal with them.

I will distinguish six economic *res publica*, or state functions:

### 1 *The Guaranteeing of Property Rights*
This guarantee is backed by forces of law: the police and armed forces. In contemporary states, one interesting area of its active application is in the protection of the integrity of self-declared fishery limits.

### 2 *Economic Liberalization*
This involves the establishment of the conditions for free, competitive exchange: the *abolition* of restrictions on the movement of goods, money or people within the territorial area and the *standardization* of currency, economic law, weights and measures and so on. The process characterizes the early stages in the establishment of an expanded territorially distinct system and is the substance of the neo-classical formulation of economic integration as the absence or progressive elimination of discrimination.[1] Indeed one of the clearest current examples of such liberalization is the European Common Market. The double process of the abolition of restrictions and standardization is the principal characteristic of the decade which has followed the coming into force of the Treaty of Rome: though it is a process nowhere near complete. Within advanced capitalist countries economic liberalization is primarily 'regressive' in character and takes the form of anti-monopoly legislation, action against restrictive practises, including resale price maintenance, and restrictions on trade unions and the use of labour's power.

### 3 *Economic Orchestration*
A matter which includes the control of the price level the regulation of business cycles, and economic planning.[2]

---

[1] B. Balassa, *Theory of Economic Integration*, London, Allen & Unwin, 1962.

[2] N. Poulantzas, in his recent 'Pouvoir Politique et Classes Sociales', Paris, 1968, sees the state as 'the factory of cohesion of a social formation and the factor of reproduction of the conditions of production of a system'. In performing this third function the state is manifestly the factor of cohesion of an economic formation.

## 4 *Input Provision*

Public bodies have been required to secure the availability of key inputs at low cost:

(a) *Labour*. States have acted to ensure (i) an increased elasticity of supply of labour, either directly or indirectly; see, for example, the statutory extension of the working day in England, the Stein–Herdenberg reforms of agrarian relations in early nineteenth-century Prussia, or the results of the Frency credit policy in Indo-china in the colonial period; (ii) the training of a labour force, visible both in public education systems or current industrial training schemes; (iii) the control of wages, as in the case of the many contemporary incomes policies. It is particularly interesting in respect to the question of labour provision that Swedish social democratic governments have put the main emphasis of their post-war economic policy not on nationalization (of which there is probably less than in other advanced Western European countries) but on the control of the labour force – its size, its quality and its redeployment.[1]

(b) *Land*. A market for land has been required not only for the development of commodity agriculture (see the state's role in the English enclosure movement) but also for the siting of public utilities, notably transport and housing (see the right of 'eminent domain' given to private corporations in the United States in the nineteenth century which enables those developing public utilities to compulsorily acquire any land needed for their operations.[2]

(c) *Capital*. Governments have acted to ensure the supply of finance to its industry through (i) the establishment and backing of a national banking system and private money market, as exemplified in the post-war history of certain countries in the British Commonwealth as well as in the history of French banking; (ii) the establishment of funds for particular industrial projects; (iii) the granting of credits, and subsidies in other ways, including tax allowances, investment grants, special interest rates, and so on: in France, for example, in the early 1960s it was estimated that 80% of business borrowers were servicing their loans at rates of interest below the market rate.[3]

(d) *Technology*. The role of states in the development of technology is well documented; the Department of Defence is estimated to finance over half of all R & D done in the US, with figures up to 90% for the aviation and spacecraft industries, and 85% for electronics.

[1] A. Shonfield, *Modern Capitalism*, Oxford, 1965, pp. 200–1.
[2] *Ibid.*, p. 306.
[3] *Ibid.*, p. 86.

Governments have also been active importers of foreign technology: the French government introduced new industrial processes from abroad by the import of machines and skilled labour in the seventeenth century, as did the Japanese in the early period of their industrial revolution. The state's pronounced role in the development of new technology rests on four factors: (i) technological research and development involves high risk; (ii) it is subject to economies of scale; (iii) it is by its nature closely connected to academic institutions, which have been public and financed by the state; (iv) technology has always been closely bound to the military which, in turn, is almost always controlled and financed by the state: indeed, it would be strange to find new military technology whose development was not considerably funded by a state.[1]

(e) *Economic infrastructure* – particularly energy and communications. These sectors are distinguished not only by their being 'natural monopolies' but by being inputs common to most productive activity: there is accordingly a particularly clear interest in the presence of cheap, secure supplies of these services. In Risorgimento, Italy, the first years of the new state were characterized by a frantic burst of railway building by the government, and although the new system was sold to private capital in 1865, the financial vicissitudes of the latter caused the government to return and by 1905 control the bulk of the system. In Germany, too, the railways were increasingly a state system after 1871, with notably low rates, while in Japan in the decade after 1868 it was the state which built and operated railways and telegraph systems, opened coal mines and established agricultural experimental stations. The public control of these utilities in contemporary Western Europe and the system of regulation in the United States is well known; what should be emphasized, of course, is their controlled rates to industry.[2]

(f) *General manufactured inputs.* These comprise those manufactured products with the strongest forward linkages for the economy in general, or for a key sector in the economy. They tend to be less general than the utilities discussed above, and are less directly controlled by the state, though often regulated. Steel is a prime example, publicly owned in Britain, Austria and to a lesser extent in Italy. Austria has nationalized a variety of electrical engineering

---

[1] The relationship of the state to the development of technology in modern capitalism is extensively discussed in a forthcoming work by Sergio Barrio and John Rickliffs.

[2] A brief discussion of the Italian and German experiences is contained in Tom Kemp, *Industrialization in Nineteenth Century Europe*, Longmans, 1969.

firms. In Italy IRI plays an important though minority role in the cement industry. The Japanese government, in the same period as it set up public utilities, also established iron foundaries, shipyards, machine shops and model factories to manufacture cement, paper and glass.

## 5 Intervention for Social Consensus

Here the public function is concerned to counteract the most evident disruptive effects which result from the unsupervized operations of the system. It covers:

(a) the prevention of public external diseconomies such as pollution, the degradation of land- and townscape, or wide regional disparities;

(b) the regulation of conditions of work, including the enforcement of industrial safety, the limitation of working hours, and some wage setting such as minimum wages or equal pay for women;

(c) the regulation of conditions of sale, as in the Swedish state consumer protection system, trade description laws, or the nationalization of pubs in Carlisle by Lloyd George to control drinking by munitions workers in Gretna;

(d) certain aspects of social security, notably unemployment provisions;

(e) ideological functions vis à vis the productive system.

## 6 The Management of the External Relations of a Capitalist System

No capitalist system is closed. The organization of the relations of this system with foreign systems, both within and outside the domestic territory of the system, has been a prime function of states at all stages of capitalist development. One part of this function is aggressive: the support of the state's own private capital in its expansion into foreign economic and territorial space. It involves the attack on monopolistic walls which discriminate against domestic capitalists, such as tariff barriers, exchange controls, discriminatory taxation, unfavourable purchasing policies by foreign monopolists or states. It also involves the support of domestic capitalists in competitive foreign markets, and the attempt not merely to reduce foreign discrimination but build up monopolistic positions for domestic capitalists abroad.

A second part of the function is defensive, and consists in defending quasi-monopolistic positions established by domestic capitalists relative to foreign capital. It involves the maintenance of discriminations against foreign capital, tariffs, exchange control, purchasing tied to domestic capital; the maintenance of preferential trading areas and monetary zones favourable to the domestic capital; the restriction of the carriage of goods abroad to national ships or airlines; and the maintenance of the property rights of nationals overseas.

The instruments used in the performance of these functions are:

(a) *Military power*, whether defensively against a foreign force, or aggressively in terms of punitive expeditions or of more permanent annexations. The defensive use of force has usually been over the challenge to property rights, not only in domestic territory but the nationalization of property overseas; we have already mentioned fishing as a less publicized area where military power is common, and it is interesting to note that over and above the defence of fishery limits, the British government sent a gunboat to support British trawlers during the Icelandic fishing dispute from 1958–61, asserting in this case a right to what it as a state regarded as common property.

(b) *Aid*, or foreign public assistance, which is used in two forms. First, it lends support to national firms engaged in foreign competition through lowering costs (either by direct subsidization as in the case of French fine linen exports in the eighteenth century, or through export credit and foreign investment guarantee programmes such as those provided by the FCIA, the Export-Import Bank and AID in the United States) and/or by tying markets (AID financing tied to US exports now accounts for 85–90% of total AID financing, while a total of 4% of all US exports are now financed by direct loans to the purchaser from the US Government). Second, the threat of withdrawing an established aid flow or withholding a new aid flow acts as a protection to the property rights of domestic firms in the foreign country, as well as an inducement to the receiving country to lower discriminations against the donor's capital: the effect of the Hickenlooper amendment on recipients of US aid lies as much in the threat as in the execution.[1]

(c) *Commercial sanctions*, in the form of trade boycotts (South Africa, Rhodesia, newly-independent Guinea, the Middle East, Cuba, North Vietnam, China) quotas, or tariff changes.[2]

---

[1] I have discussed the subject of aid as an overseas extension of state functions in the first part of a joint paper with Edith Penrose, 'Aid and Private Investment', mimeo, 1969.

[2] G. Adler-Karlsson, *Western Economic Warfare 1947–1967*, Stockholm, 1968.

(d) *Financial sanctions* in terms of the blocking of funds (the post-war history of the US film industry in Britain presents an interesting example) or the establishment of exchange premiums.

(e) *Government controls* within domestic territory, such as the reserving of certain sectors for domestic industry, the prevention of particular takeovers, discriminatory buying policies and so on.

Over and above the function of partiality to domestic capital *vis à vis* foreign competitors, whether this partiality is offensive or defensive, the state has the second function of co-ordinating or orchestrating domestic/foreign economic relations in the form of supervising the balance of payments.

These six functions seem to me the primary functions of a capitalist state: the guaranteeing of property rights; economic liberalization; economic orchestration; input provision; intervention for social consensus; and the management of the external relations of a capitalist system. Four further functions suggest themselves:

(*a*) the role of the state in securing demand in the form of mass purchases from the private sector on long-term contract: private capital is here acting as quasi-agent for the state, and this character is made explicit in the management contracts concluded by firms like Booker Brothers and ENI with the governments of underdeveloped countries;

(*b*) the state as a taxation authority, a function whose importance is particularly evident in the early development of capitalist economies;

(*c*) the state as the enforcer and protector of particular monopolies *within* a capitalist system;

(*d*) the state as a provider of first aid to ailing sectors and firms: we have mentioned above the relationship of the Italian state to its railways in the nineteenth century: the salvaging of four major banks by the Weimar Republic in 1931 and their return to private owners in 1937 when they were assured of viability is a further instance.

I have not included these among the primary functions since they all follow from those we have included. Thus, to take the question of 'first aid', it is notable that such action has been principally directed either towards those sectors producing general inputs or to those sectors which are important in foreign relations, whether in the field of exports, invisible earnings or military power. If we look

273

at those industries which have been nationalized in the advanced capitalist countries – a solution almost always accompanied by the ultimate in first aid, namely compensation, these are most commonly in the sectors providing basic inputs; there are a few in the export sector (Ireland has a number of public manufacturing concerns in this category); and almost none in the sector producing manufactured goods for final consumption (the public interest in Renault and Volkswagen is an exception, born from particular circumstances). First aid, in the form of subsidies, restructuring, and credits to particular firms, follows this pattern. I have therefore treated it as a secondary function deriving from the provision of basic inputs and the management of external relations. I would argue that the other functions are secondary in a similar manner.

The point about the primary functions is that they are found in some form at all stages of capitalist development: though the degree to which they are carried out by public bodies as well as the type of public bodies which carry them out will vary. Among the factors causing such variations we may distinguish five:

(a) the degree of international competition or to put it more strongly, critical rivalry. This is perhaps strongest in wartime and the penumbra of preparation and recovery that surrounds war: such periods feature heavy in public activity in all of the functions. But similarly the developing industries in early periods of industrialization tend to face critical external competition, as List emphasized: Japan, Germany and Italy all exemplified the principle of strong government direction in the early days of their national systems of political economy. Currently it is notable how sharp an increase in public activity followed the return to convertability of Western economies in 1958;

(b) the stage of capitalist development, for the increase in the division of labour within a system, the increase in mutual interdependence, heightens the vulnerability of the system to the failure of particular parts of the system;

(c) the strength of the labour movement, since a strong movement will win concessions in the form of greater public activity in the field of measures aimed at social consensus: further, by raising the cost of labour, a strong labour movement may (i) weaken the capital's competitive position *vis-à-vis* foreign capital; (ii) lower the rate of profit to critical levels in sectors producing general inputs;

(d) the traditional ideology with respect to the role to be played by government;

(e) the degree of concentration of capital within the economy.

This last point is important, for it should be re-emphasized that the functions we have called public are not universally exercised by government or public bodies. They may be performed by the private firms themselves. For these functions arise from the existence of externalities: whether they be Marshallian, as in the case of fish conservation, or specialized labour provision, i.e. where they are external to the firm but internal to the industry; or economies which are external to the firm and industry but internal to the productive system, such as the provision of basic inputs and the establishment of the necessary conditions for free exchange; or, finally, where they are external to the firm, the industry and the productive system, but internal to the society.

The fact that such external economies exist does not mean that single firms will not themselves undertake the function. Many firms have their own police force, the East India Company had its own army; US corporations are currently engaged in cutting down their own pollution of the atmosphere because of their fear that such external diseconomies will harm their company image. Firms build their own roads, railways and generating plants: they run their own training schemes and welfare systems. The point is rather that these are all activities which it may be relatively costly for the firm itself to undertake. Where there are indivisibilities, as in the basic utilities, it will often cost less to spread fixed costs over many firms. Where it is difficult for a firm to privatize the output from its investment, as in the case of labour training and some kinds of research, the firm will clearly prefer the investment to be shared by those who benefit. Where there is high risk, a firm which is a risk averter will clearly prefer a large body which is more indifferent to risk to finance the project. Private capital is also invariably reluctant to be seen to be the organizers of armed forces and police.

In underdeveloped countries, where a firm or small group of firms constitute the greater part of the capitalist section of the economy, these functions often are performed by the firms themselves: though they will always attempt to obtain contributions from others who benefit from their investment. Within the developed economies, too, the size of the major firms means that some of the what were traditionally external economies are becoming internal and that, in the field of communications in particular, firms are providing their own services. The British Steel Corporation owns the largest private air fleet in Britain. Fords Europe have one of the largest internal telephone systems in Europe.

Thus the public functions we have discussed are latently public by their nature; the degree to which they are exercised by public authorities will not be constant.

## STATE AND CAPITAL IN TERRITORIAL SPACE

Let us now look at the relationship of states to private capital from a geographical perspective. Capitalist systems have developed in territorially-identifiable areas, often in areas which had already been made identifiable by pre-capitalist states. During the national period of capitalisms, the roots of both private capitals and the states which performed the public functions we have just described were territorially coincident and predominantly exclusive. Both capitals and states extended beyond their own boundaries: for capitalist systems from the first have had an international dimension. But the bulk of their activities covered the same geographical space.

When any capital extends beyond its national boundaries, the historical link that binds it to its particular domestic state no longer *necessarily* holds. A capital which has extended itself in this way will require the performance of the primary public functions for its extended operations. But the body which performs them need not be the same as the body that performs them within the area of the capital's early development. The domestic state may perform the public functions abroad for its own national capital. A national state body is not territorially limited in its range of activity, even though it may be territorially identified over an exclusive area. But the geographic coincidence of the economic ranges of an extended capital with its domestic state must be empirically established and cannot be assumed.

We can identify five possible executors of the state functions for the overseas operations of an extended capital:

(*a*) The domestic state may perform these functions directly, which for the majority of the functions will involve the extension of the state's own boundaries through annexation. Since this involves an extension of the national defendenda, a considerable cost and usually a problem, to say the least, in the performance of the function of ensuring social consensus in the foreign territory, the geographic expansion of the domestic state is a method less preferred from a capitalist point of view for fulfilling the state functions over-seas. It will be supported when alternative systems are economically or politically impossible.

(b) The arrangement that foreign state structures should perform them. Such an arrangement may be made by the capital itself or its domestic state, either through persuasion, pressure or intrigue. The foreign state becomes in effect a macro-political agent. It is an arrangement which forms the basis for any conception of economic neo-colonialism: though the existence and degree of neo-colonialism will depend on the extent of the concessions to the foreign state to induce it to perform the functions in question.

The guaranteeing of the property rights of the extended firm, and the prevention of major discriminations by the foreign state against it, are backed by the type of negative sanctions outlined above in the section on the management of external relations. The provision of basic inputs, as well as the establishment of organizational struc-tures to carry out the normal business of a capitalist state (police forces, mass media, tax authorities, economic 'orchestrators') are on the other hand often directly funded. In underdeveloped coun-tries, economic services for a particular area may be financed, plan-ned and technically supervised by the public authorities and private contractors of the domestic state *after* an exploitable resource has been discovered by one of its capitalists abroad. If one looks at foreign extractive firms operating in Africa, for example, they have almost without exception got finance for necessary infrastructures from their domestic governments or international agencies – though this finance is channelled through the host government. The establish-ment of organizational structures may again involve seconded na-tionals from the home country directly fulfilling the function or the training of host nationals in domestic or host-country institutions. The performance of public functions by foreign agent states is accom-plished therefore by a mixture of positive supplies channelled through the agent states, and negative threats and sanctions.

(c) The extended capital may itself perform the functions, either singly or in conjunction with other capitals. We noted above ex-amples of this in the field of policing and input provisions.[1] It also extends to the threat of negative sanctions on foreign states discri-

---

[1] An interesting example of private policing on an international level is provided by the companies who own submarine cables. They have their own patrol vessels and helicopters operating particularly in fishing areas with a view to enforcing what would otherwise be a virtually unenforceable international public agreement regarding the damage of cables.

minating or nationalising the firms in question: the international oil majors have exercised oligopolistic solidarity against national governments on a number of occasions – notably against Iran after the nationalization of Anglo-Iranian.[1] Non-ferrous metal corporations have exercised similar threats in the form of withdrawing key imputs or closing international markets.

(*d*) Foreign states may already be performing or be willing to perform the functions of their own accord. Most advanced capitalist countries would extend protection of property rights, freedom of exchange, input provision, macro-orchestration and consensual intervention to foreign investors in their country. The major function which they may be reluctant to perform is that of partiality *vis-à-vis* other foreign interests, and impartiality in terms of their own domestic capital. Of course, many of the instruments used by a state to favour its own national capital will also apply to foreign capital which has invested within the national boundaries. This is true of tariff and monetary agreements, export credits, services of commercial branches of the country's embassies abroad, and so on. Indeed it is often this ability to enjoy the monopolistic discriminations of foreign countries that induces a firm to invest abroad: US firms invest in Britain to more cheaply service their export markets in the Sterling Area or EFTA. There are instances, too, as with ICI in Argentina, where a firm negotiates a favourable discrimination from a foreign government as a condition for investing in the country. Smaller countries, such as Ireland, go even further than this by making general offers of monopolistic advantages to foreign investors which exceed those offered to their national capital. The one notable exception to this picture of discriminations operating in favour of foreign investors comes in the field of government purchasing: the reason is clear in the case of military contracts, but the UK Government, for example, operates the principle more generally. It openly favoured British firms in the allocation of North Sea drilling blocks, while in the computor field IBM claim that they supply only two out of the seventy-two computors used by the government.[2] Yet Yet even this unfavourable discrimination is *a priori* limited to countries which have national producers of the contracted products, and in the field of advanced technology these tend to be few. The

---

[1] For a useful discussion on the operations of international oil companies, see M. Tanzer, *The Political Economy of International Oil and the Underdeveloped Countries*, London, Temple Smith, 1970.

[2] L. Turner, *Politics and the Multinational Company*, Fabian Research Series No. 279, December, 1969.

overall picture, therefore, is one of remarkably little discrimination against foreign capital which invests in a host country: extended capital has been able to rely on host governments to fulfill the public functions certainly as far as the advanced capitalist countries in Europe are concerned.

(e) The final group of executors of state functions are existing state bodies in co-operation with each other. Instances of such co-operation can be found in the following fields:

(i) property protection (mutual investment guarantees, international policing, extradition, treaties, military alliances);

(ii) implementation of free exchange and standardization between countries (free trade areas, customs unions, common markets, monetary unions);

(iii) mutual orchestration – a function performed to some extent by the IMF, the OECD, and in the BIS by central bankers;

(iv) provision of inputs; co-operation arising for reasons of scale as in technological co-operation, or in the provision of power supplies, or because the service is trans-national such as the Tan Zam railway;

(v) the exploitation of international resources, as is the case in river development schemes, or the numerous international fish conservation agreements;

(vi) supervision of mutual economic interests *vis-à-vis* other economic powers: OPEC and the meetings of the four major copper-producing countries in the underdeveloped world are examples of this form of co-operation; multilateral aid agencies could also be seen in this light.

In contrast to the intranational public functions we noted being fulfilled by foreign states, these co-operative agreements are aimed at transnational functions. But many of them have been far from successful in fulfilling their aim: this is notably so in the field of inter-governmental technological co-operation, in fishery regulation, or in OPEC. Even where the co-operation has been more successful, the success is in most cases temporary: those involving international external economies (economies which are external to the national but internal to the capitalist area of the world economy), particularly in the fields of free exchange and mutual orchestration, would be fortunate to survive a major international depression. The conditions for the establishment of a more permanent form of integrated co-operation, a *de facto* international state body, we will discuss in a moment.

The line of argument up to this point has been that a national capital extending abroad will require the primary public functions we outlined in the first section to be performed: but that the performance need not be undertaken by the capital's home government. There is no necessary link between the extended capital and its home government in the extended area. The body or bodies which do perform the functions may differ according to whether the functions are to be undertaken *within* areas with already constituted capitalist states, *between* areas with already constituted capitalist states, or *within* areas without already constituted capitalist states. In each case the home government could perform the functions; but in each case there are alternatives; and there is also the possibility – a very real one which we have underplayed until now – that the contradictions of the international system will be such as to prevent the fulfillment of the functions at all. The outcome for anyone extending capital will depend on the power of its domestic government, both economic and political, to 'follow' its own capital, on the territory of extension, and on the particular form taken by the extension. It is this last point about the form of extension which I now want to take up.

Extending capital is not homogeneous, even though many discussions of overseas investment treat it as such. More particularly the interest of the capital in the types of public function to be performed, and the bodies to perform them will differ according to the following factors:

(a) *The degree of productive centralization*, that is to say the degree to which foreign markets are served by output whose production and inputs supplies are concentrated in one country. Those companies with a high export/foreign sales ratio stand at one pole; those serving foreign markets from production and input provision in the market concerned stand at the other. Steel and parts of the electrical industry would stand nearer the first pole; service industries nearer the second. Clearly those with centralized production, with a high proportion of trade to decentralized production, will be most concerned with the establishment and maintenance of conditions of free international exchange. Productive centralization with high trade/foreign sales ratios is a characteristic of the early period of capitalist international expansion, and is reflected in the frequent international disputes over tariffs that occurred prior to this century.

The conflicting pressures relating to the international centralization of production – economies of scale tending towards centralization on the one hand, transport costs, tariff barriers, spare parts and market servicing requirements tending towards decentralization on the other – leads commonly to *regional centralization of production*. This is true of consumer durables in particular, as well as other branded goods (Colgate–Palmolive or Mars products for example). South-East Asia may be served from Australia or Malaysia, Central America from Mexico, EFTA from Britain, and the EEC from Holland. Such companies will again have a primary interest in regional free trade.

(b) *Stage of overseas company development*. Many companies have expanded abroad by what might be called an ink-blot strategy. They expand outwards from existing operations both territorially and structurally. In consumer durables, for instance, one notes an expansion path which involves exporting through overseas agents, exporting through company marketing organizations, local assembly, local full production, then regional centralization of production or regional division of labour in production, and in some cases the development of an international division of labour in production.[1] Such expansion paths have been followed by some US companies in Europe in the post-war period, with a number now reaching the stage of productive centralization or regional division of labour within the EEC. It is instructive that by the end of 1968 there were over 800 European headquarters groups in Brussels, though it is the productive rather than organizational division of labour with which we are primarily concerned.[2] Thus the stage of company development will be one of the factors determining the degree of productive centralization, or, an equally important point, the degree of *international division of labour in production*.

(c) *Forms of international flow*. Certain firms are principally concerned with the international flow of information and personnel rather than goods. Many service industries have this characteristic: with decentralized production served by a centralized information and management system. Advertising, management consultancy, data processing, film production, hotel management and department stores all exemplify the point. They may either work on a management contract (like many of the Hilton hotels) or raise capital in the local market on the strength of their international name in order to fund local operations. The size of the overseas interests in the

[1] For a discussion of the ink-blot form of foreign expansion, see Y. Aharoni, *The Foreign Investment Decision Process*, Harvard, 1966.
[2] See Newton Parks, 'The Survival of the European Headquarters' in *Harvard Business Review*, March–April 1969.

general field of management services, licensing, leasing, and so on, can be gauged by the receipts of US companies of royalties and fees. In 1968 these totalled $1·28 billion comprising $0·54 billion in the form of royalties, license fees and rentals, and $0·74 billion in the form of management fees and service charges. These figures compare with total earnings of US direct investment abroad in the same year of £7·0 billion. The important feature of this type of international operation is that in general the movement of people and information is not subject to the same restrictions as the movement goods; though they are subject to restrictions on the movement of of capital.[1]

Be that as it may, firms such as those we have discussed may in general be presumed to be less concerned with international exchange restrictions than firms depending on the international movement of goods.

(d) *Degree of dependence on state partiality*. Some companies by the nature of their operations depend more heavily on their domestic state for preferential aid. This is true of the contracting industry, of exporters to and investors in underdeveloped countries, and of firms whose sales may be predominantly in the home market but whose inputs are produced or bought from abroad. These firms will be concerned to see the maintenance of the strength of their domestic states in international markets.

(e) *The strength of foreign competition*. Where domestic states are incapable of providing preferential protection and aid to firms highly dependent on them either in domestic or foreign markets, there will be an interest among firms in this position to either transfer to stronger state structures or to encourage their own state structure to co-operate with others. There are few examples of the former move – Mars changed nationalities principally because of the rationalizing of its international operations by its founder – but in respect to the latter, European firms have evidently favoured intergovernmental European co-operation because they regard their domestic governments as inadequate in the field of protection.

We are now in a position to make an important distinction. There are some firms whose main concern with respect to their extended capital is the *intranational* performance of public functions. The current system of nation states may be largely adequate for a system, say, of decentralized production. For some, indeed, the current sys-

[1] McKinsie's experience bears this point out. They have been hampered, though only marginally, by restrictions on labour movements in Switzerland and the US.

tem shows positive advantages. We have noted already how some capitals have expanded abroad precisely in order to take advantage of other nations' sets of discriminations. We may add to this the fact that companies which are financially centralized internationally may in effect play off rival states against each other, locating where incentives are greatest either for production or profit retrieval. Given that the performance of public functions has to be paid for, such firms may minimize the costs (in terms of taxation) of the services they receive. The system of tax havens has given rise to what might be called 'accounts of convenience', firms registered in Curaçao, Malta or Luxembourg operating internationally under public 'umbrellas' financed by rival capitals. Thus, even where there is extensive territorial non-coincidence between domestic states and their extended capitals, this does not imply that the system of atomistic nation states is outdated.

In contrast, there are other firms whose interests lie not only in the intranational performance of public functions for their extended capital, but the *international* performance of them as well. We noted the following types of capital to whom this applied:

(a) those principally engaged in servicing foreign markets by trade;
(b) those with regionally centralized production;
(c) those operating with an international or regional division of labour in production;
(d) those concerned with an international exchange of goods rather than information or labour;
(e) those whose domestic government gave insufficient partial support in the face of foreign competition.

Again, the fact that these interests in favour of the international performance of state functions exist does not mean that the system of nation states cannot contain them.

A dominant state may perform them. States in co-operation may perform them. Finally, those firms pressing for international co-ordination for defensive reasons may sacrifice their identity by merging or being taken over by capital from the dominant country. This spirit of submission is characteristic of leading firms in the countries of Southern Europe: they opt for being second in Rome rather than first in a village, when it comes to a question of their identity in the face of foreign competition. Greek capital's position on their country's proposed association with the EEC provided an interesting instance of this.

At the same time, while we should note the fact that there is no necessity for the internationalization of capital to imply the passing of the nation state, even where the performance of international state functions is concerned, nevertheless there may be capitals who come to back the setting up of a unified international state power because of the insufficiency of the alternatives. If the capital is dominant, its own state may be unable to impose international co-ordination either directly or indirectly. If the capital is threatened, it may nevertheless feel itself strong enough to resist within a wider co-ordinated territory. Finally, we have noted above the difficulties of achieving such co-ordination through mutual co-operation between nation states: though forms of co-operation may constitute a stage in which the forces in favour of a unified international co-ordinated power are strengthened.

If we look at the economic origins of the Second Reich, for example, we note that the establishment of the customs union by Prussia in 1818, and its later extension as the Zollverein in 1834, appear to be the result of the need to raise revenue from customs duties plus a certain administrative convenience rather than the response to an expanding capital seeking a wider area of discriminated protection. Thus the tariff on transit goods stood much higher in 1818 than the realtively low import duty. Yet the liberalization within the area furthered industrialization, encouraged the development of a bloc system of transport (Prussian landowners who had opposed railways accepted them in the 1840s) and created vested interests in the further consolidation of this preliminary unity. Protective tariffs were heightened, particularly on British pig iron and cotton yarn, weights and measures, commercial and civil law were all standardized, and mining rights were changed to make them more accessible to capitalist exploitation. By the end of the Franco-Prussian war, in Kemp's words 'the business middle class did not mind so much how unification was to be achieved, or under whose auspices, as long as they could depend upon stable and orderly government at home and backing for their enterprise abroad'.[1] International liberalization brought about through co-operation led to an internationalization of capital which then required a unified co-ordination of state powers covering the expanded territory.

In Italy, too, there existed strong capital interests for unified political control over a territory which had many state authorities. In this case unity was supported to achieve liberalization rather than consolidate it, North Italian capital, for example, in Lombardy,

[1] Kemp, *op. cit.*, p. 103.

was hostile to customs barriers imposed by the Austrians which cut it off from the weaker systems of the South. In this case, even more than in the German one, the discordance in the interests of particular capitals and their territorial state structures is eminently clear: so, too, are their reasons for supporting a territorially consolidated state structure in both Italy and Germany.[1] Both are cases, albeit at a different stage of capitalist development, of the extension, or would-be extension, of capital calling forth new forms of political structures, and are consequently of central interest to the subject-matter of this chapter.

What I have wanted to suggest in this section is a framework for analysing the consequences for political organization of a territorial expansion of capital. I have intentionally depicted capital as politically opportunist: Germany exemplified the point but one could look equally well at the support that foreign firms have given to liberation movements in Africa. I have tried to outline the alternative forms of state organization which present themselves to such an opportunist capital, and the distinctions within the body of extending capital which may be thought to lead to differing interests among them.

## CONCLUSIONS

What general conclusions can we draw from the above discussion? To begin with, the approach throws some light on the question of the compatibility of international firms with a system of nation states. This question has been confused to my mind by being discussed in terms of a binary opposition: either the nation state will survive or it will be replaced by some set of international institutions. For some the international firm has met with a rising, and in parts effective nationalism, particularly in the underdeveloped countries. For others, like Kindleberger, 'the nation state is just about through as an economic unit'.[2] National is opposed to international, as hot is to cold, or black to white. But the problems cannot be satisfactorily put in such a form. For even if the growth of international corporations did require parallel international political organizations, nation states might well remain suitable units for the undertaking of certain economic functions, just as the states have done in the USA, the lander in

[1] See G. Luzzato, 'The Italian Economy in the first decade after Unification' in (ed.) Crouzet, Chaloner and Stern, *Essays in European Economic History, 1789–1914.*

[2] C. P. Kindleberger, *American Business Abroad*, New Haven, Yale University Press, 1969, p. 207.

Germany or the cantons in Switzerland. In other words, to argue that public international economic institutions will be required for certain functions is not to imply that the nation states will cease to perform any of their traditional economic functions, just as to argue that nation states continue to have power and some economic *raison d'être* is not to imply that there may not also be pressure towards political internationalization. The question, therefore, is not whether or not the nation state is compatible with international firms, but what functions the nation state is likely to continue to perform, in an era of international capital, whether all nation states will be similarly affected, and how 'international' will international institutions be. The relationship between firms and political structures should, in short, be seen in continuous rather than discontinuous terms, both spatially and functionally.

For an answer to these questions we have suggested two factors of importance: the interests of a country's international corporations *vis-à-vis* the performance of state functions within its operating space, and the ability of a country to perform the required functions. On the relationship between these two factors will depend a third, the continued identification of an international corporation with its state of origin, and since international firms themselves constitute a part of the body politic, their views will influence a government's view on the question of international political integration. The emphases are on the interests of private capital and the power of the state.

The question of the power of the state is of particular importance and is one on which comparatively little work has been done in the literature on the effects of foreign investment. The expansion of a national firm overseas calls into question the power of its domestic state in a double way. First, the state may be required to perform certain functions overseas either directly or indirectly which it may not have the finance or economic power to perform. Second, the internationalization of capital may blunt a nation's ability to perform the traditional economic functions within its own borders, in the field of monetary, fiscal and balance of payments policies.[1] When we also take into account the power of the state to defend its domestic capital against foreign competition in the home market, and note that powers in all these fields will differ from state to state, we are in the position to outline a model of the international economy in which states are

---

[1] An interesting recent discussion of the subject is given in R.E. Caves and G. L. Reuber, *Canadian Economic Policy and the Impact of International Capital Flows*, University of Toronto, 1969.

arranged hierarchically according to their ability to protect the inter-ests of their firms either by resisting foreign pressure on domestic conditions, or imposing conditions on other states abroad. The key point is the differential powers of nation states *vis-à-vis* domestic and foreign capital.

It follows from this that we may expect to see the acknowledgment of state weakness and the demand for some degree of international political integration to come from the relatively smaller states with still significant, independent national capitals. The history of the EEC may be seen in this light. Indigenous firms within the EEC have not only demanded liberalization and standardization in order to provide a large home market, comparable to that in the US (even though US subsidiaries in Europe have been some of the main bene-ficiaries of this market enlargement), they have also asked that the European Commission play the traditional role of supporting Euro-pean capital and trade overseas and defending it at home

UNICE, the body which represents national employers' organiza-tions at the community level, devotes a number of its declarations on community policy to such matters as a common policy of commer-cial defence against abnormal practices by third countries, the estab-lishment of a system of investment guarantees abroad, the elabora-tion of an international dumping code as part of the GATT negotia-tions, and so on. On American investments in the Common Market, UNICE is more equivocal since it represents US subsidiaries in Europe as well as native EEC firms, but the larger firms in the EEC, notably in Germany, have been quite open in their demand that the Commission should use its powers to counter the American chal-lenge. Sections of the Commission appear to agree with that position, and though the Treaty of Rome was manifestly non-discriminatory *vis-à-vis* American investors in Europe, article 86, the regulations on aids and the development of technological co-operation are all seen as ways of strengthening European firms at the expense of US subsidiaries.

Overall, it is the large firms in the EEC who have been in favour of further integration in the field of company law, patent laws, the deve-lopment of a European capital market and so on, even though the current disintegrated system in these fields gives the large firms an advantage over the medium and smaller national firms within the EEC.

The EEC experience illustrates one further general point. The approach outlined in this paper is functionalist: changes in political structures follow on a switch of interests by firms and a weakening power of the nation states to perform the requisite functions. Such change has been treated as implicitly smooth. States, however, represent more than their largest corporations: they do have an identity of their own which justifies them a primary status in any model of the international economy. One consequence of this is that, although a state's powers to fulfill its traditional functions may be weakened, it may still be reluctant to grant these formal powers to a new international body. International state functions may be demanded but not performed. There is a common fear that this is the course of events in the EEC. Individual government's powers to control their economies through monetary, fiscal and balance of payments policies are being weakened in the course of integration, without any corresponding transfer of these powers to the Commission.[1] How deep these contradictions are between political organization and economic scope is not an *a priori* matter. All we should note is that such contradictions exist and can be a significant factor in certain forms of international economic crisis.

To sum up, then, I have chosen to discuss the reactions of developed countries to the growth of the multinational enterprise in the more general context of the relations of state and private capital in territorial space. In doing so I have wanted to suggest a means by which the relationship between state and private capital could be discussed in a more continuous way, as well as emphasizing, in the course of the discussion, the importance of introducing the international firm as a primary element along with the nation state in any model of the international economy. Only an empirical study can determine how useful such an approach would be for understanding the political dynamics of the international economy.

[1] See, among others, B. Balassa, 'Whither French Planning', *Quarterly Journal of Economics*, November 1965.

*Chapter 11*

# GOVERNMENTAL POLICY ALTERNATIVES AND THE PROBLEM OF INTERNATIONAL SHARING

## JACK N. BEHRMAN

The multinational enterprise (MPE) continues to give rise to tensions with governments. These tensions are publicized as the American enterprises establish new affiliates or buy out or into existing companies abroad. The attempt by Europeans to build their own MPEs will not decrease these tensions. I have analysed the different sources of tensions elsewhere,[1] and will merely summarize them in order to introduce the analysis of policy alternatives open to governments and set the stage for an assessment of what they are likely to do and why.

Tensions over the MPE arise from pressures inside the host country and from outside. What builds the tension is the difficulty of weighing the benefits and costs. If either the costs or benefits *clearly* predominated, there would be little tension and the policy response would be evident. But the enterprise does contribute in many ways to the host country while injecting some instabilities and disturbances and even assuming some control over local economic activity. It adds to capital formation in the host country, brings managerial and technical skills, may promote regional development by moving into depressed areas, stimulates internal competition, and may contribute significantly to the expansion of export earnings of the host country. At the same time, the mere fact of its size injects a disturbance into the market; it alters competitive positions (though not necessarily the methods of competition); it alters wage rates and labour relations, personnel practices, advertising, etc. These disturbances are made more intense by the concentration of the large enterprises in a few industrial sectors – normally the technically advanced ones. This concentration points up to the host country

[1] *National Interests and the Multinational Enterprise*, Englewood-Cliffs, N.J., Prentice-Hall, 1970.

289

its dependence on the MPE for technological progress. Host governments are concerned, therefore, over the loss of control over a 'key' sector of the economy through its technological dependence. Finally, the MPE, having, significant economic power through its ability to make decisions affecting the economy of the host country, has the capacity to upset national economic plans. It may inject or accentuate economic disequilibria, requiring the host government to adopt offsetting policies – which it might prefer not to have to do.

The outside pressures are generated on the part of the government of the parent company – largely the US Government, but others may soon follow. For example, the UK policy toward Rhodesia and the Swedish toward South Africa could set precedents for governmental interference in affairs of enterprises investing abroad. The US Government has applied three sets of regulations to international business, which are quite effectively implemented through the MPE: the export control Acts, the balance of payments regulations, and the anti-trust laws. Each of these inhibits the ways in which subsidiaries (or licensees) of US enterprises may act within their host countries and alters the relationships of parents to the affiliates. Some governments feel that these restrictions are an extra-territorial reach of US laws and regulations which should stop at the water's edge and not affect the operations of locally-incorporated enterprises. But they feel hindered in taking effective counter action by the fact that they are benefiting in other ways from harmonious diplomatic relations with the US Government.

In sum, governments feel pressed by the fact that significant policies may be determined by decisions taken in another country – either by the parent company or the US Government – without regard to their national interests and without their having a chance to participate in the decisions. Host governments are placed under continuing tensions because the MPE is not holding back, waiting to see what governments are going to do.

The basic governmental response to the tensions has been to try to reduce them by increasing the benefits and decreasing the disadvantages – mainly through asking the enterprise to be a 'good corporate citizen'. But this approach has not been sufficiently successful; the tensions remain.[1] There are three policy routes available to governments. They are not mutually exclusive and may be employed simultaneously. Not all have been used as yet. In fact, no

[1] I have explained why this approach is not likely to bring satisfactory results in *International Business and Governments*, New York, McGraw-Hill, 1970, Chapter 5.

clear policies have emanated from governments toward the MPE, save *possibly* from Japan (and even here it is more implicit than explicit). The US Government itself has not officially recognized the entity in policy positions. It has, in effect, adopted a policy of 'non-recognition', which I exclude as a policy alternative, simply because I think that the tensions will demand recognition in some and at least *pro forma* treatment.

The first policy alternative is that of rejection of the MPE or restriction of its activities. Governments have the power and machinery to refuse entry or to impose conditions that affect its operations. Second, they can create a competitive industry within the nation, or in concert with others in a region, to eliminate some of the vacuums which attract the MPE. And third, they can move in concert with other governments, particularly that of the US, to build a set of intergovernmental rules and guidelines which channel the enterprise in ways satisfactory to all governments participating.

The difficulty with each of these alternatives is that there are no clear evidences as to which will work better or even what the results might be. Western governments have been built on assumptions about the rationality of man and his capacity to guide and direct himself and the society by taking a rational look at where he is and wants to go. But the pace of the growth of the MPE has been faster than governments have been able to redirect their attention to it effectively.

What governments undoubtedly would like is a breathing space in which to sort out the advantages and disadvantages and to determine long-run policy, without the tensions of continuing new pressures. This desire was the basis of French policy in the mid-sixties, when it sought a concerted policy on the part of the EEC. But, suppose that governments were given time, how should they go about making a rational determination among the alternatives? First, I suggest, comes a clear understanding of what the problem is; then an assessment of the available responses, and finally the policy determination. So far, governments have not been able to get past the first step.

The problem facing governments is a complex one of cost/benefit. The MPE is producing benefits, but for whom? – at what cost to the host country and in what 'currency'? Costs are seen in the loss of control, a disregard for national interests, and an encroachment on sovereignty. The benefits are economically real, and so are a few of the costs. But in the main the costs are not measurable. And, in any event the distribution of both benefits and costs is determined by a foreign entitity. The essential problem, therefore, is one of international sharing of costs and benefits; what it should be and how it should be decided. This is not a formulation of the problem which appeals to most Western governments, for it implies the need for new institutional arrangements.

But it seems clear that the operations of MPEs do create a particular sharing of its contributions to economic growth and stability. Some countries gain more than others. The distribution of these benefits is determined according to the decisions made by the managers as to location of production, product mix, technological processes, location of R & D efforts, trade and marketing patterns, pricing, and financial flows. The enterprises would prefer to make these decisions without regard to diverse governmental interests and will do so whenever they can. In his study of the international petroleum companies, J. E. Hartshorn described their role as essentially a logistic one, centralizing control over a variety of functions and international resources, and making decisions from 'an international viewpoint detached from the special interests of any one nation . . . '.[1]

In a similar vein, *The Statist* has eulogized this detached (non-national) orientation of MPEs:

About the nearest thing to supra-national institutions the world yet possesses are the giant international companies. The whole theory of their operation is that they should pursue global growth and profit maximization uninfluenced by the parochial interests of the countries in which they operate and trade. Capital investment, market development, and the exploitation of technological advance should all go where cold calculation indicates they will pay best, irrespective of the sensitivities of the nations which act as hosts.[2]

My own studies on the behaviour of MPEs in manufacturing supports this assessment of the *orientation* of corporate managers.[3] In fact, it is an integral part of the definition of a MPE that it is centralizing its policies and integrating its operations into a worldwide entity.

National governments have been urged by a group of prominent business and government officials to accept and foster this integrat-

[1] *Politics and World Oil Economics*, New York, F. A. Praeger, 1962, pp. 339–40.   [2] February 17, 1967, p. 267.
[3] *Some Patterns in the Rise of the Multinational Enterprise*, University of North Carolina, School of Business, Research Paper 18, 1969.

ing role of the MPE. Participants at the Fontainebleau and Croton-ville conferences on 'Atlantic Co-operation and Economic Growth' in 1965 and 1966 urged that 'Atlantic co-operation should henceforth be expanded beyond trade and investment to a conception of 'integration and resources'', and is the prerequisite of political stability, economic growth and social welfare', and that the MPE should be used to 'integrate the resources of both the US and Europe to their maximum advantage . . .' since the enterprise would provide for a 'more efficient use of resources in the entire industrialized community'.

There is no recognition in the reports of these conferences that the integrated use of resources by a private enterprise implies acceptance of its determination of the shares among nations. A similar technocratic role was seen by Berle and Means forty years ago for the giant corporation; but they recognized its effects on income distribution and assumed an overriding governmental policy: 'the great corporation should develop into a purely neutral technocracy, balancing a variety of claims by various groups in the community and assigning to each a proportion of the income stream on the basis of public policy rather than private cupidity.[1] We have not reached this juncture in any nation as yet, and it will be difficult to arrive at a solution internationally; but the problem remains much as Berle and Means saw it.

If governments do leave the enterprise free to operate across national boundaries without constraint they are, in effect, accepting the distribution of benefits as decided by the managers. But governments remain concerned over the distribution of gains, and few are willing to accept a division of international welfare determined by the decisions of MPEs, even if their share might be larger than it otherwise would be. They are concerned not only with the efficiency and the size of their share but also with their participation in the determination.[2] This concern of governments is not appreciated by economists who focus on concepts of international economic welfare, but it is understood by *political* economists who recognize the legitimate interests of governments in both wealth *and* power.

[1] *The Modern Corporation and Private Property*, New York, Macmillan, 1932, p. 356.

[2] One European economist stressed the significance of participation in the following way: 'World industry managed by giant American companies would not be desirable, no matter how efficient it might be. It makes a difference whether the bulk of the world's modern industry is controlled from one country, or whether control is more evenly spread around. Even if you had a single Atlantic nation, it would still be bad to have control of industry concentrated in one region.' (*Business Week*, November 27, 1965, p. 76.)

What governments face is a challenge to their power and control by an entity which has no legitimate claim to such power. The power of the MPE can be used to alter the policies of governments without the consent of the governed or the governing; even if it is not used to undermine governments themselves, some of the smaller state have felt that they were in a rather unequal bargaining position *vis-à-vis* MPEs. The problem of the legitimacy of the power wielded by the large corporation within the US has been finessed largely because there was a government over that corporation that could exercise final power if and when it wanted to. There is no similar supranational government to exercise similar final control over the MPE. The annals on the growth and role of the corporation are full of assessments of the legitimacy of its power, but the issue has hardly been raised in relation to the MPE. It is, in fact, the crux of the challenge, for without legitimacy the enterprise has no right to such power.

Legitimacy is a matter of representation, responsibility and responsiveness. For any entity to have legitimate power over the people the people must have some way of making it responsive to their will. It is clear that the international markets are not sufficiently free to provide such popular control on a world-wide basis, nor does the claim of responsibility to stockholders hold up on the international scene, for the stockholder of local affiliates usually is the foreign parent itself, which is neither a citizen of the host country nor owned by its citizens.

To put the matter bluntly, national governments and groups feel challenged by an entity having power, which has no clear responsibility to the people over which it exercises that power. In addition, it is the channel of a further illegitimate interference by the US Government.

Assessment of potential responses to these challenges is made difficult by the fact that the trade-off between the retention of sovereignty and the loss of benefits is not quantifiable. The loss of national control does occur; but what is its size or weight? Can one put a value on sovereignty (or parts of it)? If so, in what terms? power? security? economic growth? options? 'control over one's destiny'? opportunity? 'our way of life'? or merely identity?

The assessment by some countries of the trade-offs has become clear from their actions, if not from their policy statements. Some consider that the contributions to wealth are greater than any *additional* loss of sovereignty or control. This view results because they are already in a position of having little of sovereignty left,

294

save 'identity', and they hope to hold on to this by various means not particularly challenged by the MPE – such as language. (One may note, in passing, that the more differences that are lost among peoples, the more tenacious becomes their hold on the few left – such as the efforts to push forward the languages of the Flemish in Belgium, the French in Canada, and the Bretons in France.)

In the above category, I would put countries such as Belgium, Netherlands and Luxembourg, whose restraints on foreign investment have arisen only infrequently and from the pressures of overfull employment. For these countries, the challenge of the MPE is essentially a 'non-problem', and it has never been raised to the level of a policy debate. Note, however, that this group does not include Norway, Sweden, Finland, Denmark or Switzerland. Though small countries, they have not opened their doors to foreign investors in the same degree as have the Benelux countries. But neither have they determined their policy out of any concerted effort to decide what should be done about the MPE.

There is a second category of countries, of which Canada is the prime example, which consciously avoids raising the problem. When a national agitation develops, after the press focuses on a given action or 'insult', the government will respond with maximum apparent determination, but with minimum effect. Canada's fifteen points of 'good corporate behaviour' are a fine illustration of a slap on the wrist which does not alter behaviour. I have great sympathy for this position. Suppose, for example, that the government posed the question starkly and asked Canadians to decide: how much sovereignty can we afford to give up to gain the advantages of the MPE? And suppose that the answer came back, loud and clear: 'None!' What does the government do then? It would probably have preferred not to have raised the question. The problem is, in fact, too complex to warrant a single, simple policy response.

Consequently, we may expect that the problems surrounding the MPE will not be raised by governments as a single policy issue, requiring a single response. But, however it may be split up, it is clear that each response holds within it an attempt to resolve the problem of sharing of costs and benefits. Let us look at the sharing effects of each of the policy alternatives: restriction, competition and harmonization.

The fear by one host government that other governments would gain substantially if it imposed restraints on the MPE has been a strong factor in preventing controls on entry and operations. If one government imposes such constraints, the enterprise may simply move to another location or withhold action until a more propitious time, expanding its operations elsewhere, even selling the products of its expansion into the first host country. Therefore, a policy of restriction is made less effective by moves toward freer world trade, which permit markets to be served from any production location.

If one government is to make constraints effective it must also retain barriers to the import of similar items *and* be able to maintain a policy of restriction on trade and investment for a substantial period of time. It must also have a sufficiently attractive domestic situation to induce investment by foreign enterprises on *its* conditions. Only Japan has fulfilled these requirements. Otherwise, the enterprise will merely shift its activities to minimize the effect of the constraint, also minimizing the benefit to the host country. For example, a requirement forcing joint ventures on foreign investors may cause potential investors to look elsewhere or, even if they accept the constraint, they may alter the tax base of the host country unfavourably by eliciting payments to the foreign parent for services not generally paid for by wholly-owned affiliates. A requirement that affiliates sell shares locally will increase the drain on local capital and reduce the benefit from an inflow of capital from abroad.[1] The fact that the French lost the benefits of foreign investment without gaining significantly in terms of national sovereignty or control was a strong factor in their abandoning restrictions in the mid-sixties. French controls have become much more selective and directed at achieving a strong competitive position.

A response of strengthening competition by subsidizing national industry is acceptable if the costs incurred in a less-efficient use of resources is offset by gains of reducing relative dependence on the MPE. The national share of the benefits of growth is sacrificed for a stronger national position through greater local control over industry within the country. What is sought is greater certainty as to what the national share will be – in amount and in nature – at the cost of what could have been a greater (or lesser) share, determined by the MPE.

Similarly, strengthening the competitive posture of a group of economically-integrated countries makes the same presumption of improving collective control. But, at the same time, regional competitive responses cost each nation a loss of sovereignty – to the other

[1] **Donald T.** Brash makes these points in arguing against such restraints by Australia in *American Investment in Australian Industry*, Cambridge, Harvard University Press, 1966, pp. 77 and 274.

national entities. To date, governments have not shown themselves eager to lose sovereignty to other governments as a means of preventing its loss to the MPE.

Even an integrated, competitive response will not guarantee that Europe can retain all of its sovereignty for Europe cannot, apparently separate itself completely from the technological contributions of the MPE. The same trade-offs remain: how much economic gain for how much sovereignty? And, within an integrated Europe, there is the added problem of how to distribute the gains among the member countries.

Without a policy on industrial development, including the location and stimulation of industry within the Common Market, and without a concerted policy on development of indigenous research and development, Europe will not have taken the first steps towards resolving these problems. The recent memorandum on industrial policy approved by the EEC is directed at strengthening competition with the US enterprises. But it remains ambivalent on the role of affiliates of US companies in Europe, on dependency on US technology, and on means of sharing the benefits and costs of the integrated industrial policy among members. Though it clearly seeks to encourage transnational mergers within Europe, it offers only legal measures to assist. But these mergers have been hindered less by legal problems than by problems of sharing. How to share management among the Germans and French in a joint company; how to determine the location of various activities of the merged enterprise, especially the new facilities for research and development? And there remain strong governmental concerns over shared control – as evidenced by de Gaulle's reluctance to permit acquisition of Citroen by Fiat. The strength of these obstacles is attested by the absence of any fully-fledged, transnational mergers within Europe. Each that can be cited will be found, on examination, to have quite separate elements, resulting from an unwillingness to share a common operation and the necessity to solve sharing problems by less than full integration.

Given the inabilities of either governments or business to decide how to share the costs and benefits of policies of restriction or competition, it is not surprising that they are reluctant to move in the more difficult direction of multilateral harmonization of laws or regulations. Though such harmonization with the US Government would undoubtedly reduce tensions over the activities of the MPE, the extensive intergovernmental agreements required would raise even more difficult problems of sharing. For in every such arrangement there are implicit or explicit principles of sharing. Although governments have come a long way since World War Two in establishing international co-operative institutions, they have done so only under great pressures. And most were not given nor have developed any clear principles of sharing save in their scheduled subscriptions, which also defined their ability to benefit from the institution.

Determination of principles of sharing has been difficult enough in the most pressing area of national defence, under NATO. In the more economic and fiscal arena, precise determination will be even more difficult. Take, for example, the harmonization of tax laws – or, at the extreme, their unification into a single tax statute. Implicit within the new tax provisions is some sharing of the revenues derived from the MPEs operations. Taxes which one country considered most desirable or equitable, and more likely to produce the revenue it needed, will have to be modified to accord with those of others. But differences in business practices would alter the tax burden and revenue received in each country even if the laws were the same. Even under NATO's weapons consortia and infrastructure programmes, problems of tax sharing have been so complex as to prevent agreement and cause the nations literally to throw up their hands. Discussions in the OECD on tax issues have also been interminable.

The difficulties of arriving at acceptable criteria are magnified by the conflict between the principles of tax neutrality and tax equity. International tax neutrality means that the most economic business decisions would not be warped by international differences in tax rates or types of taxes. To achieve this result would require either similar tax rates *or* taxes which precisely offset dissimilarities in business conditions, *or* a complete disregard by business of tax burdens in making its decisions. But we know that business will not disregard taxes, that differences in tax systems do not exist for the purposes of offsetting differences in business conditions among countries, and that similar tax rates will not be seen as equitable among countries – even if they were neutral. Rather, governments insist on their own tax systems for the purpose of achieving *internal* equity or of altering business decisions to achieve *national* economic development.

Even the concept of equity means different things to taxpayers and to taxing governments. International tax equity to foreign investors, for example, means similar treatment of similar businesses in a given market, regardless of ownership of the business. To the US Government, at least, it means equal treatment of US taxpayers in similar income situations, whether the income is earned at home or abroad. It is difficult to reconcile these two views. Further to confuse the issue of tax equity, there are no principles of equity as to revenue sharing among nations. Should it be according to the benefits extended by each? or with appropriate differentials for loss of ownership and control in the host country? or with compensation for changes in the tax base made by the MPE? or according to the jurisdiction of each government over property owned by its citizens anywhere in the world? or according to some criterion of 'need'? It is quite difficult to gain a system of tax-sharing in the US among governmental levels; it will be infinitely more difficult among nations.

Faced with such a complex set of policy alternatives, most governments have tended to temporize. But reluctance to raise a problem to the level of official recognition implies acceptance of the tensions associated with it. Such behaviour may itself be quite rational and may even be dignified with the name of a 'law of tensions'. Such a law would state that if the existing tensions are less than those deemed likely to result from raising a problem and not finding an adequate solution, the present tensions will be borne instead.

This law of tensions gives rational explanation to Kant's observation that men raise only those problems that they can solve. The tensions surrounding the MPE seem to compose just such a non-raisable problem – at least not in any clear-cut fashion. The acceptable (or likely) solutions do not seem to outweigh the cost of disturbance which would result from attempting to obtain a policy determination. Some solutions, e.g. complete prohibition or nationalization, which might evolve if the problems were raised in highly-disturbed situations, are themselves not wanted by the present government leaders. Therefore the law of tensions tends to keep the issue from being raised clearly, definably, and in a form which facilitates a policy response.

Radical solutions might well result from a question posed so clearly that the public could provide an answer. This result is implied in the call by the principal author of the Watkins' report for nationalization. To some he seems to be asking the question: 'Do you want to be poor Canadians or rich Americans?' Posed in this fashion, the question is not one that the government wants answered, for they do not like the alternatives implied *nor* the means proposed. Yet to provide *no* effective response to such a question only increases the tensions.

This law also helps explain why Japan has not met the foreign investment issue completely head on, but has argued it tangentially over questions of technology transfer, ownership percentages, areas open for investment, 'over-capacity' industries, etc. Mexico also has raised specific, technical problems rather than confront the more complex, perplexing challenge of private (international) power to national power and the resulting problem of international sharing. Neither wants to start the internal arguments that would follow nor to begin a debate with the US when the position of the latter is itself so unclear.

For the United States, the aspect of the law of tensions that deters it is the high cost of raising a complex problem in a complex bureaucracy. The time spent and the drain from other problems is so great that the mere cost of raising such a problem seems exorbitant. If the problem is not at crisis level, the commitment of resources simply will not be made. It appears unlikely that the challenges of the MPE will be seen in crisis dimensions. Both this fact, and the fact that resulting policy positions within the US Government are so unpredictable, have caused it to refuse to elevate the problem to the status of policy attention. Potential responses, for example, might include its having to give up such long-cherished concepts as multilateralism and non-discrimination or national comity in investment and the right of establishment. It also does not know what to with the problems of sharing that would arise; it already has found such problems nearly intractable in the areas of multilateral aid and budgets of international institutions.

We may expect, therefore, that governmental policies toward the MPE will avoid raising the issues in a 'great debate' on the role of international private enterprise. The policy nod will go in favour of whittling away at specific tensions which seem amenable to constraint or adjustment. Technical solutions will be offered to various functional problems, avoiding the frustration of being unable to come to grips with the basic problem of sharing.

This is, of course, the 'functional' approach to international economic integration and would lead to new arrangements in patents, antitrust, taxation, standards, transport, export controls, customs formalities, accounting, exchange-rate changes, incomes policies, support for R & D, settlement of disputes, etc. But such an approach risks a lack of co-ordination among the various technical solutions; each may relate to the fundamental problem of national control and sharing in quite different and contradictory ways, because the fundamental issue remains unstated or obfuscated.

Even though unco-ordinated and contradictory, each such specific solution may be acceptable, thereby tending to ease the tensions. One reason for the acceptability is that different ministries in each government will probably work out the international agreements, with little or no co-ordination among them. But after following this road for some years, we may awaken to decide that we could have had an even better world by at least recognizing the basic problem in its complex form and seeking the new institutions necessary to guide the development of the multinational enterprise for the mutual benefit of all involved.

A vision of the world economy of the twenty-first century, which is merely a projection of the present arrangements, with the MPE increasingly pervading the interests of national economies, does not seem acceptable. But to seriously restrict its growth seems to involve too high a cost. Governments do, however, have the alternative of accepting the benefits while attempting to retain the necessary elements of sovereignty (control, diversity, opportunity and identity). But this can be done only through intergovernmental agreement which provides the necessary additional ability to protect national interests and to share the benefits equitably. This approach will lead to new international institutions.

This, then, is the fundamental challenge of the MPE: nations, in reaching for economic efficiency and growth through this enterprise, and in attempting to find solutions to its challenge to sovereignty, will have to come to grips (explicitly or implicitly) with the social values underlying the international economic system and the principles of equity on which it is based. However governments decide to respond, they will be embarking on an exercise in sharing, for which there are no acceptable principles at present. Their new answers would undoubtedly lead to new international institutions.

The paradox of this challenge is that, in seeking the appropriate principles and methods of implementation, governments can have the ready assistance of the MPE itself. The enterprise is already showing that – in situations where progress can be made only when sharing is explicitly provided for (as in the integration of markets in Latin America or in multinational weapons consortia) – it can provide a unique means of distributing the agreed-upon shares. If it is necessary that national parties share in some specified fashion in the benefits of economic integration, the enterprise can readily arrange its own operations so that these shares are secured. Governments will have to enunciate the principles of sharing, but the enterprise can translate them into practice.

The enterprise is also uniquely qualified to help quantify the trade-

offs between efficiency and equity which sharing implies, and of keeping in view the best ways of increasing the economic benefits to be
shared. But we run into another conflict in this process. In helping
to create appropriate shares, the MPE itself gains substantially,
in comparison to other (national) enterprises. Economic integration,
which is pursued for the benefit of national enterprises, becomes a
process under which the multinational (foreign-owned) enterprise
benefits.

For this result to be acceptable, a close community of interest and
much closer collaboration among the participants will be required,
including the parent company and affiliates of the enterprise and the
governments concerned.[1] For this community of interest to develop,
the enterprise must become more interested in (social) equity than
it has been, while retaining its orientation to (economic) efficiency.[2]
This does not mean that companies should become social welfare
institutions; they should and do refuse this role.[3] But business operates within many constraints, internal and external, that are non-
economic and not efficiency-orientated. Given that nations place
great emphasis on maintaining control, on providing diversity of
opportunity, on identity and on equity, MPEs can make a significant
contribution to the development of international institutions which
will have a balanced concern for both efficiency and equity. The
challenge is both to our international goals and to our international
institutions. Governments should be glad that the problems have
been raised, for the answers can produce a world with both greater
income and a more equitable distribution of it. The multinational
enterprises, having raised the problems, may find further satisfaction
in helping to resolve them.

[1] Andrew Shonfield reached a similar conclusion that a closer, more intimate
and flexible relationship between business and government must be developed
within each country to make modern capitalism successful. See *Modern
Capitalism*, London, Oxford University Press, 1965, p. 389.
[2] It certainly must appreciate better the requirements of the society and the
priorities of modern capitalism than the following view of a European business-
man: 'Sometimes, in the government official's judgment, the political and social
effect of a certain decision outweighs the economic effects it may have on business.
In our opinion this is a doubtful interpretation, because society, as we know it
it nowadays, is almost entirely dependent on economic actions, and wrong
economic decisions will in the long run cost more socially, even though they may
look brighter in the immediate political panorama.' N.I.C.B., *A World-Wide
Look at Business-Government Relations*, New York, 1967, p. 6.
[3] See the explanation of ICI's Sir Paul Chambers to a developing country of
the company's unwillingness to operate as a 'social welfare' institution in 'The
International Company', *Anglo-American Trade News*, May 1967, p. 8.

# COMMENT ON THE CHAPTER BY
# PROFESSOR BEHRMAN

GERARD CURZON

There is much in Professor Behrman's argument with which I cannot agree, and I attribute this to the fact that I do not reside on the North American Continent but in a small European country. Paradoxically, it seems to be easier to see American influence spreading throughout the world when one is not in an area which is reputedly suffering from it. I refer to Europe, which has recently received the largest share of US direct foreign investment, and readily concede that in a primitive, one-commodity economy, dominated by a single large foreign corporation, I should probably hold different views. But this rare situation is becoming rarer and is not the subject of Professor Behrman's chapter, which is concerned with relations between multinational corporations and the governments of advanced industrial nations.

Professor Behrman's play has two main characters: the multinational producing enterprise (MPE) and the nation state. Like Marx, whose Communist Manifesto contains glowing praise of the achievements of the bourgeois society, Professor Behrman does not deprive his MPE of all virtue. Good and evil are present in its make-up, though in unequal proportions. It centralizes its policies and integrates its operations into a world-wide entity, and in so doing 'adds to capital formation in the host country, brings managerial and technical skills, may promote regional development by moving into depressed areas, stimulates internal competition, and may contribute significantly to the expansion of export earnings of the host country'. (Behrman, page 289). These qualities are nevertheless overshadowed by numerous faults: 'the mere fact of its size injects a disturbance into the market; it alters competitive positions (though not necessarily methods of competition); it alters wage rates and labour relations, personnel practices, advertising, etc. . . . [it] points up to the host country its dependence on the MPE for technological progress . . . host governments are concerned, therefore, over the loss of control over a key sector of the economy . . . finally, the MPE having significant economic power through its ability to make decisions affecting the economy of the host country, has the capacity to upset national economic plans' (Behrman, page 290).

The character seems familiar. In Act I it was called 'Big Business'; in Act II it reappeared in the guise of the 'Giant Corporation'. I have also heard some of the lines before and parts of the plot have been taken from another play called 'Free Trade *versus* Protection', where one was also concerned with reliance on foreign suppliers, and the international distribution of the gains from trade.

Is the multinational enterprise essentially different from the large national enterprise? Many of the faults and qualities Professor Behrman attributes to it derive from its size, a feature shared by the large national corporation. The latter, for instance, may be as capable of thwarting or dictating national economic plans as the multinational corporation. The only difference is that it is not done by a foreign but by a native enterprise. But both types of enterprise are subject to similar constraints on their actions.

Multinational enterprises constitute a foreign element in the host country. This permits governments to treat them differently from national enterprises. Professor Behrman suggests the following alternatives:

(*a*) to reject the foreign enterprise or restrict its activities: an unprofitable course, since even the Soviet Union and other Eastern European countries, which have strong ideological reasons for excluding foreign investment, now wish to promote joint ventures with Western European firms;

(*b*) to create a competitive industry within the nation by subsidization and other aids, in order to eliminate some of the vacuums which attract the MPE: quite apart from the difficulty of making efficiency and subsidization go together, Europeans know something about subsidies. We subsidized our agriculture to compete with North America's cheap grain in the latter half of the nineteenth century and the present stage of these measures is the EEC's Common Agricultural Policy. If we pursue Professor Behrman's suggestions, we face the unhappy prospect of having, in the 1980–90s, a Common Industrial Policy along the same lines; and

(*c*) 'to build a set of intergovernmental rules and guidelines, which channel the enterprise in ways satisfactory to all governments participating'. The problem posed by the MPE would have to be of noble dimensions to justify the effort of undertaking so formidable a task. This is a point to which I shall return in my concluding remarks.

POLICY ALTERNATIVES AND INTERNATIONAL SHARING

I turn now to another question raised by the same play. It is assumed that the good guys (host countries) and the bad guys (MPEs) are easily recognizable, that the costs of multinational enterprises are born by the former and most of the benefits enjoyed by the latter, and that a redistribution is in order. But are we trying to redress the balance for the sake of the world at large, or for this or that nation state? Even within a host country there are some people who benefit from the presence of foreign direct investment and others who do not. When judging the virtues of a particular policy one has to look at how various groups within the country are affected by it. A subsidy designed to prevent a foreign firm from filling a vacuum might benefit inefficient workers as well as inefficient producers. But some citizens might object to subsidizing both. If the costs and benefits of MPEs are difficult to spot, so are those of the policies which might be used to control them. Once one takes the lid off the nation state and looks inside, it is not easy to see whom Professor Behrman is defending.

Let us look more closely at the second character of our play, the industrial nation state. Professor Behrman makes him appear rather weak and ineffective. We are made to worry over the loss of his control over the national economy: he is technologically dependent; his economic plans are upset; and, like Samson over his hair, he frets over his loss of sovereignty. I confess that I find it difficult to recognize the nation state in so poor a role. In the first place, there are some grounds for believing that MPEs behave no differently from large national enterprises, and there is some evidence that they may even behave better. But, more importantly, the nation state in Europe is not greatly to be pitied or admired. It has disgraced itself on many occasions, and some of us might even like to see its monopoly of temporal power curtailed. The OECD, EEC and EFTA are limited expressions of this desire. But the difficulties experienced by European integration show that the nation state is still very much in command of the situation. If nothing has been done to stop foreign direct investment in most European countries, it is not because the machinery is lacking but because it is usually thought to be desirable. The day foreign companies are no longer wanted they will be thrown out or nationalized, and no country would give over its right to take such a decision to an international agency.

Since I cannot agree that the nation state is an impotent hero and the MPE a powerful villain, I cannot see the need for new international machinery to keep all in order. Indeed, I see the need for no action other than that generally acceptable within a country to en-

305

sure social justice. To parody Professor Behrman's own conclusions, the MPE (which does not yet exist in its pure form) should be controlled by governments who, according to the law of tension, do not want to act.

Some parts of Professor Behrman's chapter and those of other participants, as well as much of the discussion, suggest that big business, alias the giant corporation, was just about to be captured and put under control in the United States, when it escaped abroad, disguised as the MPE. Some of our American colleagues have tried to convince us that we Europeans should try to help catch the scoundrel. But the trouble is that we rather admire him. If one looks at what passes for antitrust legislation on the continent of Europe it is clear that big business is given great latitude for unfettered development. For this very reason, the prediction that Europe is about to be eaten up by American enterprises reminds me of the old dollar gap discussion, which was discredited when the gap turned to glut overnight. In ten or fifteen years' time we may be listening to the same arguments, this time objecting that large European concerns take decisions to the detriment of the United States. It is unwise to make long-run predictions on short-run evidence. In the twenty-first century MPEs may have split up into regional components, may identify completely with national surroundings, may have created one world – we cannot tell. But in any event, the role of the MPE in the latter half of the twentieth century is likely to be less dramatic than some would have us believe.

PART SIX. THE MULTINATIONAL COMPANY IN
EUROPE

## Chapter 12

# THE MULTINATIONALLY-OWNED
# COMPANY: A CASE STUDY

### MICHAEL WHITEHEAD

#### INTRODUCTION

The chapter is divided into five sections. The following section serves
as an introduction to the main theme and discusses the most important conflicts of interest between foreign subsidiaries and host countries, particularly in the context of the European reaction. We then
turn to a discussion of the type of multi-owned national enterprise
in which we are interested at Bath, and this is followed by a description of the work now under progress. The fourth section presents a
case study of the Agfa–Gevaert merger and, finally, we offer a number of tentative conclusions on what the study at Bath has so far
indicated.

#### CONFLICTS OF INTEREST BETWEEN FOREIGN SUBSIDIARIES
#### AND HOST COUNTRIES

Direct investment overseas is not a new phenomenon; it just seems
new because, for various reasons, there has appeared over the last
decade or so a growing body of literature on the subject. Some of this
has been rhetorical, some revolutionary, some has attempted to be
analytical but, with a few notable exceptions, little has been based
on any numerical foundation or direct experience with international
firms.

#### National Fears and Hopes
Concern with some of the consequences of direct investment overseas (often referred to briefly as 'American investment abroad')

has developed in Europe from the mid-fifties onwards. Christopher Layton explains why:

> If an American firm brings competition and lower prices to the consumer, it upsets competitors. It does the same if it raises wages (or) increases its share of the market. If it brings an entire new industry, someone will be afraid that Europe is becoming 'dependent on American knowledge'.[1]

When, on August 31 1962 General Motors sacked 685 employees at their refrigerator plant near Paris, and ten days later Remington Rand announced that it would dismiss two-thirds of the workers employed at its subsidiary near Lyons, criticism came into the open.

These incidents drew attention to the emphasis placed by (some) multinational companies on 'integrated' activities,[2] and it is mainly this feature of multinational companies that can lead to conflict with host governments. Governments with employment policies will be affected by dismissals, and will also wish to see nationals in management positions in multinational companies. Governments will wish, too, to maintain future employment, and conflicts may arise if large multinational companies wish to divert a large proportion of future investment to other countries.

Multinational firms need a sophisticated financial capability if they aim to integrate their operations. This can lead to a fear that the companies may manipulate tax payments by means of transfer prices or management charges to subsidiaries. In addition, the international company will operate in the foreign exchange market, with potentially serious effects.[3]

If a country experiences balance of payments problems, discord can arise if a multinational company is financed from abroad – interest and dividends then represent a transaction across the exchanges. The multinational company can also minimize the effects of host-government policy by raising capital abroad at a time when the host government is applying 'squeeze' measures, and if the companies find it difficult or impossible to respond to import restrictions. This might be the case when, as in IBM, components are manufactured in several countries for central assembly.

[1] Christopher Layton, *Trans-Atlantic Investments*, Second Edition, The Atlanti Institute, January 1968.
[2] This is discussed by Caroline M. Miles in 'The International Corporation', *International Affairs*, 1969.
[3] See, for example, the USM case quoted from *Fortune* (September 15, 1968) by Louis Turner in *Politics and the Multi-national Company*, *Fabian Research Series*, No. 279, December 1969.

The Watkins Report[1] on foreign investment in Canadian industry recognizes this problem and concludes that national fiscal and monetary policies need not become unworkable in a situation of greater international mobility of capital, but must work differently.

Another source of conflict between the subsidiaries of multinational companies and host countries arises because the international company is itself subject to the law of the country in which the headquarters is registered. It is feared that the subsidiaries might be used as instruments of foreign policy, and that anti-monopoly policies of the HQ government might be applied extra-territorially; this need not necessarily injure the host country in any material way, but it offends national pride.

Nationalist feelings are also at the root of two more conflict areas. First, host governments wish to see national control of 'key' sectors of the economy – defence industries, the newer science-based growth industries, etc.; in the second place, there are conflicting views about the effects of multinational firms on the technology of host countries.[2]

While this is not intended in any way to be a full or complete analysis of the conflicts of interest that might arise – other papers have provided a fuller analysis – we hope that it has indicated some of the main problems associated with direct investment overseas.

On the credit side, several advantages are claimed for multinational companies. The takeover of firms is usually followed by investment, particularly in labour-saving machinery – this in turn leading to a higher productivity of labour. Multinational firms tend to have higher ratios of sales/capital employed, profit/sales, and export sales/total sales than comparable firms in the industry. The host countries' GNP is also increased and new jobs are created.

In particular, foreign-owned firms seem to respond better than national firms to incentives designed to attract industry to the development areas. The role played by international companies in the exploration of the North Sea is sometimes cited as an example of the way in which these firms bring the advantages of advanced technology to the host countries. Sometimes, too, international companies act as life-savers – for example, the Chrysler takeover of Rootes and the Philips stake in Pye. But perhaps, from the *laissez-*

[1] *Foreign Ownership and the Structure of Canadian Industry*, Queens Printer, Ottawa, 1968.

[2] In this connection, see John H. Dunning and Max Steuer, 'The Effects of United States Direct Investment in Britain on British Technology', *Moorgate and Wall Street Review*, Autumn 1969.

*faire* point of view, the most significant feature of international companies is the increase in competition their presence brings.

International companies, particularly United States companies, have brought to Europe a new conception of management. By applying the same management techniques as they employ in the United States, and by regarding Europe as a single market, many American companies have gained a significant foothold in Europe.

## The European Reaction

The host government is faced with a complex choice when weighing the advantages and drawbacks of the presence of multinational companies. The Watkins Report offers some advice:

> . . . policy should be directed towards increasing the benefits from direct investment and decreasing the costs. It is impossible to measure benefits in a precise way. There is always the problem that benefits are mostly economic whilst costs are political. How do you compare apples and oranges?[1]

European governments are beginning to grapple with this problem. Industry, however, was quicker off the mark, and we now examine some of the answers that have been put forward. As we shall see, most of the arrangements have been aimed at obtaining the benefits of large size.

The competition from efficient US companies has forced European industrialists closer together. One device – that of forming price-rings – is not tolerated by the Commission of the European Community, which in January 1970 announced that it was fining twenty-five West German steel companies for forming price-rings in the scrap metal sector.[2]

More in tune with current views on business morality has been the wave of mergers (e.g. BIMC and ICL), takeovers (GEC–English Electric) and the formation of joint subsidiaries, such as Forth Chemicals in the UK, and the Renault/Peugeot[3] link in France, designed to strengthen national industrial sectors. Other ventures are multinational in ownership, for example, the Philips–Ignis formation of Industrie Riunite Eurodomestiche[4] and the possibility of a joint company owned by Unilever and Nestle.[5]

[1] *Op. cit.*
[2] *The Times*, February 11, 1970.
[3] *The Times*, March 2, 1970.
[4] *The Times*, March 2, 1970.
[5] *The Financial Times*, November 1, 1969.

Some firms have formed joint subsidiaries with American companies; for example, Rank Xerox, the deal between Metal Box and Continental Can Company[1] and the agreement between Siemens and Allis-Chalmers.[2] Others have taken an aggressive stance and have attacked the United States market directly. BP's acquisition of Sinclair and merger with Standard Oil of Ohio is an example of this, as is the plan for Plessey to take over Alloys Unlimited.[3]

Other forms of co-operation have been the *ad hoc* consortia formed to bid for a specific project, such as the Euro-Data Computer Scheme, and collaboration on specific joint programmes, particularly in the aircraft and advanced technology industries. There are many examples of this type of collaboration – Concord, Jaguar, Panavia – and the collaboration on uranium enrichment.

These projects have involved European governments who have been open to pressure to 'buy national', and who have encouraged the strengthening of national industry by the formation of such bodies as the IRC in Britain and the French IDI. At the time of writing, there is also pressure for a similar European agency. A more recent response by government and supra-government departments has been the attempt to draw up some 'code of behaviour' as guidelines to firms to minimize any ill effects of multinational firms in the host countries.[4]

A different type of reaction by private industry which to some extent takes political considerations into account has been the formation of multinational owned companies of the Agfa-Gevaert type. Before describing the distinctive features of these ventures in some detail, we consider some more general aspects of multinational companies.

### THE SCOPE OF INTERNATIONAL COMPANIES

As Professor Dunning has shown, the definition of the adjective 'international' or 'multinational' as applied to companies varies according to the interests of particular writers: for instance, it might deal with differences in the legal structure, the objects, the geographical location, or the management philosophies of these companies. We will briefly examine some of these definitions.

---

[1] *The Financial Times*, April 6, 1970.
[2] *The Times*, February 20, 1970.
[3] *The Financial Times*, January 23, 1970.
[4] See, for example, 'Attracting the Multinationals – the Search for a Policy', Christopher Tugendhat, *The Financial Times*, March 19, 1970.

## 1 *Legal Status*

Because commercial law varies in the details of its application from country to country, the firm operating abroad is faced with the obligation to satisfy more than one legal system. The difficulties inherent in this are modified, to some extent, by treaties and, as Professor Phillipe Kahn points out:

> The nationality of a company thereby becomes its means of benefiting from a treaty (covering establishment, trade, double taxation, investment, etc.). The factors that appear to be of an international character (differing place of incorporation; seat and operational centres; control carried out by different nationalities, etc.) merely give rise to doubts regarding the exact nationality of the company in question – doubts often removed by the treaty itself which contains a definition of the national companies of one of the contracting states.[1]

In this article, Kahn quotes Professor Berthold Goldman, who asserts that there are: 'A certain number of corporations which have not been constituted by the exclusive application of one national law.'[2] Goldman had in mind such organizations as the SAS, which might be regarded as a 'half-way stage' in the development of the legal framework for a 'Societas Europaea'.

While in the past the legal aspects of international company organization has not been a widely discussed topic (outside the profession), this might change in response to reports of the case of the Barcelona Traction, Light and Power Company.[3]

## 2 *Economic Criteria*

Most manufacturing companies operate, to some extent at least, in an international environment: most import raw materials or machinery, some export finished products and a few manufacture overseas. From an economic point of view it becomes difficult to distinguish the point at which a firm adopts the 'international' label. The usual solution is to attempt to measure the percentage of, for example, sales, assets, labour employed or profits arising abroad. If the result is greater than an arbitrarily chosen number, the firm is classified with the internationals. In *The International Corporation*,

[1] Phillipe Kahn, 'International Companies', *Journal of World Trade Law*, September–October 1969.
[2] Quoted from Goldman, 'Le droit des Sociétés Internationales', *Journal du Droit International*, Clunet, 1963.
[3] See, for example, *The Financial Times*, March 17, 1970.

Sydney Rolfe[1] examines this question, and provides a useful analysis of the foreign operations of firms listed in the 1968 'Fortune Directory'.

## 3 Management Attitudes

In spite of a great deal of discussion, there is no generally accepted set of criteria defining what management theory means by 'international' firms. Professor R. Robinson, for example, distinguishes between 'international', 'multinational', 'transnational' and 'supranational' firms; Professor C. Kindleberger suggests distinctions between 'national firms with foreign operations', 'multinational firms' and 'international firms'; and Professor H. Perlmutter provides us with a conception of 'ethnocentric', 'polycentric' and 'geocentric' attitudes held by the managers of firms.[2]

These and other distinctions are doubtless useful for particular purposes. In this paper describing a study being carried out at Bath, because we wish to emphasize political differences in the ownership and management of firms, we use the term 'multinational', defined in a particular manner.

## 4 'Bath' Definition of Multinational Companies

Multinational companies are here defined as those in which the ownership and control of the companies are shared (more or less equally) between more than one country.[3] We are not concerned with examining those companies which are mainly (or wholly) owned and tightly controlled from one European national state (i.e. MPEs), though their shares might be traded in a number of countries. It is the compromise illustrated by the classic examples of Shell and Unilever that interests us here.

In these companies the structure chosen overcomes many of the legal, fiscal and taxation problems of merging across frontiers, and leaves the merged company with some degree of national identity.

### THE BATH STUDY

The essential characteristic feature of Bath multinational firms – that of internationally shared control – effectively reduces the number of firms in this category to a mere handful; so that it would be a

---

[1] Sydney E. Rolfe, *The International Corporation*, International Chamber of Commerce, 1969.
[2] S. Rolfe, *op. cit.*
[3] In Professor Dunning's terminology, MOEs and MCEs.

valid question to ask why one should be interested especially in these particular companies – the Royal Dutch/Shell Group (formed in 1906), Unilever (1928), Agfa–Gevaert (1964), Fokker–VFW (1970) and Dunlop–Pirelli (1971).

It will be noticed that each company is the result of a complete merger between two previously nationally owned (but internationally operating) companies. They are thus near one extreme of the spectrum, displaying the extent of commitment to foreign collaboration. They can be viewed as the ultimate organizational structure in certain industries in which, for a variety of reasons, governments wish to maintain a national presence, but in which the optimum size of firm is considerably larger than a single nation could support independently. It may be argued that the European computer, nuclear and aircraft industries are among those that fall into this category, but it seems that major constraints to the formation of multinational companies must first be overcome.

The first of these constraints is that there must be the will to combine across frontiers and the acceptance that the same national sovereignty must be foregone. Secondly, it appears to be essential that each party to a merger should be of approximately equal size, and hence bring more or less equal contributions (assets, profits, etc.) to the merged company, while expecting to receive roughly equal benefits.

The study being carried out at the Centre for European Industrial Studies at Bath University of Technology is concerned with the questions of the economic, political and managerial advantages and disadvantages of multinationally-owned companies, and the examination of the problems arising in developing these companies. Thus it is hoped to distinguish differences between these types of companies and nationally owned but internationally operating companies in their organizational structure, degree of integration, and means of reconciling conflicting national economic interests.

A case study approach has been adopted because, in addition to the small number of firms under discussion, differences in the external environment facing each company necessitated individual examination. Information is gleaned from a variety of sources, but particular reliance is being placed upon interviews with executives of the companies and examination of internal records.

There are a number of obvious difficulties inherent in this approach. Most firms are sensitive to the public relations aspect of information published about the company. Conflicts and failures tend to receive less attention than success. Again, conducting an interview is an art in itself. An over-structured questionnaire tends to predetermine the answers given, and inhibits the 'thinking aloud' which often provides an insight into important questions.

Another problem is that executives are not inclined to compartmentalize their actions; a decision is judged more by the resultant effect on profit than how it fits into an economic or political model of company behaviour. It is, therefore, impossible to say, without a standard of comparison whether, for example, improved sales figures are due to the fact that the sales force has been reorganized, the quality of the product changed, advertising expenditure increased, or to some other reason. However, since there is no alternative offering a means of overcoming these problems, the most one can do is to watch for the inevitable pitfalls and be suitably careful in the interpretation of the data collected.

From the case studies it is hoped to be able to give at least tentative answers to three questions. These are:

(a) What are the reasons for the success or failure, so far, of efforts to develop multinational owned and financed companies?
(b) What are the implications for policies by the European Community and by individual governments?
(c) What are the lessons for policies by management?

The validity of the conclusions will naturally be limited by the extent to which it will be possible to generalize from these cases.

In the next section we summarize the work that has so far been carried out on Agfa–Gevaert as an example of the case-study approach.


AGFA–GEVAERT – A MULTINATIONAL OWNED COMPANY

## 1 Historical Background

On February 14, 1964, Agfa – a German company – and Gevaert – a Belgian company – announced their intention to merge: on July 1st the merger became effective. The origins of Agfa AG can be traced back to 1867, when an aniline dye-stuffs factory was established in Berlin. Aktiengesellschaft fur Anilinfabrikation (Agfa) was formed in 1873 and marketed negative emulsions in 1893. By 1926 the company was marketing a range of photographic products under the Agfa brand, together with a range of cameras and processing equipment. In 1932 Agfa bought out Lenticular Colour Film, followed by Agfacolor Integral Tripack Film. The diffusion transfer process, the basis of modern copying systems, was discovered simultaneously by Agfa and Gevaert scientists in 1939. Agfacolor Cine Film appeared in 1940, followed in 1942 by Agfacolor Colour Print.

Gevaert started making photographic paper at Antwerp in 1890. In 1920 Naamloze Vennootschap Gevaert Photo-Production was formed and in 1923 motion picture film was manufactured. Gevaert marketed their first X-ray and sound-motion picture film in 1929, and in the next few years new graphic papers, and film and papers for document copying.

## 2 *Motives*

In 1964 both Agfa, which had since 1945 concentrated on re-establishing its position in the amateur field, and Gevaert, whose sales showed a leaning towards the technical side of the business, shared common problems. First, the technology was changing at an increasing pace. New developments in photo-chemistry, photo-mechanics, optics, and in other fields such as electronics, necessitated heavy expenditure on research and development. Simultaneously, the marketing situation was changing. Powerful foreign groups were thrusting into the European market, taking over a number of old-established photographic companies. In particular, Kodak already dominated the world market for photographic firms and, in 1964, was spending on research and development alone an amount roughly equivalent to the turnover of Gevaert. In addition costs, both of labour and materials, were rising fast. A press release issued at the time of the merger by the new company illustrates the position:

> Gevaert Photo-Producten NV, Mortsel/Antwerp and Agfa AG, Leverkusen, announce that the negotiations conducted during the past month to combine their industrial activity in a single economic unit, have been concluded successfully. The formation of this unit, which is in line with the progressing integration of the European market, will be accomplished on a fifty–fifty basis and will include on both sides the entire industrial activity in the scientific, technical, commercial and financial field. The co-operation will greatly increase the research potential by co-ordinating the joint scientific efforts, and it will rationalize production and distribution and strengthen the partnership's competitive position.

> Since formal mergers across the frontiers are not yet legally possible, the economic unit will be realized through the takeover

of all activities by a new German and a new Belgian operating company. Agfa AG and Gevaert Photo-Producten NV will each hold fifty per cent of the shares of both operating Companies. The Managing Boards will consist of the same directors in both Companies in equal proportion. The operating Companies will be formed shortly and will start their activity from July 1st 1964 . . .

### 3 *Mechanics of Merging*

At the beginning of 1964 Agfa AG was one of the photographic subsidiaries of Farbenfabriken Bayer AG, the German Pharmaceutical, Plastics, Dyestuffs and Chemical Group with sales in 1964 of DM3,700 million. These subsidiaries, Perutz-Photowerke GmbH, Munosa GmbH, Leonar-Werke AG, Chemische Fabrik Vaihingen/ EHZ GmbH, Gelatinefabrik Koepff and Sohne GmbH, were merged to form an enlarged Agfa AG, 91·5% of the shares being owned by Bayer, the balance of 8·5% being issued to C. F. Boehringer and Sohne GmbH in compensation for their 50% holding in Perutz-Photowerke GmbH, one of the subsidiaries merged into the new Agfa Group. This brought Agfa up to the size of Gevaert, so that each group contributed equally to the new unit. The new operating companies, Gevaert–Agfa NV with a share capital of 1,350 million BF and Agfa-Gevaert AG (110 million DM) took over the whole of the industrial activities of the parent concerns, together with all their employees. The patents and technical expertise and trade marks have been placed at the disposal of the operating companies. The buildings, land and other fixed assets held by the parent concerns as on July 1, 1964 have been leased to the new companies, and the parent companies have granted the operating companies a right of option on all the fixed assets at their disposal, together with the right to erect buildings on the land that has been leased to them.

Investments from July 1, 1964 have been undertaken by the operating companies for their own account, leading to the gradual decrease of the fixed assets of the parent companies. The operating companies have the same capital and the same financial year for accounting. The two parent companies kept to their original financial years, and share equally the total net profit of the operating companies.

The fifty–fifty theme continues in the management structure. There are, of course, two levels – the 'Supervisory Board' (College van Commissarissen/Aufsichtsrat) and the 'Board of Management' (Raad van Beheer/Vorstand). At the 'Supervisory Board' level, the personnel of each operating company is identical, with Agfa-Gevaert AG having a German chairman, while the chairman of Gevaert-Agfa NV is Belgian. The 'Board of Management' of each company is again identical, except that Agfa–Gevaert AG have, in addition to the people on the Board of Gevaert–Agfa NV, Workers' Representatives, in compliance with German law. Again, both German and Belgian operating companies have nationals as Presidents. There was originally an equal balance of Germans and Belgians on each pair of Boards, and the 'Board of Management' had five Belgian and five German representatives but, at the time of writing, one of the Belgians has retired from the 'Board of Management' and has not been replaced.

In 1964 it appears to have been desired to stress the equality of the participants in each 'politically sensitive area' of the companies' structure. There are indications now that this need has been modified with the passage of time. In 1964 it would not have been possible to publish in the Annual Report a list of an odd number on the 'Board of Management' and, in the same vein, the present-day tendency to concentrate on the Agfa–Gevaert (rather than Gevaert-Agfa) label, indicates a desire to 'tidy up' the corporate image to an extent that was out of the question at the time of the merger.

The 'twin' company device certainly overcomes a number of difficulties which would otherwise have arisen in a merger or take-over. Had Gevaert wished to take over the original Agfa company, it would have had to approach the managers of Bayer (Agfa was then a wholly-owned subsidiary), who would have been unlikely to want to dispose of a profitably operating tied outlet for its own chemical output. Certainly Bayer would have been unlikely to consider a cash sale, even supposing Gevaert could have raised the money, and the alternative of a share exchange would have resulted in Bayer obtaining a large block of Gevaert shares. Since Gevaert shares are widely owned, this might have given Bayer effective control of Gevaert.

Similarly Gevaert, situated in a Flemish part of Belgium, and looked upon as the family firm by generations of Flemish workers, would nave found it difficult to find a majority in favour of selling out to Agfa, let alone the unanimous consent of shareholders that Belgian company law requires, to move the legal location of a firm out of Belgium. This factor also ruled out the possibility of merging the two companies under a single holding company based in a third country. Moving would also have involved legal and fiscal costs. A merger would have necessitated the legal liquidation and reconstitution of the moving company. This would have meant a bill for legal advice. In addition, in Belgium there was a 30% capital gains tax on the difference between the liquidation value and the capital value of the company. There would also have been liquidation and registration taxes to pay.

A further difficulty was that since there was no double taxation agreement between Belgium and West Germany, gross profits would have to be considerably increased (to pay the higher bill) to pay shareholders the same net dividend. From a legal and fiscal viewpoint, then, the 'twin' company structure appeared to offer the only practical method of merging.

The 'twin' structure also overcomes the problem of the Bayer block vote. Gevaert Photo-Producten NV remains the publicly quoted company and, in effect, looks after shareholders' interests in the management of the two operating companies, much as Agfa AG acts on behalf of Bayer, and Bayer shareholders.

But if all this looks very neat on paper, how does it work in practice? As far as the conventional wisdom of management philosophy is concerned, the structure could hardly be described as optimal. The very equality designed to overcome political sensitivities should make decisive decision-making more difficult. Functional responsibilities are duplicated. For instance, there is a marketing director at Antwerp for technical products, and another at Leverkusen responsible for amateur sales. Subsidiaries abroad have no clear single control channel: overall financial control – for example, control of budgets – will be from either Leverkusen or Antwerp according to the location of the subsidiary. A decision on whether to employ a technical salesman at a higher salary than his equivalent amateur compatriot would involve the marketing departments of both Leverkusen and Antwerp as well as the financial control department. These sort of problems are resolved at committee meetings.

The organizational problems created by the decision to merge have not, then, been insignificant. We have seen the company press release giving summary reasons for the merger, and should now see whether the advantages were, in fact, realized.

### 4 Benefits of the Merger

The economic effects of the merger can be viewed, conceptually at least, from three points of view. Firstly, each component part can now regard itself as one-half of a much larger group. In theory, large companies are able to avail themselves of any economies of scale that exist, find it easier to raise fresh capital, have the advantage of a large cash flow within the company, and are able to exploit the image of large companies – for example, in recruiting staff.

(a) *'Size' effect*. Economies of scale can appear in every functional department of a company, from purchasing raw materials to marketing the finished product, but the optimum size to make the best use of the phenomenon will vary from function to function. The material inputs for the amateur side of photography are, to oversimplify, special chemicals, film-base material and papers. These are the products of highly capital-intensive industries, so that one might not expect to find great economies of scale in the purchase of raw materials. Purchasing could be done centrally, leading possibly to economies or, on the other hand, the firm might have grown big enough to vertically integrate production back into the manufacture of raw materials. Although by 1967 Agfa–Gevaert had a polyester film-base factory under construction, the reason for this investment is more likely to be the need to control specific technical properties of the film to fine limits than cost considerations.

As far as the manufacture of films and papers is concerned, a factor of more decisive importance is the cost of producing machines for manufacturing these products. They are extremely specialized and have, historically, been developed by each company for its own use. The larger group was able to develop a new 'generation' of machines, partly because of its increased financial resources and partly by combining the machine technology and machine producing capacity of the component companies. This has led, *ceteris paribus*, to a reduction in unit costs.

More significant, perhaps, have been the economies of scale in marketing. In part these have been due to rationalization; but in addition the size of the combined sales of the new group have made it worthwhile setting up subsidiaries in Greece, Portugal and Finland, countries in which neither group had subsidiaries before the merger.

Yet, as an executive of the company explained, perhaps the greatest benefit of the larger size has been the increased cash flow. This means that not only has it been easier to sustain a high level of research and development expenditure, rising from US $16·7 million or 5·2% of turnover in 1964–5 to US $22·4 million or nearly 6% of total sales in 1967–8, but that new products and systems could be launched in a much larger way. The 'Rapid' and 'Pak' systems – competing with the Kodak 'Instamatic' casette system – benefited from this, as did the launching of a new negative colour film, improved paper, and colour film for television, amongst other products. This increased financial strength has also enabled the companies to set up training centres for customers at Mortsel and Munich. These training centres and other technical services quickly proved their value in assisting the growth of sales.

However, some of the economies of scale a completely rationalized group might have enjoyed have had to be sacrificed to the 'twin' structure arrangement, and some have been deliberately foregone because of the social consequences that would follow – for example, the closing of uneconomic plants.

(b) *'Merger' effect*. A second aspect of the Agfa–Gevaert merger is, of course, that it represents the merging of two separate companies. There then exists, theoretically, the possibility of gaining a 'once-off' advantage by transferring techniques from one company to another. One way in which Agfa–Gevaert took advantage of this opportunity was to utilize the best coating techniques of each partner to improve machinery for manufacturing papers and films. Another example was in the marketing field. Gevaert was oriented more to technical production than Agfa and could afford to experiment with different marketing techniques for the 20% of their output which was in the amateur field. Where Agfa was tied to a formal marketing procedure for amateur products, Gevaert was able to experiment, for example, with mail-order selling.

There was also advantages from the management point of view; the Gevaert managers had, perhaps, a more entrepreneurial outlook than their Agfa counterparts. Agfa managers had the additional constraint of the responsibility to Bayer and Bayer shareholders, which entailed a rather more formal day-to-day management style. Both the Agfa and the Gevaert styles were needed by the joint companies.

There was also some possibility of rationalizing the product lines, marketing and research and development. The specialization exhibited by each company before the merger was concentrated – technical products at Mortsel and amateur at Leverkusan. This has not been carried to extremes, however, since some colour film for the amateur market is manufactured at Mortsel, and some of the products coming from the German factories, such as Megneton tapes, are supplied to both the amateur and technical markets.

(c) *'Multinational' effect*. The third aspect of this type of merger is the multinational structure of the resulting company. There are several possible advantages which come to mind here. First, it may be expected that a multinational structure offers the executives a wider field of choice when deciding, for example, where to site a new factory. The Agfa–Gevaert business was rationalized on the basis of producing at least cost. For example, the production of X-ray materials was thirteen times bigger in Antwerp than in the Agfa factories, and in addition Antwerp was marginally nearer to the market. It was, therefore, preferable to manufacture at Antwerp.

Initially, the merger resulted in the creation of a reserve of capacity, which lasted for a few years. After the slack had been taken up, the location of new plant was determined by whether the new output was mainly for the amateur market (Agfa's main field), in which case it was built in Germany, or the technical market, the Gevaert speciality. Thus a new camera factory and a plant for producing Magneton tapes were built in Germany, but a film base factory was built at Mortsel. So far then, in Agfa–Gevaert, plant location decisions appear to have been settled largely on technical arguments – the multinational structure not really being particularly advantageous in this connection.

In spite of Germany's well-publicized tight labour supply situation, there has not been much permanent movement of personnel between countries. Even at manager level such mobility was, until recently, on a small scale. At the present, movement between the two countries is being encouraged in the management development plans.

In certain situations, a multinationally merged company might be expected to benefit from an easier access to capital. Not only would the company be able to raise capital from each of the countries in which it is based, but its new status would also facilitate raising capital on the Euro-currency market. Agfa–Gevaert, however, did not find this a special advantage. Firstly, Agfa capital comes from Bayer and, on the Gevaert side, lack of capital has not, apparently, been a factor restricting the growth of business.

Again, the fact that a multinational enterprise is based in more than one country might mean that it is less dependent on the prevailing economic situation in any one of its base countries. This does not seem to have been the case with Agfa–Gevaert. There are several reasons for this: the nature of the business makes it extremely difficult, if not impossible, to change production rates in the short term; there is also the size factor – a large firm has less room for manoeuvre than smaller companies; much of Agfa–Gevaert's output is exported; and, in addition, the economies of Germany and Belgium are already, and increasingly, interrelated.

Another benefit claimed for international companies is that they can arrange their operations so that profits arise in low-tax countries. In Agfa–Gevaert, certainly as far as European operations are concerned, this question does not seem to arise. A company spokesman states that because the market is highly competitive, the 'number 2' company has to sell where it can – at a price dictated by the market. The group is horizontally rather than vertically integrated, so there is little cross-frontier intra-company trading of semi-finished goods. In the main, foreign factories produce goods for the area in which they are situated, other markets being supplied from the home-based factories. Most export markets are as competitive as the European market so that transfer pricing decisions are made in the light of the competitive situation and with a view to make some profit at each profit location.

A company merging with another from a different country also has the advantage that, compared with a merger between two firms of the same nationality, it now has a larger 'home' market. Agfa–Gevaert find that it is now easier to sell Gevaert–Agfa branded technical products in Germany, where Agfa's name is known and respected. This consideration has helped sales to the private sector and the 'twin' nationality is also used to advantage when selling to the public sector. Governments prefer to buy the strategic equipment and materials for aerial photography from companies owned by their own nationals. Agfa–Gevaert are able to 'play the market' here; sales to the German Government would be negotiated by Agfa, the Belgian content of the enterprise being played down. This is, of course, quite 'above board' as, legally, Agfa AG is a German company.

When a company has merged with another in a different country, there is the possibility that heterogeneous national attitudes and characteristics, arising from differing national mores and values, can be used to advantage in the company. It might be, for example, that highly regulated and automated production techniques would be less unacceptable to workers in one country than in another, so that production techniques might vary in different countries. For the same reason, sales techniques and management methods might differ. Dissimilar national backgrounds in science might result in distinguishable problem-solving methods and organization structures

At the time of the merger production techniques were generally alike, for similar products, in both Agfa and Gevaert, though it might be significant that Agfa has always produced cameras whereas Gevaert has not. There were differences in management techniques and sales methods between Agfa and Gevaert, but one cannot say whether this was due more to distinctions between national attitudes or whether other variables might have been equally contributory, such as, for instance, the situation of Agfa as a subsidiary of Bayer. Again, there were differences between the two companies in the type and organization of research and development effort, the reasons for which would be difficult, if not impossible, to establish.

Another possibility is that cross-frontier mergers might increase foreign exchange earnings. The financial sophistication required to carry out a merger of this type could be put to use after the merger in export marketing. Agfa–Gevaert has certainly needed sophistication in rationalizing its foreign operations. Before the merger, Gevaert had an international outlook – more than 90% of its sales being exports, while Agfa placed more emphasis on the home market. The advantages of exporting were not disregarded by the merged group. It was possible to amalgamate existing traditional export markets and, after the merger, Agfa products were carried by Gevaert foreign subsidiaries while Gevaert products were sold by the former Agfa subsidiaries in, for example, Australia and New Zealand. In some export markets both companies were represented, and here rationalization was required. Other markets, formerly too small to warrant a subsidiary, offered worthwhile investment opportunities to the merged company.

So far we have looked at some of the advantages to be gained from multinational mergers. It has not always been possible to pinpoint or to classify these advantages, and similarly it is difficult in some cases to apportion the costs resulting from a multinational merger to particular causes.

## 5 The Costs of Merging

(a) 'Size' effect. Using the categories we have taken for advantages, we may now ask first whether the increase in size has led to any disadvantages. One feature of large companies, current management theory explains, is that the organization tends to be more bureaucratic, with a larger proportion of 'non-productive' labour than small companies. This feature has not been noticed in Agfa–Gevaert, at least in the first years of its operation, partly because of the reorganization associated with rationalizing the product lines.

Another feature of bureaucratic systems[1] is the lack of flexibility with which they tend to operate. The Agfa–Gevaert management

[1] Max Weber, *The Theory of Social and Economic Organization*, London, Oxford University Press, 1947.

structure has been purposely designed to balance the power of the interested groups. Because of the need for unanimity in decision-making at Board level, it can be said that there has been some loss of flexibility. An example of this is that announcements to staff are signed by both chairmen. This sometimes results in delay, though this could in part be compensated by the greater thoroughness with which the decisions are taken.

(b) *'Merger' effect.* In addition to the special costs suffered by large companies, a company is likely to incur medium- and short-term costs when the potential benefits of size are sought in a merger. Agfa–Gevaert experienced short-term costs before obtaining the advantages of economies of scale of production and marketing that we have mentioned above. Because no outside help was available to carry out the merger, many managers had to put in extra hours. This time spent can be regarded as one of the costs of the merger.

Another short-term cost was the effect the merger had on staff. It was fairly obvious that there would have to be some rationalization, for instance, in the marketing organization, and this undoubtedly had an adverse effect on the morale of the salesmen.

Agfa–Gevaert also experienced short-term costs with the transfer between the two component groups of techniques of production, marketing and management. Rationalizing product lines and marketing also necessitated reviewing the trade marks. Some lines were dropped; for example, Gevaert amateur film. This entailed a short-term drop in total sales while the rationalization was carried through. It is quite likely that when supplies of Gevaert's film were withdrawn, retailers were as willing to yield to pressure from, for example, Kodak representatives, as they were to substitute Agfa film.

Similarly, although the merger gave Gevaert the opportunity of marketing machine systems, such as Gevefax (an electrostatic office copying machine), in the short term, costs were involved in exploiting this opportunity, since marketing arrangements etc. had to be established.

It was noted that initially after the merger the cost/sales ratio fell for most products, together with sales of some products. As new products were launched the average cost/sales ratio rose, but total sales of existing products recovered.

(c) *'Multinational' effect.* Are there any costs special to the multinational firm? Agfa–Gevaert has not so far experienced additional costs caused by either the need to share production in more than one country or the desire to ration research and development expenditure on a national basis. Perhaps Agfa–Gevaert was fortunate in the neat dovetailing of their product ranges, and it might be that these costs tend to rise in the longer term. For the present they do not worry Agfa–Gevaert.

Neither were there particular language problems: Belgians learn German as a fourth language at school, and the limited extent to which operations have been integrated has meant that the Germans have not suffered as a result of any lack of facility in Flemish they might have.

The legal and tax costs of carrying out the merger were hardly significant, apart from the costs of registering the new companies in Belgium and Germany. The Agfa–Gevaert annual report for 1964–5 reveals that:

> . . . the incorporation expenses and capital increase costs running to US $1·8 million comprise incorporation taxes and legal expenses incurred on capital increases at par and not offset against the paid-in surplus.

The professional advice needed to integrate the foreign operations was a relatively more expensive item. The decision on whether to merge subsidiaries or whether one subsidiary should take over the other was based on the desire to maximize long-term profits, but local law was, of course, one constraint.

The 'twin' nationality of the merged company might be a dis-advantage if foreigners were suspicious of the true nationality of the firm. Agfa–Gevaert, as has been pointed out already, is careful to avoid arousing fears. On the other hand, in Germany technical film had been sold partly on a national basis, so that sales were lost when the Agfa brand was withdrawn from this market.

Another cost associated with changes of this magnitude is that of the effect of the change on the labour force. The workers in Agfa–Gevaert were not affected much, since there had been no intention of carrying rationalization to an extent which would throw people out of work, and this was explained to employees early. In some foreign subsidiaries there was a noticeable fall-off in performance. Partly this was due to the fact that there was a longer time-lag before the merger resulted in the integration of foreign operations.

We have so far examined some of the advantages and drawbacks Agfa–Gevaert has experienced with their multinational venture. We have been mainly concerned with the European aspects, and will now take a brief look at foreign operations.

## 6 Foreign Subsidiaries

The full examination of the relationships between multinational firms and their foreign subsidiaries would make an interesting study in itself. It would be interesting to know whether, for example, multinational companies show a great tendency towards Perlmutter's 'geocentricity' than other international firms. In this paper we can do no more than scratch the surface of these questions.

Agfa–Gevaert lists twenty-three subsidiaries in its 1967–8 Annual Report. Most of these subsidiaries cultivate the commercial rather than manufacturing field, the exceptions being in Spain, France (where two products are made for world-wide distribution), India, Argentina (for the LAFTA market) and in the United States. Long-term investment in other subsidiaries takes the form, at present, of laboratories and training facilities. Investment decisions of any scale are taken at Group Headquarters, where policy matters are also settled.

The chief executive of a foreign subsidiary will be from Belgium or Germany and is expected to stay for the rest of his career. For example, the Argentinian Manager has held the post for eleven years.

Agfa–Gevaert denies that they manipulate prices so that profits arise in low-tax countries. Prices are set within the constraints of the competitive environment, the need to makè some profit in all operations, and cost factors. If we look at the competitive situation, we can form an opinion about the validity of this argument.

## 7 Competition

Agfa–Gevaert suffered a short-term drop in its market share initially, but the company consider that by 1968 it was at least back to the market share that Agfa and Gevaert would have held separately. In third markets, and in the United States in particular, the group's market share has increased. Has there, then, been a diminution of competition?

There is strong American competition in every field in which Agfa–Gevaert operates – from Kodak in the traditional photographic market, and from such firms as Xerox (and IBM) in office machinery. In addition, particularly in Eastern markets, Japanese competition is strong. In colour photography there are two main competitors, in black and white four other powerful firms; in the technical field there are at least six; there are four large competitors in the graphic market; and two powerful rivals in cine photography. It is unlikely that Agfa–Gevaert is in a position to exploit an

THE MULTINATIONAL ENTERPRISE

oligopolistic position, because this competition is on an international scale.

Evidence of this can be found in the behaviour of prices in the photographic industry. In spite of increases in the quality of the product, the prices of films and papers have been held from mid-1950 until 1967 at a stable level. In 1967 silver, an important raw material, displayed erratic price behaviour, jumping from an average of about US 140 cents per ounce in 1966 to 210 cents per ounce in 1967, and reaching an average of 240 cents per ounce in 1968. The prices of photographic products went up 10%. Further evidence of strong competition is that a number of other photographic product manufacturers have found themselves in difficulties since the Agfa–Gevaert merger.

The antitrust bodies took the view that the merger was in the interests of the European economy. In Belgium there is no anti-monopoly law, but this situation is different in Germany where the anti-monopoly bodies examined the case and agreed to the merger. The EEC Commission did not disagree: the company argued that, unlike the iron and steel agreement, Article 85 of the Treaty did not forbid mergers even though agreements were condemned. In June 1965 Mr Von der Groeben clarified the EEC Commission view – that certain economic mergers should not be discouraged if a monopoly situation were not thereby created. Other government bodies did not object to the merger. One explanation for this might be that governments are interested in the national control of technology.

## 8 Technology

Agfa–Gevaert is convinced that the effect of the merger has been to increase the rate of innovation in Europe. Two electrostatic machines were introduced within two years; an X-ray processing machine has been brought out, television colour film introduced, processing machinery has been marketed, and the performance of many older products improved. In this field, at least, European technology is competitive with American. Has this advantages for Europe?

## 9 Effect on the European Economy

'If one regards the subsidiaries of Kodak, Dupont and 3M as American, then the merger has strengthened the share of European trade' is the view of a manager of Agfa–Gevaert. As he was ready to point out, these value judgments mean little – the company does not think in terms of the national or supra-national implications of a decision beyond ensuring that the company behaves within the constraints set by the political, social and economic environment.

## 10 *Financial Results*

Ideally, one would like to judge the results of the merger by a comparison of the values of such variables as profits, sales, etc. of the merged Agfa–Gevaert group with the hypothetical corresponding values of the two groups operating independently over the same period. Obviously this is impossible because of the difficulty of saying what might have happened in different circumstances. A second approach to evaluating the financial results of the merger would be to compare the results obtained by the merged group with the results the two components turned in immediately before the merger. In the Agfa–Gevaert case, this too is a non-starter because the financial details of Agfa AG were, prior to the merger, consolidated with those of the Bayer parent.

The third alternative is to evaluate the performance of Agfa–Gevaert in comparison with its competitors in the industry, and work on this is at present being carried out.

## CONCLUSIONS

In spite of the fact that we have used a very particular definition of multinational companies, we find that there are significant differences between the few companies in the multinational category. Thus, while most of these companies are bi-national, this is not necessarily essential: most companies have a strict fifty-fifty relationship as far as the ownership of the shares is concerned – Shell is one exception to this; and in many cases the 'twin' company structure has resulted, though again this is not inevitable.

We can therefore expect to find differences in the behaviour of multinational-owned companies and, if we also take into account other variables (such as the effect of technology), we will be reluctant to generalize about the observable behaviour of these firms.

What we can do, however, is to draw attention to common features of the successful firms and outline the special difficulties these companies experience as a class. It is probably true to say that these firms come together as a result of a strong environmental force – usually that of competition from foreigners. Faced with a competitive threat, a firm tends to adopt one of the following strategies:

(*a*) seeks to deal with it with its own resources;

(b) enlarges its own resources by takeover;

(c) enlarges its resources by merger with a company of the same nationality;

(d) seeks outside help (e.g. sells a minority stake in the company).

Both Agfa and Gevaert no doubt did their best to maintain their business in the face of strong and increasing competition from America and Japan. They concluded that although they could remain competitive with purely European firms, this was not enough. The actions (b) and (c) above were not open to them and, for the reasons we have discussed, they decided to merge.

Agfa and Gevaert were fortunate in that several decisive factors were favourable: they were of equal size; their product mix was complementary; and their national business environments were similar.

It might also be significant that the 'bread and butter' product had reached an advanced position on the product cycle curve. It is at this stage that a fairly rigid management structure can be tolerated – so long as large-scale production etc. enables prices to be kept down; but where the external environment facing the firm is changing rapidly, the management structure needs to be more flexible.

In another case study – of a firm in the semi-conductor industry – flexible management is essential because the product is much closer to the 'take-off' stage of development, where, in some applications, price considerations come secondary to technology. It does not matter so much whether your satellite costs £100 or £110 million, so long as it functions in orbit! Does this need for adaptability mean that the 'multinational solution' to the problems of European technological advancement is doomed to failure?

In April 1970, Guido Colonna, Commissioner in charge of industrial affairs of the EEC, is quoted as saying:

... the goal is to create an industrial environment within the EEC to promote intra-EEC mergers, create more companies with a world-wide trading outlook, and more balance between EEC and United States industry through the harmonization in EEC countries of the laws affecting corporations, corporate merger regulations, corporate taxes, incentives considered necessary for industry and of foreign investment procedures and of similar matters.[1]

This appears to be a sufficiently flexible approach to the problem.

[1] *The Times*, April 22, 1970.

We have seen that Agfa–Gevaert suffered short/medium term costs because of the multinational aspect of their merger. If we wish to encourage mergers of this type, then a case can be made for giving financial help to companies in order to overcome initial costs.

If the answer to Europe's industrial problems really lies in encouraging the formation of larger units, then the proposal to create a European 'IRC-type' organization deserves further serious consideration.

So far, work at Bath has indicated that multinationally owned and operated companies are likely to provide at least a partial solution to some of the problems of scale facing industry in Europe. In some respects they offer considerable advantages over say, 'national solutions' or increased direct investment from the United States. It would be rash, however, to suggest that this formula could be applied across the board, and the EEC Commission is right to keep the options flexible while tackling some of the basic anomalies besetting European industry today.

# COMMENT ON THE CHAPTER BY
# MR WHITEHEAD

## H. WERTHEIMER

Mr Whitehead's chapter starts with a section dealing with the conflicts of interest between foreign subsidiaries and host countries. In principle, areas of potential tension exist. There is no invisible hand directing the international company such that, under all possible circumstances, its operations will optimally benefit the interests of the host country. On the other hand, as the chapter justly points out, there are also several substantial advantages accruing from the MPE to the host country. To strike a balance between the drawbacks and the benefits amounts more or less to expressing a value judgment, particularly as the different aspects are not governed by economic considerations alone. Since this relationship between the international corporation and the host countries has been discussed at length in the chapters of Professor Penrose and Professor Behrman I will confine myself to two remarks on this issue.

First, in the literature on this subject, attention is practically always focused on the relationship between the multinational enterprise and the nation state, but less on the way this relationship affects the relationship of this same MPE with *other* nation states (including the host country) in which the corporation operates. When the MPE is forced to adopt a certain conduct to accommodate the public interest of a given nation state, how does this affect the public interest of the other nation states? How should all these public interests, when they are conflicting, be evaluated and balanced against each other?

There are examples where the public interest involved in one country is of a marginal nature while that at stake in the other country is of crucial importance. A case in point is the situation of two Swiss companies, Geigy and Ciba, which have not been permitted to conclude a merger, held to be of paramount importance to the competitiveness of the Swiss economy because of the extra-territorial application of US antitrust laws. It is argued by the Department of Justice that since the American-based establishments

332

of both Swiss companies would be merged as a part of the Swiss merger this would substantially lessen competition in the USA chemical industry. It is more likely, however, that the US economy would only be marginally affected by such a merger while the chemical industry in Switzerland is vitally important to its economy – Geigy and Ciba being the second and third enterprises in that industry.

Secondly, I should like to point out there is little quantitative information on the extent to which the operations of the MPEs are not in harmony with the interests of host countries, as against the occasions when they operate in accordance with their policies. If the times a conflict of interests is shown turn out to be minimal compared with those in which their operations are beneficial it would mean that a distorted view of reality would be given if too much emphasis would be laid on the areas of tension without mentioning how often this situation occurs.

Where the report deals with the European reaction against the penetration of US firms, it may be true that the responses from European industry were quicker than those of governments' reactions, but it is open to doubt whether all the activities discussed in the paper were directly dictated by answers to those US moves. For example, BP's recent takeover of Sohio (US) was to my mind more due to the recent findings of crude oil in Alaska and should not be rated as a European counter-offensive.

When setting out the various definitions of international companies, Mr Whitehead first approaches the issue from a legal point of view. Here one is liable to tread dangerous and controversial ground. The legal international company is not necessarily the same kind of animal one has in mind when speaking of international corporations from an economic viewpoint. Under the former proposals for the creation of a so-called European company, for example, it was a matter of discussion whether the access of a company to the European status was conditional upon its indulging in intra-European operations, and if so what should then be the minimum ratio of its total operations covered by its European dealings.

According to more recent proposals, the European company will only be available for three kinds of operations, first for a merger between two companies located in different member states, second for the setting up of a joint holding company by two companies from different member states, and third, for establishing a joint subsidiary by companies from different member states. Thus it is

333

clear that the economic and legal concepts of an international corporation do not necessarily coincide.

The present paper is concerned with that type of MPE in which the ownership and control of the operating companies is shared between companies located in more than one country.

It is open to question whether a closer study of a case like that of Agfa–Gevaert provides a representative insight into the phenomenon of the multinational company in the paper's sense, all the more because of the population in this category is so small. Therefore it is welcomed that the Bath study mentioned in the paper will also study and examine other cases fitting into this category.

It may be useful to indicate in that study in what way the multinational owned and controlled firms are confronted with issues different from those encountered by other MPEs.

As to the Agfa–Gevaert merger, it was certainly triggered off by the dominating position of Kodak. The mechanics of the merger were very complicated indeed, principally because of tax reasons. This is not the place to go into further details, but Mr Whitehead should be encouraged to try and establish why the financial results of the companies involved, subsequent to the merger, have not been very impressive. How is it that the 'size-effect' has not resulted in a better rate of return, or is it too early to say anything about this yet?

The conclusions of Mr Whitehead are modest, and rightly so. Multinational companies represent birds of a varied description. In point of fact they make up quite a zoo. While some might seek them in the part occupied by the hawks, others might look for them in the section of the doves. Anyway, the paper is right in stating that the pattern of conduct of the various multinational companies cannot be generalized. It therefore seems warranted not to draw too definite conclusions from a case-study like Agfa–Gevaert.

As to the plea expressed in the paper in favour of the creation of a European 'IRC-type' organization, one may wonder whether this is not premature under present circumstances.

It should not be forgotten that the EEC Treaty contains no provisions on a common industrial policy. Community authorities have to depend wholly on the collaboration of the governments of the nation states which, for the most part, do not even have a consistent industrial policy of their own. The Commission's memorandum on a Common Industrial Policy which is more or less inspired by the French concept of a 'concerted economy' does not coincide with the Germany philosophy of a market economy. As long as no common ground exists in this direction it is unlikely that the creation of European institutions for furthering European industrialization will come to anything.

This does not imply that intra-European mergers across the borders should not be promoted. For the present time, however, the best way to do this is to eliminate barriers that stand in their way, including tax barriers which are commonly considered to constitute the greatest obstacles of them all.

*Chapter 13*

# SUMMARY OF DISCUSSION

## DAVID ROBERTSON

### THE SCOPE OF THE MULTINATIONAL ENTERPRISE

Although the conference programme was set out under separate subject headings, the discussion tended to return to certain key issues. In this summary, therefore, although the views expressed are collected under subject headings of special interest, it does not pretend to represent a chronological record of the discussion, neither is it a comprehensive summary of all that was said at the conference sessions.

Any extended discussion of the subject reveals a wide variety of different definitions of the multinational enterprise (MPE). There were some participants who wished to describe MPEs as highly-integrated operations with centralized control, and others who preferred a looser and less precise definition. For example, Professor Behrman in Chapter 11 states 'it is an integral part of the definition of a MPE that it is centralizing its policies and integrating its operations into a world-wide entity',[1] while, at the other extreme, Professor Dunning wished to define as a multinational enterprise any company producing in more than one country.[2]

There are clearly many definitions that fall between these two extremes. In fact, it is evident that some functions may be centralized while others are decentralized, and that the practice varies greatly between enterprises. Some functions may be partially centralized, such as the need for parent company approval of five-year strategic plans, while for day-to-day purposes a subsidiary may be entirely independent within these longer-term constraints. Nor is it necessary that a MPE should treat all its subsidiaries in the same

[1] J. Behrman, Chapter 11, p. 292.
[2] J. H. Dunning, Chapter 1; this chapter discusses a variety of definitions of the MPE.

manner. The variety of decision areas for a large enterprise permits many types of organization to be adopted even within the same enterprise.

When choosing a definition, therefore, it is necessary to find the one most suitable for the specific aspect or problem of the MPE that is under investigation. In particular, the character of the industry or the structure of the market is likely to be relevant to the definition adopted. Any attempts to generalize about the methods of operations or the consequences of the operations of MPEs must be treated with extreme caution. Practices vary greatly, and to generalize from specific companies or specific industries is likely to be misleading. To deal with a phenomenon as complex and as heterogenous as MPEs, however, it is necessary to simplify and to define the issues. Their effects on the world economy, and on separate national economies, can only be examined within a clearly defined model which is constructed to meet the needs of the specific aspect of multinational operations under study.

When considering the activities of MPEs it is often convenient to differentiate between their operations in the developed world, as represented by the OECD countries and in the developing world. The issues raised, however, are usually the same, although they are sometimes discussed within different institutional frameworks. The operations of MPEs in developed and developing countries were frequently considered together. It is only necessary in this summary, therefore, to accord special treatment to the operations of MPEs in developing countries where issues peculiar to these countries were highlighted in the discussion.

## STRUCTURE OF WORLD MARKETS

The rapid development of the activities of MPEs in the last twenty years is a reflection of the many changes that have occurred in the international economic environment in that period. Opportunities for overseas expansion have been revealed by the gradual removal of restrictions protecting national economies and by improved transport and communications techniques. Exploitation of these opportunities has been encouraged by various types of incentives offered by national governments and by reductions in risks and uncertainties associated with overseas operations. Proprietary knowledge and advantages obtained from the economies of scale and integration form the basis from which corporate profits and growth are realized internationally. In Chapter 1, Professor Dunning identifies three types of international extension which were accepted in the discussion.[1] When extending their international operations, however, the major MPEs are likely to be activated by a mixture of motives, or by different motives at different times.

Backward vertical integration is motivated by the pursuit and the protection of sources of raw materials and processed inputs to production. With secure markets for their main range of outputs, companies may wish to gain more control over earlier stages of production, and particularly over supplies of raw materials. Perhaps rather less important, if enterprises are uncertain about established outlets for their raw materials or semi-processed products, they may seek to extend their activities forward in an attempt to consolidate their market position.

In oligopolistic market situations, horizontal extension is often an important aim of MPEs. Currently, this is attracting great interest in developed countries. The nature of the product groups in which MPEs have shown greatest penetration – chemicals, motor cars, electrical appliances, etc. – shows a high degree of concentration on industries with oligopolistic structures supplying branded or differentiated products. The initial motive for horizontal expansion of international operations by a MPE is usually to exploit or protect a specific economic advantage over competitors. This step is presumably undertaken because exporting to that market is a less satisfactory alternative. Subsequently, competitors may be forced to follow such a lead into overseas markets for fear of losing future sales. Many commentators believe that a large proportion of overseas investment by MPEs is stimulated by defensive motives, a view that received support in the discussions.

The operations of MPEs introduce interesting problems of concentration and competition in industries on an international plane. In his paper,[2] Professor Hymer argued that the operations of MPEs tend to lead to a reduction in competition on world markets because of increased concentration. Many participants disputed this. In the first place, the method of overseas expansion adopted by MPEs is important. When an enterprise establishes a new foreign subsidiary, it appears as a new entrant to that national market. Initially this would increase the level of competition. Ultimately, it could be that rationalization may reduce the number of participating firms. Even

[1] Chapter 1 above, p. 21/22.

[2] 'The efficiency (contradictions) of multinational corporations', separately published in *American Economic Review Papers and Proceedings*, May 1970, pp. 411–49.

then, however, competition may increase efficiency in that sector; and greater efficiency may result for the economy as a whole if released resources find new employments. If, on the other hand, an MPE chooses to extend its overseas operations by a takeover of an existing national firm, the structure of competition in the national market would be unaffected, but there would be an increase in concentration in the world market because of the reduction in the number of independent operators.

Professor Caves pointed out that whether either of these sources of action are beneficial for the world depends on the circumstances in the world market before and after such a change. A new overseas subsidiary or an affiliate created by a takeover may both increase competition in the national market and the world as a whole. This is particularly true if subsidiaries operate with a high degree of autonomy. Improved communications and transport permit companies to adopt a world-wide marketing strategy and to integrate production programmes. But, for many products, separate regional markets still exist and even the most powerful MPEs are forced to operate their subsidiaries to meet the demands of particular markets. Another important consideration is the attitude of major competitors to the new investment. If they decide to safeguard their market position by means of parallel overseas investment, then competition is intensified, at least in the short term. In the longer term, rationalization may drive out some of the weaker national companies, leaving the field to the international giants. Even so, greater concentration in a market does not necessarily reduce competition; an increase in market share may encourage companies to adopt more aggressive policies in an effort to penetrate their competitors' share of the market.

## THE ISSUE OF NATIONAL SOVEREIGNTY

A subject to which the discussions returned repeatedly was the so-called conflict of interests between the nation state and MPEs. The debate, as well as the alleged conflict, was usually ill-defined and occurred in several guises. Essentially, the debate is concerned with whether the operations of MPEs which transgress national boundaries conflict with national objectives or restrict the effectiveness of national policies. Such interference can occur in two directions. Either the MPE itself operates to neutralize or reverse policies considered by a national government to be desirable, or a multinational company with its headquarters based in one particular country acts as a mechanism for transmitting the policies of that country to other territories. Both these effects may be intentional or unintentional. That is, knowingly or unknowingly a MPE may interfere in the national economic policies of a host country through its normal operations.

It is pointed out in Chapter 10 by Mr Murray that politics represent an essential aspect of the study of MPEs. Economic models are not sufficient to expose the real sources of this apparent conflict. When a company operates in only one country its activities can be regulated by means of that country's laws. But the areas of activity of a MPE stretch beyond the fixed jurisdictions of national governments. In consequence, its managers can, to some extent, shift resources and activities among its subsidiaries in different countries in order to minimize the impact of different national laws on its operations. Furthermore, by operating as a wider entity, a MPE has different space and time horizons from a competitor operating in only one national market; for instance, the former may be more, or less, interested in long-run growth, in contrast to current profits, than the latter. These observable differences in the behaviour of MPEs can be employed as evidence of a conflict of interests between its objectives and what is presumed to be one country's national interest.

Each national subsidiary is subject to the laws of the country in which it operates. And each MPE has evolved from this same environment by a succession of decisions taken in response to economic opportunities. But the scope of its operations enables a MPE, once established, to avoid more easily the laws and policies of one nation state, because these differ as between countries. One means of limiting this freedom is through international harmonization of laws and policies. During the last twenty years, national governments have been moving slowly towards greater integration of their economies through organizations such as GATT, IMF, OECD and EEC. These intergovernment efforts at economic integration, however, look meagre alongside the developments by MPEs, although the latter is not independent of the former.

Some participants believed that unless an international agreement were introduced to regulate the activities of MPEs, the *ad hoc* measures currently employed by national governments could create serious impediments to development of the international economy. In certain respects, it was suggested that MPEs would appreciate some form of regulation to provide a legal safeguard to their operations. For example, in the past they have requested international conferences to give territorial rights for oil drilling at sea and for fishing in order to establish a legal structure within which they could operate. From the point of view of national government, it was considered that this proposal would compensate for the weakening control they now exercise over the overseas activities of companies operating within their jurisdictions.

Other contributors expressed doubts as to whether an international agreement could ever be reached. The discussions revealed clearly that many of the issues supposedly raised by MPEs are unclear and ill-defined. Moreover, many aspects of the alleged conflict could be shown to arise from differences of policies and laws between nations. As such, they could be removed by harmonization of national policies, but this would require governments to surrender sovereignty over wide areas of their competence. For example, incentives and special concessions to attract foreign investment would presumably be forfeited under such an agreement.

## THE BALANCE OF PAYMENTS

One subject which occupied the conference at some length was how much consideration national authorities should give to the operations of MPEs in connection with balance of payments' policy. Obviously by definition these enterprises are involved in transactions across national frontiers, and this affects foreign receipts and payments in all countries where they operate. The balance of payments represents an aggregation of the many transactions between residents of the reporting country and residents of foreign countries during an accounting period. Some participants contended, therefore, that, as such, it is probably impossible to measure the effect on the balance of payments of a country of the operations either of a particular MPE or of all MPEs operating in or from that country. Tracing all the direct and indirect ramifications for the balance of payments of the operations of a MPE presented unsurmountable difficulties; not least because if this particular transaction had not taken place the macro-economic disposition of resources in the countries involved would have been different.

For example, if a capital outflow initiated by an investment decision by an international company leads to a negative effect on the balance of payments of the parent company's country (i.e. increasing an overall deficit or reducing a surplus), there are many ways in which this change might be offset, if that is considered necessary from a policy point of view. Assuming the investing country must seek to achieve balance of payments equilibrium in the long run, certain additional policy steps will be taken. These policy changes should be made according to macro-economic considerations. One measure that might be adopted could be to restrict overseas investment in order to reduce the impact of this kind of transaction in future, but that would be only one of a wide range of possibilities. There will, though, be differences in the policy mix for the situation where overseas direct investment is permitted and for the situation without this freedom.

In the initial period following an investment, some of the apparent outflow is returned to the investing country to pay for exports of equipment or material inputs or services required for the new plant established overseas. When the new plant begins to operate there may be continuing exports to support its production, and when it makes profits there will be remissions of profits or dividends and, possibly, service charges to the parent company. All these changes must be taken into account in assessing the situation in the domestic economies of both countries, as well as in the aggregates that compose the balance of payments accounts. Policy adjustments over different periods will vary in the light of these changes, other things being equal, which in practice they are not.

While accepting the general macro-economic considerations of this proposition, other participants thought that the operations of MPEs influenced the magnitudes of items on both the current and capital accounts of the balance of payments. Hence, before policy instruments can be decided upon, it is necessary to know how the operations of MPEs might change the effectiveness of policy instruments in a particular institutional framework, such as fixed exchange rates. The fact that a particular policy mix is necessary to maintain balance of payments equilibrium under certain assumptions is not sufficient to allow the whole impact of policies affecting the MPE to be ignored. The first stage must be to measure and understand the impact of foreign direct investment on the components of the balance of payments and to ascertain how far this might affect certain of the policy variables within the balance of payments configuration. Many items on the balance of payments accounts are affected by the operations of MPEs, directly or indirectly. Some are likely to be more clearly affected than others.

For less-developed countries, the balance of payments effects were thought to be even more crucial. A capital inflow obviously brings net benefit to the balance of payments in the short run. But, in the longer term, as repayments increase it is necessary to undertake a

343

separate type of calculation. The balance of payments of the recipient country continues to benefit so long as the remittances of profits, etc. to the overseas parent company, plus the value of any imported items, are less than the increased exports from the new plant, plus any import savings by that country as a result of the investment inflow. Eventually, however, the outflows generated by the investment may create a transfer problem for the developing country, which may already be faced with a shortage of foreign exchange as a severe constraint on its development programmes. The overall benefits of an inflow of capital, technology, management, etc. involved in the setting up of a new subsidiary by a MPE are likely to be much greater than the balance of payments effects, but the balance of payments is a particularly sensitive area of policy for developing countries.

## TRADE FLOWS

The operations of MPEs influence patterns of international trade flows in two specific ways. First, investment in new production plant generates new trade flows. Presumably one objective of the new plant is to substitute local production for imports; this represents the simplest and most direct effect on trade. Some inputs incorporated into the production process are likely to be imported either from affiliated companies or from independents; imports of associated products from the parent company are possible too. Output from the new plant may also be exported to neighbouring markets. These exports may create new trade flows, or they may simply displace exports previously made from other affiliates or the parent company. In Chapter 6 these trade flows are identified as export generating, import generating, import displacement and export displacement.

In addition, allocative decisions within the enterprise may disturb or create international trade flows. International programming of production means that components are produced at different plants within the enterprise that may be located in different countries, so that in order to assemble them they must be brought together in one country. This way intra-firm transfers appear as international trade flows.

An important consideration in this respect is the pricing of intra-firm transfers of goods and services across frontiers. It is possible for an enterprise to fix the value attached to a service or product transferred between affiliates to suit its own ends. In the case of intra-company services the value attached to these services can, theoretically, be adjusted by the parent company as a means of transferring profits or funds from one part of the company to another. In practice, of course, many governments keep a close eye on service payments from subsidiaries to the parent company in order to prevent it being used to avoid or circumvent taxes or exchange controls. The values attached to intermediate products can similarly be adjusted to the advantage of the company. Where such products are internationally traded, of course, the customs administrations have some standards of measurement for the values attached to intra-firm transfers of a similar type. In many cases, however, there is no comparable internationally traded good, in which case the company has greater freedom to adjust its prices. Specific cases were noted in the discussions; for example, certain types of pharmaceutical products.

Business representatives at the conference did not consider that transfer prices were a particularly important issue. Theoretically, transfer pricing could be used to transfer funds across frontiers to the advantage of the company. The most obvious case would be to minimize tax payments by earning profits in the country with the most favourable fiscal system. Other considerations might be avoidance of exchange control regulations on the movement of short-term funds, or speculation on exchange rate differentials, or differences in interest rates. Although such instances might occur, and in fact cases of transfer pricing being adjusted to overcome tariffs were quoted, business representatives considered that competition within the company, between subsidiaries, would mean that strong pressures would be brought to bear to obtain adequate profits in all national subsidiaries of a multinational enterprise.[1] Increasing centralization of control within a MPE might, of course, leads to a tendency for transfer pricing to be used more widely. Overhead costs in certain integrated operations must be allocated among the different subsidiaries of the multinational company, and the use of transfer pricing might be used to this end. Equally, funds could be moved by adjusting the timing of payments for intracompany exchanges in the same way as leads and lags are employed between independent companies.

---

[1] The use of transfer pricing to direct funds to an affiliates in a jurisdiction with low taxation was clearly a concern of the United States authorities when they drafted the 1962 US Revenue Act, which contains several clauses aimed at regulating the invoiced prices of goods shipped from the United States to overseas affiliated companies.

The doctrine of free trade tells us that the unrestricted movement of goods between countries leads to available resources being applied to activities in which they have comparative advantage. Trade flows result in a more efficient allocation of a given stock of resources than would be the case if no trade occurred and each country sought to be self-sufficient. A basic question with regard to the operations of MPEs, therefore, is whether their activities and the trade flows they generate bring about better allocations of resources than would occur in their absence. If the international division of labour is extended by the activities of the multinationals, then output is raised. The theory of the product cycle suggests that an mprovement is achieved. Overseas investment leads to a transfer of capital funds, organization, management and technology. In this way the efficiency of production, that is the utilization of available resources, in overseas countries is improved.

On the other hand, the fact that a subsidiary of a MPE may have a monopoly position in certain markets and may be protected from competition by imports, suggests that the allocation of resources could be improved; especially since in some cases the monopoly has government approval and protection. In these circumstances government efforts to regulate foreign investment might lead to an improvement in the allocation of resources. This case can be argued from the point of view of an individual country, or from the point of view of the world as a whole. Individual cases were quoted in the discussion. For example, the Egyptian pharmaceutical industry and the Australian motor-car industry appear to have benefited from an improvement in the allocation of resources after government intervention to regulate the entry and the activities of international companies. It was generally concluded that much wider surveys of the effects of the MPE on trade flows and the location of production are necessary before anything can be said about the effects of international investment and the operations of the multinational enterprise on the allocation of resources.

## LABOUR PRODUCTIVITY AND INDUSTRIAL RELATIONS

The discussion based on Messrs Steuer and Gennard's chapter was concerned specifically with the effects of the operations of foreign-owned enterprises in the United Kingdom on labour productivity and industrial relations. British labour relations have several peculiarities all their own; labour contracts are not legally binding for a given period, and the bargaining is usually carried out by large multi-industry unions, which leaves considerable initiative in the hands of local officers for establishing restrictive practices. Within this structure the agreements reached with unions by foreign-owned firms have had a path-breaking role.

As important innovators of industrial relations in the United Kingdom foreign-controlled subsidiaries were thought, by some participants, to have brought a net benefit to the British economy. It was pointed out, however, that they may also have had adverse effects that had not been measured directly in the paper under discussion. By breaking away from traditional conventions these foreign-controlled subsidiaries have set precedents. They were the first enterprises to introduce productivity bargaining and plant bargaining with the labour unions. Subsidiaries of foreign firms using more efficient methods of production than national competitors could afford to increase wages above the going rate in order to acquire necessary labour and to achieve a certain degree of labour peace; these subsidiaries have recorded smaller losses in labour time than their national competitors. Such increases, however, could spillover into neighbouring regions and competing or non-competing industries through other productivity bargains, which were not founded on genuine improvements in productivity. An example quoted concerned the agreement at Esso's Fawley plant being responsible for spillover effects into the Southampton labour market. It was believed by some participants that this had added to wage-cost inflation in the United Kingdom.

It was pointed out that this process of wage-transmitted inflation was formerly associated with the nationalized industries. Was it possible, therefore, that this was merely a manifestation from the development of large enterprises? Some participants argued that MPEs had been forced to concede wage increases because they are more vulnerable to pressures from labour unions than national companies. First, they are more efficient in their use of labour than local companies by definition, otherwise they would not have the competitive edge that enables them to compete overseas. Hence, they are able to pay higher wages. Secondly, as outsiders they are especially anxious to maintain good relations with the local labour unions since, in most cases, they are not entirely familiar with local labour practices and procedures. And, finally, integrated production processes in MPEs mean that they may be unable to afford drawn-out labour disputes which could disrupt production at other subsidiaries, possibly in other countries altogether.

The demonstration effect of MPEs on labour relations was thought by some discussants to have aggravated inflationary pressures in Britain. Other participants, however, asked why the demonstration effect did not spillover also as improvements in management practices? The overall conclusion was that the presence of subsidiaries of multinational enterprises had probably led to improvements in labour and management practices far outside the industrial sectors and regions where they operate. There were possibly some unfavourable consequences, too, although statistics were not available to prove this.

## TRANSMISSION OF TECHNOLOGY

A major contribution to international economic development has been made by the MPE as an effective vehicle for the transmission of technology. Some participants, however, thought that in the case of developing countries some reservations were necessary concerning the suitability of some types of technology made available by MPEs. The special problems of the developing countries are covered in a later section.

Measuring the transfer of technology is a very difficult problem. It may be transferred in a variety of ways. New technology, for example, may be embodied in producers' goods, or through copying such producers' goods or by improving upon them. Technology may also be purchased on licence from firms or individuals in other countries. Or it may be introduced into a country in association with foreign investment. Methods used to acquire new technology differ widely between countries. In Japan, foreign investment has been severely restricted and new technology acquired mainly through licensing agreements. In many cases, the technology purchased in this way is improved and developed in Japan so that the product can later be exported and sold competitively on world markets. Other developed countries allow considerable freedom for technology to be acquired through foreign investment.

The statistics available for measuring international transfers of technology are inadequate. To say that technology is embodied in overseas investment or in trade in producers' goods does not indicate any quantitative assessment of the value of technology associated with capital transfers or trade. The data on monetary payments and receipts for patents, licences and knowhow must also be interpreted with considerable caution. In some countries they include management fees, and in others authors' rights; they do not reflect barter arrangements amongst firms for the transfer of technology; and a great deal of technology gets transferred within multinational firms without any outward signs of payment. But with all these limitations, the data in Chapter 2 by Mr Pavitt suggest that international technology flows through licensing and foreign investment have been increasing over the past fifteen years at a rate greater than either economic growth or international trade, and that an increasing proportion of US technology is being exported through foreign investment by comparison with licensing.

An important consideration for governments is the different methods by which new technology can be acquired. A policy of importing technologically-advanced goods and exporting something else may be adopted; or, like Japan, it may be decided to buy technology and develop it for export advantages; or it may be decided to develop one's own technology. If the market system were perfect, then private industry could be left to make the choice. But the market is not perfect and, therefore, particularly in Europe, governments have been forced to make a choice about how advanced technology should be obtained. Governments may have a variety of objectives in seeking advanced technology. They may merely wish to use a technically advanced product; they may wish to produce a technically advanced product; or they may wish to find a new application of a specific piece of technical knowhow; or they may wish to be able to repair technically advanced goods in use; or they may need it as part of the process of educating a skilled force of research workers to establish a basic national stock of technology. In a sense the nature of a government's aim will determine what is the most suitable mix for a policy on technology.

It was pointed out by industrial representatives that the large international enterprises are becoming increasingly reluctant to license technology to their competitors. It was felt that licensing allowed competitors to catch up cheaply on a technological lead. International companies prefer to exploit a technological advantage and they have a variety of ways in which they may do so. Licensing is possibly the least suitable approach because when the licence lapses the former licensee is in a position to enter in direct competition with the licenser. Under these circumstances the association of technology with direct investment flows for MPEs is likely to become a more important mechanism for the transfer of technology. Nevertheless, the two are alternatives and national governments have some control over the transfer of technology since they are able to control investment flows. Licensing imposes a legal restraint on a market – that is selling into a market; it need not involve the same degree of transfer of knowledge.

349

## CAPITAL FLOWS

It appeared that MPEs had proved to be important integrators of world capital markets. As such they have been a stabilizing force. Exchange control regulations or exchange rate differentials or interest rate differentials are important considerations for finance officers in MPEs and their subsidiaries concerned with shifting funds between different countries. Control over capital movements was conceived by governments as a means of protecting financial markets from external influences. MPEs have access to various kinds of markets in several countries, and they are able to transfer funds directly or indirectly between capital markets. Such adaptability and flexibility weakens the impact of monetary policy as an instrument of national economic policy.

As the financial function of the MPE has become more centralized, the impact on money markets has increased. It is necessary, though, to recognize that the overall long-run strategy of an enterprise can be separated from the tactical manipulations performed by subsidiaries. That is, the long-run strategy of borrowing for development in particular markets can be offset in the short run by tactical movements of funds to maximize returns from, for example, exchange rate or interest rate differentials. It also depends on the degree of control exercised at the centre by the parent company's officers. Tight budgetary and personnel control may be excercised for the medium-term period, say five years, but within that constraint the individual freedom of subsidiaries may be considerable. To a large extent the degree of control exercised by subsidiaries depends on the overall structure of a MPE and the maturity of the subsidiaries concerned. Even a fully-integrated operation would involve a two-way flow of information between the parent centre and the outside subsidiaries.

It is difficult to isolate the relevant financial statistics for MPEs from general balance of payments statistics. Many of the financial operations of multinational enterprises are clearly included in the financial statistics of the balance of payments. Other devices, such as 'back-to-back loans', however, need not appear as movements of funds across frontiers; they are simply agreements between large companies in different countries. In particular, of course, new institutions have grown up to meet the needs of MPEs and the developing aspects of the international economy. The Euro-dollar market and the Euro-bond market are the most striking examples.

Business representatives pointed out that it is difficult to generalize even within the same international enterprise as to the financial arrangements of different subsidiaries. All medium- and long-term planning must begin with markets. Hence, in the first place subsidiaries tend to establish the financial needs of a company in a particular country. The plans of all subsidiaries may be centralized at the head office in order to co-ordinate the financial requirements of the company. The head office may determine how much should be borrowed or lent in a particular market at a particular time, but within certain limits obviously the flexibility rests with the subsidiary to optimize the day-to-day position. The first concern of the central head office is with the capital mix; that is debt to equity ratios. In a multiple currency world with different interest rate relationships there is obviously a call for flexibility in order to minimize the costs of these changing relationships.[1] The finance officers of MPEs and their affiliates are concerned to stablize the situation and as far as possible to prevent divergences in national policies that might bring about losses for their operations.

It was pointed out, though, that movements of funds between nations are only marginal to the firm under most circumstances. Capital requirements in the short and long run are linked closely to markets. Hence, it is clearly better that the borrowing should take place locally wherever possible, which involves giving considerable flexibility to subsidiaries.


## LESS-DEVELOPED COUNTRIES

It is difficult to separate the effects of MPEs on less-developed countries from wider considerations of the effects of foreign direct investment. In certain cases clearly MPEs have a specific role in the development of certain less-developed countries; the case of the large international oil companies and the Middle East states, for example. In many cases, however, it makes little difference whether it is a multinational enterprise or a national company seeking overseas outlets that undertakes investment in a less-developed country.

Doubts have arisen over the extent of the favourable impact of foreign direct investment on the economies of developing countries. Opposing views were aired during the discussions. An inflow of capital coupled with technology and management skills clearly assists economic development. But it raises two issues. National sovereignty is a sensitive area for newly independent states, and the mere presence of MPEs in these countries is sometimes interpreted as an

[1] See Professor Aliber's contribution in Chapter 2.

infringement of sovereignty. While economically, the longer run debits on the current account of the balance of payments, in the form of imported materials and equipment, repatriations of profits, etc. are often given greater emphasis than general economic benefits arising from capital investments. This raises the question of measurement of overall benefits and costs to the economy in contrast to simple balance of payments arithmetic.

In order to measure the economic benefits of a direct investment inflow to a less-developed country it is necessary to examine a number of alternatives. These are spelt out by Mr Streeten in Chapter 9. In his comments, however, Mr Hayes argued that, although many alternatives exist, only some of them are feasible. Hence, only practical considerations should be taken into account in determining whether an investment project is likely to make a country better off or worse off.

Capital transfers to less-developed countries are only one aspect of the operations of MPEs. Another involves the transfer of technology. Considerable doubts were expressed in the discussions about the suitability of technology transferred to less-developed countries by MPEs. The stock of world technology has evolved almost entirely to meet the requirements of advanced industrial countries. It is disputable whether this technology is appropriate for the requirements of less-developed countries, with their different endowments of resources and different problems of economic growth. The type of technology acquired in the advanced industrial countries tends to be labour-saving. The need of most less-developed countries is for greater use of idle or under-employed labour. The use of advanced capital-intensive techniques of production, with relatively small labour inputs, can lead through high labour productivity to high wages in the sectors of less-developed economies dominated by subsidiaries of MPEs. This aggravates 'dualism' in less-developed countries and results in the development of inflationary pressures if the high wage rates in these sectors are allowed to spillover into industries concerned with the domestic market. But, as Mr Streeten points out, spillover is not inevitable, and development along two paths – one sector of modern large-scale industry and the other labour-intensive using small units – can be complementary. The taxes levied on the incomes generated in the modern, industrial sector can be used to finance developments in infra-structure and to promote greater efficiency in the backward sectors of the economy.

The need for organizational experience and access to new industrial techniques in less-developed countries is clearly evident. The problem arises over the nature of the technology MPEs provide and its suitability for the existing stock of knowledge and skills in developing countries. In extractive industries the less-developed countries are keeping a much closer watch on the operations of the international giants and devising ways of sharing control. But in seeking to establish a base for manufacturing industry they are also dependent on the help that MPEs can provide. In many cases this may be the only way of acquiring the necessary production knowhow. It was noted earlier that licensing is becoming less popular among large companies. Proposals that the less-developed countries should try to maintain direct control over investment in industry within their borders by 'buying-in' technology and management borrowing capital abroad were criticized at some length. It was considered by some speakers that this would mean that nationalism could be extremely expensive in terms of losses in economic development. It seemed possible that this approach would lead to them either purchasing the wrong type of management or production knowhow, or getting only second-rate inputs. Such a policy could make their development less efficient than it might be through careful negotiation with the largest and most efficient international companies, who can afford to have the very best management and technology at their disposal.

The relationships between MPEs and less-developed countries' governments clearly focus on the problems of national sovereignty. The issues raised with respect to national sovereignty and MPEs in advanced industrial countries are even more emphasized in connection with less-developed countries. Here the lack of sophistication in governments may aggravate a delicate situation. Many business representatives felt that dealing with an ignorant government was far worse than dealing with one which was aware of the potential advantages and disadvantages of allowing MPEs to operate in their territories and who knew their bargaining strengths. Agreements struck between MPEs and less-developed countries' governments depend largely upon the circumstances at the time of negotiations. As attitudes in less-developed countries become more sophisticated, then their arrangements with MPEs can be expected to become more complex. In Chapter 8, Professor Penrose concludes '. . . multinational enterprises will continue to function as important international organizations, complementing and aiding the economic efforts of independent countries to develop their economies, and that such enterprises will have an important independent role in all sorts of international economic relations, but will also have to conduct continuous negotiations with states whose economic sovereignty they

353

must respect as they try to "harmonize" their own interest with those of the countries in which they operate'.[1]

It was pointed out during the discussions that although companies operating internationally have a long history, the main development of truly multinational enterprises has occurred in the last twenty years and it has been stimulated by the desire of American companies to extend their operations overseas. In one sense few of these growth companies are multinational in the same manner as European companies such as Royal Dutch Shell or Unilever, where there is a formal division of control and distribution of profits. But no single definition of the MPE was adopted by the conference, so the loosest and widest interpretation was accepted for this report.

Much of the debate on the MPE is pursued in terms of the overseas expansion of American companies, and the question was raised whether the circumstances in Western European countries do not invoke a different reaction from that most commonly expressed in attitudes coming from North America. Characteristic views about American investment in Western Europe have received wide publicity, led by Servan-Schreiber's book *Le Defi Americain*, and subsequent statements from the EEC Commission. An examination of recent experience in Western Europe, however, suggests that, in practice, expansion by large American companies has been welcomed by Western European governments and strong efforts are being made to encourage the development of transnational companies by merging competitive national companies in Western Europe, and to encourage overseas expansion by European-based international companies, particularly into the North American market. Evidence to illustrate the acceptance of the benefits from American-controlled investment was supplied from the experience of Western European governments with regard to regional development problems. American companies have proved more willing than most indigenous companies to set up new installations in backward regions and to take into account tax concessions and regional subsidies in assessing alternative locations. One reason for this is that American companies seeking a new subsidiary in Western Europe face fewer constraints from traditional regional links or committed capital; to date these companies have had greater mobility. Once one plant is established, of course, their freedom of action is diminished for

[1] Chapter 8, p. 238.

any future expansion. With these circumstances, it was argued that some governments in Western Europe have competed among themselves to offer the most favourable terms to American companies planning to expand their activities in Western Europe in an attempt to attract them to their own backward regions.

Efforts to encourage cross-frontier mergers between European companies have received considerable attention recently. Proposals for a European company statute have been under examination in EEC since 1965.[1] In addition, in February 1970, Dr Guido Colonna, Commissioner in charge of Industrial Affairs, announced a comprehensive plan for reorganizing the industrial structure of the EEC to meet competition from major United States companies. The aim would be to harmonize, in EEC countries, the laws affecting corporations, merger regulations, corporate taxes, various forms of investment incentives and foreign investment procedures. (This is clearly a response to the competitive incentive policies mentioned above.) These latest proposals are a response to the recent success of United States companies in EEC. It could be argued, though, that this attempt to safeguard European industry is misplaced, or at least premature because of the lack of real information about the effects of American investment on their main European competitors are favourable or adverse.

In a paper produced elsewhere,[2] Professor Hymer in collaboration with Mr Rowthorn, shows that the Servan–Schreiber view of the American challenge in Europe is not really supported by available statistical evidence. Europeans have been fascinated by the size and financial and managerial resources of American companies. When growth performances (measured by sales) are examined, though, it is shown that in the period 1957 to 1967 United States companies grew more slowly than their rivals up to 1962, and only managed to keep pace in the latter half of the period. Apprehension about the position of Western European companies derives principally, they suggest, from too narrow a view of company activities. American companies have been challenged in this period by the formation of the EEC and the industrial expansion in Japan. To meet this competition they have invested in new subsidiaries abroad. It seems probable, after examining the statistics, that Western European companies

[1] Dennis Thompson, *The Proposal for a European Company*, PEP/Chatham House Pamphlet, December 1969.

[2] S. Hymer and R. Rowthorn, 'Multinational Corporation and International Oligopoly: the non-American Challenge', in C. P. Kindleberger (ed.), *The International Corporation*, Cambridge M.I.T. Press, 1970.

have been looking only at the growth in the market share of these new subsidiaries in their local markets without taking into account growth in total world sales. If the wider view is taken a more complete picture is revealed. To support this, Hymer and Rawthorn put forward the apparent lack of challenge from American companies felt by Britain, in spite of the proportionately much larger American investment stake there than in EEC, which they attribute to the more international view of their activities adopted by British industry. In conclusion, they cast certain doubts on the wisdom of the desire for greater concentration in European industry as a counter to the American challenge.

Professor Dunning, in a chapter in the same symposium, also shows that United States direct investment in Europe has contributed substantially to economic growth in Western Europe.[1] Since the Second World War, West European countries have leaned heavily on United States technology which has been transferred either in association with direct investment, or through licensing agreements or through its embodiment in imported capital goods. During the 1960s, however, there seems little doubt that West European countries have improved their technological and scientific capabilities in relation to the United States. Professor Dunning indicates[2] that the transference of knowledge in association with American direct investment in research-intensive industries has contributed in no small measure to the reduction in the 'technological gap'.

These two empirical studies serve to illustrate the dangers of adopting a narrowly nationalistic or regional attitude towards the activities of MPEs. A great deal of attention at this conference was focused on the alleged 'conflict of interests' between MPEs and nation states. Considerable emphasis has already been attached to this issue in the literature on the operations of MPEs. Apparently, it is considered that any infringement or usurpation of the powers of national governments is necessarily wrong or unfavourable for the community whose interests the government serves or determines.

Very significantly, towards the end of the conference, it was suggested that this interpretation of community welfare being determined and safeguarded by national governments may not be the only interpretation, nor indeed the best. Attitudes in Western Europe,

[1] J. H. Dunning, 'Technology, United States Investment, and European Economic Growth', *op. cit.*

[2] J. H. Dunning, 'European and US Trade Patterns, US Foreign Investment and the Technological Gap', in C. P. Kindleberger and A. Shonfield (eds), *North American and Western European Economic Policies*, MacMillan, 1971.

mentioned above, toward the American challenge largely reflect this widely accepted interpretation. Professor Curzon, however, suggested that the type of MPE that is developing in Western Europe might be significantly different from the present American-controlled giants which have grown out of national companies. The Bath studies of European companies outlined by Mr Whitehead in Chapter 12 show that there are already significant structural differences within and between different MPEs. Without deeper understanding of the costs and benefits of multinational enterprises though, it will not be possible to develop a body of knowledge from which adequate and effective national policies can evolve towards this phenomenon. The case study approach proposed by Mr Whitehead may offer some help in acquiring greater knowledge of the formation and structure of European transnational enterprises, providing that a suitably rigorous analytical framework can be established for this approach.

After all, it was stated, Europe's experience of national governments as the ultimate wielders of power does not inspire confidence. Europeans have had many reasons to despair at the consequences of their governments' actions in the last fifty years. Evidence of Western Europeans' feelings has been abundant since 1945, expressed in the movement for integration and harmonization as a means of limiting the freedom of action of individual governments within a wider structure, such as OEDC and EEC. If MPE can provide a strong integrative force and constrain the actions of governments, perhaps this will be welcomed by Europeans. A great deal will obviously depend on the structure and character of the MPEs developing in Western Europe in the next few years.

FURTHER RESEARCH

All the discussions at the conference showed the need for more empirical research into all aspects of the development of multinational corporations. The present debate is largely founded on untested hypotheses and unrigorous descriptions of the institutions. What is needed is greater analysis and more empirical research.

A study of the operations of MPEs extend beyond the field of economics into other disciplines. Political science becomes involved when sovereignty is discussed, and when conflicts over the exercise of power are in dispute. Social considerations are similarly introduced when one examines the structure of MPEs. And, clearly, international relations are another aspect of the proble. In bringing the conference to a close, Mr John Heath pointed out that in order to understand the operations of MPEs it is essential to build analytical models that transcend the normal boundaries between the social sciences (see Chapter 14). Until this is done it is impossible to really understand the consequences, the costs and the benefits of the activities of MPEs for different sectors of the community and to the world as a whole. The needs for more research and for some measurement of the effects of MPEs was the fundamental conclusion of the conference.

# Chapter 14

# CONCLUDING COMMENTS

## JOHN HEATH

It is most difficult to summarize adequately the conclusions from the wide range of issues discussed, especially as the object has been to explore problem areas rather than to arrive at conclusions. What follows, therefore, are some personal impressions.

Perhaps the most striking feature is the wide variety of circumstances which studies of the MPE reveal. There are many different forms of corporate structure between parent and foreign-owned affiliates, and many different management styles, all of which may have significance for the types of behaviour which these enterprises exhibit. The size of the host country was also seen to be an important parameter, because of the high share which foreign ownership quickly assumes where there are few domestic enterprises, as well as its state of economic development. Moreover, national objectives differ, so that in one host country policies pursued by a foreign-owned enterprise may be in conflict with the national objectives, while the same actions may be welcomes elsewhere. And there seemed to be differences between the vertically integrated mineral-extracting MPEs and those engaged in manufacturing or the service trades, which could be significant in explaining the attitudes of governments. Thus, generalizations about MPEs are likely to be valueless unless accompanied by a clear specification of the circumstances concerned.

A closely related point is that study of almost any aspect of the MPE involves the use of a terminology and forms of analysis which go beyond those ordinarily familiar to economists. Concepts such as national sovereignty, conflict, tension, control, and so on require to be defined as carefully and rigorously as terms in economics such as gross national product or discriminating monopoly. Thus it is appealing to talk about a trade-off between economic gain and national sovereignty, but the social scientist is bound to ask whether both terms are commensurate; for if they cannot be compared with the use of a common measure their relationship has little meaning. Economists in the study of economics try to be analytically rigorous

359

and quantitative, and it is important not to overlook the necessity to maintain this approach when embracing other branches of social science in the study of the MPE.

It was of great benefit to the conference to have amongst its members several business representatives from international companies, who on many occasions were able to contribute information and comment on the basis of their experience, and this was most valuable. And for those undertaking further studies in this general area, no doubt many new hypotheses for future testing were derived from their remarks. But there is an obvious danger in assuming that the experiences of those businessmen present at the conference were in any way typical or representative of MPEs as a whole; anecdotal information is extremely useful to have, but generalizations cannot be derived from it.

One important conclusion which seemed to emerge from a number of the discussions, supported by more detailed studies in this area, is that the economic effects of MPEs on the economies of host countries may be either favourable or unfavourable. In this situation, it is an empirical question whether and to what extent MPEs benefit host countries. For instance, the outcome of the long discussion at the conference on transfer pricing seemed to be that, while customs and tax authorities were vigilant in trying to prevent capital movements taking place under the guise of transfer prices for materials purchased or services rendered, in many situations the authorities had no sound basis for knowing exactly how such transfer prices were derived and what they 'ought' to have been. Clearly the opportunity for capital transfer which would evade currency regulations is present in some circumstances, but whether the amount of such transfer is quantitatively significant is an empirical question, and identifying its effect on the economy of the host country may be a difficult analytical problem. It is encouraging that so many economists undertaking research into the MPE are tackling some of these difficult analytical and statistical problems.

A related issue is that the frustration of national policies in host countries would ordinarily be regarded as a disbenefit, and presumably its value should be expressed in welfare terms. But if it were to emerge that actions by a MPE which frustrated the policies of a national government were nevertheless to result in a more efficient use of domestic resources in the host country, so that their real income (including externalities) were to improve, then presumably this should be recorded as a benefit rather than the reverse (unfortunately, national governments do not invariably make decisions which promote the welfare of their citizens, although they may think they do).

In distinguishing the effects of the MPE on host countries one obvious point, that in view of some of the discussions is perhaps worth repeating, is that it is important to identify those elements in these enterprises which make them different from national enterprises. Some of what were claimed to be the substantive effects of MPEs seemed to this observer to be, at most, a question of timing (although the consequential effects of bringing forward certain changes may in themselves be very significant). Thus, in the discussion on the new techniques of wage bargaining introduced first by foreign-owned companies into the United Kingdom, it would be surprising if, given the ease of international communication, these methods which had been found successful (from the trade unionist point of view) in the United States would not ultimately have been tested in this country. The fact that it was a MPE which introduced them seems more plausibly to have brought forward in time actions which would have occurred in any event. Likewise, it is reasonable to argue that the international distribution of resources achieved by the managerial decisions of MPEs would have occurred over a much longer time-period if left to the free working of the international market mechanism. However, the more rapid international diffusion of innovations due to the internal decisions of the MPE may result in significant changes, because a high proportion of innovations prove to be unsuccessful and it is possible that the more rapid achievement of scale production may lead to some innovations being successful that would otherwise have been failures.

Finally, those undertaking research in this area should not disregard what governments regard as important, even though economists might have very different criteria, because governments may make decisions specifically about MPEs, and if they make the wrong decisions they may be reducing the welfare of their inhabitants rather than improving it, and reducing the welfare of the companies as well. Thus it is important to help governments understand what are the effects of foreign direct investment on host countries. Even exploring the logic of some of the worries of governments about foreign-owned enterprises can be helpful in decision-making, although quantifying the effects naturally would be of greater benefit.

In terms of government behaviour relating to MPEs, it may be relevant to examine how governments communicate and behave with regard to those two industries which are essentially international in their character – aviation and shipping. In the case of aviation, for example, if Pan Am wishes to perate a new service from some city in the United States to Amsterdam, then this is not a matter for negotiation between that airline and the authorities at Schipol Airport, but initially between the governments of the United States and Holland. International traffic rights are bargained by governments on behalf of airlines, and not all governments think alike on the proper basis for evaluation.

In the shipping industry, where decisions on freight rates and on freedom of entry to operate over specified routes are matters usually determined by shipping conferences, being private organizations of ship-owners, some governments are now interested in the possibility of agreeing collectively on an international code of conduct for the way in which conferences should conduct themselves. There are international jurisdictional problems involved in this in much the same way as are involved in matters relating to MPEs, and governments generally try to sustain a uniform attitude towards the limits of jurisdiction over the whole range of matters with which they are concerned (but not all governments adopt the same attitude).

It was suggested at the conference that there should be a code of conduct for MPEs. Because of the different positions of countries with regard to the share of their national output which is made by foreign direct investment, and because this may be concentrated in only a few sectors of the economy, the national interest of countries in formulating a code of conduct will vary widely. Thus, perhaps what is being sought is an international forum for discussion of these problems, and an institutional arrangement that would allow countries to enter into varying degrees of commitment about their policies towards multinational firms. Agreement may be difficult to achieve because the attitudes of host countries may be in conflict with the attitudes of governments from parent countries.

There were those at the conference who claimed that, while in many countries MPEs contributed only a small proportion of domestic production and employment, the trends were such that the rate of increase in the future might be very significant. This would seem to suggest that, even in those countries where there appear to be no problems at present, governments would be wise to keep the situation under continuous review.

## DATE DUE

| | | | |
|---|---|---|---|
| | | | |
| | | | |
| | | | |
| | | | |
| | | | |
| | | | |
| | | | |
| | | | |
| | | | |
| | | | |
| | | | |
| | | | |
| | | | |
| | | | |
| | | | |
| | | | |
| | | | |
| | | | |
| | | | |
| | | | |
| | | | |
| | | | |
| GAYLORD | | | PRINTED IN U.S.A. |